The Essayist

The Essayist

THIRD EDITION

Sheridan Baker
The University of Michigan

THOMAS Y. CROWELL COMPANY

New York   Established 1834

THE ESSAYIST, Third Edition

Copyright © 1977, 1972, 1963 by THOMAS Y. CROWELL COMPANY, INC.

Published simultaneously in Canada by Fitzhenry & Whiteside, Ltd., Toronto.

Library of Congress Cataloging in Publication Data

Baker, Sheridan Warner, 1918-
    The essayist.

        1. English language—Rhetoric.   2.   American essays.
3.   English essays.   I.   Title.
PE1417.B28   1977   808.4   76-40465
ISBN 0-690-00874-0

Contents

v

CONTENTS

Preface

These essays—newly selected and set in guiding contexts—take the student progressively through patterns of expository writing at the same time as they pose questions central to modern life. They illustrate how a thesis may organize an essay at a stroke, and how even a seasoned writer may miss the clearest opportunity to do so. They show how a structure works, how the paragraph, the sentence, and the word may work their various wiles. They illustrate the problems of writing, encouraging students to discover their own ideas and to make them persuasive, as they find their own voices and styles. Readers of *The Practical Stylist*, *The Complete Stylist and Handbook*, and the earlier *Essayist*s will recognize the rhetorical approach.

As before, the book aims for one practical point: how to write an essay. Each section concentrates on a part of the problem. We begin with the most important questions: first, *thesis*, or inner idea, then *structure*, or outer form. With a sense of this larger unity, students can more easily manage paragraphs, sentences, and words—the woods, streams, and pebbles of our verbal world—than if they were to pick up the small things first and wonder how they fit. Each section begins by describing a rhetorical focus, introduces each author with a short note to locate him or her as a human being, and heads up each essay with suggestions about what to look for, what to query—where to assay the author's faults and virtues. Each section concludes with suggestions for using the principles just seen in operation, as one applies to one's own experience the ideas set stirring—ideas running throughout the book of value and evaluation, belief and disbelief, language and meaning, thinking and knowing, and being a human being.

Among the forty-one essays, you will find some of the world's most famous authors—Woolf, Macaulay, Orwell, Schweitzer, Thoreau, Swift. After considering the essay's essential workings in general and specific ways, you will find sections on writing the personal essay, on irony, and on the critical review. The book concludes with a discussion of some varieties of evidence and the author's voice.

One
Thesis: The Argumentative Edge

Each of the three essays in this section is built around a central idea, and that idea has an edge to it, an urging, which silently says *you should believe this too*. Reading is Virginia Woolf's subject, but what she says *about* reading is her thesis: *you should read for yourself, sympathetically, joyfully, and then you will experience the ultimate pleasure of judging perceptively*. She does not state this openly, as an argumentative thesis. She might have done so, at the end of an opening paragraph that had drawn us in with her characteristically intelligent charm. Her essay would actually have been clearer, since she begins by saying that nobody can judge and ends by saying that everyone must judge. But we understand her at the end, and we forgive her inductive teasing because she has guided us to understand her thesis after all, and to believe in it as she does.

Gordon Bigelow's essay seems at first like straightforward exposition and no more—an orderly explanation of a concept. But it, too, has its argumentative edge. Existentialism is his subject; what he says *about* existentialism is: *you need to understand existentialism to read the books and grasp the attitudes of your times*. He puts his thesis to us more directly than does Virginia Woolf, bringing it home at the end of his

1

introductory paragraph, though not quite as bluntly as I have done—which might still have sharpened his edge of clarity.

Arthur Koestler's thesis is the clearest of all. It is all edge: *a new theory changes our reading of scientific facts.* Everything after that is illustration to persuade us that his thesis is right. As you read these essays, enjoy them. Three attractive people are speaking from where they live, and the breadth of their reading and learning flows with their thesis to persuade us to believe in it as they do. But as you read, keep an inquisitive pencil handy. Could they have been clearer? What does *impalpable* mean? Does Virginia Woolf contradict herself? Do you know anything that might change their tune? Sympathize, but judge, as Virginia Woolf advises.

VIRGINIA WOOLF

Virginia Woolf (1882–1941) was educated at home in London by her illustrious literary father, Sir Leslie Stephen, in whose library she browsed. After her father's death in 1904, she lived with her sister, Vanessa, and her brother, Adrian, in a house on Gordon Square, in the Bloomsbury district near the British Museum, which became the center of the vigorous aesthetic-intellectual "Bloomsbury Group." There she met and married Leonard Woolf, with whom she founded the Hogarth Press. She published her first novel, *The Voyage Out*, in 1915. *Mrs. Dalloway* (1925) and *To the Lighthouse* (1927) are the best of her nine novels, in addition to which she published a number of short stories, essays, and other studies. She was an innovator in stream-of-consciousness fiction.

HOW SHOULD ONE READ A BOOK?

This essay, first published in 1932, has never been superseded, probably because no one since Virginia Woolf has been such an omnivorous and joyous reader, with a writer's gift to match. She poses the essential question of evaluating anything, whether books or ballplayers or family tiffs: how personal perceptions can become generally valid judgments. Note what she says about *Lear* at beginning and end. How do you explain this contradiction? Note, too, how she contrasts the present reality outside the window with all those seen through the differing windows of books. As you read, underline those words that seem unusually effective or striking.

In the first place, I want to emphasize the note of interrogation at the end of my title. Even if I could answer the question for myself, the answer would apply only to me and not to you. The only advice, indeed, that one person can give another about reading is to take no advice, to follow your own instincts, to use your own reason, to come to your own conclusions. If this is agreed between us, then I feel at liberty to put forward a few ideas and suggestions because you will not allow them to fetter that independence which is the most important quality that a reader can possess. After all, what laws can be laid down about books? The battle of Waterloo was certainly fought on a certain day; but is *Hamlet* a better play than *Lear*? Nobody can say. Each must decide that question for himself. To admit authorities, however heavily furred and gowned, into our libraries and let them tell us how to read, what to read, what value to place upon what we read, is to destroy the spirit of freedom which is the breath of those sanctuaries. Everywhere else we may be bound by laws and conventions—there we have none.

But to enjoy freedom, if the platitude is pardonable, we have of course to control ourselves. We must not squander our powers, helplessly and ignorantly, squirting half the house in order to water a single rose-bush; we must train them, exactly and powerfully, here on the very spot. This, it may be, is one of the first difficulties that faces us in a library. What is "the very spot"? There may well seem to be nothing but a conglomeration and huddle of confusion. Poems and novels, histories and memoirs, dictionaries and bluebooks; books written in all languages by men and women of all tempers, races, and ages jostle each other on the shelf. And outside the donkey brays, the women gossip at the pump, the colts gallop across the fields. Where are we to begin? How are we to bring order into this multitudinous chaos and so get the deepest and widest pleasure from what we read?

It is simple enough to say that since books have classes—fiction, biography, poetry—we should separate them and take from each what it is right that each should give us. Yet few people ask from books what books can give us. Most commonly we come to books with blurred and divided minds, asking of fiction that it shall be true, of poetry that it shall be false, of biography that it shall be flattering, of history that it shall enforce our own prejudices. If we could banish all such preconceptions when we read, that would be an admirable beginning. Do not dictate to your author; try to become him. Be his fellow-worker and accomplice. If you hang back, and reserve and criticise at first, you are preventing yourself from getting the fullest possible value from what you read. But if you open your mind as widely as possible, then signs and hints of almost imperceptible fineness, from the twist and turn of the first sentences, will bring you into the presence of a human being unlike any other. Steep yourself in this, acquaint yourself with this, and soon you will find that your author is giving you, or attempting to give

you, something far more definite. The thirty-two chapters of a novel—
if we consider how to read a novel first—are an attempt to make something as formed and controlled as a building: but words are more impalpable than bricks; reading is a longer and more complicated process
than seeing. Perhaps the quickest way to understand the elements of
what a novelist is doing is not to read, but to write; to make your own
experiment with the dangers and difficulties of words. Recall, then, some
event that has left a distinct impression on you—how at the corner of
the street, perhaps, you passed two people talking. A tree shook; an
electric light danced; the tone of the talk was comic, but also tragic; a
whole vision, an entire conception, seemed contained in that moment.

novel   But when you attempt to reconstruct it in words, you will find that it
breaks into a thousand conflicting impressions. Some must be subdued;
others emphasized; in the process you will lose, probably, all grasp
upon the emotion itself. Then turn from your blurred and littered pages
to the opening pages of some great novelist—Defoe, Jane Austen, Hardy.
Now you will be better able to appreciate their mastery. It is not merely
that we are in the presence of a different person—Defoe, Jane Austen, or
Thomas Hardy—but that we are living in a different world. Here, in
Robinson Crusoe, we are trudging a plain high road; one thing happens
after another; the fact and the order of the fact is enough. But if the
open air and adventure mean everything to Defoe they mean nothing to
Jane Austen. Hers is the drawing-room, and people talking, and by the
many mirrors of their talk revealing their characters. And if, when we
have accustomed ourselves to the drawing-room and its reflections, we
turn to Hardy, we are once more spun round. The moors are round us
and the stars are above our heads. The other side of the mind is now
exposed—the dark side that comes uppermost in solitude, not the light
side that shows in company. Our relations are not toward people, but
toward Nature and destiny. Yet different as these worlds are, each is
consistent with itself. The maker of each is careful to observe the laws
of his own perspective, and however great a strain they may put upon
us they will never confuse us, as lesser writers so frequently do, by
introducing two different kinds of reality into the same book. Thus to
go from one great novelist to another—from Jane Austen to Hardy, from
Peacock to Trollope, from Scott to Meredith—is to be wrenched and
uprooted; to be thrown this way and then that. To read a novel is a
difficult and complex art. You must be capable not only of great fineness
of perception, but of great boldness of imagination if you are going to
make use of all that the novelist—the great artist—gives you.

But a glance at the heterogeneous company on the shelf will show
you that writers are very seldom "great artists"; far more often a book

makes no claim to be a work of art at all. These biographies and auto-
biographies, for example, lives of great men, of men long dead and forgotten, that stand cheek by jowl with the novels and poems, are we
to refuse to read them because they are not "art"? Or shall we read
them, but read them in a different way, with a different aim? Shall we
read them in the first place to satisfy that curiosity which possesses us
sometimes when in the evening we linger in front of a house where the
lights are lit and the blinds are not yet drawn, and each floor of the
house shows us a different section of human life in being? Then we are
consumed with curiosity about the lives of these people—the servants
gossiping, the gentlemen dining, the girl dressing for a party, the old
woman at the window with her knitting. Who are they, what are they,
what are their names, their occupations, their thoughts, and adventures?
Biographies and memoirs answer such questions, light up innumerable
such houses; they show us people going about their daily affairs, toiling,
failing, succeeding, eating, hating, loving, until they die. And sometimes
as we watch, the house fades and the iron railings vanish and we are
out at sea; we are hunting, sailing, fighting; we are among savages and
soldiers; we are taking part in great campaigns. Or if we like to stay
here in England, in London, still the scene changes; the street narrows;
the house becomes small, cramped, diamond-paned, and malodorous.
We see a poet, Donne, driven from such a house because the walls were
so thin that when the children cried their voices cut through them. We
can follow him, through the paths that lie in the pages of books, to
Twickenham; to Lady Bedford's Park, a famous meeting-ground for
nobles and poets; and then turn our steps to Wilton, the great house
under the downs, and hear Sidney read the *Arcadia* to his sister; and
ramble among the very marshes and see the very herons that figure in
that famous romance; and then again travel north with that other Lady
Pembroke, Anne Clifford, to her wild moors, or plunge into the city and
control our merriment at the sight of Gabriel Harvey in his black velvet
suit arguing about poetry with Spenser. Nothing is more fascinating
than to grope and stumble in the alternate darkness and splendour of
Elizabethan London. But there is no staying there. The Temples and the
Swifts, the Harleys and the St. Johns beckon us on; hour upon hour can
be spent disentangling their quarrels and deciphering their characters;
and when we tire of them we can stroll on, past a lady in black wearing
diamonds, to Samuel Johnson and Goldsmith and Garrick; or cross the
channel, if we like, and meet Voltaire and Diderot, Madame du Deffand;
and so back to England and Twickenham—how certain places repeat
themselves and certain names!—where Lady Bedford had her Park once
and Pope lived later, to Walpole's home at Stawberry Hill. But Walpole

introduces us to such a swarm of new acquaintances, there are so many houses to visit and bells to ring that we may well hesitate for a moment, on the Miss Berrys' doorstep, for example, when behold, up comes Thackeray; he is the friend of the woman whom Walpole loved; so that merely by going from friend to friend, from garden to garden, from house to house, we have passed from one end of English literature to another and wake to find ourselves here again in the present, if we can so differentiate this moment from all that have gone before. This, then, is one of the ways in which we can read these lives and letters; we can make them light up the many windows of the past; we can watch the famous dead in their familiar habits and fancy sometimes that we are very close and can surprise their secrets, and sometimes we may pull out a play or a poem that they have written and see whether it reads differently in the presence of the author. But this again rouses other questions. How far, we must ask ourselves, is a book influenced by its writer's life—how far is it safe to let the man interpret the writer? How far shall we resist or give way to the sympathies and antipathies that the man himself rouses in us—so sensitive are words, so receptive of the character of the author? These are questions that press upon us when we read lives and letters, and we must answer them for ourselves, for nothing can be more fatal than to be guided by the preferences of others in a matter so personal.

But also we can read such books with another aim, not to throw light on literature, not to become familiar with famous people, but to refresh and exercise our own creative powers. Is there not an open window on the right hand of the bookcase? How delightful to stop reading and look out! How stimulating the scene is, in its unconsciousness, its irrelevance, its perpetual movement—the colts galloping round the field, the woman filling her pail at the well, the donkey throwing back his head and emitting his long, acrid moan. The greater part of any library is nothing but the record of such fleeting moments in the lives of men, women, and donkeys. Every literature, as it grows old, has its rubbish-heap, its record of vanished moments and forgotten lives told in faltering and feeble accents that have perished. But if you give yourself up to the delight of rubbish-reading you will be surprised, indeed you will be overcome, by the relics of human life that have been cast out to moulder. It may be one letter—but what a vision it gives! It may be a few sentences—but what vistas they suggest! Sometimes a whole story will come together with such beautiful humour and pathos and completeness that it seems as if a great novelist had been at work, yet it is only an old actor, Tate Wilkinson, remembering the strange story of Captain Jones; it is only a young subaltern serving under Arthur Wellesley and falling in love with a pretty girl at Lisbon; it is only Maria Allen letting fall her sewing in the empty drawing-room and sighing how she wishes she had taken Dr. Burney's good advice and had never eloped with her Rishy. None of this has any value; it is negligible in the extreme; yet how absorbing it is now and again to go through the rubbish-heaps and find rings and scissors and broken noses buried in the huge past and try to piece them together while the colt gallops round the field, the woman fills her pail at the well, and the donkey brays.

But we tire of rubbish-reading in the long run. We tire of searching for what is needed to complete the half-truth which is all that the Wilkinsons, the Bunburys, and the Maria Allens are able to offer us. They had not the artist's power of mastering and eliminating; they could not tell the whole truth even about their own lives; they have disfigured the story that might have been so shapely. Facts are all that they can offer us, and facts are a very inferior form of fiction. Thus the desire grows upon us to have done with half-statements and approximations; to cease from searching out the minute shades of human character, to enjoy the greater abstractness, the purer truth of fiction. Thus we create the mood, intense and generalised, unaware of detail, but stressed by some regular, recurrent beat, whose natural expression is poetry; and that is the time to read poetry when we are most able to write it.

> Western wind, when wilt thou blow?
> The small rain down can rain.
> Christ, if my love were in my arms,
> And I in my bed again!*

The impact of poetry is so hard and direct that for the moment there is no other sensation except that of the poem itself. What profound depths we visit then—how sudden and complete is our immersion! There is nothing here to catch hold of; nothing to stay us in our flight. The illusion of fiction is gradual; its effects are prepared; but who when they read these four lines stops to ask who wrote them, or conjures up the thought of Donne's house or Sidney's secretary; or enmeshes them in the intricacy of the past and the succession of generations? The poet is always our contemporary. Our being for the moment is centered and constricted, as in any violent shock of personal emotion. Afterwards, it is true, the sensation begins to spread in wider

---

* An anonymous fragment, dated about 1300 A.D., but the spelling that has come down to us, which Virginia Woolf quotes, dates from the sixteenth century, reflecting its long popularity.—Ed.

rings through our minds; remoter senses are reached; these begin to sound and to comment and we are aware of echoes and reflections. The intensity of poetry covers an immense range of emotion. We have only to compare the force and directness of

> I shall fall like a tree, and find my grave,
> Only remembering that I grieve,

with the wavering modulation of

> Minutes are numbered by the fall of sands,
> As by an hour glass; the span of time
> Doth waste us to our graves, and we look on it;
> An age of pleasure, revelled out, comes home
> At last, and ends in sorrow; but the life,
> Weary of riot, numbers every sand,
> Wailing in sighs, until the last drop down,
> So to conclude calamity in rest,

or place the meditative calm of

> whether we be young or old,
> Our destiny, our being's heart and home,
> Is with infinitude, and only there;
> With hope it is, hope that can never die,
> Effort, and expectation, and desire,
> And something evermore about to be,

beside the complete and inexhaustible loveliness of

> The moving Moon went up the sky,
> And nowhere did abide:
> Softly she was going up,
> And a star or two beside—

or the splendid fantasy of

> And the woodland haunter
> Shall not cease to saunter
>   When, far down some glade,
> Of the great world's burning,
> One soft flame upturning,
> Seems, to his discerning,
>   Crocus in the shade,

to bethink us of the varied art of the poet*; his power to make us at once actors and spectators; his power to run his hand into character as if it were a glove, and be Falstaff or Lear; his power to condense, to widen, to state, once and for ever.

"We have only to compare"—with those words the cat is out of the bag, and the true complexity of reading is admitted. The first process, to receive impressions with the utmost understanding, is only half the process of reading; it must be completed, if we are to get the whole pleasure from a book, by another. We must pass judgment upon these multitudinous impressions; we must make of these fleeting shapes one that is hard and lasting. But not directly. Wait for the dust of reading to settle; for the conflict and the questioning to die down; walk, talk, pull the dead petals from a rose, or fall asleep. Then suddenly without our willing it, for it is thus that Nature undertakes these transitions, the book will return, but differently. It will float to the top of the mind as a whole. And the book as a whole is different from the book received currently in separate phrases. Details now fit themselves into their places. We see the shape from start to finish; it is a barn, a pig-sty, or a cathedral. Now then we can compare book with book as we compare building with building. But this act of comparison means that our attitude has changed; we are no longer the friends of the writer, but his judges; and just as we cannot be too sympathetic as friends, so as judges we cannot be too severe. Are they not criminals, books that have wasted our time and sympathy; are they not the most insidious enemies of society, corrupters, defilers, the writers of false books, faked books, books that fill the air with decay and disease? Let us then be severe in our judgments; let us compare each book with the greatest of its kind. There they hang in the mind, the shapes of the books we have read solidified by the judgments we have passed on them—*Robinson Crusoe*, *Emma*, *The Return of the Native*. Compare the novels with these— even the latest and least of novels has a right to be judged with the best. And so with poetry—when the intoxication or rhythm has died down and the splendour of words has faded, a visionary shape will return to us and this must be compared with *Lear*, with *Phèdre*, with

* These five quotations are from (1) Beaumont and Fletcher, *The Maid's Tragedy* (1619) IV.i.214–15; (2) John Ford, *The Lover's Melancholy* (1629) IV.iii.57–64; (3) William Wordsworth, *The Prelude* (1805), VI.603–8; (4) Samuel Taylor Coleridge, *The Rime of the Ancient Mariner* (1798), ll. 263–66; (5) Ebenezer Jones, "When the World Is Burning" (1860), ll. 21–27. I am grateful to Anthony W. Shipps, Librarian for English, University of Indiana, for identifying the quotations from Beaumont and Fletcher, Ford, and Jones.—Ed.

The Prelude; or if not with these, with whatever is the best or seems to us to be the best in its own kind. And we may be sure that the newness of new poetry and fiction is its most superficial quality and that we have only to alter slightly, not to recast, the standards by which we have judged the old.

It would be foolish, then, to pretend that the second part of reading, to judge, to compare, is as simple as the first—to open the mind wide to the fast flocking of innumerable impressions. To continue reading without the book before you, to hold one shadow-shape against another, to have read widely enough and with enough understanding to make such comparisons alive and illuminating—that is difficult; it is still more difficult to press further and to say, "Not only is the book of this sort, but it is of this value; here it fails; here it succeeds; this is bad; that is good." To carry out this part of a reader's duty needs such imagination, insight, and learning that it is hard to conceive any one mind sufficiently endowed; impossible for the most self-confident to find more than the seeds of such powers in himself. Would it not be wiser, then, to remit this part of reading and to allow the critics, the gowned and furred authorities of the library, to decide the question of the book's absolute value for us? Yet how impossible! We may stress the value of sympathy; we may try to sink our own identity as we read. But we know that we cannot sympathise wholly or immerse ourselves wholly; there is always a demon in us who whispers, "I hate, I love," and we cannot silence him. Indeed, it is precisely because we hate and we love that our relation with the poets and novelists is so intimate that we find the presence of another person intolerable. And even if the results are abhorrent and our judgments are wrong, still our taste, the nerve of sensation that sends shocks through us, is our chief illuminant; we learn through feelings; we cannot suppress our own idiosyncrasy without impoverishing it. But as time goes on perhaps we can train our taste; perhaps we can make it submit to some control. When it has fed greedily and lavishly upon books of all sorts—poetry, fiction, history, biography—and has stopped reading and looked for long spaces upon the variety, the incongruity of the living word, we shall find that it is changing a little; it is not so greedy, it is more reflective. It will begin to bring us not merely judgments on particular books, but it will tell us that there is a quality common to certain books. Listen, it will say, what shall we call *this?* And it will read us perhaps *Lear* and then perhaps the *Agamemnon* in order to bring out the common quality. Thus, with our taste to guide us, we shall venture beyond the particular book in search of qualities that group books together; we shall give them names and thus frame a rule that brings order into our perceptions. We shall gain a further and a rarer pleasure from that discrimination. But as a rule only lives when it is perpetually broken by contact with the books themselves—nothing is easier and more stultifying than to make rules which exist out of touch with facts, in a vacuum—now at last, in order to steady ourselves in this difficult attempt, it may be well to turn to the very rare writers who are able to enlighten us upon literature as an art. Coleridge and Dryden and Johnson, in their considered criticism, the poets and novelists themselves in their unconsidered sayings, are often surprisingly relevant; they light up and solidify the vague ideas that have been tumbling in the misty depths of our minds. But they are only able to help us if we come to them laden with questions and suggestions won honestly in the course of our own reading. They can do nothing for us if we herd ourselves under their authority and lie down like sheep in the shade of a hedge. We can only understand their ruling when it comes in conflict with our own and vanquishes it.

If this is so, if to read a book as it should be read calls for the rarest qualities of imagination, insight, and judgment, you may perhaps conclude that literature is a very complex art and that it is unlikely that we shall be able, even after a lifetime of reading, to make any valuable contribution to its criticism. We must remain readers; we shall not put on the further glory that belongs to those rare beings who are also critics. But still we have our responsibilities as readers and even our importance. The standards we raise and the judgment we pass steal into the air and become part of the atmosphere which writers breathe as they work. An influence is created which tells upon them even if it never finds its way into print. And that influence, if it were well instructed, vigorous and individual and sincere, might be of great value now when criticism is necessarily in abeyance; when books pass in review like the procession of animals in a shooting gallery, and the critic has only one second in which to load and aim and shoot and may well be pardoned if he mistakes rabbits for tigers, eagles for barndoor fowls, or misses altogether and wastes his shot upon some peaceful cow grazing in a further field. If behind the erratic gunfire of the press the author felt that there was another kind of criticism, the opinion of people reading for the love of reading, slowly and unprofessionally, and judging with great sympathy and yet with great severity, might this not improve the quality of his work? And if by our means books were to become stronger, richer, and more varied, that would be an end worth reaching.

Yet who reads to bring about an end, however desirable? Are there not some pursuits that we practise because they are good in themselves, and some pleasures that are final? And is not this among them? I have sometimes dreamt, at least, that when the Day of Judgment dawns and the great conquerors and lawyers and statesmen come to receive their rewards—their crowns, their laurels, their names carved indelibly upon imperishable marble—the Almighty will turn to Peter and will say, not without a certain envy when He sees us coming with our books under our arms, "Look, these need no reward. We have nothing to give them here. They have loved reading."

GORDON E. BIGELOW

Gordon E. Bigelow (1919–), a native of Springfield, Massachusetts, teaches American literature at the University of Florida. He served in the Army Air Force (1941–1945). His books are *Rhetoric and American Poetry of the Early National Period* (1960) and *Frontier Eden, The Literary Career of Marjorie Kinnan Rawlings* (1966).

A PRIMER OF EXISTENTIALISM

This essay outlines the essential twentieth-century concept, by whatever name it is known. Almost any twentieth-century writer will fit somewhere into its frame, convincing us as we read that Bigelow's thesis is valid: we need to understand his six points of existentialism to understand ourselves and our world. How do you and your attitudes fit into this picture? Do people you know—books, movies—also fit? How clearly does Bigelow state his thesis—and where? Underline those words in his style that seem fresh or unusual.

For some years I fought the word by irritably looking the other way whenever I stumbled across it, hoping that like dadaism and some of the other "isms" of the French *avant garde* it would go away if I ignored it. But existentialism was apparently more than the picture it evoked of uncombed beards, smoky basement cafes, and French beatniks regaling one another between sips of absinthe with brilliant variations on the theme of despair. It turned out to be of major importance to literature and the arts, to philosophy and theology, and of increasing importance to the social sciences. To learn more about it, I read several of the self-styled introductions to the subject, with the baffled sensation of a man who reads a critical introduction to a novel only to find that he must read the novel before he can understand the introduction.

Therefore, I should like to provide here something most discussions of existentialism take for granted, a simple statement of its basic characteristics. This is a reckless thing to do because there are several kinds of existentialism and what one says of one kind may not be true of another, but there is an area of agreement, and it is this common ground that I should like to set forth here. We should not run into trouble so long as we understand from the outset that the six major themes outlined below will apply in varying degrees to particular existentialists. A reader should be able to go from here to the existentialists themselves, to the more specialized critiques of them, or be able to recognize an existentialist theme or coloration in literature when he sees it.

A word first about the kinds of existentialism. Like transcendentalism of the last century, there are almost as many varieties of this *ism* as there are individual writers to whom the word is applied (not all of them claim it). But without being facetious we might group them into two main kinds, the *ungodly* and the *godly*. To take the ungodly or atheistic first, we would list as the chief spokesmen among many others Jean-Paul Sartre, Albert Camus, and Simone de Beauvoir. Several of this important group of French writers had rigorous and significant experience in the Resistance during the Nazi occupation of France in World War II. Out of the despair which came with the collapse of their nation during those terrible years they found unexpected strength in the single indomitable human spirit, which even under severe torture could maintain the spirit of resistance, the unextinguishable ability to say "No." From this irreducible core in the human spirit, they erected after the war a philosophy which was a twentieth-century variation of the philosophy of Descartes. But instead of saying "I think, therefore I am," they said "I can say No, therefore I exist." As we shall presently see, the use of the word "exist" is of prime significance. This group is chiefly responsible for giving existentialism its status in the popular mind as a literary-philosophical cult.

Of the godly or theistic existentialists we should mention first a mid-nineteenth-century Danish writer, Søren Kierkegaard; two contemporary French Roman Catholics, Gabriel Marcel and Jacques Maritain; two Protestant theologians, Paul Tillich and Nicholas Berdyaev; and Martin Buber, an important contemporary Jewish theologian. Taken together, their writings constitute one of the most significant developments in modern theology. Behind both groups of existentialists stand other important figures, chiefly philosophers, who exert powerful influence upon the movement—Blaise Pascal, Friedrich Nietzsche, Henri Bergson, Martin Heidegger, Karl Jaspers, among others. Several literary figures, notably Tolstoy and Dostoievsky, are frequently cited because existentialist attitudes and themes are prominent in their writings. The eclectic nature of this movement should already be sufficiently clear and the danger of applying too rigidly to any particular figure the general characteristics of the movement which I now make bold to describe:

1. *Existence before essence.* Existentialism gets its name from an insistence that human life is understandable only in terms of an individual man's existence, his particular experience of life. It says that a man *lives* (has existence) rather than *is* (has being or essence), and that every man's experience of life is unique, radically different from everyone else's and can be understood truly only in terms of his involvement in life or commitment to it. It strenuously shuns that view which assumes an ideal of Man or Mankind, a universal of human nature of which each man is only one example. It eschews the question of Greek philosophy, *"What is mankind?"* which suggests that man can be defined if he is ranged in his proper place in the order of nature; it asks instead the question of Job and St. Augustine, *"Who am I?"* with its suggestion of the uniqueness and mystery of each human life and its emphasis upon the subjective or personal rather than the objective or impersonal. From the outside a man appears to be just another natural creature; from the inside he is an entire universe, the center of infinity. The existentialist insists upon this latter radically subjective view, and from this grows much of the rest of existentialism.

2. *Reason is impotent to deal with the depths of human life.* There are two parts to this proposition—first, that human reason is relatively weak and imperfect, and second, that there are dark places in human life which are "nonreason" and to which reason scarcely penetrates. Since Plato, Western civilization has usually assumed a separation of reason from the rest of the human psyche, and has glorified reason as suited to command the nonrational part. The classic statement of this separation appears in the *Phaedrus,* where Plato describes the psyche in the myth of the chariot which is drawn by the white steeds of the emotions and the black unruly steeds of the appetites. The driver of the chariot is Reason who holds the reins which control the horses and the whip to subdue the surging black steeds of passion. Only the driver, the rational nature, is given human form; the rest of the psyche, the nonrational part, is given a lower, animal form. This separation and exaltation of reason is carried further in the allegory of the cave in the *Republic.* You recall the sombre picture of human life with which the story begins: men are chained in the dark in a cave, with their backs to a flickering firelight, able to see only uncertain shadows moving on the wall before them, able to hear only confused echoes of

sounds. One of the men, breaking free from his chains, is able to turn and look upon the objects themselves and the light which casts the shadows; even, at last, he is able to work his way entirely out of the cave into the sunlight beyond. All this he is able to do through his reason; he escapes from the bondage of error, from time and change, from death itself, into the realm of changeless eternal ideas or Truth, and the lower nature which had chained him in darkness is left behind.

Existentialism in our time, and this is one of its most important characteristics, insists upon reuniting the "lower" or irrational parts of the psyche with the "higher." It insists that man must be taken in his wholeness and not in some divided state, that whole man contains not only intellect but also anxiety, guilt, and the will to power—which modify and sometimes overwhelm the reason. A man seen in this light is fundamentally ambiguous, if not mysterious, full of contradictions and tensions which cannot be dissolved simply by taking thought. "Human life," said Berdyaev, "is permeated by underground streams." One is reminded of D. H. Lawrence's outburst against Franklin and his rational attempt to achieve moral perfection: "The Perfectability of Man! . . . The perfectability of which man? I am many men. Which of them are you going to perfect? I am not a mechanical contrivance. . . . It's a queer thing is a man's soul. It is the whole of him. Which means it is the unknown as well as the known. . . . The soul of man is a dark vast forest, with wild life in it." The emphasis in existentialism is not on idea but upon the thinker who has the idea. It accepts not only his power of thought, but his contingency and fallibility, his frailty, his body, blood, and bones, and above all his death. Kierkegaard emphasized the distinction between *subjective* truth (what a person *is*) and *objective* truth (what the person *knows*), and said that we encounter the true self not in the detachment of thought but in the involvement and agony of choice and in the pathos of commitment to our choice. This distrust of rational systems helps to explain why many existential writers in their own expression are paradoxical or prophetic or gnomic, why their works often belong more to literature than to philosophy.

3. *Alienation or estrangement.* One major result of the dissociation of reason from the rest of the psyche has been the growth of science, which has become one of the hallmarks of Western civilization, and an ever-increasing rational ordering of men in society. As the existentialists view them, the main forces of history since the Renaissance have progressively separated man from concrete earthy existence, have forced him to live at ever higher levels of abstraction, have collectivized individual man out of existence, have driven God from the heavens, or

what is the same thing, from the hearts of men. They are convinced that modern man lives in a fourfold condition of alienation: from God, from nature, from other men, from his own true self.

The estrangement from God is most shockingly expressed by Nietzsche's anguished cry, "God is dead," a cry which has continuously echoed through the writings of the existentialists, particularly the French. This theme of spiritual barrenness is a commonplace in literature of this century, from Eliot's "Hollow Man" to the novels of Dos Passos, Hemingway, and Faulkner. It often appears in writers not commonly associated with the existentialists as in this remarkable passage from *A Story-Teller's Story*, where Sherwood Anderson describes his own awakening to his spiritual emptiness. He tells of walking alone late at night along a moonlit road when,

> I had suddenly an odd, and to my own seeming, a ridiculous desire to abase myself before something not human and so stepping into the moonlit road, I knelt in the dust. Having no God, the gods having been taken from me by the life about me, as a personal God has been taken from all modern men by a force within that man himself does not understand but that is called the intellect, I kept smiling at the figure I cut in my own eyes as I knelt in the road. . . .
>
> There was no God in the sky, no God in myself, no conviction in myself that I had the power to believe in a God, and so I merely knelt in the dust in silence and no words came to my lips.

In another passage Anderson wondered if the giving of itself by an entire generation to mechanical things was not really making all men impotent, if the desire for a greater navy, a greater army, taller public buildings, was not a sign of growing impotence. He felt that Puritanism and the industrialism which was its offspring had sterilized modern life, and proposed that men return to a healthful animal vigor by renewed contact with simple things of the earth, among them untrammeled sexual expression. One is reminded of the unkempt and delectable raffishness of Steinbeck's *Cannery Row* or of D. H. Lawrence's quasi-religious doctrine of sex, "blood-consciousness" and the "divine otherness" of animal existence.

Man's estrangement from nature has been a major theme in literature at least since Rousseau and the Romantic movement, and can hardly be said to be the property of existentialists. But this group nevertheless adds its own insistence that one of modern man's most urgent dangers is that he builds ever higher the brick and steel walls of technology which shut him away from a health-giving life according to "nature."

Their treatment of this theme is most commonly expressed as part of a broader insistence that modern man needs to shun abstraction and return to "concreteness" or "wholeness."

A third estrangement has occurred at the social level and its sign is growing dismay at man's helplessness before the great machine-like colossus of industrialized society. This is another major theme of Western literature, and here again, though they hardly discovered the danger or began the protest, the existentialists in our time renew the protest against any pattern or force which would stifle the unique and spontaneous in individual life. The crowding of men into cities, the subdivision of labor which submerges the man in his economic function, the burgeoning of centralized government, the growth of advertising, propaganda, and mass media of entertainment and communication—all the things which force men into Riesman's "Lonely Crowd"—these same things drive men asunder by destroying their individuality and making them live on the surface of life, content to deal with things rather than people. "Exteriorization," says Berdyaev, "is the source of slavery, whereas freedom is interiorization. Slavery always indicates alienation, the ejection of human nature into the external." This kind of alienation is exemplified by Zero, in Elmer Rice's play "The Adding Machine." Zero's twenty-five years as a bookkeeper in a department store have dried up his humanity, making him incapable of love, of friendship, of any deeply felt, freely expressed emotion. Such estrangement is often given as the reason for man's inhumanity to man, the explanation of injustice in modern society. In Camus' short novel, aptly called *The Stranger*, a young man is convicted by a court of murder. This is a homicide which he has actually committed under extenuating circumstances. But the court never listens to any of the relevant evidence, seems never to hear anything that pertains to the crime itself; it convicts the young man on wholly irrelevant grounds—because he had behaved in an unconventional way at his mother's funeral the day before the homicide. In this book one feels the same dream-like distortion of reality as in the trial scene in *Alice in Wonderland*, a suffocating sense of being enclosed by events which are irrational or absurd but also inexorable. Most disturbing of all is the young man's aloneness, the impermeable membrane of estrangement which surrounds him and prevents anyone else from penetrating to his experience of life or sympathizing with it.

The fourth kind of alienation, man's estrangement from his own true self, especially as his nature is distorted by an exaltation of reason, is another theme having an extensive history as a major part of the Romantic revolt. Of the many writers who treat the theme, Hawthorne comes particularly close to the emphasis of contemporary existentialists. His Ethan Brand, Dr. Rappaccini, and Roger Chillingworth are a recurrent figure who represents the dislocation in human nature which results when an overdeveloped or misapplied intellect severs "the magnetic chain of human sympathy." Hawthorne is thoroughly existential in his concern for the sanctity of the individual human soul, as well as in his preoccupation with sin and the dark side of human nature, which must be seen in part as his attempt to build back some fullness to the flattened image of man bequeathed to him by the Enlightenment. Whitman was trying to do this when he added flesh and bone and a sexual nature to the spiritualized image of man he inherited from Emerson, though his image remains diffused and attenuated by the same cosmic optimism. Many of the nineteenth-century depictions of man represent him as a figure of power or of potential power, sometimes as daimonic, like Melville's Ahab, but after World War I the power is gone; man is not merely distorted or truncated, he is hollow, powerless, faceless. At the time when his command over natural forces seems to be unlimited, man is pictured as weak, ridden with nameless dread. And this brings us to another of the major themes of existentialism.

4. *"Fear and trembling," anxiety.* At Stockholm when he accepted the Nobel Prize, William Faulkner said that "Our tragedy today is a general and universal physical fear so long sustained by now that we can even bear it. There are no longer problems of the spirit. There is only one question: When will I be blown up?" The optimistic vision of the Enlightenment which saw man, through reason and its extensions in science, conquering all nature and solving all social and political problems in a continuous upward spiral of Progress, cracked open like a melon on the rock of World War I. The theories which held such high hopes died in that sickening and unimaginable butchery. Here was a concrete fact of human nature and society which the theories could not contain. The Great Depression and World War II deepened the sense of dismay which the loss of these ideals brought, but only with the atomic bomb did this become an unbearable terror, a threat of instant annihilation which confronted all men, even those most insulated by the thick crust of material goods and services. Now the most unthinking person could sense that each advance in mechanical technique carried not only a chromium and plush promise of comfort but a threat as well.

Sartre, following Kierkegaard, speaks of another kind of anxiety which oppresses modern man—"the anguish of Abraham"—the necessity which is laid upon him to make moral choices on his own responsibility. A military officer in wartime knows the agony of choice which forces him to sacrifice part of his army to preserve the rest, as does a man in high political office, who must make decisions affecting the lives of millions. The existentialists claim that each of us might make moral decisions in our own lives which involve the same anguish. Kierkegaard finds that this necessity is one thing which makes each life unique, which makes it impossible to speculate or generalize about human life, because each man's case is irretrievably his own, something in which he is personally and passionately involved. His book *Fear and Trembling* is an elaborate and fascinating commentary on the Old Testament story of Abraham, who was commanded by God to sacrifice his beloved son Isaac. Abraham thus becomes the emblem of man who must make a harrowing choice, in this case between love for his son and love for God, between the universal moral law which says categorically, "thou shalt not kill," and the unique inner demand of his religious faith. Abraham's decision, which is to violate the abstract and collective moral law, has to be made not in arrogance but in fear and trembling, one of the inferences being that sometimes one must make an exception to the general law because he is (existentially) an exception, a concrete being whose existence can never be completely subsumed under any universal.

5. *The encounter with nothingness.* For the man alienated from God, from nature, from his fellow man and from himself, what is left at last but Nothingness? The testimony of the existentialists is that this is where modern man now finds himself, not on the highway of upward Progress toward a radiant Utopia but on the brink of a catastrophic precipice, below which yawns the absolute void, an uncompromised black Nothingness. In one sense this is Eliot's Wasteland inhabited by his Hollow Man who is

> Shape without form, shade without color
> Paralyzed force, gesture without motion.

That is what moves E. A. Robinson's Richard Cory, the man who is everything that might make us wish that we were in his place, to go home one calm summer night and put a bullet through his head.

One of the most convincing statements of the encounter with Nothingness is made by Leo Tolstoy in "My Confession." He tells how in good health, in the prime of life, when he had everything that a man could desire—wealth, fame, aristocratic social position, a beautiful wife and children, a brilliant mind and great artistic talent in the height of their powers, he nevertheless was seized with a growing uneasiness, a nameless discontent which he could not shake or alleviate. His experience was like that of a man who falls sick, with symptoms which he disregards as insignificant; but the symptoms return again and again until they merge into a continuous suffering. And the patient suddenly is confronted with the overwhelming fact that what he took for mere indisposition is more important to him than anything else on earth, that it is death! "I felt the ground on which I stood was crumbling, that there was nothing for me to stand on, that what I had been living for was nothing, that I had no reason for living. . . . To stop was impossible, to go back was impossible; and it was impossible to shut my eyes so as to see that there was nothing before me but suffering and actual death, absolute annihilation." This is the "Sickness Unto Death" of Kierkegaard, the despair in which one wishes to die but cannot. Hemingway's short story, "A Clean, Well-Lighted Place" gives an unforgettable expression of this theme. At the end of the story, the old waiter climbs into bed late at night saying to himself, "What did he fear? It was not fear or dread. It was a nothing which he knew too well. It was all a nothing and a man was nothing too. . . . Nada y pues nada, y nada y pues nada." And then because he has experienced the death of God he goes on to recite the Lord's Prayer in blasphemous despair: "Our Nothing who are in Nothing, nothing by thy nothing. . . ." And then the Ave Maria, "Hail nothing, full of nothing. . . ." This is stark, even for Hemingway, but the old waiter does no more than name the void felt by most people in the early Hemingway novels, a hunger they seek to assuage with alcohol, sex, and violence in an aimless progress from bar to bed to bullring. It goes without saying that much of the despair and pessimism in other contemporary authors springs from a similar sense of the void in modern life.

6. *Freedom.* Sooner or later, as a theme that includes all the others, the existentialist writings bear upon freedom. The themes we have outlined above describe either some loss of man's freedom or some threat to it, and all existentialists of whatever sort are concerned to enlarge the range of human freedom.

For the avowed atheists like Sartre freedom means human autonomy. In a purposeless universe man is *condemned* to freedom because he is the only creature who is "self-surpassing," who can become something other than he is. Precisely because there is no God to give purpose to the universe, each man must accept individual responsibility for his own becoming, a burden made heavier by the fact that in choosing for himself he chooses for all men "the image of man as he ought to be." A man *is* the sum total of the acts that make up his life—no more, no less—and though the coward has made himself cowardly, it is always possible for him to change and make himself heroic. In Sartre's novel,

The Age of Reason, one of the least likable of the characters, almost overwhelmed by despair and self-disgust at his homosexual tendencies, is on the point of solving his problem by mutilating himself with a razor, when in an effort of will he throws the instrument down, and we are given to understand that from this moment he will have mastery over his aberrant drive. Thus in the daily course of ordinary life must men shape their becoming in Sartre's world.

The religious existentialists interpret man's freedom differently. They use much the same language as Sartre, develop the same themes concerning the predicament of man, but always include God as a radical factor. They stress the man of faith rather than the man of will. They interpret man's existential condition as a state of alienation from his essential nature which is God-like, the problem of his life being to heal the chasm between the two, that is, to find salvation. The mystery and ambiguity of man's existence they attribute to his being the intersection of two realms. "Man bears within himself," writes Berdyaev, "the image which is both the image of man and the image of God, and is the image of man as far as the image of God is actualized." Tillich describes salvation as "the act in which the cleavage between the essential being and the existential situation is overcome." Freedom here, as for Sartre, involves an acceptance of responsibility for choice and a *commitment* to one's choice. This is the meaning of faith, a faith like Abraham's, the commitment which is an agonizing sacrifice of one's own desire and will and dearest treasure to God's will.

A final word. Just as one should not expect to find in a particular writer all of the characteristics of existentialism as we have described them, he should also be aware that some of the most striking expressions of existentialism in literature and the arts come to us by indirection, often through symbols or through innovations in conventional form. Take the preoccupation of contemporary writers with time. In *The Sound and the Fury*, Faulkner both collapses and expands normal clock time, or by juxtapositions of past and present blurs time into a single amorphous pool. He does this by using various forms of "stream of consciousness" or other techniques which see life in terms of unique, subjective experience—that is, existentially. The conventional view of externalized life, a rational orderly progression cut into uniform segments by the hands of a clock, he rejects in favor of a view which sees life as opaque, ambiguous, and irrational—that is, as the existentialist sees it. Graham Greene does something like this in *The Power and the Glory*. He creates a scene isolated in time and cut off from the rest of the world, steamy and suffocating as if a bell jar had been placed over it. Through this atmosphere fetid with impending death and human suffering, stumbles the whiskey priest, lonely and confused, pursued by a police lieutenant who has experienced the void and the death of God. Such expressions in literature do not mean necessarily that the authors are conscious existentialist theorizers, or even that they know the writings of such theorizers. Faulkner may never have read Heidegger—or St. Augustine—both of whom attempt to demonstrate that time is more within a man and subject to his unique experience of it than it is outside him. But it is legitimate to call Faulkner's views of time and life "existential" in this novel because in recent years existentialist theorizers have given such views a local habitation and a name. One of the attractions, and one of the dangers, of existential themes is that they become like Sir Thomas Browne's quincunx: once one begins to look for them, he sees them everywhere. But if one applies restraint and discrimination, he will find that they illuminate much of contemporary literature and sometimes the literature of the past as well.

ARTHUR KOESTLER

Arthur Koestler (1905–), born in Hungary and educated in Austria, fought in the Communist forces in the Spanish Civil War (1936–1939). Captured and condemned to death, then rescued by the British, he is now a British subject and prominent author in his adopted language. In his first novel, *Darkness at Noon* (1941), he anatomizes the Russian police state; in his most recent, *The Call Girls* (1971), he deals with the world's hope for survival. This selection is from *The Act of Creation* (1964), "a study of the conscious and unconscious in science and art."

THE THINKING CAP

Koestler nicely illustrates the power of the thesis—or hypothesis—in giving meaning to what we know and even in discovering and selecting our facts, contrary to the idea, which science has inherited from Bacon, of empirically gathering our facts to reach an inductive conclusion. Notice how he states his thesis at the end of his first paragraph, then concedes a point to empirical science, then supports his thesis with two quotations from authorities and a series of persuasive examples.

I have repeatedly mentioned "shifts of attention" to previously neglected aspects of experience which make familiar phenomena appear in a new, revealing light, seen through spectacles of a different colour. At the decisive turning points in the history of science, all the data in the field, unchanged in themselves, may fall into a new pattern, and be given a new interpretation, a new theoretical frame. By stressing the importance of the *interpretation* (or reinterpretation) of facts, I may have given the impression of underestimating the importance of *collecting* facts, of having emphasized the value of theory-making at the expense of the empirical aspect of science—an unforgivable heresy in the eyes of Positivists, Behaviourists, and other theorists of the anti-theory school. Needless to say, only a fool could belittle the importance of observation and experiment—or wish to revert to Aristotelian physics which was all speculation and no experiment. But the collecting of data is a discriminating activity, like the picking of flowers, and unlike the action of a lawn-mower; and the selection of flowers considered worth picking, as well as their arrangement into a bouquet, are ultimately matters of personal taste. As T. H. Huxley has said in an oft-quoted passage:

> Those who refuse to go beyond fact rarely get as far as fact; and anyone who has studied the history of science knows that almost every step therein has been made by . . . the invention of a hypothesis which, though verifiable, often had little foundation to start with. . . .

Sir Lawrence Bragg is the only physicist who shared a Nobel Prize with his own father—for their joint work on analysing crystal structures by means of X-rays, doubtless an eminently factual preoccupation, which took two lifetimes. Yet in his book on *The History of Science* he too concluded that the essence of science "lies not in discovering facts, but in discovering new ways of thinking about them."*

New facts do emerge constantly; but they are found as the result of a search in a definite direction, based on theoretical considerations—as Galle discovered the planet Neptune, which nobody had seen before, by directing his telescope at the celestial region which Leverrier's calculations had indicated. This is admittedly an extreme case of observation guided by theory; but it remains nevertheless true that it is not enough for the scientist to keep his eyes open unless he has an idea of what he is looking for.

The telescope is, of course, the supreme eye-opener and fact-finder in astronomy; but it is rarely appreciated that the Copernican revolution came *before* the invention of the telescope—and so did Kepler's *New Astronomy*. The instruments which Copernicus used for observing the

* (London: Cohen & West, 1948), p. 167.

stars were less precise than those of the Alexandrian astronomers Hipparchus and Ptolemy, on whose data Copernicus built his theory; and he knew no more about the actual motions of stars and planets than they had known:

> Insofar as actual knowledge is concerned, Copernicus was no better off, and in some respects worse off, than the Greek astronomers of Alexandria who lived in the time of Jesus Christ. They had the same data, the same instruments, the same know-how in geometry, as he did. They were giants of "exact science"; yet they failed to see what Copernicus saw after, and Aristarchus had seen before them: that the planets' motions were obviously governed by the sun.*

Similarly, Harvey's revolutionary discoveries were made before the microscope was developed into a serviceable tool; and Einstein formulated his "Special Theory of Relativity" in 1905 based on data which . . . were by no means new. Poincaré, for instance, Einstein's senior by twenty-five years, had held all the loose threads in his hands, and the reasons for his failure to tie them together are still a matter of speculation among scientists. To quote Taton:

> Poincaré, who had so much wider a mathetical background than Einstein, then a young assistant in the Federal Patents Office of Berne, knew all the elements required for such a synthesis, of which he had felt the urgent need and for which he had laid the first foundations. Nevertheless, he did not dare to explain his thoughts, and to derive all the consequences, thus missing the decisive step separating him from the real discovery of the principle of relativity.†

Without the hard little bits of marble which are called "facts" or "data" one cannot compose a mosaic; what matters, however, are not so much the individual bits, but the successive patterns into which you arrange them, then break them up and rearrange them. "We shall find," wrote Butterfield on the opening page of his history of the Scientific Revolution, "that in both celestial and terrestrial physics—which hold the strategic place in the whole movement—change is brought about, not by new observations or additional evidence in the first instance, but by transpositions that were taking place inside the minds of the scien-

---

* A. Koestler, *The Sleepwalkers* (London: Hutchinson, 1959), p. 70.
† R. Taton, *Reason and Chance in Scientific Discovery* (London: Hutchinson, 1957), pp. 134–35.

tists themselves. . . . Of all forms of mental activity, the most difficult to induce even in the minds of the young, who may be presumed not to have lost their flexibility, is the art of handling the same bundle of data as before, but placing them in a new system of relations with one another by giving them a different framework, all of which virtually means putting on a different kind of thinking-cap for the moment. It is easy to teach anybody a new fact about Richelieu, but it needs light from heaven to enable a teacher to break the old framework in which the student has been accustomed to seeing his Richelieu."*

Once more we are facing the stubborn powers of habit, and the antithesis of habit and originality. New facts alone do not make a new theory; and new facts alone do not destroy an outlived theory. In both cases it requires creative originality to achieve the task. The facts which proved that the planetary motions depended on the sun have been staring into the face of astronomers throughout the ages—but they preferred to look away.

SUGGESTIONS FOR WRITING

1. Write a sentence that states Virginia Woolf's thesis more sharply and inclusively than she herself has done, perhaps something like "In reading a book, one should —— because ——." (This one-sentence summary, this thesis making, can help you to understand any essay or any chapter in any book. Try it and see.) Comparing these thesis-sentences in class will enable you not only to grasp more firmly Virginia Woolf's idea but also to follow her inductive strategy in spelling it out.

2. Follow Virginia Woolf's advice at the end of her third paragraph: "Recall, then, some event that has left a distinct impression on you . . . ." That will be your subject. Now write a thesis stating something *about* it, asserting its value, perhaps something like "Sometimes, as Virginia Woolf says, the whole world seems to come together in a moment of insight" or "A book [or movie] can suddenly put the whole world in a new perspective." Next write an essay in which you describe and illustrate that thesis with as much specific detail as possible ("A tree shook; an electric light danced; the tone of the talk was comic"). Try working in two or three of Virginia Woolf's words that you have underlined—*multitudinous, impalpable, trudging, heterogeneous, fancy, malodorous.* Try also, if

* H. Butterfield, *The Origins of Modern Science* (London: G. Bell, 1949), pp. 1–2.

you can, a metaphor like hers about the dark side of the mind "that comes uppermost in solitude."

3. Bigelow has written an essay explaining a concept: existentialism. See what you can do by taking an ordinary concept—education, loyalty, success, friendship, love—and developing an explanation of it, as Bigelow has done, along the lines of "though commonly used, commonly misunderstood." You might give it an even sharper argumentative edge: "You should understand the true meaning of —— to see clearly what is going on around you." Try showing what the thing you are defining is not, and what it truly is.

4. Write an essay on the thesis: "Life on this campus would be better if, in choosing for himself, everyone followed Sartre's rule of choosing for all men 'the image of man as he ought to be.'" Try to use three or four striking words from Bigelow—*gnomic, raffishness, dislocation, amorphous, steamy.* Try one sentence like Bigelow's "The crowding of men into cities . . . ."

5. Write an essay about how some new insight changed your interpretation of evidence, how discovering your parents at work one Christmas morning changed the facts as to how the presents got under the tree, how the snub by a friend on the street was the result of her losing her glasses. Your thesis might be something like "Facts are not always what they seem" or, borrowing from Koestler, "Facts may stare us in the face, but we sometimes prefer to look away."

Two
Structure: Middle Tactics

This chapter emphasizes the single most important consideration in arranging the middle of your essay: handling the opposition. In finding a thesis, you have already won most of the battle to organize your thoughts. You will have introduced your thesis with three or four sentences to acquaint the reader with where you are, and you will have produced your essay's beginning. Your middle has then described your evidence, as Woolf, Bigelow, and Koestler have done. Then, with luck, you have written a good end—a thumping last paragraph that brings your point home for good. Refer again to Koestler, since he is brief, as a convenient model for beginning and end paragraphs.

Koestler also illustrates the classic middle tactic: facing the opposition immediately after you have set your thesis, getting the opposition out of the way so you can present your evidence. The essay thus follows the inherent structure of thinking: first an assertion, then an objection from the other side of the mind, then a return to the first idea reinforced—pro and con, then pro again. This is the fundamental middle tactic. The following selections argue pro and con, and they present ideas with which you may agree and disagree to develop your own argument and handle the neighboring opposition. As you read, mark those words and phrases that seem to turn the argument from one side to the other—*but, of course, some may argue*, and the like.

ELAINE MORGAN

Elaine Morgan (1920–), born in South Wales, educated at Oxford, the mother of three sons, is a veteran television writer—everything from soap operas to documentaries—for the British Broadcasting Corporation (the BBC). *The Descent of Woman,* from which this selection comes, is her first book.

THE ESCAPE ROUTE

Mrs. Morgan is answering Darwin's *The Descent of Man* and the whole school of later anthropologists who have written about man, the aggressive hunter, and have forgotten all about woman. Formulate a thesis that might serve if she were presenting this as an independent essay, rather than as the second chapter of her book, which has already set out its point at the beginning. Notice how she handles the opposition, the "con" side of the argument.

Once upon a time . . . but which time? "Man," according to the currently fashionable concept, "is the child of the Pleistocene."

I am not going to begin with the Pleistocene. It was a vivid and dramatic period when the climate of the world went haywire and produced an era of prolific evolutionary changes, and if you're talking about Homo sapiens there is no doubt that it was the Pleistocene which first saw the finished product. The reason I'm not going to talk about it is that the most fundamental ape-into-man changes were already well under way before the Pleistocene ever began.

The Pleistocene cannot answer the really difficult questions such as how and why our ancestors first began to walk on their hind legs or how and why they first picked up a stone and used it as a tool, for the simple reason that these things happened before the Pleistocene even began. The Villafranchian (very early Pleistocene) hominids dug up in Olduvai Gorge were already walking on their hind legs. They were already using tools. All that was left to happen to them was an increase in cranial capacity, an increased elegance in their gait, and the acquisition of a chin. Before the Pleistocene came the Pliocene, and before that again the Miocene, and we are going to begin at the beginning.

Long long ago, then, back in the mild Miocene, there was a generalized vegetarian prehominid hairy ape. She had not yet developed the high-powered brain which today distinguishes woman from all other species.

She was rather like Proconsul, a primate who lived about the same time and whose remains have been dug up in large numbers. Like present-day gorillas, she got her food from the trees and slept in the branches, but spent part of her time on the ground. But she was smaller and lighter than a gorilla; and she hadn't got the gorilla's confidence that her species could lick anybody in that neck of the woods. There were several larger species around that could frighten the daylights out of her.

After a couple of million years of this peaceful existence the first torrid heat waves of the Pliocene began to scorch the African continent. All around the edges of the forest the trees began to wither in the drought and were replaced by scrub and grassland. As the forest got smaller and smaller there wasn't enough room or enough food for all the apes it had once supported. The smaller and less aggressive species, and those least intolerant of descending to ground level, were driven out onto the open savannah, and she was one of them.

She knew at once she wasn't going to like it there. She had four hands better adapted for gripping than walking and she wasn't very fast on the ground. She was a fruit eater and as far as she could see there wasn't any fruit.

When frightened by a carnivore her instinct was to climb a tree or run away and hide, but there were no trees on the plain and very few places to hide. The man in the street will be surprised by her dilemma: he's seen films about prehistory and he knows all she had to do was pop into the nearest cave. But if you dropped him down at random somewhere in the middle of the veldt, he would be even more astonished to find that it's possible to wander around for weeks or months without ever seeing a cave to pop into.

In the forest she had often varied her fruitarian diet by eating small insects and caterpillars and for a long time this was the only type of food she could find which looked to her remotely edible. She never thought of digging for roots—she wasn't very bright. She got thirsty, too, and the water holes were death traps with large cats lurking hopefully around them. She got horribly skinny and scruffy-looking.

You may be thinking that this eviction was just as bad for her brothers. Almost; but not quite. Remember, she was a primate. Primate babies are slow developers, and most primate females in the wild spend most of their adult lives either gestating or suckling a new infant or with the last one growing heavier and clinging on and slowing them down. It might be possible, in a transitional period between being vegetarian and learning to eat meat, to get by on a diet of grasshoppers; but if you're eating for two while this is happening you'll starve in half the time. Even before that, your milk dries up and the babies die.

For another thing, her brothers were probably stronger and better equipped. Her relative Proconsul, we are told, "had large, fighting canine teeth." Ardrey compares them to "the magnificent daggers sported by apes and baboons." But it just isn't true that baboons sport magnificent daggers. Only male baboons sport magnificent daggers. In vegetarian species these fangs are chiefly used for fierce intraspecies dominance-battles that females don't go in for very much. It may well have been the same for the Pliocene apes; so while her brother, when overtaken by something the size of, say, an ocelot, could inflict some very nasty lacerations, she could do little more than doggedly chew its ear while it unseamed her from top to bottom.

At this point people brought up on Tarzan will have a vague expectation that the father of her child will see what's expected of him, dash off and bring down an impala, drag it triumphantly back to her and say: "There you are, darling. Help yourself."

I'm sorry, but he'll do nothing of the kind. I've admitted she wasn't very bright—but he was just as thick as she was. Being unencumbered, he could get around faster, and like all primates he wasn't above sampling a piece of meat if it was brought to his attention. But if he happened on the remains of the lion's kill and managed to drive off the hyenas, it would never occur to him to give a piece of it to a female. Fruitarians have no need to develop these chivalrous instincts. On the contrary, if she happened to find a piece of offal on her own account he would promptly take it away from her. Ardrey rightly remarks about the dominant male that his "instinctual objects of self-sacrifice seldom among primates include the female." If they all looked likely to starve on that parching Pliocene savannah, he would make dead sure that she starved first.

In short, she found herself in an impossible situation. The only food in plentiful supply was grass, which her stomach wasn't designed to cope with. Everything in the vicinity (except the insects) was either larger, fiercer, or faster than she was. A lot of them were larger, fiercer, *and* faster.

The only thing she had going for her was the fact that she was one of a community, so that if they all ran away together a predator would be satisfied with catching the slowest and the rest would survive a little longer. This wasn't much of an advantage, though. If they all stayed together, pressure on the scarce and unfamiliar food resources would be fiercer than ever, with the females in their proper primate place at the end of the queue. The males, fresh from the trees, wouldn't have yet worked out the baboon strategy of posting fierce male outriders when the herd moved on; and if the predator always ate the slowest of the tribe, the cycle of gestation ensured that the time would soon come when the slowest would be you know who.

What, then, did she do? Did she take a crash course in walking erect, convince some male overnight that he must now be the breadwinner, and back him up by agreeing to go hairless and thus constituting an even more vulnerable and conspicuous target for any passing carnivore? Did she turn into the Naked Ape?

Of course, she did nothing of the kind. There simply wasn't time. In the circumstances there was only one thing she could possibly turn into, and she promptly did it. She turned into a leopard's dinner.

For her mate the impossible situation was just marginally less impossible. (That is why the predilection for the male pronoun has concealed the full hopelessness of their plight.) He lived a few years longer, but a chain is only as strong as its weakest link, and when he died no one came after him. Of course, the process took many more generations than this; it happened slowly over the torrid centuries as the forests dwindled, but the end was a foregone conclusion. They didn't have a cat in hell's chance. They became extinct.

At this point I anticipate a protest from the biologists and a yelp from the general reader. (I yelped myself when I first reasoned myself into this cul-de-sac.)

The specialist objection runs: "It is simply untrue to imply that arboreal primates find it impossible to adapt to terrestrial life. Baboons, mandrills, and macaques have done so with conspicuous success."

Yes, it is certainly true that the baboons survived; so why not this little ape we are talking about? My own opinion is that the baboon's ancestors must have come to earth much sooner and gradually learned to adapt to ground dwelling—by root digging, militant aggressiveness, social organization, etc.—under more propitious conditions, before the heat was on, because these adaptations take a long time to evolve. There are some solid anatomical reasons for believing that they didn't stay in the trees long enough to get as specialized for it as our own ancestors. For example, they never became brachiators, though most arboreal anthropoids begin to swing beneath the branches rather than running over them once they reach a critical size, and some of the early baboons, such as Simopithecus, were very large animals. We can be pretty sure that our own predecessors stayed aloft long enough to do a bit of brachiating, even though we never developed the elongated arms of gibbons and gorillas, because brachiating primates can move their arms in a sideways arc, through the crucifix position, while the baboon, like the dog, only moves his backward and forward.

The general objection is a more heartfelt one. If this primate who came down from the trees became extinct, what about the happy ending? *What about us?*

I will now come clean and admit she wasn't actually our grandmother, but a great-great-aunt on the maternal side who was unlucky enough to live in the middle of a continent. Hundreds of miles away near the coast lived a female cousin of the same species, another timid, hairy, undifferentiated Miocene-type ape. Her piece of forest was shrinking, too. As the heat and the dryness spread out from the baking heart of Africa, it became reduced to a narrowing strip; the larger and fiercer arboreans drove her away, just as her cousin had been driven, from poaching on their dwindling preserves.

She also couldn't digest grass; she also had a greedy and hectoring mate; she also lacked fighting canines; she also was hampered by a clinging infant; and she also was chased by a carnivore and found there was no tree she could run up to escape. However, in front of her there was a large sheet of water. With piercing squeals of terror she ran straight into the sea. The carnivore was a species of cat and didn't like wetting his feet; and moreover, though he had twice her body weight, she was accustomed like most tree-dwellers to adopting an upright posture, even though she used four legs for locomotion. She was thus able to go farther into the water than he could without drowning. She went right in up to her neck and waited there clutching her baby until the cat got fed up with waiting and went back to the grasslands.

She, too, loathed getting her feet wet. It felt so unpleasant that she sometimes wished she had no fur at all. On the other hand, when your homeland's turning into an inferno the seaside's not at all a bad place to be. She found to her delight that almost everything on the beach and in the water was either smaller or slower or more timid than she was herself.

She switched easily, almost without noticing it, from eating small scuttling insects to eating small scuttling shrimps and baby crabs. There were thousands of seabirds nesting on the cliffs, and as she had a firm handgrip and a good head for heights she filled another empty ecological niche as an egg collector.

Besides the shrimps there were larger creatures with harder shells, resembling mussels and oysters and lobsters. Her mate used to crunch through the shells or pry them open with his daggerlike canines; she was envious of this because being daggerless she couldn't always manage it. One idle afternoon after a good deal of trial and error she picked up a pebble—this required no luck at all because the beach was covered with thousands of pebbles—and hit one of the shells with it, and the shell cracked. She tried it again, and it worked every time. So she became a tool user, and the male watched her and imitated her. (This doesn't mean that she was any smarter than he was—only that necessity is the mother of invention. Later his necessities, and therefore his inventiveness, outstripped hers.)

Whenever anything alarming happened on the landward side—or sometimes just because it was getting so hot—she would go back into the water, up to her waist, or even up to her neck. This meant, of course, that she had to walk upright on her two hind legs. It was slow and ungainly, especially at first, but it was absolutely essential if she wanted to keep her head above water. She isn't the only creature who has ever had to learn to do it. Although, as we have seen, she is almost unique in having learned to walk upright all the time, there is another mammal who does it for part of the time, and probably for the same reason. The beaver, whose ancestors also spent a good deal of time in shallow water, whenever she is transporting building materials or carrying her baby around, has the habit of getting up on her hind legs and proceeding by means of a perfectly serviceable bipedal gait.

She was very relieved to notice that even the large alarming-looking things that sometimes clambered out of the sea—things like seals, and giant turtles, and various kinds of sea cow, which were much commoner in those days—all proved to be very slow and clumsy and helpless on land, and in most cases totally disinclined to fight back when attacked.

Gradually her mate extended the shell-bashing maneuver to cover skull bashing as well. When you're dealing with dugongs or baby seals there is no risk involved and no call for beginner's luck or the accurate aim that a vegetarian would take centuries, or even millennia, to learn. You simply go on clobbering them with a pebble until they die, and then you eat them.

It wasn't very glamorous, but in the end he began to get quite a kick out of it. He learned to like the taste of meat as well as that of fish (seals and sea cows are both mammals) and became more efficient at killing things. Since they were both pretty well fed and there's an awful lot of meat on a sea cow, he didn't always make her wait until he'd finished before letting her have some. It took a few million years before he began to slide imperceptibly into the role of meat provider for the family, but there were so many alternative sources of food available to her that there was no particular hurry. Sometimes the carcasses got swept into the sea before they'd finished with them, so they took to dragging them up the beach and leaving them in a cave. It was the natural thing to do because the coastline is the place where you always find caves.

She spent so much time in the water that her fur became nothing but a nuisance to her. Oftener than not, mammals who return to the water and stay there long enough, especially in warm climates, lose their hair as a perfectly natural consequence. Wet fur on land is no use to anyone, and fur in the water tends to slow down your swimming. She began to turn into a naked ape for the same reason as the porpoise turned into a naked cetacean, the hippopotamus into a naked ungulate, the walrus into a naked pinniped, and the manatee into a naked sirenian. As her fur began to disappear she felt more and more comfortable in the water, and that is where she spent the Pliocene, patiently waiting for conditions in the interior to improve.

I believe these are the "circumstances special to the point of disbelief" which explain how an anthropoid began to turn into a hominid. All the developments that otherwise appear strained and improbable, and contrary to what we know of normal behavior among primates and other quadrupeds, in these circumstances become not only credible and understandable, but natural and inevitable. Many features carelessly described as "unique" in human beings are unique only among land mammals. For most of them, as we shall see, as soon as we begin to look at *aquatic* mammals, we shall find parallels galore.

Almost everyone has hitherto taken it for granted that Australopitheca, since she was primitive and chinless and low-browed, was necessarily hairy, and the artists always depict her as a shaggy creature. I don't think there is any good reason for thinking this. Just as for a long time they "assumed" the big brain came first, before the use of tools, so they still "assume" that the hairlessness came last. If I had to visualize the Villafranchian hominids, I'd say their skin was in all probability quite as smooth as our own.

However, we haven't reached Australopithecus yet, not by a long way. When I say the ape stayed in the water until conditions began to improve, I'm not just talking about a summer season. Suppose it took a couple of million years of drought to drive her into the sea; even then the African Pliocene didn't begin to let up for another ten million after that.

And a lot of strange and upsetting things can happen to a species in the course of ten million years.

Before we go on with the story, an acknowledgment is overdue.

This aquatic theory of human evolution was first suggested by the marine biologist Professor Sir Alister Hardy, F.R.S., in an article in *The New Scientist* in 1960. Later he gave a talk on it on the BBC's Third Programme, which was reprinted in the BBC's publication *The Listener*.

I heard nothing about it at the time. Apparently it made about as much impact on the scientific world as the reading of Darwin's first paper on the evolution of species to the Linnaean Society. (The president said in his annual report for 1858: "This year has not been marked by any of those striking discoveries which at once revolutionise, so to speak, the department of science on which they bear. . . .")

Later Desmond Morris in *The Naked Ape* devoted a page or so to a full and fair summary of Professor Hardy's arguments, and acknowledged their "most appealing indirect evidence"; but something blocked him from going further. It may be that the traumatic experience of having almost drowned at the age of seven, which prevented his learning to swim for the next thirty years, prevented him also from accepting that we could ever have been beneficially molded by so dangerous an element as water. For whatever reason, he dismissed the theory as unproven and, if true, of minor importance, a "rather salutary christening ceremony."

But I felt when I read that page as if the whole evolutionary landscape had been transformed by a blinding flash of light. I was astonished that after this key had been put into their hands, people were still going on writing about the move from the trees to the plains as if nothing had happened.

Let's recapitulate a few more of Sir Alister's arguments. It wasn't only men's hairlessness that prompted him to suggest the idea. He remembered the fact noted and illustrated by Professor Wood Jones in his book *Man's Place Among the Mammals* that the vestigial hairs which remain on the human body—and which are seen still more clearly on a human fetus before it sheds its coat of hair—are arranged quite differently from the hairs of the other primates. On studying these illustrations more closely, Sir Alister perceived that in fact the arrangement of the hairs follows precisely the lines that would be followed by the flow of water over a swimming body. If the hair, for purposes of streamlining, had adapted itself to the direction of the current before it was finally discarded, this is precisely what we should expect to find.

He showed how the cracking open of shellfish would foster the use of tools. He pointed out that the ape was not the only mammal to arrive at this. Another aquatic animal, the sea otter, whenever he dives for a sea urchin, also brings up a stone in his other hand; he floats on his back, holds the stone on his belly, and uses it to break the shellfish on.

Professor Hardy wrote that wading in water would explain not only our erect walk, but the increased sensitivity of our fingertips, through the habit of groping underwater for objects we could not clearly see.

He pointed out that the best way of keeping warm in water is to develop a layer of subcutaneous fat, analogous to the whale's blubber, all over the surface of the body; that this is what all the aquatic animals have done; and that Homo sapiens, alone among the primates, has in fact developed this layer, for which no other explanation has ever been found.

The more you think about it, the more impossible it becomes to believe that hunting man discarded his fur to enable himself to become cooler, and *at the same time* developed a layer of fat, the only possible effect of which would be to make him warmer.

Fur on the outside of the skin and a layer of fat beneath it both serve essentially the same purpose. The chief distinction between them is that one is better adapted to life on land, and the other to life in the water, and there is no conceivable evolutionary reason why any animal would begin to abandon one method in favor of the other unless its environment had undergone precisely this transformation.

The Hardy theory also explains why, however far from the sea they may be found, the very earliest man-made tools unearthed in connection with hominid remains are always fashioned from "pebbles."

Above all, it gives a simple and adequate explanation of the long chronological gap between the remains of Proconsul and his contemporaries, and the remains of Australopithecus. If no traces have been found of any creature transitional between the two, it could well be because the mortal remains of the naked apes and their first animal victims were not deposited in some Kenyan lair or midden, but swept out on the tide and devoured by fishes, while the first tools they ever chipped were mixed up with a million other pebbles like single straws in a haystack.

Since this theory was first mooted, some of the possible objections to it have been steadily undermined. For instance, some people found it hard to believe in that first plunge. Were not arboreal primates known to be averse to water?

Of most of them this was perfectly true. The anthropoids in particular were believed to fear water. In the wild they will not cross the narrowest rivers. They don't even need water holes, since they get enough moisture from their food and from the little pockets of rainwater that collect in leaves and tree trunks. It was a well-known "fact" that chimps and gorillas are nonswimmers and any zoo could safely keep them in an unwalled enclosure by building a shallow moat around it. If by some accident they fell in, they would panic and drown.

But now hear Robert Golding, zoo curator at a Nigerian university, reporting on two gorillas aged six and a half and seven years.

"The female in particular enjoyed having water hosed over her. When allowed access to the moat she went right into the water. The male was at first cautious but seeing her enjoying it, he followed. They now stand in the deepest part, up to their middles, and launch themselves forward in a sort of breast stroke. They do this many times a day. They seem to enjoy it—they make a noise, splash around, and play. . . . Seeing a man swimming on the other side of the barrier, the gorilla launches himself in a horizontal position with his arms straight ahead of him. It seems to come to him quite naturally." It was clear that, given enough incentive, our ancestors would have taken the same plunge.

Moreover, we have some reason to believe that they sometimes plunged pretty deep. In truly aquatic mammals, such as the seal, there is a special physiological development enabling them to dive and hold their breath for long periods underwater without running out of oxygen as quickly as a land mammal would. When a seal dives, some of its metabolic processes slow down, reducing the body's consumption of oxygen. It can be measured most easily by the degree to which its heartbeat slows down. This physiological mechanism is known as brady-cardia, and is found in many diving mammals, even fresh water ones such as beaver and coypu. It is also found in Homo sapiens. When a man dives, his heartbeat slows down—not by any means as dramatically as a seal's, yet undoubtedly in human beings such a mechanism at some stage did at least begin to evolve. How, and when, and why? These things don't happen overnight.

Some people rejected the aquatic theory because of the problem of the primate's baby, born so immature and helpless. Children three or four years old have been known to drown in a couple of feet of water. How could an aquatic ape ever survive the hazards of those first tender years? But now we read of Hollywood's water babies, film stars' tots dogpaddling merrily around swimming pools before they can even walk. Admittedly they are carefully coached by experts. What would happen if they weren't?

Anthony Storr provides us with the answer:

"The pioneer doctors who started the Peckham Health Centre discovered that quite tiny children could be safely left in the sloping shallow end of a swimming bath. Provided no adult interfered with them, they would teach themselves to swim, exploring the water gradually and never venturing beyond the point at which they began to feel unsafe." If the prehominid's babies could do this, that Pliocene beach was the safest place for them in the whole of Africa.

The fact is that the Tarzanists, as well as forgetting the females, are constantly forgetting about the infants. It is many months before an anthropoid baby can be left alone. Its mother's existence is viable only because its fingers are strong enough almost from birth to cling onto her fur and so leave her four limbs free for going about her business. In such a perilous place as the open grassland she would need that freedom more than ever; more than ever the infant would need not only its tight grip but something to cling to. The naked baby of a naked anthropoid would never have survived.

Only in the sea could the mother afford to dispense with her fur. The baby would have very few enemies in those four-foot shallows. Leopards don't come so far into the sea, nor sharks so near to the land. The child soon gets used to the water and once in he's mobile and comparatively weightless. All he needs by way of reassurance and support is to hang on, when he gets tired, to that part of his mother remaining above water, which is of course her scalp, so from that area of her skin the hair has never disappeared.

Professor Hardy explains the hair on our heads by saying that since only our heads remained above water, exposed to the sun, the hair remained to protect us from its rays. Other evolutionists, if they explain it at all, usually dump it onto the miscellaneous heap of unique human features labeled "for sexual attraction"—a safe and lazy solution, since there are very few physical features which somebody at some time hasn't found sexually stimulating.

I feel that even protection against the sun is not a totally adequate explanation. If the hair was for this purpose it is true it would not have disappeared: it might have grown thick and tufty, as in many African tribes of course it is. But this theory leaves two things unexplained: the maiden with long flowing locks and the bald man.

In some populations of the ape there must have arisen, by mutation, the phenomenon of long hair on the head—a new departure for an ape. And the mutation must have proved adaptive. Why? I have seen this explained as a consequence of a move north or an Ice Age—protection against the cold. But this will not do. Cold is most acute when wind is blowing, and Jeannie's light brown hair, "floating like a zephyr" on the breeze, would not have kept her body warm. The fact is that when monkeys from a warm climate are moved to northern zoos like Moscow's, they adapt by growing thicker hair all over their bodies. Climate might serve to explain the hairy Ainu, but not long tresses alone. Even for an aquatic ape, there must have been some advantage to outweigh the nuisance of its sometimes getting into the eyes, and taking so long to dry when its owner went ashore to sleep.

However, it would be a powerful advantage for a baby if its mother's hair was long enough for his fingers to twine into; and if the hair floated around her for a yard or so on the surface he wouldn't have to make so accurate a beeline in swimming toward her when he wanted a rest. It would also explain the piece of dimorphism that nobody else has plausibly accounted for: in communities where the males took no part in the bringing up of the offspring there would be nothing to prevent their heads going as bald as their bodies, so long as this development remained sex-linked. Junior wouldn't mind Daddy's head being smooth and slippery because in the water, just as formerly in the trees, his mother was the one he hung on to.

There is one even more cogent reason for believing that the hair on a women's head evolved for the benefit of her offspring rather than for the enticement of her mate. In the later stage of pregnancy it still happens that the proportion of thin hairs on her scalp becomes relatively smaller and the proportion of thick hairs relatively greater. The later stage of pregnancy is not a time when she has any particular reason to acquire extra sexual allure, and anyway the total visual effect is negligible. But as providing a safer temporary anchorage for a baby treading water, the development makes very good sense.

While we're on babies, let's take another look at breasts. A chimp suckles its young quite successfully with a pair of skinny little nipples located on a fairly flat pectoral surface, and there is no immediately apparent reason why the naked ape couldn't have done the same. But women are different; and the strongly favored androcentric theory is that the difference is an esthetic improvement, and that it evolved as some sort of sexual stimulus.

This is essentially a circular argument. "I find this attribute sexy: therefore it must have evolved in order that I might find it sexy." It's like saying that a woman walks with a wiggle because this is attractive to a male. In fact, she only walks with a wiggle because her children are so intelligent. The necessity of passing a large-skulled infant's head through her pelvic ring has prevented her skeleton from adapting to bipedalism quite as gracefully as that of her brothers; and males only find this defect attractive because they associate it with femininity.

Surely, if you are considering a process as strictly functional as lactation, and you notice a modification in the arrangements for it, it would be reasonable to think about the primary beneficiary of the process—namely, the baby—rather than trying to relate it to the child's father's occupation.

So—imagine now that you are this anthropoid baby. You're having a whale of a time splashing around in the water, but after a while you get peckish. You pull your mother's hair and start bawling in her ear, so that she will come out of the water to feed you. A whale can squirt milk out to its pup rather like an aerosal container; but, as aquatic animals go, the whale is a pro and your mother is strictly in the beginners' class. Once or twice, being lazy or finding the rocks rather hard for sitting on, she's urged you to feed in the water, but there were waves, and your big brothers kept horsing around, and you swallowed great gulps of sea water and got terrible tummy upsets, so now she takes you ashore for the ten-o'clock feed. She wades up the beach, sits up straight with water dripping out of her mermaid locks, holds you on her lap in the most natural position, with your head resting comfortably in the crook of her arm, and then relaxes and gazes absently out to sea, expecting you to get on with it as you and your kind have done from time immemorial.

But now, as the astronauts put it, you have a problem here. What the stupid woman fails to realize is that things have changed. There isn't any fur. If you let your head lie in the crook of her arm, the milk is high up out of reach. You have to hoist your torso into an erect position, and try to balance your head and somehow keep your lips clamped to this chimp-sized nipple of hers, and don't think it's easy. Your arms are too short to go around her waist, and if you scrabble around trying to get a purchase on something, there's nothing there but a faintly corrugated surface of slippery wet ribs. If she's a good type she will hold you up higher and help you, but she gets fed up with this much sooner because it takes more concentration and makes her arm ache, and any dairyman will tell you a milk producer won't give down properly if she's uncomfortable or irritated.

So you really need two things: you need the nipple brought down quite a bit lower, and you need a lump of something less bony, something pliant and of a convenient size for small hands to grab hold of while you lie on her lap and guide your lips to the right place. Or, alternatively, guide the right place into your lips. And since you are what evolution is all about, what you need you ultimately get. You get two lovely pendulous dollopy breasts, as easy to hold on to as a bottle, and you're laughing.

Because of this new shape, and the fact that subcutaneous fat was being laid down all over her body at the time, a fair amount of this insulatory material naturally became concentrated in the breasts. And as Lila Leibowitz pointed out to the Northeastern Anthropological Association, the fat layer had other advantages—it cushioned the more fragile subtissue, it helped to keep the milk warm, and it stored reserve nutrients.

I don't think that in primitive conditions the form was typically hemispherical. In young females they would necessarily pass through a stage when they could be so described, and today, in civilized conditions, with high-protein feeding, and school physical training, and sexual selection for the Adolescent Look, and birth control, and well-cut brassieres, they may be coaxed into remaining that shape for quite a long time. But that's a form of neoteny—it's not the way they were originally designed as any anthropological travelogue will amply confirm. Most men regard them as intrinsically hemispherical, but that's because whenever they imagine they are thinking about *mulier sapiens*, what they are really thinking about is the Miss World Contest.

So far so good. We have a possible explanation of the Raquel Welch phenomenon in this theory of the baby deprived of a handhold. It would be greatly strengthened if we could find an animal parallel, just as the shellfish/pebble-tool theory was strenghtened by finding the sea otter. It would be nice to track down another mammal who went into the water, and found things happening to her vital statistics.

The trouble with aquatic animals is that some of them have been there so long that it's impossible to know where or how they lived before they went back to the sea. They've become as streamlined as fish. Nobody, for instance, can make a guess at the shape or habits of the unimaginable quadruped that lumbered down some prehistoric beach and began to turn into a whale (though we have reason to believe it was actually quite small).

However, it is a fact that the only nonhuman pneumatically breasted females I have been able to trace happen to be aquatic. They are the sirenians (or sea cows), that rare class of marine animals which includes the dugong and the manatee, both credited with being the original "mermaid."

Each of them has been widely reported and believed to suckle while floating upright in the water holding its single offspring in its flippers. I haven't managed to find any reliable contemporary eyewitness account of this, but that may be because they are getting very rare, and their only close relative, the massive but inoffensive Rhytina—Steller's sea cow—was subjected to a campaign of systematic slaughter and is extinct. (Or let us say, since some vague rumors of a sighting drifted out of the Russian Arctic a few years back, almost certainly extinct.)

As to their statistics, the director of the Marine Biological Station at Al Ghardaqah describes the dugong as possessing a pair of "well-developed pectoral breasts." Steller wrote of the Rhytina: "That they produce only one pup is concluded from the shortness of the teats and the number of the breasts"—which were two and pectoral.

The manatee is known colloquially in Guyana, according to David Attenborough, as the "water-mamma"; and Colin Bertram writes of it: "The breasts are indeed a single pair and pectoral, as in man. . . . In the manatee the teat seems to be almost on the actual hinder edge of the thick flipper just where it joins the body." He points out that it would be impossible to tag a manatee by clipping a marker to the base of its flipper, as is done with seals, because the breast would be in the way; and he mentions that when the manatee is lactating the gland is "large and shapely."

So far the theory holds up. But is there any evidence that there was ever a time when they (and their offspring) had hands? I admit that the word "manatee" has no connection with the Latin *manus*, a hand. But it is interesting to note that more than one keen observer, knowing more about zoology than etymology, has made the immediate assumption on looking at that jointed flat-nailed flipper that the creature must have been called manatee because of its hands.

The manatee's ancestor, of course, was nothing like a primate. It was certainly a land animal: it has the skeleton, the lungs, the vestigial hairs, to prove it. It is tempting to think of it as somewhat resembling the ancestor of her geographical neighbor the South American sloth, which must at one time have run along the branches before (like the orang) it grew too big and began to suspend itself underneath them instead. It is particularly tempting since the sloth wears her teats in the same eccentric position as the manatee—namely, under her armpits —and since the manatee and the two-toed sloth are the only two mammals in the whole of creation with six bones in their necks instead of seven.

But the taxonomists tell us that the sloth itself is not one of the sea cow's nearest living relatives. They are a small bizarrely assorted group and give us no help at all in trying to reconstruct a common ancestor. One is, improbably, the elephant. The second is a rabbitlike creature dwelling in holes in the rocks and referred to in the Bible as a "cony." The last is a small arboreal creature, the tree hyrax.

All we know for certain is that there must have been some ecological crisis (like the Pliocene for us) which induced the sea cow to leave her former habitat and take to the water; that the pectoral placing of the teats evolves most plausibly and most frequently in animals which at one time sat upright in trees; and that she has retained through all vicissitudes a vague instinct that her forelimbs were once for holding on with because she holds on to her infant with them, so that there might have been a time before she lost her fur, and when she still sat up on the beach to suckle him, when her infant likewise used his for holding on to her. If she did indeed leave the trees for the sea she is almost certainly the only creature besides ourselves that ever did so. Only instead of staying there for ten million years she stayed forever, and grew soggy and torpid, and lost her legs and most of the features of her face and degenerated into a great fat ugly six-foot blob of glup.

Poor cow, she's a far cry from Raquel Welch: one good look into those tiny watery eyes, and the mere thought that we might be sisters under the skin would send most of us scuttling hastily back to Tarzan.

It would also make us wonder why on earth those jolly pigtailed seagoing chantey-singing sailors ever took it into their heads to call her "mermaid" and tell tall tales of her fatal magnetism. It can't have been only the rum ration. . . .

ROBERT ARDREY AND LOUIS S. B. LEAKEY

Robert Ardrey (1908–), born in Chicago, American playwright and scriptwriter, who moved on to evolutionary anthropology, is best known for *The Territorial Imperative* (1966), which argues that man, like birds, beasts, and dogs, stakes out and defends his turf. His anthropological research began with *African Genesis: A Personal Investigation into the Animal Origins and Nature of Man* (1961). His plays are collected in *Plays of Three Decades* (1968). Louis S. B. Leakey (1903–1972), Fellow of the British Academy, Fellow and Honorary Fellow of St. John's College, Cambridge, was the world's leading explorer into the origins of humans and our hominid predecessors in East Africa, especially in the Olduvai Gorge in Tanzania. His books include *The Stone Age Cultures of Kenya Colony* (1931), *Adam's Ancestors* (1934, 1953), *First Lessons in Kikuyu* (1959), *The Progress and Evolution of Man in Africa* (1961), and *Olduvai Gorge* (1951).

AGGRESSION AND VIOLENCE IN MAN: A DIALOGUE

Ardrey and Leakey disagree on how and when man became aggressive, whether up from the jungle or through social abrasions. But they agree on the problem that violence poses for us today, and on the evidence for "everything going good and bad" with the dawn of individual worth. As you read, ask yourself how society as you know it, at home, in the schoolyard, on the street corner, reflects what Ardrey and Leakey suggest.

LEAKEY: I look at man and man's ancestors as creatures which until they became what Huxley and I call psycho-social men—when they were purely animal men, were like the animals themselves, and not, as far as I can see, aggressive or violent to each other. I will explain a little bit why I think that is so. I think they definitely did not have either the opportunity or the time or the means of any form to be really agressive against their own species. This was chiefly because (a) there were too few of them on the ground, there was plenty of territory for them not to squabble; and, (b) they were still not living in close contact with each other. I believe the beginning of living close together came at a much later date (which I shall discuss in a minute), and I think that is something which was linked with a change from—the animal—at the beginning, and psycho-social man—the man who developed fire, speech, abstract thought and religion, burying his dead, and magic. And I believe, although I don't think Robert would agree on this, that was the turning point at which we, man—. We had been man before that, we had been *Homo sapiens* before that. We were still *Homo sapiens* in the animal, and before that *Homo sapiens* with ancestors *Homo habilis* and his cousins the australopithecines that Dart found in South Africa and we now are finding in East Africa, too. And before that, back to *kenyapithecus wickerii*. I don't believe personally, which is where I think we will disagree, that any of those forms of man, in the widest sense, were aggressive and violent to each other. They hadn't the time, they hadn't the leisure, and I have a horrid suspicion that one of the reasons why we have become aggressive to each other more and more in an ever-increasing way is because we have turned to a way of life which throws us more and more together into great masses of people and gives us more and more leisure to think up things like jealousy, hatred, and malice, and then practice them.

At this point I'll ask Robert if he agrees with what I've said so far. I think he wants to throw some questions at me now about our earliest hominids.

ARDREY: Unfortunately, we do love each other, but we do get into trouble. You have, for example, Peking man—*Homo erectus*—who was evidently a head hunter. You find no body bones at Choukoutien, and you have heads with the underneath hollowed out to extract the brains, or at least most authorities accept it as such. You have a great deal of mayhem in the history of the developing man, but which is personal. You see, if you want to make a line between organized violence and personal violence, I'd say, absolutely, you don't get much organized violence until fairly recent times. Personal violence you get a lot. You can go back a long way and you'll find that somebody clobbered somebody. I think this is like murder today where two-thirds of murders are committed between people who know each other. And I think we had the same old instincts in the old days. But what I am more concerned about is organized violence, which we have had in more recent times. I think it is perfectly natural for a man to get mad at his wife and hit her over the head and kill her, or vice versa. But this is one of the things that happens that you call "human," and which started early. Did or did not *Homo habilis* get conked on the top of the head?

LEAKEY: I'll answer that right away. *Homo habilis* had a hole on the top of his head, the first *habilis* we ever got—the youngster, the 11-year-old. But I have never stated that he was murdered. As far as I am concerned that hole in his head was definitely a sign of death by violence. Whether it was from falling out of a tree or being hit accidently by a fellow school-boy (if you can call it that), or whether it was deliberate killing, I don't know. I personally do not think at that stage people were killing each other seriously because they were angry with each other. But it is an open question—I can't prove it.

ARDREY: No, you can't. However, there is a very clean-cut case which is Vertezollos man in Hungary, which was the first known *Homo sapiens*—unless maybe your new one is a bit earlier. But they are the same age—300,000 to 400,000 years ago—and he was definitely killed by one of the stone implements that lay beside him. His head was caved in by it, and that was the first known *Homo sapiens*—unless your son, Richard, is finding a newer (or older one, rather) this year. You do have evidence of violence all through, though. I mean, Monte Circeo man and the Neanderthals with his head cut off, and brains hollowed out, and mounted around stones. You have these things, you have evidence of violence. I don't take them all that seriously. We were dangerous animals. We were dangerous to each other. But I don't think this relates necessarily to the modern problem of violence as we know it, which is group violence, organized violence, war, etc.

LEAKEY: I agree. I'd like to take you up on two things. First I would like to discuss very briefly the Choukoutien man. It is true that there is some evidence of Choukoutien cannibalism, but at the same time Choukoutien is one of the exceptions of the rest of mankind because they were already living in a cave. In other words, there was a cave and they were living in close communities because caves were rare.

ARDREY: May I interrupt to say this is Peking man, as he is more commonly known—say 300,000 to 500,000 years ago. Peking man with a brain two-thirds the size of our own.

LEAKEY: Yes, Peking man is certainly an exception in that, surprisingly, he had fire. I don't think he had made fire, but I think he was catching wild fire and domesticating it. The evidence shows he had discontinuous fire and he was in caves. And when you start living side by side in the small area of one cave with a lot of different families, then your jealousies are going to start and your hostilities between each other are going to start. My argument is that if you go back to *Homo habilis*, or to early *Homo sapiens*, he was not in a position to really be hostile. He was living in very, very small groups, and, as far as I can see, he did not have *the leisure*, I repeat, *he did not have the leisure* in which to develop hostilities to his fellow man. Too much of his time was taken up with other business.

ARDREY: I agree; he was too busy surviving. And separation was very important, because as hunters they had to live quite far apart in groups. They could not have been next door neighbors because there wouldn't have been enough animals.

LEAKEY: Until you get to visit the caves of Dordogne, where they had moved into cave-living, cave-dwelling, which gave them shelter from the wind and the cold which they had never had before in the open. But, at that point, they were certainly in much closer communities as far as living was concerned, and they were going out farther to hunt. And I still put that down to the discovery that man could make fire himself. Have you ever thought about the significance of the making of fire in relation to human speech? I have thought about it a great deal in the last few years. I have been out on a number of occasions with hunting tribes in Tanganyika. And to my great surprise they were silent pretty well the whole day long from dawn to dark because they were either hunting, or after they made a kill, they were still not going to talk because they might make a second kill—it might be their lucky day. From dawn to dark, when they got back to camp they talked. But while they were out, their only talk was of essential things, like meat, stone—concrete things. And I was foolish; I thought that the women of the tribe, because they were food gathering, would be chatter, chatter, chattering all day long, because the nuts, berries, and fruit would not run away. But I had overlooked the fact that they, too, always had their eye for meat which they would find. They have bifocal vision.

ARDREY: Is this people like the Hadza?

LEAKEY: Yes, the Hadza. I went out with the women, and I found they didn't talk, either. Of course, they talk at night—talk, talk, talk, and the men talk, too. But they didn't talk by day. They had bifocal vision; they would come around a bush, and there would be a baby Grant's gazelle or Thompson's gazelle lying on the grass which they could see with their television and bifocal vision. And the other animals couldn't. A dog would go right past if he wasn't on the right side of the wind. But humans, no. And so they didn't talk while hunting or food gathering. But once you got fire, then after you come home in the evening, the men and the women first are cooking, then in the shelter of a cave they can talk and talk until 11 o'clock at night. And *that* to me is the beginning of our real aggression, because then was the time they began to invent words for and began to think about horrible things like hatred and malice and war—things that before had never been in their consciousness. . . . And you thus get speech. And with the arrival of real speech, although it has done a great many beautiful things, at the same time it has done certain awfully bad things, because it gave us time and leisure to invent ideas and some of those ideas, I am afraid, were the causes of our aggression.

ARDREY: So much communication is *this* kind of communication. And so much of communication as languages developed has made it absolutely impossible to understand what somebody else thinks. This is part of our problem today. Speech is not all fine. You hear some beautiful things from beautiful anthropologists about how it makes mankind one. I don't see any part of it. I agree with you down to the bottom on that.

LEAKEY: I don't think speech was present at all early. I think possibly you would regard the proto-men, hominids, and the early things like *habilis* as maybe having speech. I think they had rather more words than the chimpanzees do. Jane has now, with the help of one of our sound machines, got about 80 different sounds. I imagine our ancestors had three or four times that number, but not speech in my sense. I am trying to get you to agree with me that really the fundamental was speech and it was very late.

ARDREY: No, I don't think so. I think speech in moderately—not elaborate, but grammatical form—emerged at a fairly early date, let's say, before the big brain, in your *Homo habilis* stage because of the necessity of transmitting the social wisdom—the wisdom of the hunter—to the young. I don't think the hunter needed it so badly, but I do think there was a tremendous necessity for the young hunter—the hunter-to-be—to learn verbally from his elders the ways of the wild animals of different forms, which vary so much. So I have a feeling that speech started at a very early day, but perhaps it did not become too sophisticated until later on.

LEAKEY: I would disagree with you there. I would agree that *Homo habilis* definitely had the <u>potential</u> (I underline "potential") for speech of a far greater quality than any chimpanzee or any near-man had—even more than the australopithecines. *Homo habilis* had a speech potential created by the muscles of the root of the lower jaw. This was two million years ago. He had the potential, but I don't think he had developed that potential because he didn't have the leisure. I cannot see men or women, until they have fire, being able to develop speech to any degree—at least not abstract speech, because of having been out with these people. Until you have fire, when you come home in the evening, you just sit. And those who are not cooking or cutting up the meat and getting ready to go to bed are listening, listening. Elephants can stampede past; snakes can come wiggling up where they lie—they are not in caves. *Only* when they have got fire. Cave living is late, apart from Peking man, and fire is late. I put the whole development of articulate speech in relation to abstract ideas as late.

ARDREY: Are you getting at something with articulate speech—you developed the capacity for articulate violence along with articulate speech?

LEAKEY: Yes. Between man and man.

ARDREY: You could unite groups with speech against others. Something that was impossible before you had speech?

LEAKEY: Exactly. You could stir up emotions.

ARDREY: That's a very interesting idea.

LEAKEY: To me it's one of the key points.

ARDREY: The regular use of fire was about 40,000 years ago. The sporadic use of fire went back to Choukoutien man, 300,000 to 400,000 years. But regular use of fire, meaning control, so you could make a fire, about 40,000. So this would mean that this began only about 40,000 years ago.

LEAKEY: Yes. That's what I think, and that's why I disagree with you. I can't see it any earlier. Going back to that, once you had fire, you moved into caves, and once you moved into caves, you had freedom and leisure. But with that came concentrated groups. The number of caves in the Dordogne valley that we have both seen were limited. And for the first time I think the people went in large numbers in one and the same place to sleep and to live, although not to hunt. They had to hunt separately. I think that was a key point, as I've called it in my recent lectures, the Last Milestone in Human Evolution. . . .

ARDREY: Well, I think speech goes back farther than that. Partly because it's very difficult for me to believe that the proliferation of languages that has come on this earth all based on essential unified grammatical structure—there is no such thing as a primitive language—occurred as recently as 40,000 years ago. I feel that it must have started much earlier to have reached the last ends of the earth that it has. This, however, is just a very speculative argument which I certainly don't want to back up in front of my very speculative friend here. . . .

LEAKEY: Robert, do you think I have overstressed the importance, then, of speech? I think it is the most important factor, but I have an idea you may not agree with me on that.

ARDREY: It's a very important *contributing* factor. It's a cultural thing that happened to us which is a contributing factor of no end importance. But I think that other things are going on in the meantime, and this is where we disagree a little bit. Because I think man was a dangerous animal from way back into hominid days. He was a dangerous animal in the sense that a wolf or a lion is a dangerous animal. So we had the potentiality for violent action in us. However long we were hunters is a matter of disagreement among anthropologists, although I suspect not too great. Hunting went way back. Hunting, however, was something that encouraged, by selective necessity, a desire not to flee, a desire to attack, a pleasure in the chase, or you would be selected out. You had to be adjusted entirely towards attack. Now, we were armed hunters. And through most of our history as hunters, we were no better armed than any other hunter—wolf, or whatever. We carried a stone, wood, club, whatever weapons we had, to defend ourselves, or to attack with. But they were hand-held weapons. It is a peculiar thing that Louis and I come around to about the same date in talking about this, because the long-distance weapon—providing for killing at a distance—came about in just about the same period we're talking about—the fire thing of 40,000 years ago. A few thousand years later the long-distance weapon was invented by the very last of Neanderthal man in the Sahara Desert, which was green in those days because ice covered Europe. At this time, in between the Atlas Mountains and Algiers, in that area, you get the Aterian culture, which presents you with the very first thong weapons which have the little point at the bottom like an American arrowhead. Tanged, we call it. This meant this weapon could be fastened to a haft. If it was a light one, it could be a bow and arrow. This was the invention of the bow and arrow. A heavy one could be attached to a shaft, which would make a throwing spear. Before that we didn't have weapons that were well adapted to any kind of killing at a distance. However, this is very close to the same date we were talking about—the first, 40,000 years. This is 35–30,000 years ago.

LEAKEY: I'll let you finish first, but I'll take you up on that. I think the bolas was the weapon for attacking at a distance.

ARDREY: Well, yes, it's true. And you find these stone balls so far back

—I'll leave that to you, because you're the man that knows about them. At the same time, you didn't attack at quite the distance. The bow and arrow is effective at a great distance. I think a qualitative change came about when this weapon was invented. It was simply this. Before that we had been simply animals among animals. If we killed for a living, which we did for our meat, we killed no differently from the lion or the hunting dog, or the hyena or the wolf. We killed in close quarters, taking all the risks. But the day we had a weapon that could kill at 50 or 100 yards (there is a record of a Samoan Chief who could knock over an animal at 257 yards with a bow and arrow), we got into the new era which finally culminated with the nuclear bomb. Here the odds of the offense were changed very much in terms of the defense. In the old days we took a terrible risk going after a big animal larger than ourselves. The day we had a weapon that could kill at a distance everything was changed. The offensive weapon was greater than the defenses. Now we started talking about violence. Dr. Leakey has introduced the enormously important thing of language, which meant we could share the knowledge on how or why to do violence—or we could kid ourselves into why we should do violence—because those guys are terrible and we are fine. We could say these things to each other. We couldn't do it when we were like the wolves. Now came the problem of the mob, of the organized group, of organized killing which we came to know as war, but today we may call violence on the streets. It is all the same thing. The violent group. This I feel—the vast change in the quality of the weapon in the hands of a dangerous animal which we were and which we remain—seems to have introduced a qualitative thing into our evolving life. It didn't, in fact, have a great effect on human existence for some time. The glaciers still covered Europe. It was quite a long time, maybe 12–15,000 years ago, before these long-distance weapons began to come around. Early settlers to the American continent brought them over here and killed with them. But it seems to me this is where the predator came into his own. We talk about how in the old hunting days we were too busy making a living—making a living is tough, whatever some of our friends in the American colleges may say. And you didn't really have that much energy left at night for going out and quarreling with a neighbor. Maybe in a cave, with your very close neighbor. But going fifteen miles away to get into a battle— nonsense. You might lose someone you needed for getting the next day's hunt. Very important! I question very much that such organized violence was of anything but what I would call recent—I mean 10– 12,000 years ago. We are talking about the cultural points: the culture of language, the culture of weapons: I think these are very important. But what I want to emphasize is that we were dangerous animals to begin with. It was just that we were too busy. Wolves aren't that dangerous; they are too busy, too. When we got this thing that meant the offensive, it was so much easier, we turned into different beings in violent ways.

I would now like to get off the point that I wanted to make back to you because my thesis of the hunting way as the essential necessity or the genetic background of human propensity for violence (not that we are *all* violent, but enough of us are violent to make the rest of us have to go around with steel vests), to me this is when it started. It may have started way back in the days of your friends at the bottom of Olduvai, or Richard's friends up in Rudolph.

LEAKEY: I think on that one that you and I do disagree violently. I don't believe the earliest man even up until *Homo habilis* was anything more than a scavenger. I don't think he was killing. I believe quite definitely that he was going around scavenging animals. I have two reasons for that. The first one is that the remains we find on these very early sites at Rudolph and Olduvai never are the remains of a complete animal. We find front legs or back legs. I experimented with Richard. We went out naked, picking up some giraffe limb bones and jaws to act as rudimentary weapons, but not such as we could offend or kill anybody with, just protect ourselves a little. And we drove off the vultures and the hyenas long enough when they came in to the kill. We couldn't drive off the lions—they came in and made the kill. We watched them and the vultures watched them and the hyenas watched them, and then we rushed in as scavengers. I think for a very long time—almost until the very point of discovery of fire, we were scavengers and not weapon makers, and therefore not offensive. I don't think you agree with that.

ARDREY: I don't. Most definitely I do not. I see no reason on earth before we had a weapon that killed at a distance why anyone should be afraid of us. This is part of the scavenging hypothesis, as it is known in anthropology, that we went in and were able to frighten off animals, or that we went in and other animals did not quarrel with us. I'll refer you to *Innocent Killers*, Hugo van Lawick and Jane Goodall's book, in which they come to the conclusion that nowhere in the human past would we have been capable of scavenging regularly. We certainly swiped what we could, there is no question about that. But, then, lions swipe from hyenas. This goes on all the time in the predatory community. The question is, Can you live off it? I see no reason why we could have. The farther back you go, the more poorly were our feet developed, the slower could we run, the more inadequate we were as to what were to become men. And I see no reason why we could have competed with the natural predator scavengers. They all hunt and they all scavenge from each other. How could we have won in a competition with a hyena? A hyena would have eaten us.

LEAKEY: Well, continuing with my story, we went in for ten minutes and for a short ten minutes we were able to keep the hyenas off—they were furious. And after ten minutes I signaled to my son, "Get out, it's not safe any longer. They're going to kill us now." But we got a little zebra. And I think that the evidence at the sites does show that we were getting legs here and there, and of course we were supplementing it by the killing of small game—juvenile animals which can be done very easily, and by what I call slow game—tortoises, frogs, baby birds, rodents. And there we disagree fundamentally.

ARDREY: Louis, you forget you are talking about modern man who has been shooting animals with bow and arrow, guns, clobbering them in one way or another for so long that they have developed flight distance to get out of our way. They're scared stiff of us. They've been scared ever since the long-distance weapon, when we were separated from all other animals. You can go out today and scare hyenas off with a lot of noise or you may even bother lions; you can do it because they have an association with you as sudden death. You are sudden death. But why in the old days, when we were only four feet tall and weighed 85 lbs., and had nothing more to kill with than a stone in the hand, a piece of wood, or whatever—why should animals have been afraid of us then? I just don't think we were doing anything in the way of killing then.

LEAKEY: But we were scavenging and you can scavenge. Many times I've seen a kill with only vultures and jackals and no bigger animals on the kill at all. They didn't scavenge all the time; they'd kill other things and hunted other things, and they had nuts and berries as well. They were omnivorous, but I don't believe in the earlier days we were anything but scavengers; insofar as we ate meat at all.

ARDREY: Well, it's a big difference, but in a way it doesn't all matter that much, because we're going back so far. We're talking now about 1–2 million years ago. This isn't even recent in my terms. If we go back 500,000 years ago to *Homo sapiens*, the big-brain man, there isn't much question about what went on. They were definitely hunters. What we do know is that for only 10,000 years have we had any control of our food supply and have we not been dependent on wild food. I believe you and I agree that we didn't live much on spinach.

This is a fashionable point of view much promoted in American anthropology. Lettuce is great for diets, but not for men who have to work for a living. We had the necessity of living off meat. We had to get it somehow. We undoubtedly scavenged whenever we could, but we could not survive 365 days of the year hoping someone would leave some meat around. So we had to be able to hunt and kill. The basis of the hunting hypothesis is that the necessity lay on us for selective survival to be able to dare to go in to attack. And, unhappily, about 10,000 years ago we domesticated cereals, we domesticated cattle, goats, sheep, and so on—I say "unhappily" because in the new book *The Imperial Animal* by those ethnologically-named anthropologists, Robin Fox and Lionel Tiger—a marvelous book, incidentally—they go back to this date when we got control of our food supply and say, "Was it good or was it bad? We have sure had enough trouble since." Overpopulation, because suddenly we've got so much more food and we have so many more children and all of a sudden we begin to get the conflict of things which is important. This is where your idea and mine link together so interestingly, because your language thing meant greater differences between human beings and my weapon thing says these differences could be enforced so much more violently. And here these two ideas come together. I go with this entirely. Now we come to the point of the food supply. And it is vegetable food supply, but fortunately by that time we had invented cooking. If you ever ate some raw spaghetti you'd find out that you have to be able to cook this stuff. But by this time we had controlled fires. And now comes the population explosion, and the problem of conflicting groups for space, for areas, for food supply, and all that came in about 5–10,000 years ago. About then we all really began to get into trouble. But here are three points that add up: language, which made possible beliefs of inordinately irrational order; and, finally, food, which made possible inordinately too many people. This was more or less the road as I see it which is in our line. But, of course, from that time on you really had the possibilities of violence beautifully stated. The foundations, like the walls of Jericho, were there in front of us, to proceed and to perfect, and we have perfected them as no other species of the living world.

LEAKEY: Now, Robert, this brings us to a most terribly important thing. We can't leave our friends here thinking that you and I believe that we have become so violent now that there is no hope for the future. I personally don't believe this at all. I think we have reached a point where we certainly have a very short time in which to make up our minds what we are going to do. We can, because we're the only animal (and I say "animal" advisedly) who amongst his evolutionary developments, developed a brain and a precision grip. And, if we do not want to destroy ourselves in the very near future, we can and we must today set to work jointly, and all together—over the whole world—say to each other and to our leaders, we are not prepared to have destruction of men and the whole beauty of the arts, of the music that we have inherited from our forefathers. We insist on changing direction, now! . . .

ARDREY: . . . there is an idea that has come up in recent years that I think is marvelous. The man responsible is up at Stanford. He is a clinical psychiatrist named David Hamburg. . . .

The Hamburg hypothesis is quite simply this: Forget about instinct when you get up into the higher animals in which learning is so important. Never have the idea that people go by learning and animals by instinct. It grades so gradually—read Jane Goodall's book, *In the Shadow of Man*, about the chimpanzees. The greatest book ever written on animal observation. I urge you to read it. And you will see how much the chimp has to learn. Why it takes so long to grow up, because it has so much to learn. Ten years of observation before it becomes an adult.

Now what happens with us, and with chimps also as far as that's concerned, is Hamburg's thesis. Evolution makes easy to learn that which is of survival value. Evolution makes difficult to learn that which is not survival value. Think how quickly you learn language and how long it takes to learn the multiplication tables, which have no survival value in our evolutionary history. But language has. So we learn—bingo!—between the age of two and three. Says Hamburg, it also makes it pleasurable to learn those things that are of survival value. Go back into the hunting past and think of the necessity of being able to hunt and all that. The violence and all was pleasurable. Now it is maladaptive. It's murder. Now, what is it we are up against? You can learn to be inimical. Kids can wind up in trouble or kids can wind up angels. But you have got to work on them, because it is easier to learn to be a murderer than it is to be a peacemaker.

LEAKEY: I entirely agree, and consequently, we have to take steps now. I absolutely agree with you that we are not, as evolutionists, pessimists. We know the potential of men, and somehow, in some way, in the very near future, because we only have a very short time to go now, either we will be destroyed by overpopulation, pollution, etc., or we are going to save the world for our future generations—for our children and grandchildren and great-grandchildren. One or the other. And I think we have to do it now. That is the lesson from our study of the past.

Questions and Answers

. . . .

QUESTION: Mr. Ardrey has suggested a number of backdrops for the emergence of organized violence. One was fire, another was the emergence of speech. I wonder if we could bring in another one which would be the growth of a large brain in such an inordinately short time. Arthur Koestler says there is a relatively new brain, the neocortex, built on top of several more brains, and his suggestion is that there is a coordination between the two, but there is a lack of communication between the two. Perhaps with speech, fire, and weapons all at the same time, it was possible to draw more on the resources of the new brain and harness the violent tendencies of the older brains.

ARDREY: I spent a day last week with McLean in Washington, by the way, the Director of the National Institute of Mental Health, and Koestler, and I think that he has the answer in the sense that we too frequently refer to the brain as we do the heart, as if it were an organ. It is an evolved organ with various areas and McLean's point is that the reptilian brain still exists, circled by the early mammalian brain, and then finally by the immense cortical development of the human being. He feels that this cortical development is so recent that we haven't developed proper connections yet. We don't have in all the switchboard. And this means that the old animal brain in us (which is a delightful phrase, because it means that nature never throws anything away), we are stuck with the old brain. It still operates, but without the inhibition we'd like to believe the cortex could give. The problem is that we have somehow to work awfully hard on the communication between the cortex which tells us that something isn't going to do. That the violent life, for example, is simply annihilation in the end. But the trouble is that we have one of those Spanish postal systems when it comes to dropping a message into the box and getting it down to the old brain. We don't know how soon the message will get there, if at all. And so we are fighting against something that is very tough. But you can't take your eye off it—you have to work on it all the time. You can't just believe that the old brain is angelic in any sense.

LEAKEY: I must add, though, that there is no correlation at all scientifically between absolute size of the brain and the function of the brain itself. It depends on two things, (1) the relative size of the brain to body size, and (2) the complicated development of the brain itself within the actual brain capacity. Some of the best mathematicians who ever lived have recently had their skulls exhumed, by permission, and they had smaller brains than the average. But they were brilliant. We did an experiment some time ago in England where we exhumed the brains of a number of other well-known people in other fields, such as sports, and although they were not very intellectual, they had big brains. And I would remind you that Neanderthal man and early *Homo sapiens* (250,000) before he was psycho-social man had a much bigger brain than the average person in this room.

· · · ·

QUESTION: This isn't a scientific question, but I'd like to ask Dr. Leakey if we are going to have to define ways of teaching peace, we're going to have to find these patterns that must exist to teach peace. Where are we to look for those of us who work with young people? Where shall you suggest that we look? Will it be in medicine? Will it be studying animal behavior? What is the field in your intuitive guess that would be the most favored place to look for those patterns?

LEAKEY: First and foremost I would encourage more and more mixing of people from different backgrounds, until they realized that they are all one and the same. That they think differently, in certain respects, that their colors may vary, their hair may be different, but, nevertheless, they are all men and women and that they, therefore, must work together for better things. As soon as people start mixing together, of different races and backgrounds, they begin to find so much in common with each other that the other things that are different fall apart. This is heresy in some circles, but I am certain it is true. Secondly, I think you have to distinguish in teaching the young between what I would call a "faith" as distinct from "religion." Today, as I see it, we are losing all faith—the faith that man has grown to a point where he has some awareness, some consciousness of right and wrong. But because of the destructive influence of dogmas and doctrines as distinct from faith, we are letting our young people lose faith, which they don't need to lose. And having lost faith, because they confuse faith with religion, they are not willing to abandon violence. You can't really kill people if you have a real feeling that they also have a faith and are meaningful in this life and the world. And in this connection I took some years ago a random sample of dossiers of people who had committed kinds of violence in this country. This is very important. Out of 100 random files which I was allowed to see, only three individuals admitted to any faith. All the others had no faith. If you have no faith of any kind, if you think you are just body, hair, skin, flesh, and nothing more, then obviously if I snuff you out today instead of letting you go on, it doesn't matter. But if you believe that that person is something worthwhile, you don't snuff him out. And I believe that you have to differentiate with the young people between real faith and false religion.

QUESTION: You have spoken of the time about 40,000 years ago when there was fire, long-range weapons, and about that time, abstract speech began. Where in this time spectrum—Dr. Leakey has now spoken about faith and the worth of the individual—when did the burying of the dead begin?

LEAKEY: At just about that same time—40,000 years ago, with the development of speech and art, and there is some evidence now of music and magic. At the same time there was evidence of burying of the dead and a belief in some kind of religion.

ARDREY: Red ochre. Very interesting. Burial with red ochre. There was not much with the Neanderthal, if any, but with Cromagnon who came in about 35,000 years ago came in the red ochre, which is an evident blood symbol, and life symbol, connected with the dead, which we find on the bones. It was a critical time.

LEAKEY: It was the last major milestone.

ARDREY: Everything went good and everything went bad.

KARL R. POPPER

Karl R. Popper (1902–). Born in Vienna, Popper educated himself as a part-time student at the University of Vienna, as an assistant to psychiatrist Alfred Adler, and as apprentice cabinetmaker, earning a Ph.D. in 1928. He became professor of philosophy and scientific method at the University of London in 194͡5, holding the post until his retirement in 1969. He was knighted in 1965. His central books are *The Logic of Scientific Discovery* (1935), *The Open Society and Its Enemies* (1947), *The Poverty of Historicism* (1957), *Conjectures and Refutations: The Growth of Scientific Knowledge* (1963), and *Objective Knowledge: An Evolutionary Approach* (1972).

UTOPIA AND VIOLENCE

In this essay the world's leading rationalist makes the case for rationality, as he handles the opposition. Note especially the phrases with which he admits the cons to the discussion—*I do not overlook, but I must admit*—and how he turns back to his own side: *But in spite of all this.* Mark these turns as you read. See if you can make a fully explicit thesis for his argument: "Violence *can* be reduced and brought under the control of reason by ＿＿＿ and by ＿＿＿."

There are many people who hate violence and are convinced that it is one of their foremost and at the same time one of their most hopeful tasks to work for its reduction and, if possible, for its elimination from human life. I am among these hopeful enemies of violence. I not only hate violence, but I firmly believe that the fight against it is not at all hopeless. I realize that the task is difficult. I realize that, only too often in the course of history, it has happened that what appeared at first to be a great success in the fight against violence was followed by defeat. I do not overlook the fact that the new age of violence which was opened by the two world wars is by no means at an end. Nazism and Fascism are thoroughly beaten, but I must admit that their defeat does not mean that barbarism and brutality have been defeated. On the contrary, it is no use closing our eyes to the fact that these hateful ideas achieved something like victory in defeat. I have to admit that Hitler succeeded in degrading the moral standards of our Western world, and that in the world of today there is more violence and brutal force than would have been tolerated even in the decade after the first World War. And we must face the possibility that our civilization may ultimately be destroyed by those new weapons which Hitlerism wished upon us, perhaps even within the first decade* after the second World War; for no doubt the spirit of Hitlerism won its greatest victory over us when, after its defeat, we used the weapons which the threat of Nazism had induced us to develop. But in spite of all this I am today no less hopeful than I have ever been that violence can be defeated. It is our only hope; and long stretches in the history of Western as well as of Eastern civilizations prove that it need not be a vain hope—that violence *can* be reduced, and brought under the control of reason.

This is perhaps why I, like many others, believe in reason; why I call myself a rationalist. I am a rationalist because I see in the attitude of reasonableness the only alternative to violence.

When two men disagree, they do so either because their opinions differ, or because their interests differ, or both. There are many kinds of disagreement in social life which must be decided one way or another. The question may be one which must be settled, because failure to settle it may create new difficulties whose cumulative effects may cause an intolerable strain, such as a state of continual and intense preparation for deciding the issue. (An armaments race is an example.) To reach a decision may be a necessity.

How can a decision be reached? There are, in the main, only two

* This was written in 1947. Today I should alter this passage merely by replacing "first" by "second."

possible ways: argument (including arguments submitted to arbitration, for example, to some international court of justice) and violence. Or, if it is interests that clash, the two alternatives are a reasonable compromise or an attempt to destroy the opposing interest.

A rationalist, as I use the word, is a man who attempts to reach decisions by argument and perhaps, in certain cases, by compromise, rather than by violence. He is a man who would rather be unsuccessful in convincing another man by argument than successful in crushing him by force, by intimidation and threats, or even by persuasive propaganda.

We shall understand better what I mean by reasonableness if we consider the difference between trying to convince a man by argument and trying to persuade him by propaganda.

The difference does not lie so much in the use of argument. Propaganda often uses argument too. Nor does the difference lie in our conviction that our arguments are conclusive, and must be admitted to be conclusive by any reasonable man. It lies rather in an attitude of give and take, in a readiness not only to convince the other man but also possibly to be convinced by him. What I call the attitude of reasonableness may be characterized by a remark like this: "I think I am right, but I may be wrong and you may be right, and in any case let us discuss it, for in this way we are likely to get nearer to a true understanding than if we each merely insist that we are right."

It will be realized that what I call the attitude of reasonableness or the rationalistic attitude presupposes a certain amount of intellectual humility. Perhaps only those can take it up who are aware that they are sometimes wrong, and who do not habitually forget their mistakes. It is born of the realization that we are not omniscient, and that we owe most of our knowledge to others. It is an attitude which tries as far as possible to transfer to the field of opinions in general the two rules of every legal proceeding: first, that one should always hear both sides, and secondly, that one does not make a good judge if one is a party to the case.

I believe that we can avoid violence only in so far as we practise this attitude of reasonableness when dealing with one another in social life; and that any other attitude is likely to produce violence—even a one-sided attempt to deal with others by gentle persuasion, and to convince them by argument and example of those insights we are proud of possessing, and of whose truth we are absolutely certain. We all remember how many religious wars were fought for a religion of love and gentleness; how many bodies were burned alive with the genuinely kind intention of saving souls from the external fire of hell. Only if we give up our authoritarian attitude in the realm of opinion, only if we establish the attitude of give and take, of readiness to learn from other people, can we hope to control acts of violence inspired by piety and duty.

There are many difficulties impeding the rapid spread of reasonableness. One of the main difficulties is that it always takes two to make a discussion reasonable. Each of the parties must be ready to learn from the other. You cannot have a rational discussion with a man who prefers shooting you to being convinced by you. In other words, there are limits to the attitude of reasonableness. It is the same with tolerance. You must not, without qualification, accept the principle of tolerating all those who are intolerant; if you do, you will destroy not only yourself, but also the attitude of tolerance. (All this is indicated in the remark I made before—that reasonableness must be an attitude of *give and take*.)

An important consequence of all this is that we must not allow the distinction between attack and defence to become blurred. We must insist upon this distinction, and support and develop social institutions (national as well as international) whose function it is to discriminate between aggression and resistance to aggression.

I think I have said enough to make clear what I intend to convey by calling myself a rationalist. My rationalism is not dogmatic. I fully admit that I cannot rationally prove it. I frankly confess that I choose rationalism because I hate violence, and I do not deceive myself into believing that this hatred has any rational grounds. Or to put it another way, my rationalism is not self-contained, but rests on an irrational faith in the attitude of reasonableness. I do not see that we can go beyond this. One could say, perhaps, that my irrational faith in equal and reciprocal rights to convince others and be convinced by them is a faith in human reason; or simply, that I believe in man.

If I say that I believe in man, I mean in man as he is; and I should never dream of saying that he is wholly rational. I do not think that a question such as whether man is more rational than emotional or *vice versa* should be asked: there are no ways of assessing or comparing such things. I admit that I feel inclined to protest against certain exaggerations (arising largely from a vulgarization of psycho-analysis) of the irrationality of man and of human society. But I am aware not only of the power of emotions in human life, but also of their value. I should never demand that the attainment of an attitude of reasonableness should become the one dominant aim of our lives. All I wish to assert is that this attitude can become one that is never wholly absent—not even in relationships which are dominated by great passions, such as love.*

My fundamental attitude towards the problem of reason and violence will by now be understood; and I hope I share it with some of my readers and with many other people everywhere. It is on this basis that I now propose to discuss the problem of Utopianism.

I think we can describe Utopianism as a result of a form of rationalism, and I shall try to show that this is a form of rationalism very different from the form in which I and many others believe. So I shall try to show that there exist at least two forms of rationalism, one of which I believe is right and the other wrong; and that the wrong kind of rationalism is the one which leads to Utopianism.

As far as I can see, Utopianism is the result of a way of reasoning which is accepted by many who would be astonished to hear that this apparently quite inescapable and self-evident way of reasoning leads to Utopian results. This specious reasoning can perhaps be presented in the following manner.

An action, it may be argued, is rational if it makes the best use of the available means in order to achieve a certain end. The end, admittedly, may be incapable of being determined rationally. However this may be, we can judge an action rationally, and describe it as rational or adequate, only relative to some given end. Only if we have an end in mind, and only relative to such an end, can we say that we are acting rationally.

Now let us apply this argument to politics. All politics consists of actions; and these actions will be rational only if they pursue some end. The end of a man's political actions may be the increase of his own power or wealth. Or it may perhaps be the improvement of the laws of the state, a change in the structure of the state.

In the latter case political action will be rational only if we first determine the final ends of the political changes which we intend to bring about. It will be rational only relative to certain ideas of what a state ought to be like. Thus it appears that as a preliminary to any rational political action we must first attempt to become as clear as possible about our ultimate political ends: for example the kind of state which we should consider the best; and only afterwards can we begin to determine the means which may best help us to realize this state, or

---

* The existentialist Jaspers writes "This is why love is cruel, ruthless; and why it is believed in, by the genuine lover, only if it is so." This attitude, to my mind, reveals weakness rather than the strength it wishes to show; it is not so much plain barbarism as an hysterical attempt to play the barbarian. (Cf. my *Open Society*, 4th edn., vol. II, p. 317.)

to move slowly towards it, taking it as the aim of a historical process which we may to some extent influence and steer towards the goal selected.

Now it is precisely this view which I call Utopianism. Any rational and nonselfish political action, on this view, must be preceded by a determination of our ultimate ends, not merely of intermediate or partial aims which are only steps towards our ultimate end, and which there-fore should be considered as means rather than as ends; therefore rational political action must be based upon a more or less clear and detailed description or blueprint of our ideal state, and also upon a plan or blueprint of the historical path that leads towards this goal.

I consider what I call Utopianism an attractive and, indeed, an all too attractive theory; for I also consider it dangerous and pernicious. It is, I believe, self-defeating, and it leads to violence.

That it is self-defeating is connected with the fact that it is impossible to determine ends scientifically. There is no scientific way of choosing between two ends. Some people, for example, love and venerate violence. For them a life without violence would be shallow and trivial. Many others, of whom I am one, hate violence. This is a quarrel about ends. It cannot be decided by science. This does not mean that the attempt to argue against violence is necessarily a waste of time. It only means that you may not be able to argue with the admirer of violence. He has a way of answering an argument with a bullet if he is not kept under control by the threat of counter-violence. If he is willing to listen to your arguments without shooting you, then he is at least infected by ration-alism, and you may, perhaps, win him over. This is why arguing is no waste of time—as long as people listen to you. But you cannot, by means of argument, make people listen to argument; you cannot, by means of argument, convert those who suspect all argument, and who prefer violent decisions to rational decisions. You cannot prove to them that they are wrong. And this is only a particular case, which can be gen-eralized. No decision about aims can be established by *purely* rational or scientific means. Nevertheless argument may prove extremely helpful in reaching a decision about aims.

Applying all this to the problem of Utopianism, we must first be quite clear that the problem of constructing a Utopian blueprint cannot pos-sibly be solved by science alone. Its aims, at least, must be given before the social scientist can begin to sketch his blueprint. We find the same situation in the natural sciences. No amount of physics will tell a scien-tist that it is the right thing for him to construct a plough, or an aero-plane, or an atomic bomb. Ends must be adopted by him, or given to him; and what he does *qua* scientist is only to construct means by which these ends can be realized.

In emphasizing the difficulty of deciding, by way of rational argument, between different Utopian ideals, I do not wish to create the impression that there is a realm—such as the realm of ends—which goes altogether beyond the power of rational criticism (even though I certainly wish to say that the realm of ends goes largely beyond the power of *scientific* argument). For I myself try to argue about this realm; and by pointing out the difficulty of deciding between competing Utopian blueprints, I try to argue rationally against choosing ideal ends of this kind. Similarly, my attempt to point out that this difficulty is likely to produce violence is meant as a rational argument, although it will appeal only to those who hate violence.

That the Utopian method, which chooses an ideal state of society as the aim which all our political actions should serve, is likely to produce violence can be shown thus. Since we cannot determine the ultimate ends of political actions scientifically, or by purely rational methods, differences of opinion concerning what the ideal state should be like cannot always be smoothed out by the method of argument. They will at least partly have the character of religious differences. And there can be no tolerance between these different Utopian religions. Utopian aims are designed to serve as a basis for rational political action and discussion, and such action appears to be possible only if the aim is definitely decided upon. Thus the Utopianist must win over, or else crush, his Utopianist competitors who do not share his own Utopian aims, and who do not profess his own Utopianist religion.

But he has to do more. He has to be very thorough in eliminating and stamping out all heretical competing views. For the way to the Utopian goal is long. Thus the rationality of his political action demands constancy of aim for a long time ahead; and this can only be achieved if he not merely crushes competing Utopian religions, but as far as possible stamps out all memory of them.

The use of violent methods for the suppression of competing aims becomes even more urgent if we consider that the period of Utopian construction is liable to be one of social change. In such a time ideas are liable to change also. Thus what may have appeared to many as desirable at the time when the Utopian blueprint was decided upon may appear less desirable at a later date. If this is so, the whole approach is in danger of breaking down. For if we change our ultimate political aims while attempting to move towards them we may soon discover that we are moving in circles. The whole method of first establishing an ultimate political aim and then preparing to move towards it must be futile if the aim may be changed during the process of its realization. It may easily turn out that the steps so far taken lead in fact away from the new aim. And if we then change direction in accordance with our new aim we expose ourselves to the same risk. In spite of all the sacrifices which we may have made in order to make sure that we are acting rationally, we may get exactly nowhere—although not exactly to that "nowhere" which is meant by the word "Utopia."

Again, the only way to avoid such changes of our aims seems to be to use violence, which includes propaganda, the suppression of criticism, and the annihilation of all opposition. With it goes the affirmation of the wisdom and foresight of the Utopian planners, of the Utopian engineers who design and execute the Utopian blueprint. The Utopian engineers must in this way become omniscient as well as omnipotent. They become gods. Thou shalt have no other Gods before them.

Utopian rationalism is a self-defeating rationalism. However benevolent its ends, it does not bring happiness, but only the familiar misery of being condemned to live under a tyrannical government.

It is important to understand this criticism fully. I do not criticize political ideals as such, nor do I assert that a political ideal can never be realized. This would not be a valid criticism. Many ideals have been realized which were once dogmatically declared to be unrealizable, for example, the establishment of workable and untyrannical institutions for securing civil peace, that is, for the suppression of crime within the state. Again, I see no reason why an international judicature and an international police force should be less successful in suppressing international crime, that is, national aggression and the ill-treatment of minorities or perhaps majorities. I do not object to the attempt to realize such ideals.

Wherein, then, lies the difference between those benevolent Utopian plans to which I object because they lead to violence, and those other important and far-reaching political reforms which I am inclined to recommend?

If I were to give a simple formula or recipe for distinguishing between what I consider to be admissible plans for social reform and inadmissible Utopian blueprints, I might say:

Work for the elimination of concrete evils rather than for the realization of abstract goods. Do not aim at establishing happiness by political means. Rather aim at the elimination of concrete miseries. Or, in more practical terms: fight for the elimination of poverty by direct means—for example, by making sure that everybody has a minimum income. Or fight against epidemics and disease by erecting hospitals and schools of medicine. Fight illiteracy as you fight criminality. But do all this by direct means. Choose what you consider the most urgent evil of the society in which you live, and try patiently to convince people that we can get rid of it.

But do not try to realize these aims indirectly by designing and working for a distant ideal of a society which is wholly good. However you may feel indebted to its inspiring vision, do not think you are obliged to work for its realization, or that it is your mission to open the eyes of others to its beauty. Do not allow your dreams of a beautiful world to lure you away from the claims of men who suffer here and now. Our fellow men have a claim to our help; no generation must be sacrificed for the sake of future generations, for the sake of an ideal of happiness that may never be realized. In brief, it is my thesis that human misery is the most urgent problem of a rational public policy and that happiness is not such a problem. The attainment of happiness should be left to our private endeavours.

It is a fact, and not a very strange fact, that it is not so very difficult to reach agreement by discussion on what are the most intolerable evils of our society, and on what are the most urgent social reforms. Such an agreement can be reached much more easily than an agreement concerning some ideal form of social life. For the evils are with us here and now. They can be experienced, and are being experienced every day, by many people who have been and are being made miserable by poverty, unemployment, national oppression, war, and disease. Those of us who do not suffer from these miseries meet every day others who can describe them to us. This is what makes the evils concrete. This is why we can get somewhere in arguing about them; why we can profit here from the attitude of reasonableness. We can learn by listening to concrete claims, by patiently trying to assess them as impartially as we can, and by considering ways of meeting them without creating worse evils.

With ideal goods it is different. These we know only from our dreams and from the dreams of our poets and prophets. They cannot be discussed, only proclaimed from the housetops. They do not call for the rational attitude of the impartial judge, but for the emotional attitude of the impassioned preacher.

The Utopianist attitude, therefore, is opposed to the attitude of reasonableness. Utopianism, even though it may often appear in a rationalist disguise, cannot be more than a pseudo-rationalism.

What, then, is wrong with the apparently rational argument which I outlined when presenting the Utopianist case? I believe that it is quite true that we can judge the rationality of an action only in relation to some aims or ends. But this does not necessarily mean that the rationality of a political action can be judged only in relation to an *historical* end. And it surely does not mean that we must consider every social or political situation merely from the point of view of some preconceived historical ideal, from the point of view of an alleged ultimate aim of the development of history. On the contrary, if among our aims and ends there is anything conceived in terms of human happiness and misery, then we are bound to judge our actions in terms not only of possible contributions to the happiness of man in a distant future, but also of their more immediate effects. We must not argue that a certain social situation is a mere means to an end on the grounds that it is merely a transient historical situation. For all situations are transient. Similarly we must not argue that the misery of one generation may be considered as a mere means to the end of securing the lasting happiness of some later generation or generations; and this argument is improved neither by a high degree of promised happiness nor by a large number of generations profiting by it. All generations are transient. All have an equal right to be considered, but our immediate duties are undoubtedly to the present generation and to the next. Besides, we should never attempt to balance anybody's misery against somebody else's happiness.

With this the apparently rational arguments of Utopianism dissolve into nothing. The fascination which the future exerts upon the Utopianist has nothing to do with rational foresight. Considered in this light the violence which Utopianism breeds looks very much like the running amok of an evolutionist metaphysics, of an hysterical philosophy of history, eager to sacrifice the present for the splendours of the future, and unaware that its principle would lead to sacrificing each particular future period for one which comes after it; and likewise unaware of the trivial truth that the ultimate future of man—whatever fate may have in store for him—can be nothing more splendid than his ultimate extinction.

The appeal of Utopianism arises from the failure to realize that we cannot make heaven on earth. What I believe we can do instead is to make life a little less terrible and a little less unjust in each generation. A good deal can be achieved in this way. Much has been achieved in the last hundred years. More could be achieved by our own generation. There are many pressing problems which we might solve, at least partially, such as helping the weak and the sick, and those who suffer under oppression and injustice; stamping out unemployment; equalizing opportunities; and preventing international crime, such as blackmail and war instigated by men like gods, by omnipotent and omniscient leaders. All this we might achieve if only we could give up dreaming about distant ideals and fighting over our Utopian blueprints for a new world and a new man. Those of us who believe in man as he is, and who have therefore not given up the hope of defeating violence and unreason, must demand instead that every man should be given the right to arrange his life himself so far as this is compatible with the equal rights of others.

We can see here that the problem of the true and the false rationalisms is part of a larger problem. Ultimately it is the problem of a sane attitude towards our own existence and its limitations—that very problem of which so much is made now by those who call themselves "Existentialists," the expounders of a new theology without God. There is, I believe, a neurotic and even an hysterical element in this exaggerated emphasis upon the fundamental loneliness of man in a godless world, and upon the resulting tension between the self and the world. I have little doubt that this hysteria is closely akin to Utopian romanticism, and also to the ethic of hero-worship, to an ethic that can comprehend life only in terms of "dominate or prostrate yourself." And I do not doubt that this hysteria is the secret of its strong appeal. That our problem is part of a larger one can be seen from the fact that we can find a clear parallel to the split between true and false rationalism even in a sphere apparently so far removed from rationalism as that of religion. Christian thinkers have interpreted the relationship between man and God in at least two very different ways. The sane one may be expressed by: "Never forget that men are not Gods; but remember that there is a divine spark in them." The other exaggerates the tension between man and God, and the baseness of man as well as the heights to which men may aspire. It introduces the ethic of "dominate or prostrate yourself." into the relationship of man and God. Whether there are always either conscious or unconscious dreams of godlikeness and of omnipotence at the roots of this attitude, I do not know. But I think it is hard to deny that the emphasis on this tension can arise only from an unbalanced attitude towards the problem of power.

This unbalanced (and immature) attitude is obsessed with the problem of power, not only over other men, but also over our national environment—over the world as a whole. What I might call, by analogy, the "false religion," is obsessed not only by God's power over men but also by His power to create a world; similarly, false rationalism is fascinated by the idea of creating huge machines and Utopian social worlds. Bacon's "knowledge is power" and Plato's "rule of the wise" are different expressions of this attitude which, at bottom, is one of claiming power on the basis of one's superior intellectual gifts. The true rationalist, by contrast, will always know how little he knows, and he will be aware of the simple fact that whatever critical faculty or reason he may possess he owes to intellectual intercourse with others. He will be inclined, therefore, to consider men as fundamentally equal, and human reason as a bond which unites them. Reason for him is the precise opposite of an instrument of power and violence: he sees it as a means whereby these may be tamed.

SUGGESTIONS FOR WRITING

Write an essay arguing for some idea that interests you: the similarities or differences between men and women, the intelligence or ignorance of animals, social proximity as a promoter of togetherness or discord, violence as natural or acquired, controlling population, racial mixing, "real faith and false religion," funerals or no funerals, political platforms, propaganda, the possibility or impossibility of rational discussion. Quote anything from the foregoing selections that will fit your argument, pro or con.

If the opposition can be met with one swing, as in Koestler's essay, for instance, use a simple pro-con structure. Write an introductory paragraph that ends with your thesis: "Animals are more intelligent than many people suppose." Then bring in the opposition: "Of course, they have no speech or lofty ideals. They never learn that the door to the garage won't let them outside." And so on to the end of the paragraph. Then back to your main line: "But my dog can talk with his eyes and his ears, his whines and his yips." The structure might be diagramed as follows:

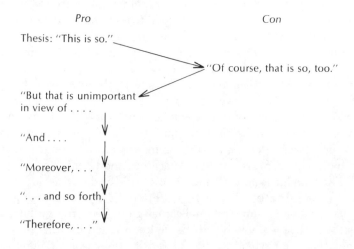

If your argument demands more swinging from pro to con, do not hesitate to swing more than once, as Popper has done. You might have been repelled by a funeral, for instance. You write a thesis asserting that "Funerals are inappropriate remnants from barbaric times." You then admit your first con: "Of course, some people still need the comfort of ritual." You swing back to your pro side with "But these needs can be met without public display and embarrassing pomp." You then find another con: "I admit that anyone's life deserves some acknowledgment, some tribute in conclusion." Then back to your pro side: "But let us eliminate all empty show." Such a complex or multiple pro-con would follow a structure something like this:

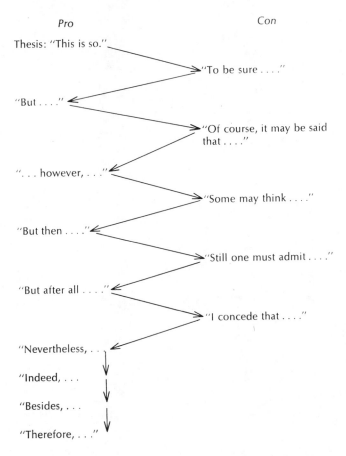

Pro   Con

Thesis: "This is so."

"To be sure . . . ."

"But . . . ."

"Of course, it may be said that . . . ."

". . . however, . . ."

"Some may think . . . ."

"But then . . . ."

"Still one must admit . . . ."

"But after all . . . ."

"I concede that . . . ."

"Nevertheless, . . .

"Indeed, . . .

"Besides, . . .

"Therefore, . . ."

Three
Middle Tactics:
Interest and Contrast

Once you have grasped the essential "middle" structuring of pro and con, you need only two more structural principles: the order of interest and the order of contrast. To keep your reader's interest, save your best till last. To keep your contrasts clear, contrast point by point. Each of these simply serves the psychological needs of your reader, that is, the one whom you hope to please and convince. To hold your reader's interest, begin with your most obvious point and follow it with two or three more and more interesting points. Your contrasts follow the same principle too—from least interesting to most interesting.

But contrasts add a second dimension. "Least to most" still obtains, but it may tempt you to write all about the poorer subject first and then to lay out all the glories of the good one. This is fatal. Your reader will not see where you are driving with the first, will be surprised when you bring in the second, and will lose all the points of contrast, unless you repeat them, growing redundant and wasting paper. So line up your two specimens item by item, as Macaulay has done in the last essay of this section. Arrange them in an ascending order of interest, but, at each item, bring in both members of the contrast. If you mention plot in one, contrast plot in the other. If you mention the hero in one, contrast the hero in the other—*point by point.*

Study the four essays in this section to see how well their authors have fulfilled the principle of arranging their "middles" from least to most. Notice also the different kinds of "middle" order. After a paragraph on Sartre to clarify his thesis, Stace, for instance, uses a historical arrangement to illustrate his first point, moving backward in time from Russell to Darwin to Plato, and then forward again to Galileo and modern man. Next he shifts to a reasonable progression, from what he thinks least important (religion) to what he considers most important (moral courage). Greene progresses from "science" to "spirit"; Bettelheim, from inner self to outer moral obligation; Macaulay, from arithmetic to medicine.

As you read, check your own experience. *Does* the world seem dark and lonely? Has the ideal shriveled before the real? What are the fantasies we live by?

W. T. STACE

W. T. Stace (1886–1967), born in England, served for twenty-two years in the British Civil Service in Ceylon, after graduating from Trinity College, Dublin (1910). His *Philosophy of Hegel* (1924) earned him a professorship in philosophy at Princeton (1932–1955). His last book was *Mysticism and Philosophy* (1961).

MAN AGAINST DARKNESS

This essay presents the philosophical background for the existential stance of the modern world, which Bigelow has outlined. Science has changed our picture of the world; the facts have taken on new meanings, as Koestler has suggested. The old absolutes have dissolved to particulars, and Stace does not want "to invent yet another absolute." The world is meaningless, he says, but he wants us "to walk straightly and to live honorably." Does he assume some meaning after all? Compare this with Sartre's anguish about making choices with nothing to go on, as if we were choosing for all men "the image of man as he ought to be."

1

The Catholic bishops of America recently issued a statement in which they said that the chaotic and bewildered state of the modern world is due to man's loss of faith, his abandonment of God and religion. For my part I believe in no religion at all. Yet I entirely agree with the bishops. It is no doubt an oversimplification to speak of the cause of so complex a state of affairs as the tortured condition of the world today. Its causes are doubtless multitudinous. Yet allowing for some element of oversimplification, I say that the bishops' assertion is substantially true.

M. Jean-Paul Sartre, the French existentialist philosopher, labels himself an atheist. Yet his views seem to me plainly to support the statement of the bishops. So long as there was believed to be a God in the sky, he says, men could regard him as the source of their moral ideals. The universe, created and governed by a fatherly God, was a friendly habitation for man. We could be sure that, however great the evil in the world, good in the end would triumph and the forces of evil would be routed. With the disappearance of God from the sky, all this has changed. Since the world is not ruled by a spiritual being, but rather by blind forces, there cannot be any ideals, moral or otherwise, in the universe outside us. Our ideals, therefore, must proceed only from our own minds; they are our own inventions. Thus the world which surrounds us is nothing but an immense spiritual emptiness. It is a dead universe. We do not live in a universe which is on the side of our values. It is completely indifferent to them.

Years ago Mr. Bertrand Russell, in his essay *A Free Man's Worship*, said much the same thing.

> Such in outline, but even more purposeless, more void of meaning, is the world which Science presents for our belief. Amid such a world, if anywhere, our ideals henceforward must find a home. . . . Blind to good and evil, reckless of destruction, omnipotent matter rolls on its relentless way; for man, condemned today to lose his dearest, tomorrow himself to pass through the gate of darkness, it remains only to cherish, ere yet the blow falls, the lofty thoughts that ennoble his little day; . . . to worship at the shrine his own hands have built; . . . to sustain alone, a weary but unyielding Atlas, the world that his own ideals have fashioned despite the trampling march of unconscious power.

It is true that Mr. Russell's personal attitude to the disappearance of religion is quite different from either that of M. Sartre or the bishops or myself. The bishops think it a calamity. So do I. M. Sartre finds it "very distressing." And he berates as shallow the attitude of those who think that without God the world can go on just the same as before, as if nothing had happened. This creates for mankind, he thinks, a terrible crisis. And in this I agree with him. Mr. Russell, on the other hand, seems to believe that religion has done more harm than good in the world, and that its disappearance will be a blessing. But his picture of the world, and of the modern mind, is the same as that of M. Sartre. He stresses the *purposelessness* of the universe, the facts that man's ideals are his own creations, that the universe outside him in no way supports them, that man is alone and friendless in the world. Mr. Russell notes that it is science which has produced this situation. There is no doubt that this is correct. But the way in which it has come about is not generally understood. There is a popular belief that some particular scientific discoveries or theories, such as the Darwinian theory of evolution, or the views of geologists about the age of the earth, or a series of such discoveries, have done the damage. It would be foolish to deny that these discoveries have had a great effect in undermining religious dogmas. But this account does not at all go to the root of the matter. Religion can probably outlive any scientific discoveries which could be made. It can accommodate itself to them. The root cause of the decay of faith has not been any particular discovery of science, but rather the general spirit of science and certain basic assumptions upon which modern science, from the seventeenth century onwards, has proceeded.

2

It was Galileo and Newton—notwithstanding that Newton himself was a deeply religious man—who destroyed the old comfortable picture of a friendly universe governed by spiritual values. And this was effected, not by Newton's discovery of the law of gravitation nor by any of Galileo's brilliant investigations, but by the general picture of the world which these men and others of their time made the basis of the science, not only of their own day, but of all succeeding generations down to the present. That is why the century immediately following Newton, the eighteenth century, was notoriously an age of religious skepticism. Skepticism did not have to wait for the discoveries of Darwin and the geologists in the nineteenth century. It flooded the world immediately after the age of the rise of science.

Neither the Copernican hypothesis nor any of Newton's or Galileo's particular discoveries were the real causes. Religious faith might well have accommodated itself to the new astronomy. The real turning point between the medieval age of faith and the modern age of unfaith came when the scientists of the seventeenth century turned their backs upon what used to be called "final causes." The final cause of a thing or event meant the purpose which it was supposed to serve in the universe.

its cosmic purpose. What lay back of this was the presupposition that there is a cosmic order or plan and that everything which exists could in the last analysis be explained in terms of its place in this cosmic plan, that is, in terms of its purpose.

Plato and Aristotle believed this; and so did the whole medieval Christian world. For instance, if it were true that the sun and the moon were created and exist for the purpose of giving light to man, then this fact would explain why the sun and the moon exist. We might not be able to discover the purpose of everything, but everything must have a purpose. Belief in final causes thus amounted to a belief that the world is governed by purposes, presumably the purposes of some overruling mind. This belief was not the invention of Christianity. It was basic to the whole of Western civilization, whether in the ancient pagan world or in Christendom, from the time of Socrates to the rise of science in the seventeenth century.

The founders of modern science—for instance, Galileo, Kepler, and Newton—were mostly pious men who did not doubt God's purposes. Nevertheless they took the revolutionary step of consciously and deliberately expelling the idea of purpose as controlling nature from their new science of nature. They did this on the ground that inquiry into purposes is useless for what science aims at: namely, the prediction and control of events. To predict an eclipse, what you have to know is not its purpose but its causes. Hence science from the seventeenth century onwards became exclusively an inquiry into causes. The conception of purpose in the world was ignored and frowned on. This, though silent and almost unnoticed, was the greatest revolution in human history, far outweighing in importance any of the political revolutions whose thunder has reverberated through the world.

For it came about in this way that for the past three hundred years there has been growing up in men's minds, dominated as they are by science, a new imaginative picture of the world. The world, according to this new picture, is purposeless, senseless, meaningless. Nature is nothing but matter in motion. The motions of matter are governed, not by any purpose, but by blind forces and laws. Nature on this view, says Whitehead—to whose writings I am indebted in this part of my paper—is "merely the hurrying of material, endlessly, meaninglessly." You can draw a sharp line across the history of Europe dividing it into two epochs of very unequal length. The line passes through the lifetime of Galileo. European man before Galileo—whether ancient pagan or more recent Christian—thought of the world as controlled by plan and purpose. After Galileo European man thinks of it as utterly purposeless. This is the great revolution of which I spoke.

It is this which has killed religion. Religion could survive the discoveries that the sun, not the earth, is the center; that men are descended from simian ancestors; that the earth is hundreds of million of years old. These discoveries may render out of date some of the details of older theological dogmas, may force their restatement in new intellectual frameworks. But they do not touch the essence of the religious vision itself, which is the faith that there is plan and purpose in the world, that the world is a moral order, that in the end all things are for the best. This faith may express itself through many different intellectual dogmas, those of Christianity, of Hinduism, of Islam. All and any of these intellectual dogmas may be destroyed without destroying the essential religious spirit. But that spirit cannot survive destruction of belief in a plan and purpose of the world, for that is the very heart of it. Religion can get on with any sort of astronomy, geology, biology, physics. But it cannot get on with a purposeless and meaningless universe.

If the scheme of things is purposeless and meaningless, then the life of man is purposeless and meaningless too. Everything is futile, all effort is in the end worthless. A man may, of course, still pursue disconnected ends, money, fame, art, science, and may gain pleasure from them. But his life is hollow at the center. Hence the dissatisfied, disillusioned, restless, spirit of modern man.

The picture of a meaningless world, and a meaningless human life, is, I think, the basic theme of much modern art and literature. Certainly it is the basic theme of modern philosophy. According to the most characteristic philosophies of the modern period from Hume in the eighteenth century to the so-called positivists of today, the world is just what it is, and that is the end of all inquiry. There is no reason for its being what it is. Everything might just as well have been quite different, and there would have been no reason for that either. When you have stated what things are, what things the world contains, there is nothing more which could be said, even by an omniscient being. To ask any question about why things are thus, or what purpose their being so serves, is to ask a senseless question, because they serve no purpose at all. For instance, there is for modern philosophy no such thing as the ancient problem of evil. For this once famous question pre-supposes that pain and misery, though they seem so inexplicable and irrational to us, must ultimately subserve some rational purpose, must have their places in the cosmic plan. But this is nonsense. There is no such overruling rationality in the universe. Belief in the ultimate irrationality of everything is the quintessence of what is called the modern mind.

It is true that, parallel with these philosophies which are typical of the modern mind, preaching the meaninglessness of the world, there has run a line of idealistic philosophies whose contention is that the world is after all spiritual in nature and that moral ideals and values are inherent in its structure. But most of these idealisms were simply philosophical expressions of romanticism, which was itself no more than an unsuccessful counterattack of the religious against the scientific view of things. They perished, along with romanticism in literature and art, about the beginning of the present century, though of course they still have a few adherents.

At the bottom these idealistic systems of thought were rationalizations of man's wishful thinking. They were born of the refusal of men to admit the cosmic darkness. They were comforting illusions within the warm glow of which the more tender-minded intellectuals sought to shelter themselves from the icy winds of the universe. They lasted a little while. But they are shattered now, and we return once more to the vision of a purposeless world.

3

Along with the ruin of the religious vision there went the ruin of moral principles and indeed of all values. If there is a cosmic purpose, if there is in the nature of things a drive towards goodness, then our moral systems will derive their validity from this. But if our moral rules do not proceed from something outside us in the nature of the universe— whether we say it is God or simply the universe itself—then they must be our own inventions. Thus it came to be believed that moral rules must be merely an expression of our own likes and dislikes. But likes and dislikes are notoriously variable. What pleases one man, people, or culture displeases another. Therefore morals are wholly relative.

This obvious conclusion from the idea of a purposeless world made its appearance in Europe immediately after the rise of science, for instance in the philosophy of Hobbes. Hobbes saw at once that if there is no purpose in the world there are no values either. "Good and evil," he writes, "are names that signify our appetites and aversions; which in different tempers, customs, and doctrines of men are different. . . . Every man calleth that which pleaseth him, good; and that which displeaseth him, evil."

This doctrine of the relativity of morals, though it has recently received an impetus from the studies of anthropologists, was thus really implicit in the whole scientific mentality. It is disastrous for morals because it destroys their entire traditional foundation. That is why philosophers who see the danger signals, from the time at least of Kant, have been trying to give to morals a new foundation, that is, a secular or nonreligious foundation. This attempt may very well be intellectually successful. Such a foundation, independent of the religious view of the world, might well be found. But the question is whether it can ever be a *practical* success, that is, whether apart from its logical validity and its influence with intellectuals, it can ever replace among the masses of men the lost religious foundation. On that question hangs perhaps the future of civilization. But meanwhile disaster is overtaking us.

The widespread belief in "ethical relativity" among philosophers, psychologists, ethnologists, and sociologists is the theoretical counterpart of the repudiation of principle which we see all around us, especially in international affairs, the field in which morals have always had the weakest foothold. No one any longer effectively believes in moral principles except as the private prejudices either of individual men or of nations or cultures. This is the inevitable consequence of the doctrine of ethical relativity, which in turn is the inevitable consequence of believing in a purposeless world.

Another characteristic of our spiritual state is loss of belief in the freedom of the will. This also is a fruit of the scientific spirit, though not of any particular scientific discovery. Science has been built up on the basis of determinism, which is the belief that every event is completely determined by a chain of causes and is therefore theoretically predictable beforehand. It is true that recent physics seems to challenge this. But so far as its practical consequences are concerned, the damage has long ago been done. A man's actions, it was argued, are as much events in the natural world as is an eclipse of the sun. It follows that men's actions are as theoretically predictable as an eclipse. But if it is certain now that John Smith will murder Joseph Jones at 2.15 P.M. on January 1, 1963, what possible meaning can it have to say that when that time comes John Smith will be *free* to choose whether he will commit the murder or not? And if he is not free, how can he be held responsible?

It is true that the whole of this argument can be shown by a competent philosopher to be a tissue of fallacies—or at least I claim that it can. But the point is that the analysis required to show this is much too subtle to be understood by the average entirely unphilosophical man. Because of this, the argument against free will is generally swallowed whole by the unphilosophical. Hence the thought that man is not free, that he is the helpless plaything of forces over which he has no control, has deeply penetrated the modern mind. We hear of economic determinism, cultural determinism, historical determinism. We are not responsible for what we do because our glands control us, or because we are the products of environment or heredity. Not moral self-control, but the doctor, the psychiatrist, the educationist, must save us from doing evil. Pills and injections in the future are to do what Christ and the prophets have failed to do. Of course I do not mean to deny that doctors and educationists can and must help. And I do not mean in any way to belittle their efforts. But I do wish to draw attention to the weakening of moral controls, the greater or less repudiation of personal responsibility which, in the popular thinking of the day, result from these tendencies of thought.

4

What, then, is to be done? Where are we to look for salvation from the evils of our time? All the remedies I have seen suggested so far are, in my opinion, useless. Let us look at some of them.

Philosophers and intellectuals generally can, I believe, genuinely do something to help. But it is extremely little. What philosophers can do is to show that neither the relativity of morals nor the denial of free will really follows from the grounds which have been supposed to support them. They can also try to discover a genuine secular basis for morals to replace the religious basis which has disappeared. Some of us are trying to do these things. But in the first place philosophers unfortunately are not agreed about these matters, and their disputes are utterly confusing to the non-philosophers. And in the second place their influence is practically negligible because their analyses necessarily take place on a level on which the masses are totally unable to follow them.

The bishops, of course, propose as remedy a return to belief in God and in the doctrines of the Christian religion. Others think that a new religion is what is needed. Those who make these proposals fail to realize that the crisis in man's spiritual condition is something unique in history for which there is no sort of analogy in the past. They are thinking perhaps of the collapse of the ancient Greek and Roman religions. The vacuum then created was easily filled by Christianity, and it might have been filled by Mithraism if Christianity had not appeared. By analogy they think that Christianity might now be replaced by a new religion, or even that Christianity itself, if revivified, might bring back health to men's lives.

But I believe that there is no analogy at all between our present state and that of the European peoples at the time of the fall of paganism. Men had at that time lost their belief only in particular dogmas, particular embodiments of the religious view of the world. It had no doubt become incredible that Zeus and the other gods were living on the top of Mount Olympus. You could go to the top and find no trace of them. But the imaginative picture of a world governed by purpose, a world driving towards the good—which is the inner spirit of religion—had at that time received no serious shock. It had merely to re-embody itself in new dogmas, those of Christianity or some other religion. Religion itself was not dead in the world, only a particular form of it.

But now the situation is quite different. It is not merely that particular dogmas, like that of the virgin birth, are unacceptable to the modern mind. That is true, but it constitutes a very superficial diagnosis of the present situation of religion. Modern skepticism is of a wholly different order from that of the intellectuals of the ancient world. It has attacked and destroyed not merely the outward forms of the religious spirit, its particularized dogmas, but the very essence of that spirit itself, belief in a meaningful and purposeful world. For the founding of a new religion a new Jesus Christ or Buddha would have to appear, in itself a most unlikely event and one for which in any case we cannot afford to sit and wait. But even if a new prophet and a new religion did appear, we may predict that they would fail in the modern world. No one for long would believe in them, for modern men have lost the vision, basic to all religion, of an ordered plan and purpose of the world. They have before their minds the picture of a purposeless universe, and such a world-picture must be fatal to any religion at all, not merely to Christianity.

We must not be misled by occasional appearances of a revival of the religious spirit. Men, we are told, in their disgust and disillusionment at the emptiness of their lives, are turning once more to religion, or are searching for a new message. It may be so. We must expect such wistful yearnings of the spirit. We must expect men to wish back again the light that is gone, and to try to bring it back. But however they may wish and try, the light will not shine again—not at least in the civilization to which we belong.

Another remedy commonly proposed is that we should turn to science itself, or the scientific spirit, for our salvation. Mr. Russell and Professor Dewey both make this proposal, though in somewhat different ways. Professor Dewey seems to believe that discoveries in sociology, the application of scientific method to social and political problems, will rescue us. This seems to me to be utterly naïve. It is not likely that science, which is basically the cause of our spiritual troubles, is likely also to produce the cure for them. Also it lies in the nature of science that, though it can teach us the best means for achieving our ends, it can never tell us what ends to pursue. It cannot give us any ideals. And our trouble is about ideals and ends, not about the means for reaching them.

5

No civilization can live without ideals, or to put it in another way, without a firm faith in moral ideals. Our ideals and moral ideas have in the past been rooted in religion. But the religious basis of our ideals has been undermined, and the superstructure of ideals is plainly tottering. None of the commonly suggested remedies on examination seems likely to succeed. It would therefore look as if the early death of our civilization were inevitable.

Of course we know that it is perfectly possible for individual men, very highly educated men, philosophers, scientists, intellectuals in general, to live moral lives without any religious convictions. But the question is whether a whole civilization, a whole family of peoples, composed almost entirely of relatively uneducated men and women, can do this.

It follows, of course, that if we could make the vast majority of men as highly educated as the very few are now, we might save the situation. And we are already moving slowly in that direction through the techniques of mass education. But the critical question seems to concern the time-lag. Perhaps in a few hundred years most of the population will, at the present rate, be sufficiently highly educated and civilized to combine high ideals with an absence of religion. But long before we reach any such stage, the collapse of our civilization may have come about. How are we to live through the intervening period?

I am sure that the first thing we have to do is to face the truth, however bleak it may be, and then next we have to learn to live with it. Let me say a word about each of these two points. What I am urging as regards the first is complete honesty. Those who wish to resurrect Christian dogmas are not, of course, consciously dishonest. But they have that kind of unconscious dishonesty which consists in lulling oneself with opiates and dreams. Those who talk of a new religion are merely hoping for a new opiate. Both alike refuse to face the truth that there is, in the universe outside man, no spirituality, no regard for values, no friend in the sky, no help or comfort for man of any sort. To be perfectly honest in the admission of this fact, not to seek shelter in new or old illusions, not to indulge in wishful dreams about this matter, this is the first thing we shall have to do.

I do not urge this course out of any special regard for the sanctity of truth in the abstract. It is not self-evident to me that truth is the supreme value to which all else must be sacrificed. Might not the discoverer of a truth which would be fatal to mankind be justified in suppressing it, even in teaching men a falsehood? Is truth more valuable than goodness and beauty and happiness? To think so is to invent yet another absolute, another religious delusion in which Truth with a capital T is substituted for God. The reason why we must now boldly and honestly face the truth that the universe is non-spiritual and indifferent to goodness, beauty, happiness, or truth is not that it would be wicked to suppress it, but simply that it is too late to do so, so that in the end we cannot do anything else but face it. Yet we stand on the brink, dreading the icy plunge. We need courage. We need honesty.

Now about the other point, the necessity of learning to live with the truth. This means learning to live virtuously and happily, or at least contentedly, without illusions. And this is going to be extremely difficult because what we have now begun dimly to perceive is that human life in the past, or at least human happiness, has almost wholly depended upon illusions. It has been said that man lives by truth, and that the truth will make us free. Nearly the opposite seems to me to be the case. Mankind has managed to live only by means of lies, and the truth may very well destroy us. If one were a Bergsonian one might believe that nature deliberately puts illusions into our souls in order to induce us to go on living.

The illusions by which men have lived seem to be of two kinds. First, there is what one may perhaps call the Great Illusion—I mean the religious illusion that the universe is moral and good, that it follows a wise and noble plan, that it is gradually generating some supreme value, that goodness is bound to triumph in it. Secondly, there is a whole host of minor illusions on which human happiness nourishes itself. How much of human happiness notoriously comes from the illusions of the lover about his beloved? Then again we work and strive because of the illusions connected with fame, glory, power, or money. Banners of all kinds, flags, emblems, insignia, ceremonials, and rituals are invariably symbols of some illusion or other. The British Empire, the connection between mother country and dominions, is partly kept going by illusions surrounding the notion of kingship. Or think of the vast amount of human happiness which is derived from the illusion of supposing that if some nonsense syllable, such as "sir" or "count" or "lord," is pronounced in conjunction with our names, we belong to a superior order of people.

There is plenty of evidence that human happiness is almost wholly based upon illusions of one kind of another. But the scientific spirit, or the spirit of truth, is the enemy of illusions and therefore the enemy of human happiness. That is why it is going to be so difficult to live with the truth.

There is no reason why we should have to give up the host of minor illusions which render life supportable. There is no reason why the lover should be scientific about the loved one. Even the illusions of fame and glory may persist. But without the Great Illusion, the illusion of a good, kindly, and purposeful universe, we shall *have* to learn to live. And to ask this is really no more than to ask that we become genuinely civilized beings and not merely sham civilized beings.

I can best explain the difference by a reminiscence. I remember a fellow student in my college days, an ardent Christian, who told me that if he did not believe in a future life, in heaven and hell, he would rape, murder, steal, and be a drunkard. That is what I call being a sham civilized being. On the other hand, not only could a Huxley, a John Stuart Mill, a David Hume, live great and fine lives without any religion, but a great many others of us, quite obscure persons, can at least live decent lives without it.

To be genuinely civilized means to be able to walk straightly and to live honorably without the props and crutches of one or another of the childish dreams which have so far supported men. That such a life is likely to be ecstatically happy I will not claim. But that it can be lived in quiet content, accepting resignedly what cannot be helped, not expecting the impossible, and thankful for small mercies, this I would maintain. That it will be difficult for men in general to learn this lesson I do not deny. But that it will be impossible I would not admit since so many have learned it already.

Man has not yet grown up. He is not adult. Like a child he cries for the moon and lives in a world of fantasies. And the race as a whole has perhaps reached the great crisis of its life. Can it grow up as a race in the same sense as individual men grow up? Can man put away childish things and adolescent dreams? Can he grasp the real world as it actually is, stark and bleak, without its romantic or religious halo, and still retain his ideals, striving for great ends and noble achievements? If he cannot, he will probably sink back into the savagery and brutality from which he came, taking a humble place once more among the lower animals.

THEODORE M. GREENE

Theodore M. Greene (1897–) was born in Constantinople and educated at Amherst and Edinburgh. A professor of philosophy at Yale since 1946, he taught at Princeton from 1923 to 1945, where he was Stace's colleague.

MAN OUT OF DARKNESS: RELIGION HAS NOT LOST ITS POWER

This essay replied to Stace's "Man Against Darkness" in the pages of *The Atlantic Monthly,* where Stace's article appeared. How successful is Greene's? What other points might you bring against Stace? Does Greene fail to meet Stace fully at any point?

1

When Professor Stace says that the question of purpose in the universe is the crucial cultural issue of our times, he is certainly right. He is also right in urging us to face the truth, whatever it is, and to live with it honestly and courageously. The question is, Is "the truth" what he thinks it is? Has science, as Professor Stace claims, given us a new imaginative picture of the world—a picture of a meaningless and purposeless universe indifferent to all human aspiration? This picture in its large outline is certainly not "new"—in our tradition it is at least as old as Democritus and Lucretius. Nor is it correct to say that science has given us a picture of reality *as a whole* which logically *excludes* meaning and purpose. All that can fairly be said is that the scientific account of the "world of nature" does not, at least at present, include moral or religious purpose and meaning. The picture science paints is neutral with respect to such purpose and meaning because the scientific enterprise, in and of itself, simply ignores these issues.

It must be admitted, however, that the concept of a purposeless universe has been judged by many people to have received the endorsement of modern science. We must also grant that this picture, with its prestige thus greatly enhanced, has profoundly influenced the thought and the unconscious attitudes of a lot of people, particularly the intelligentsia, but also the man in the street.

But this is *not* the whole story. Not only has organized Christianity lost no ground during the last decades; it is actually increasing its following in this country, in England, and in some portions of Europe. More people are going to church with, in many cases, a deeper sense of spiritual need. Theological seminaries are crowded with students who are, on the whole, abler than their pre-war predecessors, yet seminaries are unable to satisfy the demand of churches for more clergy. Missionary activity is increasing in scope and improving in quality. Christianity is more widely spread geographically and more deeply rooted among more peoples than it has ever been. The Christian ecumenical movement is making rapid strides: through it Christians are coming together on a world-wide scale as never before. There is also increasingly evident in various branches of the Church a growing tendency to take stock of their inadequacies and failures, to indulge in contrite self-examination, and to seek to promote a revitalization of Christian belief, thought, and social action.

No less significant is the renewed interest of college students in a faith to live by. Most of these eager inquirers are largely ignorant of the Bible, Christian doctrine, and the Christian tradition. Many of them are highly critical of Christian orthodoxy and traditionalism and are indignant at what they (often justly) regard as self-righteousness, wishful thinking, and cant in organized religion. Few are properly equipped to grapple intelligently with the basic problems of religious faith in our secular society. But they are neither complacent nor dogmatic; they are deeply troubled and sincerely anxious to find whatever light and strength religion can provide. In short, the "spirit of religion" is a vital force in their lives.

Who, then, is the common man who, according to Professor Stace, has absorbed the idea of a purposeless universe so completely that he has lost all belief not only in God but in moral principles, freedom of the will, and moral responsibility, and could not now be persuaded to abandon or modify this idea even if the intellectual and spiritual leaders in his community were convinced that it was erroneous? In so far as he is impervious to philosophy, he will not greatly be affected by naturalism in its modern scientific dress. If, on the other hand, he has been impressed—indeed, very deeply impressed—by the "new world picture," is there any reason why philosophers and scientists, in combination, could not gradually impress another picture of the world upon his mind?

This leaves us with the question, Can we formulate a constructive argument in support of a critical religious faith? I believe we can.

2

The scientific method has amply demonstrated its validity and power in the areas of inquiry, and for the purposes, for which it has been designed. Witness the spectacular advance of science over the past three hundred years, the large measure of agreement among reputable scientists, and the technological achievements of applied science, every one of which is a pragmatic demonstration of the scientist's understanding of natural processes.

Science also invites, and supports, more embracing philosophical accounts of the nature of the physical world, and no responsible interpretation of reality as a whole can ignore, or contradict, careful philosophical generalizations based upon well-established scientific conclusions. The position I would defend is therefore committed to affirmative reliance on scientific evidence and to the full incorporation, at any point in history, of accepted scientifically supported interpretations of nature.

Science, however, in the stricter sense of the term, is not all-inclusive; it addresses itself to a specific type of inquiry into a specific area of reality for a specific purpose. Pure science concerns itself solely with temporal events, both "physical" and "psycho-physical." It studies these to discover and formulate recurrences and uniformities, commonly called "laws of nature"; and it does so partly to satisfy man's native curiosity, partly to facilitate his control of nature for greater human welfare. But, as Professor Stace admits, it is by its very nature unqualified to deal with values; "it can teach us the best means for achieving our ends, it can never tell us what ends to pursue." This fact is enormously important, for it means that science, in its strict sense, simply has nothing to say about God or goodness or beauty.

Hence the "imaginative picture of the world" which science, in and of itself, supports is *of course* a picture of a valueless, meaningless universe. How could it be otherwise? But this doesn't prove that there are no values and no God in the universe; it merely proves that science can't possibly discover these values and this Deity if they do exist.

Furthermore, no scientific conclusions, at any point in history, are final, definitive, or certain. They are *necessarily* hypothetical and tentative. It follows that philosophical extrapolations of science are equally tentative and hypothetical. For example, late-nineteenth-century science supported the philosophical doctrine of strict mechanistic determinism; some qualified philosophers today are not sure that the most recent scientific thinking justifies any such philosophical conclusion. In any case, the farther science advances, the less disposed are first-rate scientists to believe that they have fathomed the mysteries even of the world of nature, let alone the whole of reality. Their attitude is humble and cautious, not dogmatic and assured.

→ If my analysis is correct thus far, it follows that science cannot properly deny that there *may* be meaning and purpose, or even a God, in the universe, though it cannot itself make any such assertions. Responsible belief in God and in a cosmic purpose is possible, however, only if affirmative evidence can be adduced for its support. Without such evidence, moral and religious belief would have to be wholly blind, and I would condemn blind faith as heartily as does Professor Stace. What kind of evidence, then, would be relevant and coercive? On what kind of experience can an enlightened belief in God and cosmic meaning be based?

The obvious answer would seem to be: on man's moral and religious experiences. Moralists like Socrates and Kant based their beliefs in a meaningful cosmos on man's moral experiences at their best. Christian theologians have based their beliefs on man's Christian experiences, individual and corporate. Is this procedure invalid? Is it wrong to believe that we can achieve reliable knowledge of objective moral values by means of a critical interpretation of man's experience of duty, his respect for his fellow man, his loyalty to moral ideals, or that we can achieve reliable knowledge of God by critical interpretation of man's religious experiences as described, for example, in the New Testament?

It is precisely at this point that we can relate man's search for, and knowledge of, God and moral values to man's scientific study of, and knowledge of, nature. The scientific method is, in essence, the method of rational interpretation of sensory evidence. (I will ignore here the complications raised by psychology.) This means that *both* sensory evidence *and* rational interpretation are essential for scientific knowledge; that sensory data without interpretation are blind, and that reasoning, however consistent, which is not based on sensory evidence is empty of content.

If we can accept the basic scientific assumption that logical interpretation of *sensory* evidence gives us an ever increasing understanding of the world of *nature*, why can we not similarly assume that the logical interpretation of *moral and religious* data, if such exist, can give us an ever increasing understanding of a *spiritual*—that is, a moral and religious—dimension of reality which is related to, but not identical with, the world of nature? If this were possible, it would then be the task of philosophy to try to give an account of reality which does justice *both* to sensory *and* to moral and religious experiences, to science *and* to ethics and theology at their best.

The crucial point in the entire constructive argument is thus the concept of "experience." If the only type of experience which can be taken seriously—that is, accepted as providing contact with reality and clues to its nature—is sensory experience, then Professor Stace's conclusions inevitably follow. But why must experience be so narrowly defined? What is to prevent us from being really empirical and believing that man's moral and religious experiences, which are no less coercive, vivid, sharable, and rationally interpretable than his sensory experiences, provide further contacts with reality and further clues to its nature?

3

Reflective religious faith (in contrast to blind superstition and uncritical faith) rests on precisely this more liberal and inclusive conception of experience. It is always anchored in the primary religious experiences of the individual believer, set in the context of the religious experiences of other individuals in the same and other religious traditions. That is, it rests on the deep conviction of reflective religious believers that only in and through such experiences do we confront a living God. But religious faith, if it is reflective, is never identified with mere experience, however intense, however often repeated, and however widely shared by others. The factor of reasonable interpretation is as essential as the factor of the primary experience itself.

What we actually find in the history of religions, therefore, parallels what we find in the history of science. The earliest attempts in our tradition at a "scientific" understanding of nature were those of the pre-Socratic thinkers who tried to explain the whole of nature in terms of one or more of the four basic "elements"—earth, air, fire, and water. Only very gradually did this attempt grow out of its primitive crudities into the rich pattern of concepts, principles, and methods that constitute modern science. Similarly, primitive religious beliefs and practices were crude, uncritical, and superstitious; it is only gradually that religious experience and belief have developed into what we find them to be, at their best, in the higher religions.

I do not wish to press this analogy between science and religion too hard. Pure science is merely a way of knowing; religion is a way of life based on a way of knowing. Science can use quantitative measurement as theology cannot. And scientists, at least in principle, can hope for a degree of mutual understanding and agreement which theologians have not yet achieved. This disagreement, however, need not invalidate the belief that man can in some measure know God. If God is the infinite and mysterious Being that religious people believe He is, it is to be expected that man, with his finite mind, will have the greatest difficulty in apprehending His nature at all adequately. I must admit that men of religion have had great difficulty in achieving and maintaining an attitude of humble open-minded search, and are tempted to be dogmatic and intolerant towards conflicting beliefs regarding the Deity. I do insist, however, on the validity of the religious quest—the belief that man can and does encounter the Divine, that he can and should reflect upon these encounters, and that such reflection can progressively increase our understanding of God and render our belief in Him less superstitious and more responsible and mature.

Many people feel obliged to repudiate religious belief because they identify religion with one of its cruder, more superstitious forms, or because they interpret more enlightened religious beliefs and practices in a crudely anthropomorphic manner. Anyone who thinks that enlightened Christians believe that God is literally in the sky, or that the phrase in the Nicene Creed "sitteth on the right hand of the Father" literally means that God has a body with a right and left hand, must of course, as an intelligent man, reject such rubbish. It is true that most professing Christians are deplorably uninformed regarding the language of religious utterance and inclined to a crude anthropomorphism in their thinking about God. But the fact that most people are also scientifically illiterate does not justify us in reading this illiteracy into science and in repudiating science on that score. Similarly, Christianity at its enlightened best should not be identified with its unenlightened distortions.

Let us therefore be fair to religion before we decide to brand all religious faith as the "Great Illusion." We can and should distinguish man's everyday encounters with nature and his unscientific conceptions of physical objects from the scientist's much more precise observations and much more critical interpretations of them. We need not, in making this distinction, condemn the common man's experiences or beliefs as illusory, but we should recognize their limitations. We can say that he possesses "opinions" rather than "knowledge," defining opinions as beliefs which may be valid so far as they go but which a man who cannot rise above opinions cannot rationally refine or test.

Similarly, we can and should distinguish between the common man's coercive religious experiences which he rather crudely interprets in terms of an inadequate theology, and the far deeper experiences of the saint and the far more refined interpretations of the competent theologian and philosopher of religion. This does not mean that the religious beliefs of the common man are necessarily false, or that he fails to find strength and joy in his religious life; it does not mean that Christianity is available only to intellectual and spiritual aristocrats. Far from it— witness Jesus' concern for children and uneducated people. "Come unto me, *all* ye that labor and are heavy laden." But Jesus was also concerned to eradicate inadequate conceptions of God in the minds of his disciples, and for twenty centuries his followers have tried to refine and clarify man's understanding of God—witness the long history of progressive theological clarification. Every honest man must of course make his own final decision as to what he believes and what his ultimate loyalties are to be; but a man is less than honest with himself if he fails to inform himself as best he can what Christianity, or any other religion, is at its *best* before he rejects it as illusory.

I must add a word regarding the vexed problem of authority. The position I have been sketching, most inadequately, might be labeled "Liberal Christian Protestantism." This position, on the question of authority, is at variance with Christian positions which assert the literal truth of every word of the Bible or the infallibility of certain ecclesiastical dogmas. I cannot recognize the "absolute" authority of either a book or a church. I do, however, recognize the impressive authority, in a non-absolutistic sense, of the accumulated wisdom of the Church and of the Bible as a uniquely rich and revealing record of authentic religious experiences and vital beliefs, and I also agree with those who believe that Jesus taught "as one having authority." Such a belief is not only completely credible: it is, to me, quite inescapable.

This authority of the Bible (interpreted in the light of the best available Biblical scholarship), and of the Church (interpreted in the light of the best, religiously informed, historical wisdom) and of Jesus Christ, encountered not only in the New Testament but in Christian devotion through the centuries and today by countless sincere Christians, is an enormously impressive testimony that the venture of Christian faith is not illusory, escapist, or irrational, but is magnificently rooted in the poignant experience of Christian love and helpfully elucidated in enlightened Christian doctrine. This faith is *not*, I believe, to be confused with omniscience or infallibility—it is still faith, not absolute knowledge. But it need not be blind faith, superstitious and irrational; it can become, for each individual and for mankind, a knowledge of God which is more and more deeply rooted in experience, more and more enlightened, more and more productive of that reflective commitment which is the mark of responsible maturity.

4

Where does this leave us with regard to Professor Stace's major thesis? It leaves us, I believe, with a way of approaching reality which he does not seriously envisage and which, if followed out, may lead us to a conception of the universe very different from the one which he offers us as the only possible conception today. Of course I have not been able to describe what Christians accept as crucial experiences of God, any more than he was able to describe the crucial scientific contacts with nature upon which scientists base their scientific theories. Nor have I been able to summarize the interpretations of these religious experiences offered by competent theologians, any more than he was able to summarize the major conclusions of modern science.

Anyone who wishes to verify science at first hand must train himself in the scientific method, participate in scientific experiment, and test scientific theories for belief. And even if he does so he must accept on the authority of other scientists the reports of countless other experiments and vast areas of detailed scientific theory.

Similarly, really to explore the religious approach to reality, a man

correct

must submit himself to a spiritual discipline, participate in crucial religious experiences at first hand, and test their theological interpretations for himself. The most deeply religious and thoughtful of men, moreover, must rely on the testimony of other members of the religious community, past and present, since he cannot hope, in a single lifetime, to duplicate all the religious experiences and to explore all the theological interpretations which are to be found in his own and other religious traditions. I have therefore in no sense offered a "proof" of God's existence and nature; I have merely pointed to the empirical method whereby religious beliefs can be generated and tested.

I should not wish to suggest that Christianity is the only religion which should be taken seriously. A responsible philosophy of religion will study all the religions of mankind, the more primitive as well as the higher, in the same sympathetic and critical spirit. Nor would I insist on any exclusive reliance on any, or all, orthodox ecclesiastical approaches to God. "God moves in a mysterious way," and *all* of man's spiritual aspirations, experiments, and reflections deserve encouragement and open-minded scrutiny. It is in this spirit that I should always welcome the secular and humanistic search for whatever can give meaning and purpose to human life. This does not mean that all roads are equally illuminating and promising. Some must certainly be dead-ends and others painfully indirect and tortuous. But no one who wishes to avoid dogmatism can presume to deny categorically that genuine light and strength may be available to those who are searching for a cosmic meaning along some other road than the one he himself is traveling.

I have not been able to demonstrate God's existence; neither have I proved that the universe is meaningful and purposive; nor do I wish to assert that it is with the dogmatic assurance of those who deny cosmic purpose. I can, however, record my own conviction, in company with countless others, that these moral and religious approaches to reality provide evidence which justifies, nay, compels, the conclusion that there is a meaning and purpose at the heart of things. But no one can hope to encounter and comprehend this value-dimension of reality who does not feel a sense of need sufficient to motivate a humble, honest search for what others claim to have found. Philosophers, scientists, and all men capable of sincere idealism can themselves enter upon this search only in this spirit of eager inquiry.

Religion cannot, it is true, "get on with a purposeless and meaningless universe," but it alone—or, at best, its moral equivalent—can reveal to us a universe which has a purpose and a meaning. Only to the man of religion do the "heavens declare the glory of God"; but to him they do declare this glory. Hence the peculiar responsibility of those who feel that the religious spirit is alive in them, and particularly the responsibility of organized religion. The Churches could do far more than they are doing now to educate their clergy and laity, to vitalize the Christian experience of their people, to translate Christian belief into social action, to combat racial prejudice and social privilege within the Christian community, and, above all, to cultivate the tolerance and the humility that should be the first fruits of Christian love. Were the Christian leaven in the Churches purer and more powerful, it would be far more effective in quickening the religious spirit which today, though far from dead, is often dormant and lethargic.

Professor Stace is, I think, quite right in insisting that the vitality of our culture depends essentially upon the vitality of the religious spirit in it. That is why his charges against religion are so serious and his prophecies so ominous. The implication of his argument, and of my counterargument thus far, has been that the chief function of religion is to vitalize a human culture. In any informed religious perspective, however, and certainly in the Christian perspective, this is to put second things first.

The prime motive for religious revival cannot be the saving of our own or any other civilization, for that would involve the attempt to make God simply serve human ends and satisfy human desires. In the Great Commandment of Christianity, the love of God and His worship is man's supreme privilege and duty; the exhortation to love your neighbor as yourself follows as a necessary corollary. A true Christian does believe that only in and through God's love for man, and man's responsive love for God, can individual men, or mankind, be saved, in this world or the next, and the New Testament is eloquent in its condemnation of those who profess to love God but fail to translate this love into charity toward their fellow men. But God alone is holy, not mankind or any human culture. Religion, if valid, is first of all an end in itself, though *also* an essential condition of cultural vitality. Only in this perspective can we hope to avoid a sentimentalized and distorted interpretation of religion.

My final word to Mr. Stace, then, is this. Man finds himself today not in "darkness" but in a cultural and spiritual twilight which T. S. Eliot describes as a "place of disaffection . . . in a dim light," a state of "neither plenitude nor vacancy," "a twittering world." It may be that we must, as Eliot believes we must, "descend lower" into

> Internal darkness, deprivation
> And destitution of all property,
> Desiccation of the world of sense,
> Evacuation of the world of fancy,
> Inoperancy of the world of spirit

before we can hope, as individuals or as a race, to achieve the requisite sense of need and humility. The Christian Gospel directs us not to a romantic primrose path of comforting illusions, but to the painful road of suffering and sacrifice, to the way of the Cross. Men have never really *lived* by illusions: they have merely existed, in some kind of fool's paradise. Men cannot now *really* live, fully and deeply, on illusions, either the "minor" illusions of "fame, glory, power, or money" which Professor Stace rather cynically invites us not to give up, or the Great Illusion which he identifies with religious faith but which should perhaps rather be identified with Stygian disbelief in God. We are "standing on the brink." We do indeed need courage and honesty, *not*, however, to face an inevitable loss of faith, but rather to search our own hearts and minds to see whether we may not ourselves have generated this "darkness" and inadvertently invented the myth that the "light will not shine again." May it perchance be true that "the light shineth in darkness; and the darkness comprehended it not"?

Each of us must finally assume the responsibility of deciding whether to believe the grim injunction: Since faith is impossible and civilization doomed, resign yourselves to quiet contentment and be thankful for small mercies—this is the test of secular maturity; or, alternatively, the sober but heart-warming injunction to achieve religious maturity and joy: "These things I have spoken unto you, that in me ye might have peace. In the world ye shall have tribulation: but be of good cheer; I have overcome the world."

BRUNO BETTELHEIM

Bruno Bettelheim (1903–) was born in Vienna. With a Ph.D. from the University of Vienna (1938), he came to America in 1939 to begin a distinguished career in child psychology at the University of Chicago, whence he retired to California. He is one of the world's leading authorities on disturbed children.

THE USES OF ENCHANTMENT

Contrary to many who have banned or rewritten fairy tales as unrealistic and harmful, Bettelheim makes a case for their psychic reality and educational power. How does his view of inner ordering compare with Stace's outer chaos? Explain what Bettelheim means by moral education. Would he and Stace agree as to what morality is? What fairy tales have helped to form your assumptions? Are these illusions or realities?

If we do not live just from moment to moment but try to be conscious of our existence, then our greatest need and most difficult achievement is to find meaning in life. It is well known that many people lose the will to live because such meaning evades them. An understanding of the meaning of life is not suddenly acquired at the age of chronological maturity, or at any particular age. On the contrary, gaining this understanding is what constitutes having attained psychological maturity. This achievement is the result of a long development; wisdom is built up, small step by small step, from most irrational beginnings. Unfortunately, too many parents want their children's minds to function as their own do—as if a child's understanding of himself and the world did not have to develop as slowly as his body does. To find meaning in life, the child must become able to transcend the confines of a self-centered existence and believe that he will make a significant contribution—if not right now, then at some future time. This belief is necessary if he is to be satisfied with himself and with what he is doing; only hope for the future can sustain us in the adversities we unavoidably encounter.

As an educator and therapist, I have had as my main task giving meaning to the lives of severely disturbed children. This work has made it obvious to me that if children are reared so that their lives are meaningful to them they will not need special help. I have been confronted with the problem of deducing what experiences are suitable to promote a child's ability to find meaning in his own life and thereby endow life in general with more meaning. Of the first importance in providing such experiences is the impact of parents and others who take care of the child; second is our cultural heritage, if it is transmitted to the child in the right manner. Because it quickly became apparent to me that when the child is young this heritage reaches him best through literature, I grew deeply dissatisfied with much of the literature intended to develop the child's mind and personality, finding that it fails to stimulate and nurture those resources he needs most in order to cope with his difficult inner problems. The pre-primers and primers from which he learns to read in school are designed to teach merely that skill, irrespective of the meaning of what is read. The overwhelming majority of the rest of the so-called "children's books" currently available attempt to entertain or inform, or both, but are so shallow that little of significance can be gained from them. The idea that by learning to read one may be able later to enrich one's life is experienced as an empty promise when the stories that the child listens to or reads are vacuous. For a story to truly hold the child's attention, it must entertain him and arouse his curiosity. But for a story to enrich his life it must stimulate his imagination, help him to develop his intellect and to clarify his emotions, be attuned to his anxieties and aspirations, give full recognition to his difficulties, suggest solutions to the problems that perturb him, and promote confidence in himself and his future.

In all these respects and many others, nothing in the entire range of "children's literature"—with rare exceptions—can be as enriching and satisfying to child and adult alike as the folk fairy tale. True, fairy tales teach little overtly about the specific conditions of life in modern mass society; these tales were created long before modern society came into being. But from them a child can learn more about the inner problems of man, and about solutions to his own (and our) predicaments in any society, than he can from any other type of story within his comprehension. Since the child is exposed at every moment to the society in which he lives, he will learn to cope with its conditions—provided, that is, that his inner resources permit him to do so. The child must therefore be helped to bring order into the turmoil of his feelings. He needs—and the point hardly requires emphasis at this moment in our history—a moral education that subtly, by implication only, conveys to him the advantages of moral behavior, not through abstract ethical concepts but through that which seems tangibly right and therefore has meaning for him. The child can find meaning through fairy tales. Like so many other modern psychological insights, this one was anticipated long ago by poets. The German poet Schiller wrote, "Deeper meaning resides in the fairy tales told to me in my childhood than in the truth that is taught by life." Through the centuries (if not millennia) during which fairy tales, in their retelling, became ever more refined, they came to convey overt and covert meanings at the same time; came to speak simultaneously to all levels of the human personality, communicating in a manner that reaches the uneducated mind of the child as well as the sophisticated mind of the adult. In terms of the psychoanalytic model of the human personality, fairy tales carry important messages to the conscious, the preconscious, and the unconscious mind, on whatever level these are functioning. By dealing with universal human problems, and especially with those that preoccupy the child's mind, these stories speak to his budding ego and encourage its development, and at the same time relieve preconscious and unconscious pressures. As the stories unfold, they give conscious credence and body to id pressures and show how to satisfy these in ways that are in line with ego and superego requirements.

But my interest in fairy tales is not a result of such technical analysis of their merits. It is, on the contrary, a consequence of my asking myself why, in my experience, children—normal and abnormal alike, and at every level of intelligence—have found folk fairy tales more satisfying than all other children's stories. The more I tried to understand why these stories are so successful in enriching the inner life of the child, the clearer it became to me that, in a much deeper sense than any other reading material, they start where the child really is in his psychological and emotional being. They speak about his severe inner pressures in a way that the child unconsciously understands and, without belittling the serious inner struggles that growing up entails, offer examples of both temporary and permanent solutions to acute psychological difficulties.

In order to master the psychological problems of growing up—overcoming narcissistic disappointments, oedipal dilemmas, sibling rivalries, becoming able to relinquish childhood dependencies, gaining a feeling of selfhood and self-worth and a sense of moral obligation—a child needs to be able to cope with what goes on in his unconscious. He can achieve this ability not by attaining rational comprehension of the nature and content of his unconscious but by becoming familiar with it through spinning out daydreams—ruminating on, rearranging, and fantasizing about suitable story elements in response to unconscious pressures. By doing this, the child fits into conscious fantasies matter from his unconscious, which he is then able to deal with. Here fairy tales have an unequaled value, because they offer new dimensions to the child's imagination, suggesting to him images with which he can structure his daydreams.

In child or adult, the unconscious is a powerful determinant of behavior. When the unconscious is repressed and its content denied entrance into awareness, the person's conscious mind will eventually become partly overwhelmed by derivatives of these unconscious elements, or else he will be forced to keep such rigid, compulsive control over them that his personality may be severely crippled. But when unconscious material is to some degree permitted to come to awareness and to be worked through in imagination, its propensity to cause harm—to him or others—is much reduced; indeed, some of its forces can be made to serve positive purposes. However, the prevalent parental belief is that a child must be diverted from what troubles him most: his formless, nameless anxieties and his chaotic, angry, and even violent fantasies. Many parents believe that only conscious reality or pleasant and wish-fulfilling images should be presented to the child—that he should be exposed only to the sunny side of things. But such one-sided fare nourishes the mind only in a one-sided way, and real life is not all sunny. There is a widespread disinclination to let children know that the source of much that goes wrong in life is due to our own natures—the propensity of all men to act aggressively, asocially, selfishly, out of anger and anxiety. Instead, we want our children to believe that all men are inherently good. But every child knows that *he* is not always good, and that even when he is he would often prefer not to be. This contradicts what he is told by his parents, and therefore makes the child a monster in his own eyes.

Psychoanalysis was created to enable man to accept life's problematic nature without being defeated or giving in to escapism. Freud's prescription is that only by struggling courageously against what seem like overwhelming odds can man succeed in wringing meaning out of human existence. This is exactly the message that fairy tales get across to the child in manifold form: that a struggle against severe difficulties in life is unavoidable—is part of the human condition—but that if, instead of shying away, one steadfastly meets unexpected and often unjust hardships, one masters all obstacles in the end and emerges victorious. Modern stories written for young children mainly avoid these existential problems, which are such crucial issues for all of us. The child needs most particularly to be given suggestions in symbolic form about how he may deal with these issues and grow successfully to maturity. "Safe" stories mention neither death nor aging, neither the limits to our existence nor the wish for eternal life. The fairy tale, by contrast, confronts the child squarely with the basic human predicaments. For example, many fairy tales begin with the death of a mother or father; in these tales the death of a parent creates the most agonizing problems, as it (or the fear of it) does in real life. Other fairy tales tell about an aging parent who has decided that the time has come to let the new generation take over. But before this can happen, the successor has to prove himself capable and worthy. The Brothers Grimm's story "The Three Feathers" begins, "There was once upon a time a king who had three sons. . . . When the king had become old and weak, and was thinking of his end, he did not know which of his sons should inherit the kingdom after him." In order to decide, the king sets all his sons a number of difficult tasks; the son who meets them best "shall be king after my death." It is characteristic of fairy tales to state an existential dilemma briefly and pointedly. This permits the child to come to grips with the problem in its most essential form; a more complex plot would merely confuse matters for him. The fairy tale simplifies all situations. Its figures are clearly drawn, and details, unless they are very important, are eliminated. All characters are typical rather than unique.

Unlike many modern stories for children, fairy tales present evil as being no less omnipresent than virtue. In practically every fairy tale, both good and evil are given body in the form of figures and their actions, as both good and evil are omnipresent in life and the propensities for both are present in every man. It is this duality that poses the moral problem and requires the struggle to solve it. Evil is not without its attractions—symbolized by the might of the giant or dragon, the power of the witch, the cunning of the queen in "Snow White"—and often it is temporarily in the ascendancy. In many fairy tales, a usurper succeeds for a time in seizing the place that rightfully belongs to the hero—as the wicked stepsisters do in "Cinderella." It is not so much that the evildoer is punished at the story's end which makes immersing oneself in fairy tales an experience in moral education, although this is part of it. In fairy tales, as in life, punishment or fear of it is a limited deterrent to crime. The conviction that crime does not pay is much more effective as a deterrent, and in fairy tales the bad person always loses out. However, it is not even the fact that virtue wins in the end that promotes morality but that the hero is the most attractive figure to the child, who thus identifies with the hero in all his struggles and triumphs with him when virtue is victorious. The child makes such identifications on his own, and the inner and outer struggles of the hero imprint morality on him.

The figures in fairy tales are not good and bad at the same time, as we all are in reality. But polarization dominates the child's mind, and that is another reason he is so receptive to fairy tales. In the tales, a person is either good or bad—not both, and nothing in between. One brother is stupid, the other is clever. One sister is virtuous and industrious, the others are vile and lazy; one is beautiful, the others are ugly. One parent is all good, the other evil. But opposite characters are not juxtaposed merely for the purpose of stressing right behavior, as in cautionary tales. (There are some amoral fairy tales, in which goodness and badness, beauty and ugliness play no role at all.) Rather, the polarities simply exist as the basis for the tale that is to be told. Being presented with the polarities of character in this way permits the child to comprehend easily the difference between the two, which he could not do if the figures were drawn more true to life, with all the complexities that characterize real people. Ambiguities must wait until a relatively firm personality has been established, on the basis of positive identifications—until the child comes to understand that there are great differences between people, and that therefore one has to make choices about the kind of person one wants to be. This fundamental decision, on which all later personality development will build, is facilitated by the polarizations of the fairy tale.

Amoral fairy tales, which show no polarization or juxtaposition of good and bad persons, serve an entirely different purpose. Puss in Boots, who arranges for the hero's success through trickery, and Jack, in "Jack and the Beanstalk," who steals the giant's treasure, both answer needs very different from those answered by the good heroes. These amoral stories or motifs build character not by promoting choices between good and bad but by giving the child the hope that even the lowliest can succeed in life. After all, what's the use of choosing to become a good person when you feel so insignificant that you fear you will never amount to anything: In these tales, the issue is not morality but assurance that one can succeed. Whether one meets life with a belief in the possibility of mastering its difficulties or with the expectation of certain defeat is also, of course, a very important existential problem.

The child is subject to desperate feelings of loneliness and isolation, and often experiences mortal anxiety. More often than not, he is unable to express these feelings in words, or can do so only by indirection: by claiming fear of the dark or of some animal, for instance. Since it creates discomfort in parents to recognize negative emotions in their child, the parents tend to overlook them, or they belittle the spoken fears out of their own anxiety, believing that such a response will allay the child's fears. The fairy tale, by contrast, takes these existential anxieties and dilemmas very seriously and addresses itself directly to them: to the need to be loved and the fear that one is thought worthless; to the love of life and the fear of death. Further, the fairy tale offers solutions on the child's level of understanding. For example, fairy tales recognize the dilemma of wishing to live eternally by occasionally concluding, "If they have not died, they are living still." As for the ending "And they lived happily ever after," it does not for a moment fool the child into believing that eternal life is possible. Instead, it indicates that which alone can take the sting out of recognition of the narrow limits of our time on this earth: forming a truly satisfying bond to another. The tales teach that when one has done this, one has reached the ultimate in emotional security and permanency of relation available to man, and that this alone can dissipate the fear of death. If one has found true adult love, the fairy tale makes plain, one doesn't need to wish for eternal life. This is also suggested by another ending found in fairy tales: "They lived for a long time afterward, happy and contented."

An uninformed view of fairy tales sees in this type of ending an unrealistic wish fulfillment, and misses completely the important message that it conveys to the child. These stories tell him that by forming a true interpersonal relation one escapes separation anxiety, which haunts the child—and which sets the stage for many fairy tales but is always resolved at the story's ending. Furthermore, these stories indicate that this desirable condition is not to be achieved by holding on to Mother eternally, as the child wishes and believes. If we try to escape anxiety about separation and death by desperately keeping our grasp on our parents, we will be cruelly forced out, like Hansel and Gretel. Only by going out into the world can the fairy-tale hero (child) find himself there; and as he does, he will also find the other with whom he will be able to live happily ever after—that is, without ever again having to experience separation anxiety. The fairy tale is future-oriented and guides the child—in terms he can understand in both his conscious and his unconscious mind—to relinquish his infantile wishes for dependency and achieve an independent existence, which the fairy tale helps him to perceive as more satisfying. Children no longer grow up within the security of an extended family or of a well-integrated community. Therefore, it is even more important than it was when fairy tales were invented that the child be provided with images of heroes who have to go out into the world by themselves and, although they are originally ignorant of the ultimate things, find themselves secure places by following the way that is right for them with deep inner confidence.

In most cultures, there is no clear line separating fairy tales from myths; together, the two forms constitute the literature of pre-literate societies. Myths and fairy tales alike attain a definite form only when they are committed to writing, for then they are no longer subject to continuous change. Up to that point, these stories would be sometimes condensed, sometimes vastly elaborated in their retelling over the centuries. Some stories would merge with others. All would be modified by what the teller thought was of greatest interest to his listeners, by his concerns of the moment, and by the special problems of his era.

Myths and fairy tales have much in common. Both speak to us in the language of symbols representing certain aspects of the unconscious. The appeal of both is simultaneously to the conscious and the unconscious, to all three of the mind's aspects—id, ego, and superego. But there are also inherent differences between myths and fairy tales. Although the same exemplary figures and situations are found in the two forms, and equally miraculous events occur in the two, these are not communicated in the same way. Put simply, the dominant feeling that a myth conveys is: this is unique; it could not have happened to any other creature, or in any other setting; such events are grandiose, awe-inspiring, and could never be duplicated in the lives of ordinary mortals like you and me. The reason is not so much that what takes place is miraculous as that it is described as such. By contrast, although the events that occur in fairy tales are often unusual and most improbable, they are always presented as quite ordinary—as something that could happen to you or me or the person next door while taking a walk in the woods.

An even more significant difference in these two kinds of stories concerns the ending. The myth is pessimistic, while the fairy tale, no matter how terrifyingly serious some of its features may be, is optimistic. Whether the happy outcome is due to the virtues of the hero, to chance, or to the intervention of supernatural figures, it sets the fairy tale apart from all other stories in which fantastic events occur. Because the fairy tale, with its promise of a happy ending, reassures by giving hope for the future, Lewis Carroll called it a love gift—a term hardly applicable to a myth. Obviously, not every story contained in a collection called "Fairy Tales" necessarily meets these criteria. For example, Hans Christian Andersen's "The Little Match Girl" and "The Steadfast Tin Soldier" are beautiful but extremely sad; they do not convey the feeling of consolation so characteristic of fairy tales. But Andersen's "The Snow Queen" comes quite close to being a true fairy tale. Many of the stories in fairy-tale collections may be simply diversions, fables, cautionary tales. If they are fables, they tell by means of words, actions, or events—implausible though these may be—what one ought to do. Cautionary tales demand and threaten—they are moralistic—and the diversions just entertain. Not a bad way of deciding whether a story is a fairy tale or something else might be to consider whether it could rightly be called a love gift to a child.

The child asks himself, "Who am I? Where did I come from? How did the world come into being? Who created man and all the animals? What is the purpose of life?" True, he ponders these vital questions not in the abstract but mainly as they pertain to him. He worries not about whether there is justice for individual man but about whether *he* will be treated justly. He wonders who or what brings adversity upon him, and what can protect him against it. Are there benevolent powers in addition to his parents? *Are* his parents benevolent powers? How should he form himself, and why? Is there hope for him, though he may have done wrong? Why did all this happen to him? What will it mean for his future? Fairy tales provide answers to these questions—questions that, pressing though they are, the child may become aware of only as he follows the stories.

From an adult point of view and in terms of modern science, the answers that fairy tales offer are fantastic rather than true. As a matter of fact, these answers seem so wrong to many adults, who have become estranged from the ways in which young people experience the world, that they object to having children exposed to such "false" information. However, a realistic explanation is usually incomprehensible to children, because they lack the abstract understanding required to make sense of it. While scientifically correct answers make an adult think that he has clarified things for the child, they leave the child confused, overpowered, intellectually defeated. A child can derive security only from the conviction that he understands now what baffled him before; being given facts that create *new* uncertainties simply makes everything seem more precarious. As the child accepts such a factual answer, he comes to doubt whether he has asked the right question. Since the explanation fails to make sense to him, it must apply to some unknown problem, not the one he asked about.

To tell a child that the earth floats in space, attracted by gravity into circling around the sun, but that the earth doesn't fall to the sun, as the child falls to the ground, is very confusing to him. The child knows from his experience that everything has to rest on something or be held up by something. Only an explanation based on that knowledge can make him feel that he understands better about the earth in space. What is more important, in order for the child to feel secure on earth he needs to believe that this world is held firmly in place. Therefore, a more satisfactory explanation for him will be a myth that tells him that the earth rests on a turtle or is held up by a giant. Considerable intellectual maturity is needed to believe that there can be stability to one's life when the ground one walks on (the firmest thing around, on which everything rests) rotates with incredible speed on an invisible axis, that in addition it revolves around the sun, and furthermore that the entire solar system is itself hurtling through space. I have seldom encountered a child under ten who could comprehend all these combined movements, although I have known many who could repeat the information. A child will parrot explanations that according to his own experience of the world are lies, feeling that he must believe them to be true because some adult has said so. The consequence is that the child comes to distrust his own experience, and therefore himself and what his mind can do for him.

In trying to get a child to accept scientifically correct explanations, parents all too frequently discount scientific findings of how a child's mind works. Research on the child's mental processes—most notably by Piaget—convincingly demonstrates that the young child is not able to comprehend two vital abstract concepts: the conservation of quantity, and reversibility; for instance, that the same quantity of water rises high in a narrow receptacle and falls low in a wide one, and that subtraction reverses the process of addition. Until the child can understand abstract concepts such as these, he can experience the world only subjectively.

I have known many young people who, particularly in late adolescence, come to a belief in magic, to compensate for their having been deprived of it prematurely in childhood. It is as if such young people felt that now was their last chance to make up for a severe deficiency in their life experience—that without having had a period of belief in magic they would be unable to meet the rigors of adult life. Many of the young people who today suddenly seek escape in drug-induced dreams, apprentice themselves to a guru, believe in astrology, practice "black magic," or in some other fashion escape from reality into daydreams about magic experiences were prematurely pressed to view reality as adults view it. Trying to evade reality by the methods these adolescents adopt has its ultimate cause in early experiences that prevented the development of the conviction that life can be mastered in realistic ways. It is apparently desirable for the individual to repeat in his life span the process involved historically in the genesis of scientific thought. For a good part of human history, men used emotional projections (such as gods) born of their immature hopes and anxieties to explain man, his society, and the universe; these explanations gave men a feeling of security. Then, slowly, by their own social, scientific, and technological progress, men freed themselves of the constant fear for their very existence. Feeling more secure in the world, and also within themselves, they could now begin to question the validity of the images they had used in the past as explanatory tools. From there, men's "childish" projections dissolved and more rational explanations took their place.

"True" stories about the "real" world may provide children with some interesting and often useful information. But the way such stories unfold is as alien to the way the child's mind functions as the supernatural events of the fairy tale are to the way the mature intellect comprehends the world. Strictly realistic stories run counter to the child's inner experiences; he will listen to them and maybe get something out of them, but he cannot extract from them much personal meaning that transcends their obvious content. These stories inform without enriching, and the same thing is unfortunately true of much learning in school. Factual knowledge profits the total personality only when it is turned into personal knowledge. Outlawing realistic stories for children would be as foolish as banning fairy tales; there is an important place in the life of the child for each. Yet a fare of nothing but realistic stories is barren. When realistic stories are combined with ample and psychologically sound exposure to fairy tales, the child receives information that speaks to both parts of his budding personality—the rational and the emotional.

The child who is familiar with fairy tales understands that they speak to him in the language of symbols, not that of everyday reality. The fairy tale conveys from its first words, throughout its plot, and by its ending that the things he is being told about are not tangible facts or real persons and places. "Once upon a time," "In a certain country," "A thousand years ago, or longer," "At a time when animals still talked," "There was once an old castle in the midst of a large and dense forest"—such beginnings suggest that what follows does not pertain to the here and now that we know. This deliberate vagueness in the beginnings of fairy tales symbolizes a departure from the concrete world of ordinary reality. The old castles, the dark caves, the locked rooms one is forbidden to enter, the impenetrable woods all suggest that something normally hidden will be revealed, and the "long ago" implies that we are going to learn about the most archaic events. The Brothers Grimm could not have begun their collection of fairy tales with a more telling sentence than the one that introduces their first story, "The Frog King": "In olden times when wishing still helped, there lived a king whose daughters were all beautiful, but the youngest was so beautiful that the sun itself, which has seen so much, was astonished whenever it shone in her face." This beginning very clearly locates the story in a unique fairy-tale time: the archaic period when we all believed that our wishes could, if not move mountains, change our fate, and when, in our animistic view of the world, the sun took notice of us and reacted to events. After the age of approximately five—the age when fairy tales really begin to have meaning—no normal child takes these stories as true to external reality. Much as the little girl wishes to imagine that she is a princess living in a castle and spins elaborate fantasies that she is, when her mother calls her to dinner she knows that she is not. And while a grove in a park may be experienced at times as a deep, dark forest full of hidden secrets, the little boy knows what it really is, just as the little girl knows that her doll is not really her baby, even though she calls it that and treats it as such. . . .

The fairy-tale motif of the child abused and rejected by older siblings is well known all through history, especially in the form of "Cinderella." But the stories centering on a stupid child, of which "The Three Languages" and "The Three Feathers" are examples, tell a different tale. The unhappiness of the "dumb" child, whom the rest of the family holds in such low esteem, is not mentioned. His being considered stupid is stated as a fact of life, and one that does not seem to concern him much. Sometimes one gets the feeling that the "simpleton" does not mind this condition, because as a result of it others expect nothing of him. Such stories begin to unfold when the simpleton's uneventful life is interrupted by some demand.

A small child, bright though he may be, feels himself stupid and inadequate when he is confronted with the complexity of the world that surrounds him. Everybody else seems to know so much more than he, and to be so much more capable. In the same way, many fairy tales begin with the hero's being depreciated and considered stupid. These are the child's feelings about himself, which are projected not so much onto the world at large as onto his parents and older brothers and sisters. Even when in some fairy stories, like "Cinderella," we are told that the child lived in bliss before the advent of misfortune, the happy time is not described as one during which the child was competent. The child was so happy because nothing was expected of him; everything was provided for him. A young child's inadequacy, which makes him fear that he is stupid, is not his fault, and so the fairy tale that never explains why the child is considered stupid is psychologically sound.

As far as a child's consciousness is concerned, nothing happened during his first years, because in the normal course of events the child remembers no inner conflicts before parents began making specific demands that ran counter to his desires. It is in part because of these demands that the child experiences conflicts with the world, and internalization of these demands contributes to the establishment of the superego and the awareness of inner conflicts. Hence, these few first years are remembered as conflict-free and blissful, but empty. This situation is represented in the fairy tale by an absence of events in the child's life before he awakens to the conflicts between him and his parents and, with those, to the conflicts within himself. Being "dumb" suggests an undifferentiated stage of existence, which precedes the struggles between the id, the ego, and the superego of the complex personality.

On the simplest and most direct level, fairy tales in which the hero is the youngest and most inept offer the child consolation and hope for the future. Though the child thinks little of himself—a view he projects onto others' views of him—and fears he will never amount to anything, the story shows that he has already started on the process of realizing his potential. As the son learns the language of dogs and later those of birds and frogs in "The Three Languages," the father sees in this only a clear indication of the boy's stupidity, while the boy has actually taken very important steps toward selfhood. The outcome of these stories tells the child that he who regarded himself, or was viewed by others, as the least able nonetheless surpasses all.

Such a message can best carry conviction through repeated telling of the story. Upon first being told a story with a "dumb" hero, a child may not be able to identify with him, stupid though the child feels himself to be. That would be too threatening, too contrary to his self-love. Only when the child feels completely assured of the hero's superiority, through repeated hearings, can he afford to identify with the hero from the beginning. And only on the basis of such identification can the story encourage the child to believe that his depreciated view of himself is erroneous. Before such identification occurs, the story means little to the child as a person. But as the child comes to identify with the stupid or degraded hero of the fairy tale, who he knows will eventually show his superiority, the child himself is started on the process of realizing his potential. . . .

The first steps toward achieving a well-integrated personality are made as the child begins to struggle with his deep and ambivalent attachments to his parents—that is, during his oedipal conflicts. In regard to these, too, fairy tales help the child to comprehend the nature of his difficulties and offer him hope for their successful resolution. In the throes of oedipal conflict, a young boy resents his father for standing in the way of his receiving Mother's exclusive attention. The boy wants Mother to admire *him* as the greatest hero of all; that means that somehow he has to get Father out of the way. This idea creates anxiety in the child, though, because without Father to protect them, what will happen to the family? And what if Father were to find out that the little boy wanted him out of the way? Might he not take a most terrible revenge?

One can tell a small boy many times—without avail—that someday he will grow up, marry, and be like his father. Such realistic advice provides no relief from the pressures that the child feels right now. But the fairy tale tells the child how he can live with his conflicts: it suggests fantasies he could never invent for himself. For example, the fairy tale offers the story of the little unnoticed boy who goes out into the world and makes a great success of life. Details may differ, but the basic plot is always the same: the unlikely hero proves himself through slaying dragons, solving riddles, and living by his wits and his goodness until eventually he frees the beautiful princess, marries her, and lives happily ever after. No little boy has ever failed to see himself in this starring role. The story implies: It's not Father whose jealousy prevents you from having Mother all to yourself; it's an evil dragon. What you really have in mind is to slay an evil dragon. Further, the story gives veracity to the boy's feeling that the most desirable female is kept in captivity by an evil figure, while implying that it is not Mother whom the child wants for himself but a marvelous and wonderful woman he hasn't met yet but certainly will meet. The story tells more of what the boy wants to hear and believe: that it is not of her own free will that this wonderful female (Mother) abides with this bad male figure. On the contrary, if she just could, she would much prefer to be with a young hero (the child). The dragon slayer always has to be young, like the child, and innocent. The innocence of the hero with whom the child identifies proves by proxy the child's innocence; thus, far from having to feel guilty about these fantasies, the child can feel himself to be the hero.

The oedipal problems of a girl are different from those of a boy, and so the fairy tales that help her to cope with her oedipal situation are of a different character. What blocks the oedipal girl's uninterrupted bliss-ful existence with Father is an older, ill-intentioned female (Mother). But since the little girl wants very much to continue enjoying Mother's loving care, there is also a benevolent female in the past or in the back-ground of the fairy tale the happy memory of whom is kept intact, although she has become inoperative. A little girl wishes to see herself as a young and beautiful maiden—a princess or the like—who is kept captive, and hence unavailable to the male lover, by the selfish, evil female figure. The captive princess's real father is depicted as benevolent but helpless to come to the rescue of his lovely girl. In "Rapunzel," it is a vow that stymies him. In "Cinderella" and "Snow White," he seems unable to hold his own against the all-powerful stepmother. The mother is split into two figures: the pre-oedipal wonderful, good mother, and the oedipal evil stepmother. (Sometimes there are bad stepmothers in fairy tales about boys, but such tales deal with problems other than oedipal ones.) The good mother, so the fantasy goes, would never have been jeal-ous of her daughter or have prevented the prince (Father) and the girl from living happily together. So for the oedipal girl belief and trust in the good-ness of the pre-oedipal mother, and deep loyalty to her, tend to reduce the guilt about what the girl wishes would happen to the (step)mother who stands in her way.

Thus, thanks to the fairy tale, both oedipal girls and boys can have the best of two worlds: they can fully enjoy oedipal satisfactions in fantasy and can keep good relations with both parents in reality. For the oedipal boy, if Mother disappoints him there is the fairy princess in the back of his mind—that wonderful woman of the future who will com-pensate for all his present hardships, and so makes it much easier to bear up under them. If Father is less attentive to his little girl than she desires, she can endure such adversity, because a prince will arrive who will prefer her to all competitors. Since everything takes place in never-never land, the child need not feel guilty or anxious about casting Father in the role of the dragon or evil giant, or Mother in the role of a mis-erable stepmother or witch.

If one would believe in a grand design to human life, one could admire the wisdom with which it is arranged that a wide variety of psychological events coincide to reinforce each other and propel the young human being out of infancy into childhood. Because of the child's growing ability to cope, he can have more contact with people outside the family, and with wider aspects of the world. Also, because the child is able to do more, his parents feel that the time has come to expect more of him, and they become less ready to do for him. This change in their relations is an enormous disappointment of the child's hope that he will always receive endlessly; it is the most severe disillusionment of his young life, made infinitely worse because it is inflicted by those who he believes owe him unlimited care. Because of his new experiences with the outside world, however, the child can afford to become aware of the "limitations" of his parents—that is, their shortcomings as seen in the light of his unrealistic expectations of them. In consequence, the child grows so disgusted with his parents that he ventures to seek satisfaction elsewhere. When this comes about, so overwhelming are the new challenges presented to the child by his enlarging experiences, and so very small is his ability to meet them, that he needs fantasy satisfactions in order not to give up in despair. Considerable as the child's real achievements are, they all seem to vanish into insignificance whenever he fails in any respect—if only because he has no comprehension of what is actually possible. This disillusionment may lead to such severe disappointment in himself that he gives up all effort and withdraws into himself completely, unless fantasy comes to his rescue. If any one of the various steps the child is taking in growing up could be viewed in isolation, it might be said that the ability to spin fantasies beyond the present is the new achievement that makes all others possible—because it makes bearable the frustrations experienced in reality. . . .

It seems quite understandable that when children are asked to name their favorite fairy tales, hardly any modern tales are among their choices. Many of the new tales have sad endings, which fail to provide the escape and consolation that the fearsome events in the fairy tale require if the child is to be strengthened for meeting the vagaries of his life. Without such encouraging conclusions, the child, after listening to the story, feels that there is indeed no hope for extricating himself from his despairs. In the traditional fairy tale, the hero is rewarded and the evil person meets his well-deserved fate, thus satisfying the child's deep need for justice to prevail. How else can a child hope that justice will be done to him, who so often feels unfairly treated? And how else can he convince himself that he must act correctly, when he is so sorely tempted to give in to the asocial proddings of his desires? Chesterton once remarked that some children with whom he saw Maeterlinck's play "The Blue Bird" were dissatisfied, "because it did not end with a Day of Judgment, and it was not revealed to the hero and the heroine that the Dog had been faithful and the Cat faithless." He added, "For children are innocent and love justice, while most of us are wicked and naturally prefer mercy."

One may rightly question Chesterton's belief in the innocence of children, but he is absolutely correct in observing that the appreciation of mercy for the unjust, while characteristic of a mature mind, baffles the child. It seems particularly appropriate to a child that exactly what the evildoer wishes to inflict on the hero should be the bad person's fate—as in the case of the witch in "Hansel and Gretel," who wants to cook children in the oven and is pushed into it and burned to death, or of the usurper in "The Goose Girl," who names her own punishment and suffers it. Consolation requires that the right order of the world be restored, and this means punishment of the evildoer.

Prettified or bowdlerized fairy tales are rightly rejected by any child who has heard them in their original form. It does not seem fitting to the child that Cinderella's evil stepsisters should go scot-free, or actually be elevated by Cinderella. Such magnanimity does not impress the child favorably, nor will he learn it from a parent who bowdlerizes the story so that the just and the wicked are both rewarded. The child knows better what he needs to be told. When a seven-year-old was read the story of Snow White, an adult, anxious not to disturb the child's mind, ended the story with Snow White's wedding. The child, who knew the story, immediately demanded, "What about the red-hot shoes that killed the wicked queen?" The child feels that all's well with the world, and he can be secure in it, only if the wicked are punished in the end.

Perhaps the greatest consolation offered to the child by fairy tales, however, is not the promise that justice will be done but the promise that he will never be deserted. There is no greater threat in life than that we will be left all alone. Psychoanalysis has given this—man's greatest fear—the name separation anxiety; and the younger we are, the more excruciating is our anxiety when we feel deserted, for the young child actually perishes when he is not adequately protected and taken care of. There is a cycle of Turkish fairy tales in which the heroes again and again find themselves in the most impossible situations but succeed in evading or overcoming the danger as soon as they have gained a friend. For example, in one famous tale, the hero, Iskender, arouses the enmity of his mother, who forces his father to put Iskender into a casket and set him adrift on the ocean. Iskender's helper is a green bird, which rescues him from this danger, and later from innumerable others, each more threatening than the preceding one. The bird reassures Iskender each time with the words "Know that you are never deserted." This, then, is the ultimate consolation—the one that is implied in the common fairy-tale ending "And they lived happily ever after." . . .

Goethe wrote that he gained from his mother his pleasure in spinning fantasies, and with it his cheerful outlook on life. It all had begun in his childhood with his mother's telling him fairy tales. And his mother recounted in her old age, "Air, fire, water, and earth I presented to him as beautiful princesses, and everything in all nature took on a deeper meaning. We invented roads between stars, and what great minds we would encounter. . . . He devoured me with his eyes; and if the fate of one of his favorites did not go as he wished, this I could see from the anger in his face, or his efforts not to break out in tears. Occasionally he interfered by saying, 'Mother, the princess will *not* marry the miserable tailor, even if he slays the giant,' at which I stopped and postponed the catastrophe until the next evening. So my imagination was often replaced by his; and when the following morning I arranged fate according to his suggestions and said, 'You guessed it, that's how it came out,' he was all excited, and one could see his heart beating." Not every parent can invent stories as well as Goethe's mother, who during her lifetime was known as a great teller of fairy tales. She told the stories in line with her listeners' inner feelings of how things should proceed in the tale, and this was considered the right way. Unfortunately, many modern parents have never known how it felt to be told fairy tales. Having been deprived as children of realizing how enjoyable fairy tales are, and how much they enrich the inner life of the child, even the best of parents cannot be spontaneous in providing his child with such experiences. In such cases, an intellectual understanding of how significant a fairy tale can be for a child, and why, must replace direct empathy based on recollections of one's own childhood.

When we speak of an intellectual understanding of the meaning of a fairy tale, it should be emphasized that it will not do to approach the telling of fairy tales with didactic intentions. When I say that a fairy tale helps the child to understand himself, guides him to find solution to the problems that beset him, and so on, I always mean it metaphorically. The purpose in telling a fairy tale ought to be that of Goethe's mother— a shared experience of enjoying the story, even though what makes for this enjoyment may be quite different for child and adult. While the child enjoys the fantasy, the adult may well derive his pleasure from the child's enjoyment; while the child may be elated because he now understands something about himself better, the adult's delight in telling the story may derive from the child's experiencing a sudden shock of recognition. Telling a fairy tale with a purpose other than that of enriching the child's experience turns it into a cautionary tale, a fable, or some other didactic experience. One must never "explain" to the child the meanings of fairy tales. If the parent tells his child fairy tales in the right spirit—that is, with a feeling for the meaning that the story had for him when he was a child, and for its different present meaning to him, and with sensitivity to the reasons why his child may derive some personal meaning from hearing the tale—then the child feels understood in his most tender longings, his most ardent wishes, his most severe anxieties and feelings of misery. The child feels that he is not alone in his fantasy life—that it is shared by the person he needs and loves most. Under such favorable conditions, fairy tales communicate to the child an intuitive, subconscious understanding of his own nature and of what his future may hold if he develops his potential. He senses that to be a human being means having to accept difficult challenges, but also means encountering the most wondrous adventures.

THOMAS BABINGTON MACAULAY

Thomas Babington Macaulay (1800–1859), member of Parliament, literary critic, essayist, and historian, is remembered for his breadth, energy, and style. His father, a former governor of Sierra Leone, dedicated his life to abolishing the British slave trade; and Macaulay, at age twenty-four, made his first public speech at an antislavery rally. In Parliament (1833), he laid his position and his sole income on the line for the same cause. At a post in India (1833–1838), he drafted the basic Indian criminal code, which upheld the equality of Indians and Europeans before the law. His *History of England* (five volumes, 1848, 1855) was an instant and enormous success on both sides of the Atlantic, bringing him wealth, an unheard-of elevation to the peerage (as Baron Macaulay of Rothley) for literary achievement, and burial in the Poets' Corner in Westminster Abbey. His liberalism was wholly practical: no one should be unjustly barred from the things of this world. His style derived from wide reading in Greek, Latin, and modern languages, together with brilliant conversation and careful polish.

PLATO AND BACON

This essay is a classic contrast of idealism and realism, as well as an outstanding example of contrasting point by point. As you read, underline the points under which Macaulay marshals Plato and Bacon. Notice how he can expand his evidence by a wholly imaginary, though valid, illustration of the aged invalid. Notice also how he repeats phrases to balance and contrast opposites, especially in his next-to-last paragraph beginning "To sum up the whole." You might have some fun, and strengthen your style, by imitating or parodying that paragraph: "The aim of Smith's game was to hit a home run. The aim of Jones's game was to hit anything at all."

The difference between the philosophy of Bacon and that of his predecessors cannot, we think, be better illustrated than by comparing his views on some important subjects with those of Plato. We select Plato, because we conceive that he did more than any other person towards giving to the minds of speculative men that bent which they retained till they received from Bacon a new impulse in a diametrically opposite direction.

It is curious to observe how differently these great men estimated the value of every kind of knowledge. Take Arithmetic for example. Plato, after speaking slightly of the convenience of being able to reckon and compute in the ordinary transactions of life, passes to what he considers as a far more important advantage. The study of the properties of numbers, he tells us, habituates the mind to the contemplation of pure truth, and raises it above the material universe. He would have his disciples apply themselves to this study,—not that they may be able to buy or sell,—not that they may qualify themselves to be shopkeepers or travelling merchants,—but that they may learn to withdraw their minds from the ever-shifting spectacle of this visible and tangible world, and to fix them on the immutable essence of things.

Bacon, on the other hand, valued this branch of knowledge only on account of its uses with reference to that visible and tangible world which Plato so much despised. He speaks with scorn of the mystical arithmetic of the later Platonists; and laments the propensity of mankind to employ, on mere matters of curiosity, powers, the whole exertion of which is required for purposes of solid advantage. He advises arithmeticians to leave these trifles, and to employ themselves in framing convenient expressions, which may be of use in physical researches.

The same reasons which led Plato to recommend the study of arithmetic, led him to recommend also the study of mathematics. The vulgar crowd of geometricians, he says, will not understand him. They have practice always in view. They do not know that the real use of the science is to lead man to the knowledge of abstract, essential, eternal truth. Indeed, if we are to believe Plutarch,* Plato carried this feeling so far,

* Plutarch (c. 46–120 A.D.). A Greek who lectured on philosophy in Rome and educated the future emperor Hadrian. His famous *Parallel Lives*—twenty-three Romans paired with twenty-three Greeks—was one of Shakespeare's principal sources.—Ed.

that he considered geometry as degraded by being applied to any purpose of vulgar utility. Archytas,* it seems, had framed machines of extraordinary power, on mathematical principles. Plato remonstrated with his friend; and declared that this was to degrade a noble intellectual exercise into a low craft, fit only for carpenters and wheelwrights. The office of geometry, he said, was to discipline the mind, not to minister to the base wants of the body. His interference was successful; and from that time, according to Plutarch, the science of mechanics was considered as unworthy of the attention of a philosopher.

Archimedes† in a later age imitated and surpassed Archytas. But even Archimedes was not free from the prevailing notion that geometry was degraded by being employed to produce any thing useful. It was with difficulty that he was induced to stoop from speculation to practice. He was half ashamed of those inventions which were the wonder of hostile nations; and always spoke of them slightingly as mere amusements—as trifles in which a mathematician might be suffered to relax his mind after intense application to the higher parts of his science.

The opinion of Bacon on this subject was diametrically opposed to that of the ancient philosophers. He valued geometry chiefly, if not solely, on account of those uses which to Plato appeared so base. And it is remarkable that the longer he lived the stronger this feeling became. When, in 1605, he wrote the two books on the "Advancement of Learning," he dwelt on the advantages which mankind derived from mixed mathematics; but he at the same time admitted, that the beneficial effect produced by mathematical study on the intellect, though a collateral advantage, was "no less worthy than that which was principal and intended." But it is evident that his views underwent a change. When, nearly twenty years later, he published the *De Augmentis*, which is the treatise on the "Advancement of Learning," greatly expanded and carefully corrected, he made important alterations in the part which related to mathematics. He condemned with severity the high pretensions of the mathematicians,—"delicias et fastum mathematicorum." Assuming the well-being of the human race to be the end of knowledge, he pronounced that mathematical science could claim no higher rank than that of an appendage, or an auxiliary to other sciences. Mathematical

---

* Archytas (c. 428–347 B.C.). Intimate friend of Plato, flutist, statesman, general, philosopher, mathematician; invented the rattle to amuse his slaves' children and a wooden pigeon that flew by compressed air on a pulley—Ed.

† Archimedes (c. 287–212 B.C.). Inventor and mathematician of Syracuse, the Greek colony on Sicily; famous for jumping from the bath and running home naked shouting "Eureka!" ("I've found it") when he discovered the principle of hydrostatics; and for saying that he could move the whole earth with a lever, if he had a place to stand on.—Ed.

science, he says, is the handmaid of natural philosophy—she ought to demean herself as such—and he declares that he cannot conceive by what ill chance it has happened that she presumes to claim precedence over her mistress. He predicts,—a prediction which would have made Plato shudder,—that as more and more discoveries are made in physics, there will be more and more branches of mixed mathematics. Of that collateral advantage, the value of which, twenty years before, he rated so highly, he says not one word. This omission cannot have been the effect of mere inadvertence. His own treatise was before him. From the treatise he deliberately expunged whatever was favorable to the study of pure mathematics, and inserted several keen reflections on the ardent votaries of that study. This fact in our opinion, admits of only one explanation. Bacon's love of those pursuits which directly tend to improve the condition of mankind, and his jealousy of all pursuits merely curious, had grown upon him, and had, it may be, become immoderate. He was afraid of using any expression which might have the effect of inducing any man of talents to employ in speculations, useful only to the mind of the speculator, a single hour which might be employed in extending the empire of man over matter. If Bacon erred here, we must acknowledge that we greatly prefer his error to the opposite error of Plato.—We have no patience with a philosophy which, like those Roman matrons who swallowed abortives in order to preserve their shapes, takes pains to be barren for fear of being homely. . . .

On the greatest and most useful of all inventions,—the invention of alphabetical writing,—Plato did not look with much complacency. He seems to have thought that the use of letters had operated on the human mind as the use of the go-cart in learning to walk, or of corks in learning to swim, is said to operate on the human body. It was a support which soon became indispensable to those who used it,—which made vigorous exertion first unnecessary, and then impossible. The powers of the intellect would, he conceived, have been more fully developed without this delusive aid. Men would have been compelled to exercise the understanding and the memory; and, by deep and assiduous meditation, to make truth thoroughly their own. Now, on the contrary, much knowledge is traced on paper, but little is engraved in the soul. A man is certain that he can find information at a moment's notice when he wants it. He therefore suffers it to fade from his mind. Such a man cannot in strictness be said to know any thing. He has the show without the reality of wisdom. . . .

Bacon's views, as may easily be supposed, were widely different. The powers of the memory, he observes, without the help of writing, can do little towards the advancement of any useful science. He acknowledges that the memory may be disciplined to such a point as to be able to perform very extraordinary feats. But on such feats he sets little value. The habits of his mind, he tells us, are such that he is not disposed to rate highly any accomplishment, however rare, which is of no practical use to mankind. As to these prodigious achievements of the memory, he ranks them with the exhibitions of rope-dancers and tumblers. "The two performances," he says, "are of much the same sort. The one is an abuse of the powers of the body; the other is an abuse of the powers of the mind. Both may perhaps excite our wonder; but neither is entitled to our respect."

To Plato, the science of medicine appeared one of very disputable advantage. He did not indeed object to quick cures for acute disorders, or for injuries produced by accidents. But the art which resists the slow sap of a chronic disease—which repairs frames enervated by lust, swollen by gluttony, or inflamed by wine—which encourages sensuality, by mitigating the natural punishment of the sensualist, and prolongs existence when the intellect has ceased to retain its entire energy—had no share of his esteem. A life protracted by medical skill he pronounced to be a long death. The exercise of the art of medicine ought, he said, to be tolerated so far as that art may serve to cure the occasional distempers of men whose constitutions are good. As to those who have bad constitutions, let them die;—and the sooner the better. Such men are unfit for war, for magistracy, for the management of their domestic affairs. That however is comparatively of little consequence. But they are incapable of study and speculation. If they engage in any severe mental exercise, they are troubled with giddiness and fulness of the head; all which they lay to the account of philosophy. The best thing that can happen to such wretches is to have done with life at once. He quotes mythical authority in support of this doctrine; and reminds his disciples that the practice of the sons of Aesculapius,* as described by Homer, extended only to the cure of external injuries.

Far different was the philosophy of Bacon. Of all the sciences, that which he seems to have regarded with the greatest interest was the science which, in Plato's opinion, would not be tolerated in a well-regulated community. To make men perfect was no part of Bacon's plan. His humble aim was to make imperfect men comfortable. The beneficence of his philosophy resembled the beneficence of the common Father, whose sun rises on the evil and the good—whose rain descends

---

* The legendary father of medicine, son of Apollo, and a nymph. In the *Iliad*, Homer mentions his skill. His two sons were doctors with the Greek army besieging Troy.—Ed.

for the just and the unjust. In Plato's opinion man was made for philosophy; in Bacon's opinion philosophy was made for man; it was a means
to an end;—and that end was to increase the pleasures and to mitigate
the pains of millions who are not and cannot be philosophers. That a
valetudinarian who took great pleasure in being wheeled along his ter-
race, who relished his boiled chicken and his weak wine and water, and
who enjoyed a hearty laugh over the Queen of Navarre's tales, should
be treated as a *caput lupinum** because he could not read the Timaeus†
without a headache, was a notion which the humane spirit of the English school of wisdom altogether rejected. Bacon would not have thought
it beneath the dignity of a philosopher to contrive an improved garden
chair for such a valetudinarian—to devise some way of rendering his
medicines more palatable—to invent repasts which he might enjoy, and
pillows on which he might sleep soundly; and this though there might
not be the smallest hope that the mind of the poor invalid would ever
rise to the contemplation of the ideal beautiful and the ideal good. As
Plato had cited the religious legends of Greece to justify his contempt
for the more recondite parts of the art of healing, Bacon vindicated the
dignity of that art by appealing to the example of Christ; and reminded
his readers that the great physician of the soul did not disdain to be also
the physician of the body.

When we pass from the science of medicine to that of legislation, we
find the same difference between the systems of these two great men.
Plato, at the commencement of the fine Dialogue on Laws, lays it down
as a fundamental principle that the end of legislation is to make men
virtuous. It is unnecessary to point out the extravagant conclusions to
which such a proposition leads. Bacon well knew to how great an extent
the happiness of every society must depend on the virtue of its members; and he also knew what legislators can, and what they cannot do
for the purpose of promoting virtue. The view which he has given of the
end of legislation and of the principal means for the attainment of that
end, has always seemed to us eminently happy; even among the many
happy passages of the same kind with which his works abound. . . . The
end is the well-being of the people. The means are the imparting of
moral and religious education; the providing of every thing necessary
for defence against foreign enemies; the maintaining of internal order;

* "A wolfish head." The sentence *Caput gerat lupinum* ("Let him wear a wolf's
head") was handed down on outlaws—to be shot on sight, like wolves.—Ed.

† Plato's last complete *Dialogue*, in which the Pythagorean philosopher, Timaeus,
attempts to outline the origin of the universe down to the creation of man, going
beyond Plato's earlier limits of rationality.—Ed.

the establishing of a judicial, financial, and commercial system, under which wealth may be rapidly accumulated and securely enjoyed.

Even with respect to the form in which laws ought to be drawn, there is a remarkable difference of opinion between the Greek and the Englishman. Plato thought a preamble essential; Bacon thought it mischievous. Each was consistent with himself. Plato, considering the moral improvement of the people as the end of legislation, justly inferred that a law which commanded and threatened, but which neither convinced the reason nor touched the heart, must be a most imperfect law. He was not content with deterring from theft a man who still continued to be a thief at heart,—with restraining a son who hated his mother from beating his mother. The only obedience on which he set so much value, was the obedience which an enlightened understanding yields to reason, and which a virtuous disposition yields to precepts of virtue. He really seems to have believed that, by prefixing to every law an eloquent and pathetic exhortation, he should, to a great extent, render penal enactments superfluous. Bacon entertained no such romantic hopes; and he well knew the practical inconveniences of the course which Plato recommended. . . .

To sum up the whole: we should say that the aim of the Platonic philosophy was to exalt man into a god. The aim of the Baconian philosophy was to provide man with what he requires while he continues to be man. The aim of the Platonic philosophy was to raise us far above vulgar wants. The aim of the Baconian philosophy was to supply our vulgar wants. The former aim was noble; but the latter was attainable. Plato drew a good bow; but, like Acestes in Virgil, he aimed at the stars; and therefore, though there was no want of strength or skill, the shot was thrown away. His arrow was indeed followed by a track of dazzling radiance, but it struck nothing. . . . Bacon fixed his eye on a mark which was placed on the earth and within bow-shot, and hit it in the white. The philosophy of Plato began in words and ended in words,—noble words indeed,—words such as were to be expected from the finest of human intellects exercising boundless dominion over the finest of human languages. The philosophy of Bacon began in observation and ended in arts.

The boast of the ancient philosophers was, that their doctrine formed the minds of men to a high degree of wisdom and virtue. This was indeed the only practical good which the most celebrated of those teachers even pretended to effect; and undoubtedly if they had effected this, they would have deserved the greatest praise. But the truth is, that in those very matters in which alone they professed to do any good to mankind, in those very matters for the sake of which they neglected all the vulgar interests of mankind, they did nothing, or worse than nothing. They promised what was impracticable; they despised what was practicable; they filled the world with long words and long beards; and they left it as wicked and as ignorant as they found it. . . .

SUGGESTIONS FOR WRITING

1. Write an essay on the thesis: "Human happiness nourishes itself on a whole host of minor illusions." Pick out four or five of our minor (or major) obsessions, such as dreams of clothes, cars, waterskiing, love, fraternities, family life, money. The problem is to arrange your items in an order of ascending interest—humorous or serious. Give each item no less than a paragraph.
2. Attack or defend Stace's assertion about "the real world as it actually is, stark and bleak."
3. Write an essay in which you defend or attack some reading you remember from early schooling or childhood, bringing in quotations from Bettelheim for support. Or do the same with a television fantasy or science fiction program.
4. Write an essay in which you contrast Stace with Greene, working from a thesis that supports one against the other. Conduct your comparison as Macaulay does with Plato and Bacon; treat both men under each of your points.
5. Write a passage of straight imitation or parody of Macaulay, taking as your opposites two baseball players, two movie actresses, or perhaps two types of persons, like the freshman and the sophomore: "To sum up the whole: we should say that the aim of the freshman is to learn everything. The aim of the sophomore is to appear as if he had already learned it."
6. Write an essay in which you clearly favor one side, but in which you fully and fairly contrast your side with its opposite—for instance, baseball is better than football, one team over another, big college over small, realism over fantasy, or the ideal over the practical (using Macaulay against himself). Again, treat both sides under each of your points, as Macaulay does.

Four
Paragraphs:
Beginning, Middle, End

These four essays show four different writers, with four different subjects, facing the problems of getting started and of concluding, and they suggest how important it is to set the thesis clearly at the beginning and to round it off at the end, usually in a single paragraph for the beginning and another for the conclusion. Sapir clearly says that he will show how the law of a writer's medium will assert its force; Foster, that the translator must walk a wire between accuracy and poetry. Santayana, although a bit more open in structure, nevertheless clearly announces his demonstration of how the writer's environment shaped everything in his book, from characters to incidents to ultimate message. Orwell suggests that, contrary to prevailing assumptions, we can shape language for our purposes, and perhaps preserve its best expression in the process.

Thus these essays illustrate, with natural variations, the three essential kinds of paragraph: (1) the beginning paragraph, (2) the end paragraph, and (3) the middle paragraph—the standard one, the norm. Think of the beginning paragraph as a funnel which begins somewhat broadly with an opening invitation and then narrows down sharply to state the thesis at its end. Think of the end paragraph as the funnel inverted, starting with a sentence restating the essay's thesis, then opening out to wider and deeper implications, with a touch of fervor and finality.

Think of the middle paragraph as a standard frame of four or five sentences, and as a miniature of the essay as a whole, with its own small beginning, middle, and end. Its beginning is its *topic sentence*— its own small thesis, which the middle of the paragraph then unfolds and illustrates. Its end sentence should have some sense of conclusion, like the entire essay's end paragraph.

One final point. For full control, to keep your essay flowing smoothly, to link paragraphs together, give each of your topic sentences some touch of *transition*—a word such as *But, This, Nevertheless,* or a word or phrase from the end sentence of the preceding paragraph.

These are three ideal forms of the paragraph, the forms-in-your-head, which you will use and vary as the flow of your language and subject demand. Each of the essays in this section is ably paragraphed. Each writer, as if working from a preconceived norm, measures his thoughts more or less into equal paragraphs, occasionally coming up short for emphasis, occasionally expanding for clarity. Notice how almost every paragraph begins with its topic sentence. Notice the ways in which each essay begins and ends—Foster taking two paragraphs for his beginning, for instance, and Orwell setting his thesis by its negative. As you read, underline the first sentence of each paragraph (except the beginning one), and ask yourself how good a topic sentence it is, or if it is one at all.

EDWARD SAPIR

Edward Sapir (1884–1939), pioneering student of American Indian languages, came to the United States from Pomerania at age five with his parents. He taught at Yale from 1927 until his death. His *Language* (1921) remains one of the foundations of modern linguistics.

LANGUAGE AND LITERATURE

This essay describes the central wonder of language: how languages, like personalities, are unique and yet how they share a common ground of meaning too. This, as Sapir suggests, is the individual writer's paradox as well. Our personal thoughts must find their clothing in the common idiom we share. Will we find a perfect fit, or will we walk around in hand-me-downs three sizes too big or too small? Notice the imaginative wonders of Sapir's own language.

Languages are more to us than systems of thought-transference. They are invisible garments that drape themselves about our spirit and give a predetermined form to all its symbolic expression. When the expression is of unusual significance, we call it literature.* Art is so personal an expression that we do not like to feel that it is bound to predetermined form of any sort. The possibilities of individual expression are infinite; language in particular is the most fluid of mediums. Yet some limitation there must be to this freedom, some resistance of the medium. In great art there is the illusion of absolute freedom. The formal restraints imposed by the material—paint, black and white, marble, piano tones, or whatever it may be—are not perceived; it is as though there were a limitless margin of elbow-room between the artist's fullest utilization of form and the most that the material is innately capable of. The artist has intuitively surrendered to the inescapable tyranny of the material, made its brute nature fuse easily with his conception.† The material "disappears" precisely because there is nothing in the artist's conception to indicate that any other material exists. For the time being, he, and we with him, move in the artistic medium as a fish moves in the water, oblivious of the existence of an alien atmosphere. No sooner, however, does the artist transgress the law of his medium than we realize with a start that there is a medium to obey.

Language is the medium of literature as marble or bronze or clay are the materials of the sculptor. Since every language has its distinctive peculiarities, the innate formal limitations—and possibilities—of one literature are never quite the same as those of another. The literature fashioned out of the form and substance of a language has the color and the texture of its matrix. The literary artist may never be conscious of just how he is hindered or helped or otherwise guided by the matrix, but when it is a question of translating his work into another language, the nature of the original matrix manifests itself at once. All his effects have been calculated, or intuitively felt, with reference to the formal

* I can hardly stop to define just what kind of expression is "significant" enough to be called art or literature. Besides, I do not exactly know. We shall have to take literature for granted.

† This "intuitive surrender" has nothing to do with subservience to artistic convention. More than one revolt in modern art has been dominated by the desire to get out of the material just what it is really capable of. The impressionist wants light and color because paint can give him just these; "literature" in painting, the sentimental suggestion of a "story," is offensive to him because he does not want the virtue of his particular form to be dimmed by shadows from another medium. Similarly, the poet, as never before, insists that words mean just what they really mean.

"genius" of his own language; they cannot be carried over without loss or modification. Croce* is therefore perfectly right in saying that a work of literary art can never be translated. Nevertheless literature does get itself translated, sometimes with astonishing adequacy. This brings up the question whether in the art of literature there are not intertwined two distinct kinds or levels of art—a generalized, non-linguistic art, which can be transferred without loss into an alien linguistic medium, and a specifically linguistic art that is not transferable.† I believe the distinction is entirely valid, though we never get the two levels pure in practice. Literature moves in language as a medium, but that medium comprises two layers, the latent content of language—our intuitive record of experience—and the particular conformation of a given language —the specific how of our record of experience. Literature that draws its sustenance mainly—never entirely—from the lower level, say a play of Shakespeare's, is translatable without too great a loss of character. If it moves in the upper rather than in the lower level—a fair example is a lyric of Swinburne's—it is as good as untranslatable. Both types of literary expression may be great or mediocre.

There is really no mystery in the distinction. It can be clarified a little by comparing literature with science. A scientific truth is impersonal, in its essence it is untinctured by the particular linguistic medium in which it finds expression. It can as readily deliver its message in Chinese‡ as in English. Nevertheless it must have some expression, and that expression must needs be a linguistic one. Indeed the apprehension of the scientific truth is itself a linguistic process, for thought is nothing but language denuded of its outward garb. The proper medium of scientific expression is therefore a generalized language that may be defined as a symbolic algebra of which all known languages are translations. One can adequately translate scientific literature because the original scientific

---

* See Benedetto Croce, *Aesthetic*.

† The question of the transferability of art productions seems to me to be of genuine theoretic interest. For all that we speak of the sacrosanct uniqueness of a given art work, we know very well, though we do not always admit it, that not all productions are equally intractable to transference. A Chopin étude is inviolate; it moves altogether in the world of piano tone. A Bach fugue is transferable into another set of musical timbres without serious loss of esthetic significance. Chopin plays with the language of the piano as though no other language existed (the medium "disappears"); Bach speaks the language of the piano as a handy means of giving outward expression to a conception wrought in the generalized language of tone.

‡ Provided, of course, Chinese is careful to provide itself with the necessary scientific vocabulary. Like any other language, it can do so without serious difficulty if the need arises.

expression is itself a translation. Literary expression is personal and concrete, but this does not mean that its significance is altogether bound up with the accidental qualities of the medium. A truly deep symbolism, for instance, does not depend on the verbal associations of a particular language but rests securely on an intuitive basis that underlies all linguistic expression. The artist's "intuition," to use Croce's term, is immediately fashioned out of a generalized human experience—thought and feeling—of which his own individual experience is a highly personalized selection. The thought relations in this deeper level have no specific linguistic vesture; the rhythms are free, not bound, in the first instance, to the traditional rhythms of the artist's language. Certain artists whose spirit moves largely in the non-linguistic (better, in the generalized linguistic) layer even find a certain difficulty in getting themselves expressed in the rigidly set terms of their accepted idiom. One feels that they are unconsciously striving for a generalized art language, a literary algebra, that is related to the sum of all known languages as a perfect mathematical symbolism is related to all the roundabout reports of mathematical relations that normal speech is capable of conveying. Their art expression is frequently strained, it sounds at times like a translation from an unknown original—which, indeed, is precisely what it is. These artists—Whitmans and Brownings—impress us rather by the greatness of their spirit than the felicity of their art. Their relative failure is of the greatest diagnostic value as an index of the pervasive presence in literature of a larger, more intuitive linguistic medium than any particular language.

Nevertheless, human expression being what it is, the greatest—or shall we say the most satisfying—literary artists, the Shakespeares and Heines, are those who have known subconsciously to fit or trim the deeper intuition to the provincial accents of their daily speech. In them there is no effect of strain. Their personal "intuition" appears as a completed synthesis of the absolute art of intuition and the innate, specialized art of the linguistic medium. With Heine, for instance, one is under the illusion that the universe speaks German. The material "disappears."

Every language is itself a collective art of expression. There is concealed in it a particular set of esthetic factors—phonetic, rhythmic, symbolic, morphological—which it does not completely share with any other language. These factors may either merge their potencies with those of that unknown, absolute language to which I have referred—this is the method of Shakespeare and Heine—or they may weave a private, technical art fabric of their own, the innate art of the language intensified or sublimated. The latter type, the more technically "literary" art of Swinburne and of hosts of delicate "minor" poets, is too fragile for endurance. It is built out of spiritualized material, not out of spirit. The successes of the Swinburnes are as valuable for diagnostic purposes as the semi-failures of the Brownings. They show to what extent literary art may lean on the collective art of the language itself. The more extreme technical practitioners may so over-individualize this collective art as to make it almost unendurable. One is not always thankful to have one's flesh and blood frozen to ivory.

An artist must utilize the native esthetic resources of his speech. He may be thankful if the given palette of colors is rich, if the springboard is light. But he deserves no special credit for felicities that are the language's own. We must take for granted this language with all its qualities of flexibility or rigidity and see the artist's work in relation to it. A cathedral on the lowlands is higher than a stick on Mont Blanc. In other words, we must not commit the folly of admiring a French sonnet because the vowels are more sonorous than our own or of condemning Nietzsche's prose because it harbors in its texture combinations of consonants that would affright on English soil. To so judge literature would be tantamount to loving *Tristan und Isolde* because one is fond of the timbre of horns. There are certain things that one language can do supremely well which it would be almost vain for another to attempt. Generally there are compensations. The vocalism of English is an inherently drabber thing than the vowel scale of French, yet English compensates for this drawback by its greater rhythmical alertness. It is even doubtful if the innate sonority of a phonetic system counts for as much, as esthetic determinant, as the relations between the sounds, the total gamut of their similarities and contrasts. As long as the artist has the wherewithal to lay out his sequences and rhythms, it matters little what are the sensuous qualities of the elements of his material.

The phonetic groundwork of a language, however, is only one of the features that give its literature a certain direction. Far more important are its morphological peculiarities. It makes a great deal of difference for the development of style if the language can or cannot create compound words, if its structure is synthetic or analytic, if the words of its sentences have considerable freedom of position or are compelled to fall into a rigidly determined sequence. The major characteristics of style, in so far as style is a technical matter of the building and placing of words, are given by the language itself, quite as inescapably, indeed, as the general acoustic effect of verse is given by the sounds and natural accents of the language. These necessary fundamentals of style are hardly felt by the artist to constrain his individuality of expression. They rather point the way to those stylistic developments that most suit the natural bent of the language. It is not in the least likely that a truly great style can seriously oppose itself to the basic form patterns of the language. It not only incorporates them, it builds on them. The merit of such a style as W. H. Hudson's or George Moore's* is that it does with ease and economy what the language is always trying to do. Carlylese, though individual and vigorous, is yet not style; it is a Teutonic mannerism. Nor is the prose of Milton and his contemporaries strictly English; it is semi-Latin done into magnificent English words.

It is strange how long it has taken the European literatures to learn that style is not an absolute, a something that is to be imposed on the language from Greek or Latin models, but merely the language itself, running in its natural grooves, and with enough of an individual accent to allow the artist's personality to be felt as a presence, not as an acrobat. We understand more clearly now that what is effective and beautiful in one language is a vice in another. Latin and Eskimo, with their highly inflected forms, lend themselves to an elaborately periodic structure that would be boring in English. English allows, even demands, a looseness that would be insipid in Chinese. And Chinese, with its unmodified words and rigid sequences, has a compactness of phrase, a terse parallelism, and a silent suggestiveness that would be too tart, too mathematical, for the English genius. While we cannot assimilate the luxurious periods of Latin nor the pointillist style of the Chinese classics, we can enter sympathetically into the spirit of these alien techniques.

I believe that any English poet of today would be thankful for the concision that a Chinese poetaster attains without effort. Here is an example:†

> Wu-river‡ stream mouth evening sun sink,
> North look Liao-Tung,§ not see home.
> Steam whistle several noise, sky-earth boundless,
> Float float one reed out Middle-Kingdom.

These twenty-eight syllables may be clumsily interpreted: "At the mouth of the Yangtsze River, as the sun is about to sink, I look north toward Liao-Tung but do not see my home. The steam-whistle shrills several times on the boundless expanse where meet sky and earth. The steamer, floating gently like a hollow reed, sails out of the Middle Kingdom."‖

---

* Aside from individual peculiarities of diction, the selection and evaluation of particular words as such.

† Not by any means a great poem, merely a bit of occasional verse written by a young Chinese friend of mine when he left Shanghai for Canada.

‡ The old name of the country about the mouth of the Yangtsze.

§ A province of Manchuria.

‖ That is, China.

But we must not envy Chinese its terseness unduly. Our more sprawling mode of expression is capable of its own beauties, and the more compact luxuriance of Latin style has its loveliness too. There are almost as many natural ideals of literary style as there are languages. Most of these are merely potential, awaiting the hand of artists who will never come. And yet in the recorded texts of primitive tradition and song there are many passages of unique vigor and beauty. The structure of the language often forces an assemblage of concepts that impresses us as a stylistic discovery. Single Algonkin words are like tiny imagist poems. We must be careful not to exaggerate a freshness of content that is at least half due to our freshness of approach, but the possibility is indicated none the less of utterly alien literary styles, each distinctive with its disclosure of the search of the human spirit for beautiful form.

Probably nothing better illustrates the formal dependence of literature on language than the prosodic aspect of poetry. Quantitative verse was entirely natural to the Greeks, not merely because poetry grew up in connection with the chant and the dance,* but because alternations of long and short syllables were keenly live facts in the daily economy of the language. The tonal accents, which were only secondarily stress phenomena, helped to give the syllable its quantitative individuality. When the Greek meters were carried over into Latin verse, there was comparatively little strain, for Latin too was characterized by an acute awareness of quantitative distinctions. However, the Latin accent was more markedly stressed than that of Greek. Probably, therefore, the purely quantitative meters modeled after the Greek were felt as a shade more artificial than in the language of their origin. The attempt to cast English verse into Latin and Greek molds has never been successful. The dynamic basis of English is not quantity,† but stress, the alternation of accented and unaccented syllables. This fact gives English verse an entirely different slant and has determined the development of its poetic forms, is still responsible for the evolution of new forms. Neither stress nor syllabic weight is a very keen psychologic factor in the dynamics of French. The syllable has great inherent sonority and does not fluctuate significantly as to quantity and stress. Quantitative or accentual metrics would be as artificial in French as stress metrics in clas-

---

* Poetry everywhere is inseparable in its origins from the singing voice and the measure of the dance. Yet accentual and syllabic types of verse, rather than quantitative verse, seem to be the prevailing norms.

† Quantitative distinctions exist as an objective fact. They have not the same inner, psychological value that they had in Greek.

sical Greek or quantitative or purely syllabic metrics in English. French prosody was compelled to develop on the basis of unit syllable-groups. Assonance, later rhyme, could not but prove a welcome, an all but necessary, means of articulating or sectioning the somewhat spineless flow of sonorous syllables. English was hospitable to the French suggestion of rhyme, but did not seriously need it in its rhythmic economy. Hence rhyme has always been strictly subordinated to stress as a somewhat decorative feature and has been frequently dispensed with. It is no psychologic accident that rhyme came later into English than in French and is leaving it sooner.* Chinese verse has developed along very much the same lines as French verse. The syllable is an even more integral and sonorous unit than in French, while quantity and stress are too uncertain to form the basis of a metric system. Syllable-groups—so and so many syllables per rhythmic unit—and rhyme are therefore two of the controlling factors in Chinese prosody. The third factor, the alternation of syllables with level tone and syllables with inflected (rising or falling) tone, is peculiar to Chinese.

To summarize, Latin and Greek verse depends on the principle of contrasting weights; English verse, on the principle of contrasting stresses; French verse, on the principles of number and echo; Chinese verse, on the principles of number, echo, and contrasting pitches. Each of these rhythmic systems proceeds from the unconscious dynamic habit of the language, falling from the lips of the folk. Study carefully the phonetic system of a language, above all its dynamic features, and you can tell what kind of a verse it has developed—or, if history has played pranks with its psychology, what kind of verse it should have developed and some day will.

Whatever be the sounds, accents, and forms of a language, however these lay hands on the shape of its literature, there is a subtle law of compensations that gives the artist space. If he is squeezed a bit here, he can swing a free arm there. And generally he has rope enough to hang himself with, if he must. It is not strange that this should be so. Language is itself the collective art of expression, a summary of thousands upon thousands of individual intuitions. The individual goes lost in the collective creation, but his personal expression has left some trace in a certain give and flexibility that are inherent in all collective works of the human spirit. The language is ready, or can be quickly made

---

* Verhaeren was no slave to the Alexandrine, yet he remarked to Symons, à propos of the translation of Les Aubes, that while he approved of the use of rhymeless verse in the English version, he found it "meaningless" in French.

ready, to define the artist's individuality. If no literary artist appears, it is not essentially because the language is too weak an instrument, it is because the culture of the people is not favorable to the growth of such personality as seeks a truly individual verbal expression.

JOHN L. FOSTER

John L. Foster (1930–), Professor of English and Speech at Roosevelt University, Chicago, has won two fellowships for study in Egypt. His *Love Songs of the New Kingdom* appeared in 1974.

ON TRANSLATING HIEROGLYPHIC LOVE SONGS

In this beautifully paragraphed essay,* Foster admirably illustrates Sapir's point about translation as he describes both the process and the irresistible challenge to translate in spite of the odds. Notice his unusual and effective beginning: two paragraphs opening with the thesis itself and closing with it in fuller recapitulation.

Every translator of poetry walks a tightrope across an abyss, trying to keep his balance on a thread of meaning until he can arrive at the far side of his text intact. For the translator is a sort of acrobat, an aerialist; and each step must be faultless. And his performance seldom satisfies all his audience, which divides into two groups of partisans, the philologist and the poet, each calling upon him to lean a little more to the right or the left. If he leans too far in either direction, of course, the act suddenly ends. Nevertheless, his is the necessary and proper audience; the callings of philologist and poet are honorable each in itself, both deal with verbal communication, and each of the partisans can sit in legitimate judgment upon at least part of the translator's performance. The poet—limited only by the scope of his own imagination, his skill with words, and the richness of his feelings, and working with his native language—can ask: Is the performance a poem? The philologist— expert in and respecting the vocabulary, grammatical structures, idioms, and the whole means of communication of the language in which the original was expressed—can ask: Is the performance accurate? Does the performer do justice to the native style of acting?

The translator must respect and satisfactorily answer both kinds of

* Professor Foster has revised and condensed his original essay for *The Essayist*.

question; for otherwise there is no translation. If he has an ear only for the philologists in the audience, he comes up with a literal translation —one which will surely satisfy only the philologist, and one which should have been left to that expert in the first place. If he listens only to the poet's, he comes up (if he is good enough) with a poem—an original poem of his own, but not one that catches the texture or meaning (and, perhaps, the strangeness) of the original. Which is all very fine, and literary, but is not a literary translation. So, for the translator-acrobat it really does come down to a matter of balance: he must exhibit enough of both the philologist and the poet to move ahead upright and astride the meaning, enough of both knowledge and intuition to sense when a shift of balance to the left or the right is needed to keep his feet.

Balancing the claims of philology and poetry is of course a commonplace in the theory of verse translation; but, when one comes to think of it, masterly performances are few. There is Fitzgerald's *Rubaiyat*, or Pound's *Cathay*, or the other Fitzgerald's *Odyssey* in the Anglo-American tradition (I accept opinion here; for I do not know any of the originals); but definitive literary translations seem not to be common. Why? I suspect that without too much oversimplification one can argue that the bent, the basic urge, the attitudes toward the job exhibited by the philologist and poet are different, conflicting, and even antithetical. The philologist insists upon respect for the facts of his chosen language; he gathers data—occurrences, instances, parallels, contexts of words, usages, and grammatical forms. And he builds what he finds into sets of rules and a system which describes the way meaning in that language is communicated according to the best evidence he has. But, respecting his facts, he is cautious: "There is as yet no occurrence of that word with that particular shade of meaning." "The grammatical structure of the language does not allow for that particular interpretation of the passage." "Our evidence suggests the image or the idiom you use is not native to the language." Translating too "imaginatively" is dangerous; it is not scholarly; it goes beyond the facts. The poet, of course, functions quite another way. For him, imagination is everything. Confronted by rules, or even the current linguistic description of his native language, he is a lawbreaker and a nonconformist, always looking for new ways to speak, to express thought and feeling. He has faith in the resilience of his language; and he seeks what is fresh and novel to convey what he has to say. He tries to force fallen words back toward image and metaphor, back to their prelapsarian state. And he is a gambler with language, always hoping to snatch the grace beyond the reach of art; he takes chances with words, knowing that so often it is catching the main chance that makes the poem.

If these two portraits are at all accurate, they perhaps explain why the good literary translation is relatively rare. The translator *is* a tightrope walker; and the concept of balance *is* of profound importance to his art. For somewhere down at the very wellspring of his urge to write he must strike the balance between conflicting claims—the scholar's rightful caution and the poet's right to gamble, rights which inherently tend to cancel each other out, or which lead at the very least to an unpleasant wavering along the rope. The translator is such, then, by virtue of his double calling: he somehow has the talent to integrate his respect for the uniqueness of his original with an equal respect for the uniqueness of the living language of his own time. The art and the role are in the balance, which he must preserve at all costs—keeping an ear out for the claims and cautions of both sides but never, despite all cries of the experts seated there (and in this he finds his proper use), leaning too far to the left or to the right.

Keeping one's balance is a particularly formidable task with a language like ancient Egyptian hieroglyphic, which is both exotic and dead. It is, after all, only during the past century and a half that a language whose history and development spanned more than three millennia has begun to be recovered. For most of the Christian era (and for some centuries before that) the hieroglyphs on the monuments of ancient Egypt have been only pretty little pictures for tourists to goggle at and scrawl their graffiti beside in Greek, Latin, Arabic, French, and English. Decipherment of hieroglyphic only began around 1800 when Napoleon's soldiers, digging a fort, found the Rosetta stone, a trilingual inscription in Greek, demotic, and hieroglyphic. Since then, enough progress has been made for scholars to compile dictionaries and grammars and compose what seem to be accurate literal translations of most of the surviving texts. But there is much still to be learned; and discussion still goes on about the exact meaning of words, the implications of grammatical structures, and the relationship of sentences.

The translator who would render the ancient hieroglyphic into modern English faces many problems; and for him who is interested primarily in the literature, and most particularly in the verse, the problems are compounded. First of all, the ancient Egyptian did not draw the vowels when writing his words; he knew what sounds to expect and how to pronounce the words, so that showing them in the writing was unnecessary. But since knowledge of hieroglyphic died out, the sounds of the words were lost. All we have now are their consonantal skeletons; and the language is unpronounceable. Since the Egyptian philologist must speak the words somehow, he simply fakes the pronunciation by adding the sound of short *e* between consonants; but the claim is never made that this convention approximates the actual sounds of the ancient language. Thus, the hieroglyph of the wave of water (the alphabetic sign for the consonant *n*) is pronounced "en"; the chessboard (designating the biliteral *mn*) is pronounced "men"; and the heart and windpipe sign (for the triliteral *nfr*) is sounded "nefer." This makeshift at least enables one to "speak" a hieroglyphic sentence or line of verse after a fashion; and thus one can, for instance, approximate the number of syllables in the total length of a line. This, fortunately, is sufficient evidence to demonstrate that the lines of verse in an ancient poem were of unequal length—a point of importance to the translator, as we shall see later.

But ignorance of the sound system of hieroglyphic is still a profound loss to the translator aiming at a version of literary caliber: he cannot know the rhythm of the original piece. Though he can roughly tell the line lengths of a poem, he cannot know exactly how the words were accented, whether a slow, heavy rhythm or a light, skipping rhythm was employed, where stressed words were clustered for emphasis, or where patterns of dark or light vowels were used to color the meaning of a passage. The verse translator is in the rather ridiculous situation of knowing whether or not a passage alliterates but unable to tell if assonance was employed in the same passage. He simply must live with the fact that he cannot at present approximate either the sound or rhythmic system of the original. That part is almost pure guesswork.

Another kind of problem for the translator centers on uncertainties about the tense and mood of the Egyptian verb. Though the problem is too complicated to detail here, it seems that the ancient Egyptians thought of an action not so much in terms of when it occurred (past, present, or future—our tenses) but rather according to its duration—how long it took or whether it was a distinct, completed act or one which was continuous, repeated, or habitual. Durative acts tended to employ a tense analogous to our present tense, since they were not finished yet and hence not yet in the past; completed acts were over and hence tended to use a tense analogous to our past tense. The philologist is all too often forced back to the context of a passage in order to determine the tense of specific verbs. The translator of course faces the same problems; and although at times it does not particularly matter whether a passage is translated as present or past, at other times (say, in an historical document) the very basis of interpretation rests on the time of the action. Similar uncertainties of interpretation also occur with regard to the moods of the verb—whether a statement is made or a question asked, whether the verb includes a notion of wishing, commanding, or stating a condition to be fulfilled, or whether some special part of the sentence, other than the verb, is meant to be emphasized. It can be demonstrated from those verbs whose stems are mutable that indicators for such moods occurred in the language; but with most verbs such knowledge is masked by the absence of the vowels.

Understanding hieroglyphic is not all a darkness, however. The grammar is known, after all, and the language can be translated, even if many of its nuances are uncertain. Even though Sir Alan Gardiner in his *Egyptian Grammar* can begin one chapter by listing eighteen different ways in which the phrase, "His majesty went forth," can be written in hieroglyphs (each way originally having some special nuance of meaning or emphasis), the situation for the translator is not that hopeless. The bedrock of translation from this language is syntax—the word order of the individual sentence: verb, subject, indirect object, adverb or prepositional phrase. Often an indicator (a "particle") occurs at the beginning of the sentence to signal the special way in which the entire sentence is to be read (question, condition, new paragraph, dependency on previous sentence, and in some cases, tense). And if the syntax of the sentence varies from the basic pattern, one understands that some part of the sentence is being awarded special emphasis. The language itself provides some means for dispelling the ignorance generated by the loss of the vowel system.

Another major problem for the translator of the hieroglyphs lies with the ancient Egyptian vocabulary, the meanings of the individual words themselves. For anyone desiring a literary translation, especially of verse texts, the situation is critical; for so often in looking up the meaning of an unfamiliar word in even the monumental *Wörterbuch der Ägyptische Sprache*, one finds only citations of the texts where the word occurs (usually not one's own text) and a question mark. Even the brute denotations of many of the less familiar words are unknown, as indeed are the secondary meanings and connotations of a good many fairly common ones, particularly those words dealing with private and personal life or with human moods and feelings—the very stuff of literature. The student of ancient Egyptian is reduced to compiling his own dictionary as he goes, accumulating file-drawers full of 3×5 cards, each bearing a hieroglyphic word, the text where it occurred, and all too often another question mark for its translation.

The Egyptian language is constituted from picture signs, some of which represent ideas of concrete things (ideograms) and some of which represent sounds (phonograms). The latter consist primarily of alphabetic, biliteral, and triliteral signs (representing one, two, and three consonants respectively). The situation is somewhat complicated by the fact that the language is not merely alphabetic and that some of the signs can be used either for their ideogrammic or phonetic values. In addition, there is a third very significant category of signs called determinatives, which indicate the general area of meaning of a word; they might be thought of as determining the broader "genus" of the "species" of word spelled out by phonograms preceding the determinative. Thus, one may not be able to tell if an unknown word signifies berries or pomegranates, but from the determinative he can at least be sure it is some kind of fruit. Since the meanings of almost all determinatives are known, they are a great help to the translator slogging through unfamiliar terrain. As with much of the grammar, the nuances may be elusive, but the general outlines are known.

Although Egyptian hieroglyphic employs picture signs, it is not really picture writing (ideogrammic), since the language had advanced to a proto-alphabet and words in most cases were spelled out. One unfamiliar with the language sees only the appeal of the things depicted by the signs; but to the philologist an owl, no matter how beautifully drawn, is after all simply the letter *m*. And he would argue that to an ancient Egyptian this sign no more meant "owl" than our letter *A* means "head of a bull."

And yet, for us today, the hieroglyphs do have an important appeal as pictures—there is an aesthetic dimension in simply seeing a well-drawn hieroglyphic text. Additionally, I think one can argue that ancient Egyptian is at least residually ideogrammic, enough of the signs still *can* mean the object depicted for one to say that the idea meant to be conveyed is also often *seen*. Three wavy horizontal lines, one under the other, *do* mean "water"; one does *see* the female silhouette in the sign for "woman"; one can distinguish between a certain kind of tree and its fruit by looking at the determinatives of the words. This ideogrammic dimension to the language—of seeing the idea mentioned—has a special importance for anyone interested in the aesthetic values and the literature of the language. One has only to recall Ezra Pound's interest in Chinese as an ideogrammic language and the rather elaborate theory of poetry his artist's imagination developed from the insight: an ideogrammic language is automatically the language of poetry par excellence because it is inherently so concrete and imagistic. One of the cornerstones of modernist poetic theory has been an insistence upon concrete language and a direct presentation of the subject matter—the poet must not merely describe his subject, he must show it, dramatize it, present it concretely before his reader's imagination. The mind's eye must *see* the subject of the poem in action. Pound argued that any pictorial language was inherently more poetic than one like English because one can see something going on, in no matter how rudimentary a manner, at the same time he is thinking and feeling about the meaning conveyed. Egyptian hieroglyphic is this kind of language.

In addition to its ideogrammic value as a poetic language, ancient Egyptian exhibits a vocabulary rich in sensory appeal, in concrete words and phrases. At least some students of ancient Egypt argue that the consciousness of an ancient Egyptian was "pre-logical" or "mythopoeic," innocent of or not interested in the processes of abstraction and generalization developed by the Greeks. However accurate that might be historically, it does seem that the surviving texts concerned with such problems are not "philosophic" in our sense but rather "wisdom" texts: instead of the generalization or principle we have the observation; instead of the syllogism we have the maxim. In the Egyptian texts the emphasis is more limited to the individual instance or situation, the practical, the actual, the moral—the accumulations of experience gained over a career and passed on to a son. Such writings seem more limited to the concrete and particular.

And the Egyptian vocabulary in general seems to reflect this situation. It is especially rich in concrete words, words for objects, words for the natural world to which the ancient Egyptian was so closely tied, epithets concretely describing the qualities and powers of the invisible gods. And unless it is our ignorance of an entire level of the ancient language speaking, we can say that Egyptian was grudging in its employment of abstract, general words. So far as we know, there was a single word ("maat") to express what to us would be the differing concepts of "justice," "truth," and "order." The Egyptian would tend to speak, not of the concept of "love" (though a noun for "love" does exist), but the activity of "loving," the condition of "being in love," or the person "beloved." The difference, I think, is fundamental to the translator of the literature because it shifts emphasis from the general or the abstract to the particular and concrete, to the more personal and sensory. And (again) of such stuff is literature made.

A similar kind of example, perhaps more clearly demonstrating the concrete, "poetic" emphasis in the language, concerns the circumlocutions often used to describe personal qualities, moods and feelings, and aspects of human character. Thus one who is joyful is described as "long of heart"; one who is generous is called "long of hand." A presumptuous person is "high of back," while the alert is called "sharp of face." There is a whole vocabulary of such phrases, most dealing with human attributes; and in them, where the philologist may see only a clumsy periphrasis, the translator, if he has the wit to catch it, perceives the very concreteness of image and vigor of phrase so necessary to modern literary idiom. As with the residual ideograms, these phrases demonstrate that certain highly literary qualities are inherent in the language —it is wonderfully rich in sensory appeal. Both characteristics are a kind of compensation to the translator for the loss of the sounds and rhythms of ancient Egyptian.

But here are other problems to be faced from an entirely different quarter, especially for one working with literary texts. Almost all the latter appear either on papyri or on ostraca (pieces of pottery or stone smoothed and used for writing). Such texts are not written in hieroglyphic at all but in hieratic, the cursive form of ancient Egyptian adapted to the use of brush on either of these two surfaces (whereas the hieroglyphs proper resulted from use of chisel on stone). The two kinds of writing are merely variants of the same language; but the understanding of hieratic does require additional study, and it displays conventions of its own. There is the added problem (sometimes insurmountable) of trying to decipher the handwriting of someone who lived and wrote three or four thousand years ago. So, as well as knowing what the cursive form of the hieroglyphic signs are, the translator must know his scribe—the idiosyncrasies of his handwriting, his flourishes and abbreviations, the method at his period of forming given signs. And often (though not so much with literary texts), the translator is faced with the work of a writer who is hurried, careless, or even semi-illiterate. Or just plain hungry: one man from the New Kingdom village where workers on the royal tombs were housed scrawled, "Go get me one fat goose—quick, quick, quick!"

Many of the texts, both on papyri and ostraca, are schoolboy exercises, copied out as the young student was learning his profession of scribe; and some still exhibit in the margins the instructor's corrections of badly formed hieratic signs. Such texts are sometimes horribly garbled, full of misspellings, undecipherable tracks, and obviously wrong words; but we are forced to be thankful for them, since some of the most important and charming literary productions of ancient Egypt survive only because of the sweat of these fledgling professionals. And if one is lucky, enough fragmentary "duplicates" of the more renowned works survive for the modern philologist to piece together a fairly respectable synthetic version of what the original must have been like.

But completely apart from the intricacies of hieratic and the whims of student compositions, the translator is faced with the brute facts of the condition of his texts. The first fact is that the texts are between three and four thousand years old; and the second, that things deteriorate: papyrus tatters, stone and pottery flake and crumble. Perhaps the miracle is that any texts survive at all. Anyway, one can say without too much exaggeration that there is scarcely a text from ancient Egypt fully intact; the Egyptologist is at home with lacunae. Most of the surviving "classics" of ancient Egypt are fragmentary: the beginning or end of a papyrus lost or its entirety so threadbare with age that it is full of holes and its writing faded into the remaining fibers, or an ostracon broken in half, chipped at the corners and around the edges, or its surface flaking—or worse: only the broken corner surviving. These things, unfortunately, are the rule rather than the exception. Some papyri (obviously untranslated) are only heaps of crumbs in a box. Shorter pieces, by their very brevity, fare better: individual lyrics and letters have often survived almost intact. The philologist does what he can with the remains; and enough has endured for the scholar to reconstruct the general outlines of ancient Egyptian literature, filling it in here and there with specific pieces, and now and then a masterwork.

And there is a compensation here too. Though faced with fragments, the translator can hope for, and even expect, the appearance of new texts with some regularity. They are always emerging from the sand or appearing from tomb excavations. When I was in Luxor not long ago, news came to Chicago House that the French expedition had just the day before unearthed a new cache of ostraca in the ancient workmen's village across the River in Western Thebes. There is probably more of the literature still in the sand than has come to light during the past two centuries. At another point during my trip to Egypt, as my guide was driving us out into the desert to look at Zoser's Step Pyramid, and as we approached it on a "road" consisting of a double rut through the sand, he said, "You realize, of course, that we are driving over the tops of tombs." So, the translator of hieroglyphic, despite having largely to view only remains of texts, is a sort of eternal optimist: there is so much sand —so much unexcavated—that something will turn up to keep him busy, to fill in a passage of a text, to clarify the working of an inscription or a point of grammar or clinch the meaning of a word.

As for the love songs of ancient Egypt, those known to date survive in four main collections, none of them very extensive by our standards: Papyrus Chester Beatty I and P. Harris 500 (both in the British Museum), P. Turin 1966 (in the Egyptian Museum of Turin, Italy), and Cairo Ostracon 25218 (in the Cairo Museum). Beatty I is in fine condition, well written, with few lacunae, and with only the first part of the roll missing—a philologist's delight. Harris 500, like Beatty I a literary "anthology," is currently on display in an Egyptian gallery of the British Museum; it is fragmentary, threadbare, and full of lacunae, but contains the single most extensive group of the surviving love songs. The

Turin Love Papyrus consists of four pieces originally constituting two full columns (pages) from a more extensive roll; what survives here (the last three of a group of love songs) is in good condition, but translation originally was thwarted by the fact that the pieces were mounted in the wrong sequence and no one could make any sense of them. The Cairo Ostracon is a piece of broken pottery, with a good deal of the original text apparently missing and with the remaining surface fading and flaking. Scholars date all four of these collections to the later New Kingdom of ancient Egypt, Dynasties XIX and XX, or about 1300–1100 B.C. The total of the love songs amounts to only about sixty pieces— and some of these too fragmentary to recover as poems. There are hints of a few other such songs appearing on ostraca scattered here and there in various museum collections in Europe and America; but most present texts, too fragmentary to translate meaningfully, are identified as love songs only by a characteristic word or phrase or by some small clue as to situation or setting. . . .

One pleasure of translating these lyrics comes with the knowledge that, amid the turbulence of history, love endures; for, fused with the portrait of a life and civilization so different from our own occur characters— lovers and other speakers—and a spectrum of moods, feelings, and tones quite like those known from our own experience. The whole range is there, all the varieties of loving. The themes, despite the exotic setting, are perennial. There is the set description of the beloved—for the speaker she is "one and only," and he catalogues her beauties head to toe. There are the standard situations of lovelonging, unrequited love, wish-fulfillment, dreams of mastery, even prayers to deity to aid in conquest. There are the devices of enticement, deception, duplicity—clever moves on the chessboard of love. There are the moments of absence and separation; invitations, sports, activities, and the games people play; the conversations of lovers; union and the act of love; its loss and the aftermath of love.

And we see all the characters of lovers, usually young, and both sexes speaking. There is the featherheaded neophyte, off for a chat with her girlfriend, who suddenly sights her secret love on the road, and all brashness gone, is paralyzed with uncertainty. There is the girl out walking at night for a glimpse of her beloved (and he is found conveniently standing in the doorway of his house). Or, there is the couple sitting in the twilight in their garden to catch the evening breeze after a hot day. Or, the young sophisticate kneeling for an ironic prayer to Hathor, goddess of love, to retrieve his wandering girlfriend. Or the girl coaxing her friend to go bathing with her by promising to wear her new swimsuit (which, as she carefully explains to him, goes sheer in the water). One young man takes to his bed, feigning violent illness and hoping his love will come to visit him out of pity, and another, in the single case where character and theme overlap in different lyrics, imagines a similar ploy as his lucidity begins to falter under the pressure of his girlfriend's week-long absence. Still others spur themselves with erotic daydreams of the cornering and conquest of maidens not yet brought to bed. And there are young lady speakers with parallel thoughts and dreams.

In one instance from P. Harris 500 there is an entire cycle of eight poems linked by a narrative thread. Telling a story by concentrating only on the "poetic" lyric peaks of emotion and drama while omitting the "prosaic" connecting events—an idea developed by modernist poets like Pound, Eliot, and Williams—is not so new after all. In the Egyptian analogue the story is a simple one of unrequited love. The speaker of all eight lyrics is a virginal young girl swept away by her feelings, perhaps a first love; and we watch the progress of the affair from her initial stratagems, through her hopes and fears concerning her success, to the physical culmination, her discovery of her lover's duplicity, and her final loneliness. The ancient poet has given us an appealing persona and presented her deepest feelings in a unified sequence of lyric moments as the experience works to its inevitable conclusion. After three millennia the modern reader can still be moved by her disappointment and emptiness.

One other "character" deserves mention. She is Hathor, the Egyptian goddess of love; and her function in these lyrics is much like that of the Greek Aphrodite. Lovers regularly appeal to her for aid, usually to provide the elusive beloved for them; they are always aware of her invisible presence and power; and at least one attributes the imminent conquest of his latest lady to long and faithful service in her behalf. Though there is no machinery of Cupid and his amorous darts in the Egyptian conception, the capriciousness of love is simply and obviously Hathor at work manipulating Egyptian heartstrings.

The variety of tone in these lyrics thus is seen to express most of the moods of love. The speakers can, on the one hand, be innocent and pure of heart, hesitant, or self-sacrificing in love's duties; but on the other hand, they can be intensely passionate, patently physical in their desire, or even given to sexual innuendo, bawdry, and lust. The tones in which they express these attitudes and conditions thus range the entire gamut from the romantic and idyllic, through the simple and naive, to the humorously realistic and even satirical, and on to the openly sexual and erotic.

The most prevalent tone gives an impression of grace, liveliness, and charm—of a kind observed over and over again in the scenes of daily life depicted on the tomb walls of Western Thebes (paintings for which these songs must be the verbal equivalent): the noble ladies in their finest party dresses, the riot of food and drink, the female singers, musicians, and dancers, the naked servant girls and entertainers, and the harpers (often, like Homer, blind) plucking out dinner music. It is as if life and eternity alike were an unending banquet. Sometimes, written in hieroglyphs beside their portraits, we even have snatches of the songs being sung and played by the performers. And mural and song alike attest that these ancient people, far from being in love with death, as misinformation has it, were so delighted with life in the Nile valley that they took great pains to preserve those bodies which had served them so well in this world in order to use them with equal happiness forever.

The liveliness and the grace are certainly there; but in the Egyptian songs there is almost always an element of physical attraction and delight which will often become an expression of erotic longing. I return to this aspect because it seems to have been passed over too lightly by students of Egyptology. Perhaps it is because earlier phases of Egyptology were an outgrowth of Biblical studies, where all too often emphasis was placed not on daily life but upon another world and transcendence of the urges and mundane loves of the flesh. One philologist, footnoting a lyric he had translated, excused the ancient Egyptian delight in the body as due to the hot blood of the Mediterranean temperament. But the broadening of subject matter which has occurred in modern poetry makes possible what I think is a more genuine response to the presence of the erotic in the anciet poetry. This is another parallel to modernist poetry; and one can cite the love poems of Cummings and Williams or the more "classic" early love songs of Pound.

But graceful and charming or erotic and physical, the Egyptian lyrics sometimes plumb deeper than the surfaces of human experience. The young girl who falls in and out of love is appealing, and the intricacies of the game of love are pleasant and often amusing; but now and then, there is more. The woman who tries to persuade her lover not to leave her bed begins with the teasing speeches of love combat; but by the end of the poem her light words seem to mask a more enduring feeling, a strength of attachment that will be genuinely injured by the looming separation. Elsewhere, a young man breaks his daily routine, gives in to his wanderlust, and heads for the big city—taking a boat trip downriver to Memphis, capital of the Old Kingdom. A girl is one of his goals, to be sure; but the poem is based fundamentally on the human urge to wander, to seek adventure, to answer the call of the city lights. On board the ferry, as he watches the Nile go by in the twilight, he experiences an almost mystical communion with the triad of gods who watch over Memphis, sensing their presence around him and projecting their influence over his future activities in the city of his dreams. Such expressions of deeper experiences are the exception rather than the rule in the love songs; but they do occur, showing that at times the ancient authors could and would probe beyond the conventions of the genre to profounder experience. . . .

The would-be translator of such songs must try never to forget that it was not a printing press or a photoduplicating machine but the living hand of some now forgotten Egyptian that once carefully (or sometimes not so carefully) formed the hieratic characters on a clean, untattered papyrus or an unchipped, unflaked ostracon. He was probably not the author of the song, and he may have been only a scribe copying out the text for his master (for we today have only copies); but someone thought enough of these lyrics to have them written down for his own library. For himself, not for us; but we have them, and they are ours now too.

If some Egyptian then could be moved and delighted by these songs, the modern translator, keeping faith with that dead hand from the past, must honor them as poems, making them new for his own time. These ancient verses must sing as poetry to our modern ear, and they must be as faithful as our knowledge of the ancient Egyptian language allows to the texture and idiom—the feel—of the original. We want to know the exact words of these speakers; but we also want to know the implications of their words, how they felt—about to love, in love, or the far side of love. The speakers must come alive again for us, after their millennia of frozen silence in the limbo of a forgotten language. Only in this way, in this kind of a translation, can the continuity of human imagination and feeling over the centuries be perceived. . . .

There are four steps in the literary translation of an ancient Egyptian poem, illustrated here by the fifth lyric of the first cycle of love songs in Papyrus Harris 500, "The Memphis Ferry." The first step is simply obtaining a photographic copy of the text. It is written in hieratic, the cursive form of hieroglyphic adapted for the use of brush (i.e., pen) on papyrus. The characters are written continuously and without punctuation from right to left. An approximation of the hieratic appears in Figure 1. As the hieratic is deciphered, it is rewritten in the corresponding hieroglyphs. These are usually written from right to left and, for verse texts, divided into lines of poetry (Figure 2). From his hieroglyphic text, the translator develops a line-by-line translation, at this stage attempting to be accurate rather than poetic. The last stage, of course, is the poem in the new language (text of "The Memphis Ferry").

The shaded portions in my approximation of the hieratic original indicate gaps, or holes, in the papyrus manuscript. I have also indicated these gaps with shading in my hieroglyphic transcription. The literal translation contains my restorations, most of which are based on the surrounding context. A few words and phrases were inserted because of the similarity of the surrounding passages with those in other hieratic love poems, in terms of structure and poetic conventions.

The translator's aim is a poem, of course, but more specifically (and more accurately) it is a feeling that the final version catches not what the original said but what its author must have meant by employing the words he did. With a language as long dead as Egyptian hieroglyphic, that goal is a gamble against rather long odds. All too often there is, perhaps, *a* poem, but without the inner conviction that it recreates *the* poem; and the translator sadly recalls the clever observation that a poem is never finished, it is only abandoned. No matter how convincing the tonal equivalent seems to be when freshly finished, it should always be set aside for several weeks or months and then examined again to see if any cracks have developed in its construction. Often what one thought

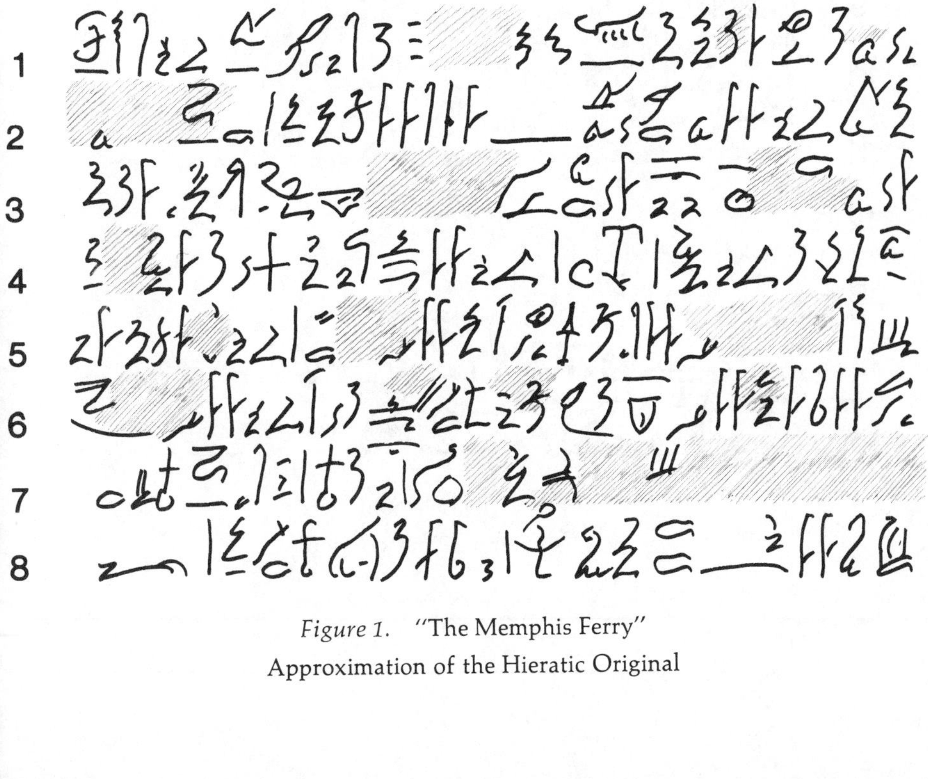

Figure 1. "The Memphis Ferry"
Approximation of the Hieratic Original

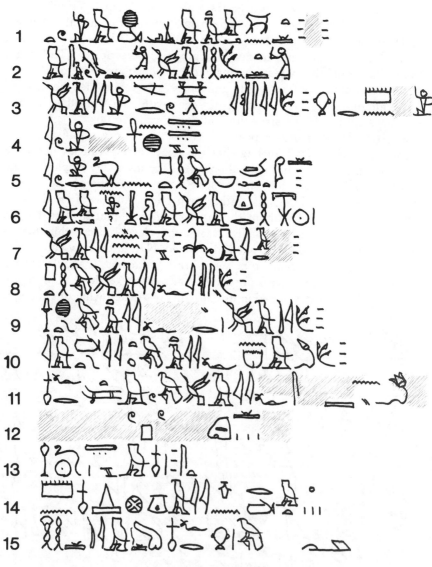

Figure 2. "The Memphis Ferry"
Hieroglyphic Transcription

"The Memphis Ferry"
Literal Translation from Hieroglyphic Transcription

1 I am going downstream in the ferryboat
2 Like (?) one who strains (?) against the command
3 My bundle of old clothes (?) upon my shoulder
4 I shall go to "The Life-of-the-Two-Lands"
5 I shall say to [Ptah,] Lord of Justice
6 Give to me a sister in the night
7 The sea—it is among rushes (?)
8 Ptah is its reeds
9 Sakhmet is its lotus pads
10 She-who-is-the-Dew (?) is its lotus buds
11 Nefertem is its lotus blossoms
12 . . . . [joy?]
13 When dawn comes with her beauties
14 "The Enduring-of-Beauty" is a bowl of love-apples (?)
15 Set in the presence of the "Beautiful-of-Face"

"The Memphis Ferry"
Poetic Translation

Oh I'm bound downstream on the Memphis ferry,
        like a runaway, snapping all ties,
With my bundle of old clothes over my shoulder.

I'm going down there where the living is,
        going down there to that big city,
And there I'll tell Ptah (Lord who loves justice):
        "Give me a girl tonight!"

Look at the River! eddying,
        in love with the young vegetation.
Ptah himself is the life of these reedshoots,
        Lady Sakhmet of the lilies—
Yes, Our Lady of Dew dwells among lilypads—
        and their son, Nefertem, sweet boy,
Blossoms newborn in the blue lotus.
        Twilight is heavy with gods. . . .

And the quiet joy of tomorrow,
        dawn whitening over her loveliness:
Oh Memphis my city, beauty forever!—
        you are a bowl of love's own berries,
Dish set for Ptah your god,
        god of the handsome face.

was a fine phrase or a lively image dries and deadens with time, need-
ing change. So, one tries to revise, checking, teasing, and polishing.

And once in a while, with a new word or phrase the poem is finally
and really there; the translator feels he can do no more with it. Nor does
he wish to, for it now is as right as he can make it. He feels he has
caught the life of the ancient text and time in words and rhythms that
are alive now: he has really been back there, and returned. It is a good
feeling; for it is a victory, no matter how small or momentary, over
death and decay and time—the death of lovers, of papyri, of authors and
civilizations, of emotions and consciousness. And I hope that it is not
too pretentious a way of putting it; for that, it seems to me, is the way
it is—the ultimate motive for translation: keeping traditions of civilization alive, recreating people of flesh and blood out of the distant past.

GEORGE SANTAYANA

George Santayana (1863–1925), born in Madrid, emigrated to the United
States with his parents at the age of nine. Educated at Harvard, he taught
philosophy there from 1889 to 1912, before returning to Europe to travel
and write. *The Sense of Beauty* (1896) is still a basic study of aesthetics.
Poems appeared in 1923; his novel, *The Last Puritan,* in 1936.

CERVANTES

This is a classic study of a masterpiece from Santayana's native Spain. In
bringing the author and the work together, in translating the life into the
art, Santayana explains that great book more clearly and simply than anyone before or since, suggesting the meaning behind the comic clash of
idealism and reality. Notice how Cervantes discovered and deepened his
meaning as he wrote, as you and I do when we put pen to paper.

Cervantes is known to the world as the author of *Don Quixote,* and
although his other works are numerous and creditable, and his pathetic
life is carefully recorded, yet it is as the author of *Don Quixote* alone
that he deserves to be generally known or considered. Had his wit not
come by chance on the idea of the Ingenious Hidalgo, Cervantes would
never have attained his universal renown, even if his other works and
the interest of his career should have sufficed to give him a place in the
literary history of his country. Here, then, where our task is to present
in miniature only what has the greatest and most universal value, we
may treat our author as playwrights are advised to treat their heroes,
saying of him only what is necessary to the understanding of the single

action with which we are concerned. This single action is the writing of *Don Quixote*; and what we shall try to understand is what there was in the life and environment of Cervantes that enabled him to compose that great book, and that remained imbedded in its characters, its episodes, and its moral.

There was in vogue in the Spain of the sixteenth century a species of romance called books of chivalry. They were developments of the legends dealing with King Arthur and the Knights of the Table Round, and their numerous descendants and emulators. These stories had appealed in the first place to what we should still think of as the spirit of chivalry: they were full of tourneys and single combats, desperate adventures and romantic loves. The setting was in the same vague and wonderful region as the Coast of Bohemia where, to the known mountains, seas, and cities that have poetic names, was added a prodigious number of caverns, castles, islands, and forests of the romancer's invention. With time and popularity this kind of story had naturally intensified its characteristics until it had reached the greatest extravagance and absurdity, and combined in a way the unreality of the fairy tale with the bombast of the melodrama.

Cervantes had apparently read these books with avidity, and was not without a great sympathy with the kind of imagination they embodied. His own last and most carefully written book, the *Travails of Persiles and Sigismunda*, is in many respects an imitation of them; it abounds in savage islands, furious tyrants, prodigious feats of arms, disguised maidens whose discretion is as marvelous as their beauty, and happy deliverances from intricate and hopeless situations. His first book also, the *Galatea*, was an embodiment of a kind of pastoral idealism: sentimental verses being interspersed with euphuistic prose, the whole describing the lovelorn shepherds and heartless shepherdesses of Arcadia.

But while these books, which were the author's favorites among his own works, expressed perhaps Cervantes's natural taste and ambition, the events of his life and the real bent of his talent, which in time he came himself to recognize, drove him to a very different sort of composition. His family was ancient but impoverished, and he was forced throughout his life to turn his hand to anything that could promise him a livelihood. His existence was a continuous series of experiments, vexations, and disappointments. He adopted at first the profession of arms, and followed his colors as a private soldier upon several foreign expeditions. He was long quartered in Italy; he fought at Lepanto against the Turks, where among other wounds he received one that maimed his left hand, to the greater glory, as he tells us, of his right; he was captured by Barbary pirates and remained for five years as a slave in Algiers; he was ransomed, and returned to Spain only to find official favors and recognitions denied him; and finally, at the age of thirty-seven, he abandoned the army for literature.

His first thought as a writer does not seem to have been to make direct use of his rich experience and varied observation; he was rather possessed by an obstinate longing for that poetic gift which, as he confesses in one place, Heaven had denied him. He began with the idyllic romance, the *Galatea*, already mentioned, and at various times during the rest of his life wrote poems, plays, and stories of a romantic and sentimental type. In the course of these labors, however, he struck one vein of much richer promise. It was what the Spanish call the *picaresque*; that is, the description of the life and character of rogues, pickpockets, vagabonds, and all those wretches and sorry wits that might be found about the highways, in the country inns, or in the slums of cities. Of this kind is much of what is best in his collected stories, the *Novelas Exemplares*. The talent and the experience which he betrays in these amusing narratives were to be invaluable to him later as the author of *Don Quixote*, where they enabled him to supply a foil to the fine world of his poor hero's imagination.

We have now mentioned what were perhaps the chief elements of the preparation of Cervantes for his great task. They were a great familiarity with the romances of chivalry, and a natural liking for them; a life of honorable but unrewarded endeavor both in war and in the higher literature; and much experience of Vagabondia, with the art of taking down and reproducing in amusing profusion the typical scenes and languages of low life. Out of these elements a single spark, which we may attribute to genius, to chance, or to inspiration, was enough to produce a new and happy conception: that of a parody on the romances of chivalry, in which the extravagances of the fables of knighthood should be contrasted with the sordid realities of life. This is done by the ingenious device of representing a country gentleman whose naturally generous mind, unhinged by much reading of the books of chivalry, should lead him to undertake the office of knight-errant, and induce him to ride about the country clad in ancient armor, to right wrongs, to succor defenseless maidens, to kill giants, and to win empires at least as vast as that of Alexander.

This is the subject of *Don Quixote*. But happy as the conception is, it could not have produced a book of enduring charm and well-seasoned wisdom, had it not been filled in with a great number of amusing and lifelike episodes, and verified by two admirable figures, Don Quixote and Sancho Panza, characters at once intimately individual and truly universal.

Don Quixote at first appears to the reader, and probably appeared to the author as well, as primarily a madman,—a thin and gaunt old village squire, whose brain has been turned by the nonsense he has read and taken for gospel truth; and who is punished for his ridiculous mania by an uninterrupted series of beatings, falls, indignities, and insults. But the hero and the author together, with the ingenuity proper to madness and the inevitableness proper to genius, soon begin to disclose the fund of intelligence and ideal passion which underlies this superficial insanity. We see that Don Quixote is only mad north-north-west, when the wind blows from the quarter of his chivalrous preoccupation. At other times he shows himself a man of great goodness and fineness of wit; virtuous, courageous, courteous, and generous, and in fact the perfect ideal of a gentleman. When he takes, for instance, a handful of acorns from the goat-herds' table and begins a grandiloquent discourse upon the Golden Age, we feel how cultivated the man is, how easily the little things of life suggest to him the great things, and with what delight he dwells on what is beautiful and happy. The truth and pathos of the character become all the more compelling when we consider how naturally the hero's madness and calamities flow from this same exquisite sense of what is good.

The contrast to this figure is furnished by that of Sancho Panza, who embodies all that is matter-of-fact, gross, and plebeian. Yet he is willing to become Don Quixote's esquire, and by his credulity and devotion shows what an ascendency a heroic and enthusiastic nature can gain over the most sluggish of men. Sancho has none of the instincts of his master. He never read the books of chivalry or desired to right the wrongs of the world. He is naturally satisfied with his crust and his onions, if they can be washed down with enough bad wine. His good drudge of a wife never transformed herself in his fancy into a peerless Dulcinea. Yet Sancho follows his master into every danger, shares his discomfiture and the many blows that rain down upon him, and hopes to the end for the governorship of that Insula with which Don Quixote is some day to reward his faithful esquire.

As the madness of Don Quixote is humanized by his natural intelligence and courage, so the grossness and credulity of Sancho are relieved by his homely wit. He abounds in proverbs. He never fails to see the reality of a situation, and to protest doggedly against his master's visionary flights. He holds fast as long as he can to the evidence of his senses, and to his little weaknesses of flesh and spirit. But finally he surrenders to the authority of Don Quixote, and of the historians of chivalry, although not without a certain reluctance and some surviving doubts.

The character of Sancho is admirable for the veracity with which its details are drawn. The traits of the boor, the glutton, and the coward come most naturally to the surface upon occasion, yet Sancho remains a patient, good-natured peasant, a devoted servant, and a humble Christian. Under the cover of such lifelike incongruities, and a pervasive humor, the author has given us a satirical picture of human nature not inferior, perhaps, to that furnished by Don Quixote himself. For instance: Don Quixote, after mending his helmet, tries its strength with a blow that smashes it to pieces. He mends it a second time, but now, without trial, deputes it to be henceforth a strong and perfect helmet. Sancho, when he is sent to bear a letter to Dulcinea, neglects to deliver it, and invents an account of his interview with the imaginary lady for the satisfaction of his master. But before long, by dint of repeating the story, he comes himself to believe his own lies. Thus self-deception in the knight is the ridiculous effect of courage, and in the esquire the not less ridiculous effect of sloth.

The adventures these two heroes encounter are naturally only such as travelers along the Spanish roads would then have been likely to come upon. The point of the story depends on the familiarity and commonness of the situations in which Don Quixote finds himself, so that the absurdity of his pretensions may be overwhelmingly shown. Critics are agreed in blaming the exceptions which Cervantes allowed himself to make to the realism of his scenes, where he introduced romantic tales into the narrative of the first part. The tales are in themselves unworthy of their setting, and contrary to the spirit of the whole book. Cervantes doubtless yielded here partly to his story-telling habits, partly to a fear of monotony in the uninterrupted description of Don Quixote's adventures. He avoided this mistake in the second part, and devised the visit to the Duke's palace, and the intentional sport there made of the hero, to give variety to the story.

More variety and more unity may still, perhaps, seem desirable in the book. The episodes are strung together without much coherence, and without any attempt to develop either the plot or the characters. Sancho, to be sure, at last tastes the governorship of his Insula, and Don Quixote on his death-bed recovers his wits. But this conclusion, appropriate and touching as it is, might have come almost anywhere in the course of the story. The whole book has, in fact, rather the quality of an improvisation. The episodes suggest themselves to the author's fancy as he proceeds; a fact which gives them the same unexpectedness and sometimes the same incompleteness which the events of a journey naturally have. It is in the genius of this kind of narrative to be a sort of imaginary diary, without a general dramatic structure. The interest depends on the characters and the incidents alone; on the fertility of the author's invention, on the ingenuity of the turns he gives to the story, and on the incidental scenes and figures he describes.

When we have once accepted this manner of writing fiction—which might be called that of the novelist before the days of the novel—we can only admire the execution of *Don Quixote* as masterly in its kind. We find here an abundance of fancy that is never at a loss for some probable and interesting incident; we find a graphic power that makes living and unforgettable many a minor character, even if slightly sketched; we find the charm of the country rendered by little touches without any formal descriptions; and we find a humorous and minute reproduction of the manners of the time. All this is rendered in a flowing and easy style, abounding in both characterization and parody of diverse types of speech and composition; and the whole is still but the background for the figures of Don Quixote and Sancho, and for their pleasant discourse, the quality and savor of which is maintained to the end. These excellences unite to make the book one of the most permanently delightful in the world, as well as one of the most diverting. Seldom has laughter been so well justified as that which the reading of *Don Quixote* continually provokes; seldom has it found its causes in such genuine fancy, such profound and real contrast, and such victorious good-humor.

We sometimes wish, perhaps, that our heroes were spared some of their bruises, and that we were not asked to delight so much in promiscuous beatings and floggings. But we must remember that these three hundred years have made the European race much more sensitive to physical suffering. Our ancestors took that doubtful pleasure in the idea of corporal writhings which we still take in the description of the tortures of the spirit. The idea of both evils is naturally distasteful to a refined mind; but we admit more willingly the kind which habit has accustomed us to regard as inevitable, and which personal experience very probably has made an old friend.

Don Quixote has accordingly enjoyed a universal popularity, and has had the singular privilege of accomplishing the object for which it was written, which was to recall fiction from the extravagances of the books of chivalry to the study of real life. This is the simple object which Cervantes had and avowed. He was a literary man with literary interests, and the idea which came to him was to ridicule the absurdities of the prevalent literary mode. The rich vein which he struck in the conception of Don Quixote's madness and topsy-turvy adventures encouraged him to go on. The subject and the characters deepened under his hands, until from a parody of a certain kind of romance the story threatened to become a satire on human idealism. At the same time

Cervantes grew fond of his hero, and made him, as we must feel, in some sort a representative of his own chivalrous enthusiasms and constant disappointments.

We need not, however, see in this transformation any deep-laid malice or remote significance. As the tale opened out before the author's fancy and enlisted his closer and more loving attention, he naturally enriched it with all the wealth of his experience. Just as he diversified it with pictures of common life and manners, so he weighted it with the burden of human tragedy. He left upon it an impress of his own nobility and misfortunes side by side with a record of his time and country. But in this there was nothing intentional. He only spoke out of the fullness of his heart. The highest motives and characters had been revealed to him by his own impulses, and the lowest by his daily experience.

There is nothing in the book that suggests a premeditated satire upon faith and enthusiasm in general. The author's evident purpose is to amuse, not to upbraid or to discourage. There is no bitterness in his pathos or despair in his disenchantment; partly because he retains a healthy fondness for this naughty world, and partly because his heart is profoundly and entirely Christian. He would have rejected with indignation an interpretation of his work that would see in it an attack on religion or even on chivalry. His birth and nurture had made him religious and chivalrous from the beginning, and he remained so by conviction to the end. He was still full of plans and hopes when death overtook him, but he greeted it with perfect simplicity, without lamentations over the past or anxiety for the future.

If we could have asked Cervantes what the moral of Don Quixote was to his own mind, he would have told us perhaps that it was this: that the force of idealism is wasted when it does not recognize the reality of things. Neglect of the facts of daily life made the absurdity of the romances of chivalry and of the enterprise of Don Quixote. What is needed is not, of course, that idealism should be surrendered, either in literature or in life; but that in both it should be made efficacious by a better adjustment to the reality it would transform.

Something of this kind would have been, we may believe, Cervantes's own reading of his parable. But when parables are such direct and full transcripts of life as is the story of Don Quixote, they offer almost as much occasion for diversity of interpretation as does the personal experience of men in the world. That the moral of Don Quixote should be doubtful and that each man should be tempted to see in it the expression of his own convictions is after all the greatest possible encomium of the book. For we may infer the truth has been rendered in it, and that men may return to it always, as to Nature herself, to renew their theories or to forget them, and to refresh their fancy with the spectacle of a living world.

GEORGE ORWELL

George Orwell (1903–1950), whose real name was Eric Arthur Blair, was born in Motihari, Bengal, of British parents. He won a scholarship to Eton, and, at nineteen, joined the Indian Imperial Police in Burma (1922–1927). He joined the Communist movement, and fought in the Spanish Civil War, which added the Communists to the imperialists in his aversion to authoritarian governments. Two of his well-known books are *Animal Farm* (1945) and *Nineteen Eighty-Four* (1949).

POLITICS AND THE ENGLISH LANGUAGE

This is the classic case against the concept that no one can or should tamper with the "accepted" usages of language. Orwell argues that the writer indeed can contribute to usage and stem decay by making his words mean what they say and by throwing into the dustbin all those words that blur or conceal meaning, especially those propagandists use deliberately to conceal. Ask, as you read, how Orwell's view of language compares with Sapir's. Make a list of worn-out and useless phrases to avoid in your own writing.

Most people who bother with the matter at all would admit that the English language is in a bad way, but it is generally assumed that we cannot by conscious action do anything about it. Our civilization is decadent and our language—so the argument runs—must inevitably share in the general collapse. It follows that any struggle against the abuse of language is a sentimental archaism, like preferring candles to electric light or hansom cabs to aeroplanes. Underneath this lies the half-conscious belief that language is a natural growth and not an instrument which we shape for our own purposes.

Now, it is clear that the decline of a language must ultimately have political and economic causes: it is not due simply to the bad influence of this or that individual writer. But an effect can become a cause, reinforcing the original cause and producing the same effect in an intensified form, and so on indefinitely. A man may take to drink because he feels himself to be a failure, and then fail all the more completely because he drinks. It is rather the same thing that is happening to the

English language. It becomes ugly and inaccurate because our thoughts are foolish, but the slovenliness of our language makes it easier for us to have foolish thoughts. The point is that the process is reversible. Modern English, especially written English, is full of bad habits which spread by imitation and which can be avoided if one is willing to take the necessary trouble. If one gets rid of these habits one can think more clearly, and to think clearly is a necessary first step towards political regeneration: so that the fight against bad English is not frivolous and is not the exclusive concern of professional writers. I will come back to this presently, and I hope that by that time the meaning of what I have said here will have become clearer. Meanwhile, here are five specimens of the English language as it is now habitually written.

These five passages have not been picked out because they are especially bad—I could have quoted far worse if I had chosen—but because they illustrate various of the mental vices from which we now suffer. They are a little below the average, but are fairly representative samples. I number them so that I can refer back to them when necessary:

(1) I am not, indeed, sure whether it is not true to say that the Milton who once seemed not unlike a seventeenth-century Shelley had not become, out of an experience ever more bitter in each year, more alien [sic] to the founder of that Jesuit sect which nothing could induce him to tolerate.

PROFESSOR HAROLD LASKI
(ESSAY IN Freedom of Expression)

(2) Above all, we cannot play ducks and drakes with a native battery of idioms which prescribes such egregious collocations of vocables as the Basic *put up with* for *tolerate* or *put at a loss* for *bewilder*.

PROFESSOR LANCELOT HOGBEN
(Interglossa)

(3) On the one side we have the free personality: by definition it is not neurotic, for it has neither conflict nor dream. Its desires, such as they are, are transparent, for they are just what institutional approval keeps in the forefront of consciousness; another institutional pattern would alter their number and intensity; there is little in them that is natural, irreducible, or culturally dangerous. But *on the other side*, the social bond itself is nothing but the mutual reflection of these self-secure integrities. Recall the definition of love. Is not this the very picture of a small academic? Where is there a place in this hall of mirrors for either personality or fraternity?

ESSAY ON PSYCHOLOGY IN Politics (NEW YORK)

(4) All the "best people" from the gentlemen's clubs, and all the frantic fascist captains, united in common hatred of Socialism and bestial horror of the rising tide of the mass revolutionary movement, have turned to acts of provocation, to foul incendiarism, to medieval legends of poisoned wells, to legalize their own destruction of proletarian organizations, and rouse the agitated petty-bourgeoisie to chauvinistic fervor on behalf of the fight against the revolutionary way out of the crisis.

COMMUNIST PAMPHLET

(5) If a new spirit *is* to be infused into this old country, there is one thorny and contentious reform which must be tackled, and that is the humanization and galvanization of the B.B.C.* Timidity here will bespeak canker and atrophy of the soul. The heart of Britain may be sound and of strong beat, for instance, but the British lion's roar at present is like that of Bottom in Shakespeare's *Midsummer Night's Dream*—as gentle as any sucking dove. A virile new Britain cannot continue indefinitely to be traduced in the eyes or rather ears of the world by the effete languors of Langham Place, brazenly masquerading as "standard English." When the voice of Britain is heard at nine o'clock, better far and infinitely less ludicrous to hear aitches honestly dropped than the present priggish, inhibited, school-ma'amish arch braying of blameless bashful mewing maidens!

LETTER IN Tribune

Each of these passages has faults of its own, but, quite apart from avoidable ugliness, two qualities are common to all of them. The first is staleness of imagery; the other is lack of precision. The writer either has a meaning and cannot express it, or he inadvertently says something else, or he is almost indifferent as to whether his words mean anything or not. This mixture of vagueness and sheer incompetence is the most marked characteristic of modern English prose, and especially of any kind of political writing. As soon as certain topics are raised, the concrete melts into the abstract and no one seems able to think of turns of speech that are not hackneyed: prose consists less and less of *words* chosen for the sake of their meaning, and more and more of *phrases* tacked together like the sections of a prefabricated hen-house. I list below, with notes and examples, various of the tricks by means of which the work of prose-construction is habitually dodged:

Dying metaphors. A newly invented metaphor assists thought by evoking a visual image, while on the other hand a metaphor which is

---

* British Broadcasting Corporation.

technically "dead" (e.g. *iron resolution*) has in effect reverted to being an ordinary word and can generally be used without loss of vividness. But in between these two classes there is a huge dump of worn-out metaphors which have lost all evocative power and are merely used because they save people the trouble of inventing phrases for themselves. Examples are: *Ring the changes on, take up the cudgels for, toe the line, ride roughshod over, stand shoulder to shoulder with, play into the hands of, no axe to grind, grist to the mill, fishing in troubled waters, on the order of the day, Achilles' heel, swan song, hotbed.* Many of these are used without knowledge of their meaning (what is a "rift," for instance?), and incompatible metaphors are frequently mixed, a sure sign that the writer is not interested in what he is saying. Some metaphors now current have been twisted out of their original meaning without those who use them even being aware of the fact. For example, *toe the line* is sometimes written *tow the line*. Another example is *the hammer and the anvil*, now always used with the implication that the anvil gets the worst of it. In real life it is always the anvil that breaks the hammer, never the other way about: a writer who stopped to think what he was saying would be aware of this, and would avoid perverting the original phrase.

Operators or verbal false limbs. These save the trouble of picking out appropriate verbs and nouns, and at the same time pad each sentence with extra syllables which give it an appearance of symmetry. Characteristic phrases are *render inoperative, militate against, make contact with, be subjected to, give rise to, give grounds for, have the effect of, play a leading part (role) in, make itself felt, take effect, exhibit a tendency to, serve the purpose of, etc. etc.* The keynote is the elimination of simple verbs. Instead of being a single word, such as *break, stop, spoil, mend, kill,* a verb becomes a *phrase,* made up of a noun or adjective tacked on to some general-purpose verb such as *prove, serve, form, play, render.* In addition, the passive voice is wherever possible used in preference to the active, and noun constructions are used instead of gerunds (*by examination of* instead of *by examining*). The range of verbs is further cut down by means of the *-ize* and *de-* formations, and the banal statements are given an appearance of profundity by means of the *not un-* formation. Simple conjunctions and prepositions are replaced by such phrases as *with respect to, having regard to, the fact that, by dint of, in view of, in the interests of, on the hypothesis that;* and the ends of sentences are saved from anticlimax by such resounding commonplaces as *greatly to be desired, cannot be left out of account, a development to be expected in the near future, deserving of serious* *consideration, brought to a satisfactory conclusion,* and so on and so forth.

Pretentious diction. Words like *phenomenon, element, individual* (as noun), *objective, categorical, effective, virtual, basic, primary, promote, constitute, exhibit, exploit, utilize, eliminate, liquidate,* are used to dress up simple statements and give an air of scientific impartiality to biased judgments. Adjectives like *epoch-making, epic, historic, unforgettable, triumphant, age-old, inevitable, inexorable, veritable,* are used to dignify the sordid processes of international politics, while writing that aims at glorifying war usually takes on an archaic color, its characteristic words being: *realm, throne, chariot, mailed fist, trident, sword, shield, buckler, banner, jackboot, clarion.* Foreign words and expressions such as *cul de sac, ancien régime, deus ex machina, mutatis mutandis, status quo, gleichschaltung, weltanschauung,* are used to give an air of culture and elegance. Except for the useful abbreviations *i.e., e.g.,* and *etc.,* there is no real need for any of the hundreds of foreign phrases now current in English. Bad writers, and especially scientific, political and sociological writers, are nearly always haunted by the notion that Latin or Greek words are grander than Saxon ones, and unnecessary words like *expedite, ameliorate, predict, extraneous, deracinated, clandestine, subaqueous* and hundreds of others constantly gain ground from their Anglo-Saxon opposite numbers.* The jargon peculiar to Marxist writing (*hyena, hangman, cannibal, petty bourgeois, these gentry, lacquey, flunkey, mad dog, White Guard,* etc.) consists largely of words and phrases translated from Russian, German or French; but the normal way of coining a new word is to use a Latin or Greek root with the appropriate affix and, where necessary, the *-ize* formation. It is often easier to make up words of this kind (*deregionalize, impermissible, extramarital, non-fragmentary* and so forth) than to think up the English words that will cover one's meaning. The result, in general, is an increase in slovenliness and vagueness.

Meaningless words. In certain kinds of writing, particularly in art criticism and literary criticism, it is normal to come across long pas-

---

* An interesting illustration of this is the way in which the English flower names which were in use till very recently are being ousted by Greek ones, *snapdragon* becoming *antirrhinum, forget-me-not* becoming *myosotis,* etc. It is hard to see any practical reason for this change of fashion: it is probably due to an instinctive turning-away from the more homely word and a vague feeling that the Greek word is scientific.

sages which are almost completely lacking in meaning.* Words like *romantic, plastic, values, human, dead, sentimental, natural, vitality,* as used in art criticism, are strictly meaningless, in the sense that they not only do not point to any discoverable object, but are hardly ever expected to do so by the reader. When one critic writes, "The outstanding feature of Mr. X's work is its living quality," while another writes, "The immediately striking thing about Mr. X's work is its peculiar deadness," the reader accepts this as a simple difference of opinion. If words like *black* and *white* were involved, instead of the jargon words *dead* and *living,* he would see at once that language was being used in an improper way. Many political words are similarly abused. The word *Fascism* has now no meaning except in so far as it signifies "something not desirable." The words *democracy, socialism, freedom, patriotic, realistic, justice,* have each of them several different meanings which cannot be reconciled with one another. In the case of a word like *democracy,* not only is there no agreed definition, but the attempt to make one is resisted from all sides. It is almost universally felt that when we call a country democratic we are praising it: consequently the defenders of every kind of régime claim that it is a democracy, and fear that they might have to stop using the word if it were tied down to any one meaning. Words of this kind are often used in a consciously dishonest way. That is, the person who uses them has his own private definition, but allows his hearer to think he means something quite different. Statements like *Marshal Pétain was a true patriot, The Soviet Press is the freest in the world, The Catholic Church is opposed to persecution,* are almost always made with intent to deceive. Other words used in variable meanings, in most cases more or less dishonestly, are: *class, totalitarian, science, progressive, reactionary, bourgeois, equality.*

Now that I have made this catalogue of swindles and perversions, let me give another example of the kind of writing that they lead to. This time it must of its nature be an imaginary one. I am going to translate a passage of good English into modern English of the worst sort. Here is a well-known verse from *Ecclesiastes:*

"I returned and saw under the sun, that the race is not to the swift, nor the battle to the strong, neither yet bread to the wise, nor yet riches

---

* Example: "Comfort's catholicity of perception and image, strangely Whitmanesque in range, almost the exact opposite in aesthetic compulsion, continues to evoke that trembling atmospheric accumulative hinting at a cruel, an inexorably serene timelessness. . . . Wrey Gardiner scores by aiming at simple bull's-eyes with precision. Only they are not so simple, and through this contented sadness runs more than the surface bittersweet of resignation." (*Poetry Quarterly.*)

to men of understanding, nor yet favour to men of skill; but time and chance happeneth to them all."

Here it is in modern English:

"Objective consideration of contemporary phenomena compels the conclusion that success or failure in competitive activities exhibits no tendency to be commensurate with innate capacity, but that a considerable element of the unpredictable must invariably be taken into account."

This is a parody, but not a very gross one. Exhibit (3), above, for instance, contains several patches of the same kind of English. It will be seen that I have not made a full translation. The beginning and ending of the sentence follow the original meaning fairly closely, but in the middle the concrete illustrations—race, battle, break—dissolve into the vague phrase "success or failure in competitive activities." This had to be so, because no modern writer of the kind I am discussing—no one capable of using phrases like "objective consideration of contemporary phenomena"—would ever tabulate his thoughts in that precise and detailed way. The whole tendency of modern prose is away from concreteness. Now analyse these two sentences a little more closely. The first contains forty-nine words but only sixty syllables, and all its words are those of everyday life. The second contains thirty-eight words of ninety syllables: eighteen of its words are from Latin roots, and one from Greek. The first sentence contains six vivid images, and only one phrase ("time and chance") that could be called vague. The second contains not a single fresh, arresting phrase, and in spite of its ninety syllables it gives only a shortened version of the meaning contained in the first. Yet without a doubt it is the second kind of sentence that is gaining ground in modern English. I do not want to exaggerate. This kind of writing is not universal, and outcrops of simplicity will occur here and there in the worst-written page. Still, if you or I were told to write a few lines on the uncertainty of human fortunes, we should probably come much nearer to my imaginary sentence than to the one from *Ecclesiastes*.

As I have tried to show, modern writing at its worst does not consist in picking out words for the sake of their meaning and inventing images in order to make the meaning clearer. It consists in gumming together long strips of words which have already been set in order by someone else, and making the results presentable by sheer humbug. The attraction of this way of writing is that it is easy. It is easier—even quicker, once you have the habit—to say *In my opinion it is not an unjustifiable assumption that* than to say *I think*. If you use ready-made phrases, you not only don't have to hunt about for words; you also don't have to bother with the rhythms of your sentences, since these phrases are generally so arranged as to be more or less euphonious. When you are composing in a hurry—when you are dictating to a stenographer, for instance, or making a public speech—it is natural to fall into a pretentious, Latinized style. Tags like *a consideration which we should do well to bear in mind* or *a conclusion to which all of us would readily assent* will save many a sentence from coming down with a bump. By using stale metaphors, similes and idioms, you save much mental effort, at the cost of leaving your meaning vague, not only for your reader but for yourself. This is the significance of mixed metaphors. The sole aim of a metaphor is to call up a visual image. When these images clash—as in *The Fascist octopus has sung its swan song, the jackboot is thrown into the melting pot*—it can be taken as certain that the writer is not seeing a mental image of the objects he is naming; in other words he is not really thinking. Look again at the examples I gave at the beginning of this essay. Professor Laski (1) uses five negatives in fifty-three words. One of these is superfluous, making nonsense of the whole passage, and in addition there is the slip *alien* for akin, making further nonsense, and several avoidable pieces of clumsiness which increase the general vagueness. Professor Hogben (2) plays ducks and drakes with a battery which is able to write prescriptions, and, while disapproving of the everyday phrase *put up with*, is unwilling to look *egregious* up in the dictionary and see what it means; (3), if one takes an uncharitable attitude towards it, is simply meaningless: probably one could work out its intended meaning by reading the whole of the article in which it occurs. In (4), the writer knows more or less what he wants to say, but an accumulation of stale phrases chokes him like tea leaves blocking a sink. In (5), words and meaning have almost parted company. People who write in this manner usually have a general emotional meaning—they dislike one thing and want to express solidarity with another—but they are not interested in the detail of what they are saying. A scrupulous writer, in every sentence that he writes, will ask himself at least four questions, thus: What am I trying to say? What words will express it? What image or idiom will make it clearer? Is this image fresh enough to have an effect? And he will probably ask himself two more: Could I put it more shortly? Have I said anything that is avoidably ugly? But you are not obliged to go to all this trouble. You can shirk it by simply throwing your mind open and letting the ready-made phrases come crowding in. They will construct your sentences for you—even think your thoughts for you, to a certain extent—and at need they will perform the important service of partially concealing your meaning even from yourself. It is at this point that the special connection between politics and the debasement of language becomes clear.

In our time it is broadly true that political writing is bad writing. Where it is not true, it will generally be found that the writer is some kind of rebel, expressing his private opinions and not a "party line." Orthodoxy, of whatever color, seems to demand a lifeless, imitative style. The political dialects to be found in pamphlets, leading articles, manifestos, White Papers and the speeches of under-secretaries do, of course, vary from party to party, but they are all alike in that one almost never finds in them a fresh, vivid, home-made turn of speech. When one watches some tired hack on the platform mechanically repeating the familiar phrases—*bestial atrocities, iron heel, bloodstained tyranny, free peoples of the world, stand shoulder to shoulder*—one often has a curious feeling that one is not watching a live human being but some kind of dummy: a feeling which suddenly becomes stronger at moments when the light catches the speaker's spectacles and turns them into blank discs which seem to have no eyes behind them. And this is not altogether fanciful. A speaker who uses that kind of phraseology has gone some distance towards turning himself into a machine. The appropriate noises are coming out of his larynx, but his brain is not involved as it would be if he were choosing his words for himself. If the speech he is making is one that he is accustomed to make over and over again, he may be almost unconscious of what he is saying, as one is when one utters the responses in church. And this reduced state of consciousness, if not indispensable, is at any rate favorable to political conformity.

In our time, political speech and writing are largely the defence of the indefensible. Things like the continuance of British rule in India, the Russian purges and deportations, the dropping of the atom bombs on Japan, can indeed be defended, but only by arguments which are too brutal for most people to face, and which do not square with the professed aims of political parties. Thus political language has to consist largely of euphemism, question-begging and sheer cloudy vagueness. Defenceless villages are bombarded from the air, the inhabitants driven out into the countryside, the cattle machine-gunned, the huts set on fire with incendiary bullets: this is called *pacification*. Millions of peasants are robbed of their farms and sent trudging along the roads with no more than they can carry: this is called *transfer of population* or *rectification of frontiers*. People are imprisoned for years without trial or shot in the back of the neck or sent to die of scurvy in Arctic lumber camps: this is called *elimination of unreliable elements*. Such phraseology is needed if one wants to name things without calling up mental pictures of them. Consider for instance some comfortable English professor defending Russian totalitarianism. He cannot say outright, "I believe in killing off your opponents when you can get good results by doing so." Probably, therefore, he will say something like this:

"While freely conceding that the Soviet régime exhibits certain features which the humanitarian may be inclined to deplore, we must, I think, agree that a cetrain curtailment of the right to political opposition is an unavoidable concomitant of transitional periods, and that the rigors which the Russian people have been called upon to undergo have been amply justified in the sphere of concrete achievement."

The inflated style is itself a kind of euphemism. A mass of Latin words falls upon the facts like soft snow, blurring the outlines and covering up all the details. The great enemy of clear language is insincerity. When there is a gap between one's real and one's declared aims, one turns as it were instinctively to long words and exhausted idioms, like a cuttlefish squirting out ink. In our age there is no such thing as "keeping out of politics." All issues are political issues, and politics itself is a mass of lies, evasions, folly, hatred and schizophrenia. When the general atmosphere is bad, language must suffer. I should expect to find—this is a guess which I have not sufficient knowledge to verify— that the German, Russian and Italian languages have all deteriorated in the last ten or fifteen years, as a result of dictatorship.

But if thought corrupts language, language can also corrupt thought. A bad usage can spread by tradition and imitation, even among people who should and do know better. The debased language that I have been discussing is in some ways very convenient. Phrases like *a not unjustifiable assumption, leaves much to be desired, would serve no good purpose, a consideration which we should do well to bear in mind*, are a continuous temptation, a packet of aspirins always at one's elbow. Look back through this essay, and for certain you will find that I have again and again committed the very faults I am protesting against. By this morning's post I have received a pamphlet dealing with conditions in Germany. The author tells me that he "felt impelled" to write it. I open it at random, and here is almost the first sentence that I see: "[The Allies] have an opportunity not only of achieving a radical transformation of Germany's social and political structure in such a way as to avoid a nationalistic reaction in Germany itself, but at the same time of laying the foundations of a cooperative and unified Europe." You see, he "feels impelled" to write—feels, presumably, that he has something new to say—and yet his words, like cavalry horses answering the bugle, group themselves automatically into the familiar dreary pattern. This invasion of one's mind by read-made phrases (*lay the foundations, achieve a radical transformation*) can only be prevented if one is constantly on guard against them, and every such phrase anaesthetizes a portion of one's brain.

I said earlier that the decadence of our language is probably curable. Those who deny this would argue, if they produced an argument at all, that language merely reflects existing social conditions, and that we cannot influence its development by any direct tinkering with words and constructions. So far as the general tone or spirit of a language goes, this may be true, but it is not true in detail. Silly words and expressions have often disappeared, not through any evolutionary process but owing to the conscious action of a minority. Two recent examples were *explore every avenue* and *leave no stone unturned*, which were killed by the jeers of a few journalists. There is a long list of flyblown metaphors which could similarly be got rid of if enough people would interest themselves in the job; and it should also be possible to laugh the *not unformation* out of existence,* to reduce the amount of Latin and Greek in the average sentence, to drive out foreign phrases and strayed scientific words, and, in general, to make pretentiousness unfashionable. But all these are minor points. The defence of the English language implies more than this, and perhaps it is best to start by saying what it does *not* imply.

To begin with it has nothing to do with archaism, with the salvaging of obsolete words and turns of speech, or with the setting up of a "standard English" which must never be departed from. On the contrary, it is especially concerned with the scrapping of every word or idiom which has outworn its usefulness. It has nothing to do with correct grammar and syntax, which are of no importance so long as one makes one's meaning clear, or with the avoidance of Americanisms, or with having what is called a "good prose style." On the other hand it is not concerned with fake simplicity and the attempt to make written English colloquial. Nor does it even imply in every case preferring the Saxon word to the Latin one, though it does imply using the fewest and shortest words that will cover one's meaning. What is above all needed is to let the meaning choose the word, and not the other way about. In prose, the worst thing one can do with words is to surrender to them. When you think of a concrete object, you think wordlessly, and then, if you want to describe the thing you have been visualizing

---

* One can cure oneself of the *not un-* formation by memorizing this sentence: *A not unblack dog was chasing a not unsmall rabbit across a not ungreen field.*

you probably hunt about till you find the exact words that seem to fit it. When you think of something abstract you are more inclined to use words from the start, and unless you make a conscious effort to prevent it, the existing dialect will come rushing in and do the job for you, at the expense of blurring or even changing your meaning. Probably it is better to put off using words as long as possible and get one's meaning as clear as one can through pictures or sensations. Afterwards one can choose—not simply *accept*—the phrases that will best cover the meaning, and then switch round and decide what impression one's words are likely to make on another person. This last effort of the mind cuts out all stale or mixed images, all prefabricated phrases, needless repetitions, and humbug and vagueness generally. But one can often be in doubt about the effect of a word or a phrase, and one needs rules that one can rely on when instinct fails. I think the following rules will cover most cases:

(i)   Never use a metaphor, simile or other figure of speech which you are used to seeing in print.
(ii) Never use a long word where a short one will do.
(iii) If it is possible to cut a word out, always cut it out.
(iv) Never use the passive where you can use the active.
(v)   Never use a foreign phrase, a scientific word or a jargon word if you can think of an everyday English equivalent.
(vi) Break any of these rules sooner than say anything outright barbarous.

These rules sound elementary, and so they are, but they demand a deep change of attitude in anyone who has grown used to writing in the style now fashionable. One could keep all of them and still write bad English, but one could not write the kind of stuff that I quoted in those five specimens at the beginning of this article.

I have not here been considering the literary use of language, but merely language as an instrument for expressing and not for concealing or preventing thought. Stuart Chase and others have come near to claiming that all abstract words are meaningless, and have used this as a pretext for advocating a kind of political quietism. Since you don't know what Fascism is, how can you struggle against Fascism? One need not swallow such absurdities as this, but one ought to recognize that the present political chaos is connected with the decay of language, and that one can probably bring about some improvement by starting at the verbal end. If you simplify your English, you are freed from the worst follies of orthodoxy. You cannot speak any of the necessary dialects, and when you make a stupid remark its stupidity will be obvious, even to yourself. Political language—and with variations this is true of all political parties, from Conservatives to Anarchists—is designed to make lies sound truthful and murder respectable, and to give an appearance of solidity to pure wind. One cannot change this all in a moment, but one can at least change one's own habits, and from time to time one can even, if one jeers loudly enough, send some worn-out and useless phrase —some *jackboot, Achilles' heel, hotbed, melting pot, acid test, veritable inferno* or other lump of verbal refuse—into the dustbin where it belongs.

SUGGESTIONS FOR WRITING

1. To get the feel of using your thesis to connect beginning and end, and to see how even the work of experienced writers may sometimes be improved, write a good, clear thesis sentence for each of the four essays in this chapter. As you go, match each of your thesis sentences with a "restated thesis" that would serve to open the end paragraph. Example:

   Wisdom is more precious than rubies.
   Wisdom, then, is a great deal more precious and useful than rubies.

2. Write a smooth, complete middle paragraph for one (or more) of the following topic sentences:
   (a) Writing is more difficult than one might think.
   (b) The translator walks a tightrope between the literal and the poetic.
   (c) Idealism is a broader kind of realism.
   (d) Language can conceal as well as reveal.

3. To grasp how an able essayist unfolds his thought paragraph by paragraph, take one of the essays in this chapter and draw up a list of topic sentences—one for each of the paragraphs. Use the actual topic sentence when it seems to cover everything in the paragraph; when it seems inadequate, expand and sharpen it in your own words. First, set down the writer's thesis as clearly as you can in your own words. Then write down the topic sentence for each succeeding paragraph, as it announces the paragraph's own little thesis. Be particularly careful in devising the topic sentence of the concluding paragraph; ideally, it should include and reaffirm the central thesis of the whole essay. Had you been an editor, would you have recommended that these authors reparagraph or rephrase their conclusions?

4. Write an essay, illustrating from some experience or observation of your own that "The force of idealism is wasted when it does not recognize the reality of things."

5. Write an essay on any point suggested by Sapir, Foster, Santayana, or Orwell, using (or attacking) a thesis such as one of the following:

    (a) The foreign language requirement should be abolished.

    (b) This campus needs a Don Quixote.

    (c) All cultures are different.

    (d) The "Students for X" conceal their real intentions.

Five
Sentences in Exposition

Now that we have the structure of the essay in mind—its organizing thesis, its frame of beginning, middle, and end, its march of paragraphs —we will look at varieties of the sentence, to give your style individuality. You can orchestrate your sentences infinitely in differing lengths and loops and chords, but three modes stand out:

I.   Coordination

Here you deal in straightforward statements, all on the same level, either separately, in short sentences, or joined together by semicolons or conjunctions such as *and* or *but.*

> All men are beasts. They feed, couple, sleep, and die; they satisfy only themselves. But they have souls too, and these can move them to greatness.

The quality here is forcefulness, like a hammer on an anvil. This mode frequently produces the short epigrammatic sentence: "Writing makes thought visible."

II.   Subordination.

Here you attach a number of statements to one principal statement, putting them in a "sub" order to it, tying them in with prepositions, relative pronouns, adverbs, or any other subordinating word—*with, in, who, which, when, after.*

> Man of today, the atomic manipulator, the aeronaut who flies faster than sound, has precisely the same brain and body as his ancestors of twenty thousand years ago who painted the last Ice Age mammoths on the walls of caves in France.

The main statement is *Man has the same brain and body;* all the rest is *subordinate* to it.

III.   Parallelism

You put parallel thoughts in parallel constructions. Witness the following example of introductory phrases in parallel:

> Having studied hard,
> having gone to bed early,
> having reviewed the main points in the morning,
>   she still wrote a poor exam.

Or you may use paralleling coordinators such as *either/or, not only/ but also, first/second/third.*

> He is *either* an absolute piker *or* a fool.
> This is true *not only* of the young voters *but also* of their parents.

Finally, the richest style is one that can move among these three modes to vary the short and emphatic sentence against the long and interestingly subordinated one.

As you read the five writers in this group, notice which mode each seems to favor. In their different ways, Nietzsche, Schweitzer, and Chesterton are mostly coordinators. Nietzsche's opening statements, for instance, are all coordinate, and their force is evident. Eiseley and Canby are subordinators, and their writing is more graceful. The subordinator, of course, must parallel his thoughts extensively to keep his long sentences clear. All five writers, however, use parallels as their thoughts require. See if you can mark off one good paralleled sentence in each.

FRIEDRICH W. NIETZSCHE

Friedrich W. Nietzsche (1844–1900), German philosopher, son of one Lutheran pastor, and grandson of two more, shook the world in 1882 by declaring God dead in *The Joyful Science (Die Fröhliche Wissenschaft)*, the book from which this selection comes. He taught philosophy at Basel, became a Swiss citizen, and befriended his older German compatriot, Richard Wagner, who was also living in Switzerland. He based his first book, *The Birth of Tragedy* (1872), mostly on Wagner's operas. His *Thus Spake Zarathustra (Also Sprach Zarathustra,* 1883-84) reiterates the death of God in a series of imaginative visions, quite unrelated to the historical Zarathustra (Zoroaster, sixth century B.C.) of whom Schweitzer speaks in the essay that follows.

WHAT PRESERVES THE SPECIES?

In this vigorous iconoclastic assertion, Nietzsche carries Darwin's "survival of the fittest" to its logical conclusion. Can you agree that "the new is always *the evil,*" by which society must be awakened? What in contemporary life would seem to agree with Nietzsche? Notice how his coordinate style enforces his thought.

The strongest and most evil spirits have so far advanced humanity the most: they have always rekindled the drowsing passions—all ordered society puts the passions to sleep; they have always reawakened the sense of comparison, of contradiction, of joy in the new, the daring, and the untried; they force men to meet opinion with opinion, model with model; for the most part by arms, by the overthrow of boundary stones, and by offense to the pieties, but also by new religions and moralities. The same "malice" is to be found in every teacher and preacher of the new. . . . The new is always *the evil,* as that which wants to conquer, to overthrow the old boundary stones and the old pieties; and only the old is the good. The good men of every age are those who dig the old ideas deep down and bear fruit with them, the husbandmen of the spirit. But all land is finally exhausted, and the plow of evil must always return.

There is a fundamentally erroneous doctrine in contemporary morality, celebrated particularly in England: according to this, the judgments "good" and "evil" are condensations of the experiences concerning "expedient" and "inexpedient"; what is called good preserves the species, while what is called evil is harmful to the species. In truth, however, the evil urges are expedient and indispensable and preserve the species to as high a degree as the good ones—only their function is different.

ALBERT SCHWEITZER

Albert Schweitzer (1875–1965), like Nietzsche the son of a Lutheran minister, earned a doctorate in theology at Berlin. But he pursued a parallel career as organist and musicologist, writing on organ building and playing, and, in two volumes in French, on the poetry of Bach's cantatas, working simultaneously on *The Quest for the Historical Jesus* (1906). But, in 1905, he announced a decision of ten years earlier: after a decade devoted to music and scholarship, and another decade in studying medicine so he could go to French Equatorial Africa and found a hospital, he would repay God for his tremendous gifts of intellectual and physical vigor. He built his hospital at Lambaréné in 1913 and maintained it for the rest of his life, with the tireless assistance of his wife, also a gifted historical scholar, who joined him in studying medicine.

THE EVOLUTION OF ETHICS

In an application of Darwinian thinking quite different from Nietzsche's, Schweitzer argues that human ethics has evolved, and proceeds to trace that evolutionary history. Note especially his contrast of affirmation and negation as a way of classifying philosophies, and the crucial tension between egoism and altruism. What are the limits of altruism? What would Schweitzer say to the question of suicide—the right to take one's own life?

In a very general sense, ethics is the name we give to our concern for good behavior. We feel an obligation to consider not only our own personal well-being but also that of others and of human society as a whole, and it is in the extension of this notion of solidarity with others that the first evolution of ethics is to be seen.

For the primitive man the circle of solidarity is limited to those whom he can look upon as his blood relatives—that is to say, the members of his tribe, who are to him his family. I am speaking from experience. In my hospital I have primitives. When I happen to ask a hospitalized tribesman, who is not himself bedridden, to render little services to a bedridden patient, he will consent only if the latter belongs to his tribe. If not, he will answer me candidly: "This, no brother for me," and neither attempts to persuade him nor threats will make him do this favor for a stranger.

However, as man starts reflecting upon himself and his behavior toward others, he gradually realizes that all men are his brothers and neighbors. Slowly he reaches a point where he sees the circle of his responsibilities enlarged to comprise all human beings with whom he is in contact.

In the history of man, this idea of responsibility toward others has been wholly or partially formulated in various cultures at various times. It was reached by the Chinese thinkers: Lao-tse, born in 604 B.C.; Kung Fu-tse (Confucius), 551–479 B.C.; Meng-tse, 372–289 B.C.; Tchouang-tse, fourth century B.C. It was also proclaimed by the Israelite prophets of the eighth century B.C.: Amos, Hosea, and Isaiah. As proclaimed by Jesus and Saint Paul, the idea that man obligates himself to all human beings became an integral part of the Christian system of ethics.

For the great thinkers of India, too, whether they belonged to Brahmanism, Buddhism, or Hinduism, the idea of the brotherhood of man was included in their metaphysical notion of existence, but they had difficulty giving it the proper importance in their ethics because they could not abolish the barriers erected between men in India by the different castes sanctioned by tradition.

Zarathustra, who lived in about the seventh century B.C., was also prevented from reaching the notion of the full brotherhood of man because he had to differentiate between those who believed in Ormuzd, the god of Light and Good, and the nonbelievers who remained in the power of devils. This forced the believers to fight for the coming of the reign of Ormuzd and to consider the nonbelievers as enemies and treat them as such. To understand this, one must remember that the believers were Bactrian tribes who had become sedentary and aspired to live as honest and peaceful families, while the nonbelievers were nomadic tribes who dwelt in the desert and lived from pillage.

Plato and Aristotle and the other thinkers of the classic period of Greek philosophy limited their consideration to the Greek freeman, who did not have to earn his subsistence. All those who did not belong to this aristocracy were dismissed as men of inferior quality in whom there was no need to be concerned.

It was not until the second epoch of Greek thought, when the simultaneous blossoming of Stoicism and Epicureanism occurred, that the idea of the equality of men and of the sympathy which attaches us to all human beings was recognized by these two schools. The most remarkable protagonist of this new conception was the Stoic Panaetius, who lived in the second century B.C. He was the prophet of humanism, and even though the idea of the brotherhood of man never became popular in antiquity, the very fact that philosophy had proclaimed it as a concept dictated by reason was of great importance for its future.

However, this concept has never enjoyed the full authority which it deserves. Down to our time, it has ceaselessly been compromised by the stressing of differences—differences of race, of religious beliefs, and of nationalities—which turn our fellow man into a stranger to whom we owe nothing but indifference, if not contempt.

As we trace the evolution of ethics, we are aware of the influence exerted by the various concepts of the material world. There are the affirmative concepts which insist that interest must be taken in material matters and in the existence we lead on this earth. Others, on the contrary, advocate a negative attitude, urging that we detach ourselves from whatever has to do with the world, including our own existence on earth. Affirmation conforms with our natural feeling. Negation contradicts it. Affirmation invites us to be at home in this world and to throw ourselves voluntarily into action; negation requires that we live in the world as strangers and that we choose a passive role. By its very nature, ethics is affiliated with affirmation. One must be active if one is to serve the ideal of Good. An affirmative concept of the world produces a favorable climate for the development of ethics, while negation, on the contrary, hampers it. Negation of the world was professed by the thinkers of India and by the Christians of antiquity and of the Middle Ages; affirmation by the Chinese thinkers, the Israelite prophets, Zarathustra, and the European thinkers of the Renaissance and of the modern day.

In the thinkers of India, this negative concept of the world was the result of their conviction that true existence is immaterial, immutable, and external and that the worldly existence is fictitious, deceitful, and transient. The world that we consider as real was for them but a mirage of the immaterial world in time and space. By taking interest in this phantasmagoria and in the part he plays in it, they argued, man made a mistake. The only behavior compatible with the true knowledge of the nature of existence is nonactivity.

To a degree, nonactivity does have ethical characteristics. By detaching himself from worldly matters, man renounces the egotism that material interests and mere covetousness arouse in him. Furthermore, an essential aspect of nonactivity is nonviolence.

The thinkers of Brahmanism, of Samkhya, of Jainism, as well as of Buddhism, exalt nonviolence, which they call ahimsa; indeed, they consider it as the sublime principle. However, it is imperfect and incomplete because it concedes to man the egotism to be preoccupied entirely with his salvation. It does not command him in the name of compassion but in the name of metaphysical theories. It demands merely abstention from evil, rather than the positive activity inspired by the notion of Good.

Only a system of ethics affiliated with the affirmation of the world can be natural and complete. Buddha, who rises against the cold Brahmanic doctrine by preaching pity, cannot completely resist the temptation to forgo the principle of nonactivity. He gives in, more than once, unable to keep himself from accomplishing acts of charity or from recommending them to his disciples. Under the cover of ethics the affirmation of the world carries on, in India, a persistent struggle against the principle of nonactivity. In Hinduism, which is a religious movement against the exigencies of Brahmanism, affirmation is recognized as the equal of nonactivity. The reconciliation of the two is set forth in the *Bhagavad Gita.*

Man can believe that he is authorized to take part in the material world only as a spectator. But likewise he has the right to believe that he is called to play an active part. Activity, then, is justified by the spirit which guides it. The man who practices it with the intention of accomplishing the will of God is as right as he who raises the question of nonactivity. Nowadays, the thinkers of India make great concessions to the principle of activity, claiming that it is found in the Upanishads. This is true. The explanation is that the Aryans of India in ancient times, as we learn it from the Veda, had an existence penetrated with naïve *joie de vivre.* The Brahmanic doctrine of negation of the world appears side by side with the concept of affirmation only in the Upanishads, the sacred texts of the first thousand years B.C.

Christianity in early times and in the Middle Ages professed negation of the world without, however, reaching the extremes of nonactivity. Its denial of the world was of a different nature from that of the thinkers of India: to the early Christians the world was not a phantasmagoria, it was an imperfect world destined to be transformed into the perfect world of the kingdom of God. The idea of the kingdom of God was created by the Israelite prophets of the eighth century B.C.

In announcing the imminence of the transformation of the material world into the kingdom of God, Jesus exhorted men to seek the perfection required for participation in the new world. He asked man to detach himself from this world, the better to be preoccupied by the practice of Good. He allowed man to detach himself from material things, but not from his duties toward other men. In Jesus' ethics, activity kept all its rights and all its obligations. This is where Christianity differs from Buddha's religion, with which it shares the idea of compassion. Because it is animated by the spirit of activity, Christian ethics has a certain affinity with the affirmation of the world.

The transformation of the world into the kingdom of God was what the early Christians were looking for immediately, but it never occurred.

During antiquity and the Middle Ages, Christianity remained in a situation of having to lose hope in this world, without the compensating hope, which had sustained the early Christians, of seeing the new world at hand. In the Middle Ages there was no enthusiastic affirmation of the world; actually this did not take place until the Renaissance. Christianity identified itself with this new enthusiastic affirmation of the world during the sixteenth and seventeenth centuries. Renaissance ethics—apart from the ideal of perfecting oneself, which came from Jesus—attempted subsequently to create new and better material and spiritual conditions for the existence of human society. From then on, Christian ethics found a goal for its activity and so reached its full bloom. From the union of the Christian and the Renaissance enthusiasm for the world is born the civilization in which we live and which we have to maintain and improve.

In the first century of the Christian era, thinkers of Stoicism—Seneca, Epictetus, and the emperor Marcus Aurelius—following the steps of Panaetius, the creator of the idea of humanism, came to consider Love as the virtue of virtues. Their system of ethics is about the same as that of the great Chinese thinkers. They have in common not only the principle of Love, but also the conviction that it proceeds from reason and is thoroughly reasonable.

During the first and second centuries of the Christian era, the Greco-Roman philosophy seemed to profess the same ethical ideal as that of Christianity. The possibility of agreement between the ancient and Christian worlds existed, but it did not happen. Ethical Stoicism did not become popular. Moreover, it accused Christianity of being a superstition because Christianity claimed that a divine revelation had taken place in Jesus Christ, and was awaiting the miraculous coming of a new world. Christianity, on the other hand, scorned philosophy as a guiding wisdom for this world. What separated Christianity and Stoicism was the fact that the Greco-Roman philosophy adhered to the idea of the affirmation of the world, whereas Christianity adhered to the idea of its negation. No agreement was possible.

Agreement did occur, but only after centuries. When Christianity became more familiar with the enthusiastic affirmation of the world, which the Renaissance had bequeathed to European thought; it at the same time became acquainted with ethical Stoicism and noted with surprise that Jesus' principle of Love had also been stated as a rational truth. Thus it was deduced that the fundamental ideas of religion were revealed truths, confirmed afterwards by reason. Among the thinkers who felt that they belonged to both Christianity and Stoicism were Erasmus and Hugo Grotius.

Under the influence of Christianity, philosophy's ethics acquired an enthusiasm that it had not possessed earlier. Under the influence of philosophy, Christian ethics, on the other hand, started reflecting upon what it owed itself and upon what it should accomplish in this world. Thus was born a spirit which did not allow the ethics of Love any longer to tolerate injustice, cruelties, and superstitions. Torture was abolished, the scourge of the witchcraft trials ceased. Inhuman laws gave way to others more human. A reform without precedent in the previous history of humanity had begun and was accomplished in the first enthusiasm of the discovery that the principle of Love is also taught by reason.

To demonstrate the rationality of altruism, philosophers of the eighteenth century, among whom are Hartley, Baron Holbach, Helvetius, and Bentham, thought that it was enough to show that love of others had a utility value. The Chinese thinkers and the representatives of ethical Stoicism admitted the utility value, but also insisted on other values. According to the eighteenth-century thinkers, altruism would be a well-understood egotism, taking into account the fact that the well-being of the individual and of society can be guaranteed only by the self-sacrifice which men make for their fellow men.

Kant and David Hume refuted this superficial thesis. Kant, in order to defend the dignity of ethics, went so far as to pretend that its utility ought not to be taken into consideration. Obvious as it is, it must not be admitted as a motive of ethics. Ethics, according to the doctrine of the categorical imperative, rules, absolutely. It is our conscience which reveals to us what is Good and what is evil. We have but to obey the moral law that we carry within ourselves to gain the certitude that we not only belong to the world as it appears to us in time and space, but that we are at the same time citizens of the spiritual world.

Hume, in order to refute the utilitarian thesis, proceeded in an empirical way. He analyzed the motives of ethics and came to the conclusion that ethics is primarily a matter of feeling. Nature, he argued, endowed us with the faculty of sympathy, which permits and obliges us to feel the joy, apprehensions, and sufferings of others as if they were our own. We are, after an image employed by Hume, like strings vibrating in unison with others. It is this sympathy which leads us to devotion toward others and to the desire to contribute to their well-being and to the well-being of society.

After Hume, philosophy—if we set aside the enterprise of Nietzsche —did not dare seriously to doubt the fact that ethics is primarily a matter of compassion.

But, if this is the case, is ethics capable of defining and setting a limit to the obligations of self-sacrifice, and thereby placing egoism and altruism in accord, as was attempted by the utilitarian theories?

Hume is not much preoccupied by this question. The philosophers who followed him likewise did not think it necessary to take into consideration the consequences of the principle of self-sacrifice through compassion. It is as if they had the presentiment that these consequences might prove to be a little disturbing.

They are indeed. The ethic of self-sacrifice by compassion no longer has the characteristic of a law. It no longer comprises any clearly established and clearly formulated commandments. It is thoroughly subjective, because it leaves to each one the responsibility of deciding how much he will sacrifice himself.

And not only does it cease to give precise commandments: it is no longer satisfied, as the law must be, by the limitations of the possible. It constantly forces us to attempt the impossible, to carry devotion to others so far as to endanger our own existence. In the horrible times we have lived through, there were many of these perilous situations and many persons who sacrificed themselves for others. Even in daily life, the ethic of self-sacrifice asks from each of us that we abdicate selfish interests and renounce advantages for the sake of others. Alas, we too often succeed in silencing our conscience, the guardian of our feeling of responsibility.

How many are the struggles in which the ethic of self-sacrifice abandons us to ourselves! It is seldom that the heads of firms give a job, through compassion, to the man who needs it most, rather than to the man who is most qualified. But evil unto them who think themselves authorized, by such experiences, *never* to take into account the principle of compassion.

A final consequence is to be drawn from the principle of self-sacrifice: it does not allow us to be preoccupied only by human beings, but obliges us to have the same behavior toward all living beings whose fate may be influenced by us. They also are our fellows, for they, too, aspire to happiness. They know fear and suffering, and they dread annihilation.

The man who has kept intact his sensibility finds it quite natural to have pity on all living beings. Why does not philosophy at long last recognize that our behavior toward all life should be an integral part of the ethics which it teaches?

The reason is very simple. Philosophy fears, and rightly so, that this huge enlargement of the circle of our responsibilities will take away from ethics the small hope which it still has to formulate reasonable and satisfactory commandments.

In fact, if we are preoccupied by the fate of all living beings with whom we come in contact, we face conflicts more numerous and more disturbing than those of devotion toward human beings. We are constantly in situations which compel us to harm other creatures or affect their lives. The farmer cannot let all his animals survive. He can keep only those he can feed and the breeding of which assures him necessary income. In many instances, there is the obligation of sacrificing some lives to save others. Whoever shelters a crippled bird finds it necessary to kill insects to feed him. In so doing, he makes an arbitrary decision. By what right does he sacrifice a multitude of lives in order to save a single life? He must also make an arbitrary choice when he exterminates animals which he thinks are harmful, in order to protect others.

It is then incumbent upon each of us to judge whether we must harm or kill, and thus become, by necessity, guilty. We should seek forgiveness by never missing an occasion to rescue living creatures.

What an advance it would be if men started to reflect upon the kindness due all creatures and refrained from harming them by carelessness! We must intensify the struggle against inhuman traditions and feelings remaining in our time if our civilization is to keep any respect for itself. Among inhuman customs which our civilization should no longer tolerate, I must name two: bullfights with their inevitable death, and hunting for sport.

It is finally the exigency of compassion with all beings which makes ethics as complete as it should be.

There is another great change in the evolution of ethics: today it cannot expect help from a concept of the world which justifies what it teaches.

In the past, ethics seemed convinced that it was only requiring a behavior in harmony with the knowledge of the true nature of the world. On this conviction are based not only the religions, but also the rationalist philosophy of the seventeenth and eighteenth centuries.

But it happens that the concept of the world that ethics called upon was the result of the optimistic interpretation of this very world which ethics gave and is still giving. It loaned to the universal will qualities and intentions which give satisfaction to its own way of feeling and judging.

But in the course of the nineteenth century, research which seeks only objective truth was obliged to face the evidence that ethics had nothing to expect from an ever-closer knowledge of the world. The progress of science consisted in a more precise ascertainment of the processes of nature. It allowed us to use the energies of the universe. But, at the same time, it obliged us to renounce an understanding of the intentions of the universe. The world offers us the disconcerting spectacle of the will to live in conflict with itself. One life maintains itself at the cost of another. The world is horror within magnificence, absurdity within intelligibility, suffering within joy.

How can the ethic of self-sacrifice maintain itself without being justified by an adequate concept of the world? It seems doomed to sink into skepticism. This, however, will not be its fate.

In the beginning, ethics needed to call upon a concept of the world which gave it satisfaction. Having reached the knowledge that the fundamental principle is devotion to others, it becomes fully aware of itself, and thereby self-sufficient.

We are now able to understand its origins and its foundation by meditating upon the world and upon ourselves. We lack a complete and satisfactory knowledge of the world. We are reduced to merely ascertaining that everything in it is living, as we ourselves are, and that all life is a mystery. Our true knowledge of the world consists in being penetrated by the mystery of existence and of life. This mystery becomes ever more mysterious by the progress of scientific research. To be penetrated by the mystery of life corresponds to what is called in the language of the mystic "learned ignorance."

The fundamental idea in our conscience, to which we come back each time we want to reach comprehension of ourselves and of our situation in the world, is: I am life wanting to live, surrounded by life wanting to live. Meditating upon life, I feel the obligation to respect any will-to-live around me as equal to mine and as having a mysterious value.

A fundamental idea of Good then consists in preserving life, in favoring it, in wanting to raise it to its highest value, and evil consists in annihilating life, injuring it, and impeding its growth.

The principle of this veneration of life corresponds to the one of Love, which has been discovered by religion and philosophy seeking an understanding of the fundamental notion of Good.

The term Reverence for Life is larger and at the same time dimmer than the term Love. But it bears within itself the same potentialities. The essentially philosophical notion of Good has the advantage of being more complete than the notion of Love. Love comprises only our obligations toward other beings, but not toward ourselves. It is, for instance, impossible to deduce from it the notion of veracity, the primary quality of the ethical personality in addition to the one of Love. The respect which man owes to his own life obliges him to be faithful to himself by renouncing any self-deceit and by becoming himself in the noblest and deepest way.

By having reverence for life, we enter into a spiritual relation with the world. The absolute is so abstract that we can have no communion with it. It is not given to us to serve the creative will, infinite and unfathomable, by comprehending its nature and its intentions. But we come into spiritual contact with it by the feeling of the mystery of life and by devoting ourselves to all the living beings whom we are able to serve. The ethics which obliges us to be concerned only with men and with society cannot have this same significance. Only a universal ethics which obliges us to be occupied with all beings puts us in a complete relation with the universe and the will manifested in it. In the world, the will to live is in conflict with itself. In us it wants, by a mystery that we do not understand, to be at peace with itself. In the world it manifests itself; in us it reveals itself. To be other than the world is our spiritual destiny. By conforming to it we live our existence instead of submitting to it. By practicing reverence for life we become good, deep, and alive.

LOREN EISELEY

Loren Eiseley (1907–) was born in Nebraska and educated at the University of Nebraska. He has been professor of anthropology, chairman of the department, and dean at the University of Pennsylvania, and Curator of Early Man at the university's museum. His principal books on evolution are *The Immense Journey* (1957) and *Darwin's Century* (1958). In *Francis Bacon and the Modern Dilemma* (1962), he considers the problem of scientific knowledge somewhat as Karl Popper does in "Utopia and Violence." His autobiography is entitled *All the Strange Hours* (1975).

THE REAL SECRET OF PILTDOWN

This essay, published in 1955, and the hoax it describes testify to the enduring human curiosity about our origins. Anthropologists, such as Louis S. B. Leakey and his wife and son, have uncovered evidence thrusting human origins back unimaginable distances since Eiseley wrote, and since Darwin and Wallace pondered the size of the human brain. But Wallace's shattering question remains: if we have evolved only by an edge of survival, how did the brain develop beyond the needs of survival? Compare Wallace's assumptions, and Eiseley's, with those of Elaine Morgan, Robert Ardrey, and Leakey. Note how Eiseley's style, and mind, turn naturally to subordination. Starting with a direct question and direct statements, he soon moves into elaboration: "A skull, a supposedly very ancient skull . . . ." And his prose swells to subordinative grandeur as, toward the end, he marvels at the galaxy overhead.

How did man get his brain? Many years ago Charles Darwin's great contemporary, and co-discover with him of the principle of natural selection, Alfred Russel Wallace, propounded that simple question. It is a question which has bothered evolutionists ever since, and when Darwin received his copy of an article Wallace had written on this subject he was obviously shaken. It is recorded that he wrote in anguish across the paper, "No!" and underlined the "No" three times heavily in a rising fervor of objection.

Today the question asked by Wallace and never satisfactorily answered by Darwin has returned to haunt us. A skull, a supposedly very ancient skull, long used as one of the most powerful pieces of evidence documenting the Darwinian position upon human evolution, has been proven to be a forgery, a hoax perpetrated by an unscrupulous but learned amateur. In the fall of 1953 the famous Piltdown cranium, known in scientific circles all over the world since its discovery in a gravel pit on the Sussex Downs in 1911, was jocularly dismissed by the world's press as the skull that had "made monkeys out of the anthropologists." Nobody remembered in 1953 that Wallace, the great evolutionist, had protested to a friend in 1913, "The Piltdown skull does not prove much, if anything!"

Why had Wallace made that remark? Why, almost alone among the English scientists of his time, had he chosen to regard with a dubious eye a fossil specimen that seemed to substantiate the theory to which he and Darwin had devoted their lives? He did so for one reason: he did not believe what the Piltdown skull appeared to reveal as to the nature of the process by which the human brain had been evolved. He did not believe in a skull which had a modern brain box attached to an apparently primitive face and given, in the original estimates, an antiquity of something over a million years.

Today we know that the elimination of the Piltdown skull from the growing list of valid human fossils in no way affects the scientific acceptance of the theory of evolution. In fact, only the circumstance that Piltdown had been discovered early, before we had a clear knowledge of the nature of human fossils and the techniques of dating them, made the long survival of this extraordinary hoax possible. Yet in the end it has been the press, absorbed in a piece of clever scientific detection, which has missed the real secret of Piltdown. Darwin saw in the rise of man, with his unique, time-spanning brain, only the undirected play of such natural forces as had created the rest of the living world of plants and animals. Wallace, by contrast, in the case of man, totally abandoned this point of view and turned instead toward a theory of a divinely directed control of the evolutionary process. The issue can be made clear only by a rapid comparison of the views of both men.

As everyone who has studied evolution knows, Darwin propounded the theory that since the reproductive powers of plants and animals potentially far outpace the available food supply, there is in nature a constant struggle for existence on the part of every living thing. Since animals vary individually, the most cleverly adapted will survive and leave offspring which will inherit, and in their turn enhance, the genetic endowment they have received from their ancestors. Because the struggle for life is incessant, this unceasing process promotes endless slow changes in bodily form, as living creatures are subjected to different natural environments, different enemies, and all the vicissitudes against which life has struggled down the ages.

Darwin, however, laid just one stricture on his theory: it could, he maintained, "render each organized being only as perfect or a little more perfect than other inhabitants of the same country." It could allow any animal only a relative superiority, never an absolute perfection—otherwise selection and the struggle for existence would cease to operate. To explain the rise of man through the slow, incremental gains of natural selection, Darwin had to assume a long struggle of man with man and tribe with tribe.

He had to make this assumption because man had far outpaced his animal associates. Since Darwin's theory of the evolutionary process is based upon the practical value of all physical and mental characters in the life struggle, to ignore the human struggle of man with man would have left no explanation as to how humanity by natural selection alone managed to attain an intellectual status so far beyond that of any of the animals with which it had begun its competition for survival.

To most of the thinkers of Darwin's day this seemed a reasonable explanation. It was a time of colonial expansion and ruthless business competition. Peoples of primitive cultures, small societies lost on the world's margins, seemed destined to be destroyed. It was thought that Victorian civilization was the apex of human achievement and that other races with different customs and ways of life must be biologically inferior to Western man. Some of them were even described as only slightly superior to apes. The Darwinians, in a time when there were no satisfactory fossils by which to demonstrate human evolution, were unconsciously minimizing the abyss which yawned between man and ape. In their anxiety to demonstrate our lowly origins they were throwing modern natives into the gap as representing living "missing links" in the chain of human ascent.

It was just at this time that Wallace lifted a voice of lonely protest. The episode is a strange one in the history of science, for Wallace had, independently of Darwin, originally arrived at the same general conclusion as to the nature of the evolutionary process. Nevertheless, only a few years after the publication of Darwin's work, *The Origin of Species*, Wallace had come to entertain a point of view which astounded and troubled Darwin. Wallace, who had had years of experience with natives of the tropical archipelagoes, abandoned the idea that they were of mentally inferior cast. He did more. He committed the Darwinian heresy of maintaining that their mental powers were far in excess of what they really needed to carry on the simple food-gathering techniques by which they survived.

"How, then," Wallace insisted, "was an organ developed so far beyond the needs of its possessor? Natural selection could only have endowed the savage with a brain a little superior to that of an ape, whereas he actually possesses one but little inferior to that of the average member of our learned societies."

At a time when many primitive people were erroneously assumed to speak only in grunts or to chatter like monkeys, Wallace maintained his view of the high intellectual powers of natives by insisting that "the capacity of uttering a variety of distinct articulate sounds and of applying to them an almost infinite amount of modulation . . . is not in any way inferior to that of the higher races. An instrument has been developed in advance of the needs of its possessor."

Finally, Wallace challenged the whole Darwinian position on man by insisting that artistic, mathematical, and musical abilities could not be explained on the basis of natural selection and the struggle for existence. Something else, he contended, some unknown spiritual element, must have been at work in the elaboration of the human brain. Why else would men of simple cultures possess the same basic intellectual powers which the Darwinists maintained could be elaborated only by competitive struggle?

"If you had not told me you had made these remarks," Darwin said, "I should have thought they had been added by someone else. I differ grievously from you and am very sorry for it." He did not, however, supply a valid answer to Wallace's queries. Outside of murmuring about the inherited effects of habit—a contention without scientific validity today—Darwin clung to his original position. Slowly Wallace's challenge was forgotten and a great complacency settled down upon the scientific world.

For seventy years after the publication of *The Origin of Species* in 1859, there were only two finds of fossil human skulls which seemed to throw any light upon the Darwin-Wallace controversy. One was the discovery of the small-brained Java Ape Man, the other was the famous Piltdown or "dawn man." Both were originally dated as lying at the very beginning of the Ice Age, and, though, these dates were later to be modified, the skulls, for a very long time, were regarded as roughly contemporaneous and very old.

Two more unlike "missing links" could hardly be imagined. Though they were supposed to share a million-year antiquity, the one was indeed quite primitive and small-brained; the other, Piltdown, in spite of what seemed a primitive lower face, was surprisingly modern in brain. Which of these forms told the true story of human development? Was a large brain old? Had ages upon ages of slow, incremental, Darwinian increase produced it? The Piltdown skull seemed to suggest such a development.

Many were flattered to find their anthropoid ancestry seemingly removed to an increasingly remote past. If one looked at the Java Ape Man, one was forced to contemplate an ancestor, not terribly remote in time, who still had a face and a brain which hinted strongly of the ape. Yet, when by geological evidence this "erect walking ape-man" was finally assigned to a middle Ice Age antiquity, there arose the immediate possibility that Wallace could be right in his suspicion that the human brain might have had a surprisingly rapid development. By contrast, the Piltdown remains seemed to suggest a far more ancient and slow-paced evolution of man. The Piltdown hoaxer, in attaching an ape jaw to a human skull fragment, had, perhaps unwittingly, created a creature which supported the Darwinian idea of man, not too unlike the man of today, extending far back into pre-Ice Age times.

Which story was the right one? Until the exposé of Piltdown in 1953, both theories had to be considered possible and the two hopelessly unlike fossils had to be solemnly weighed in the same balance. Today Piltdown is gone. In its place we are confronted with the blunt statement of two modern scientists, M. R. A. Chance and A. P. Mead.

"No adequate explanation," they confess over eighty years after Darwin scrawled his vigorous "No!" upon Wallace's paper, "has been put forward to account for so large a cerebrum as that found in man."

We have been so busy tracing the tangible aspects of evolution in the *forms of animals* that our heads, the little globes which hold the midnight sky and the shining, invisible universes of thought, have been taken about as much for granted as the growth of a yellow pumpkin in the fall.

Now a part of this mystery as it is seen by the anthropologists of today lies in the relation of the brain to time. "If," Wallace had said, "researches in all parts of Europe and Asia fail to bring to light any proofs of man's presence far back in the Age of Mammals, *it will be at least a presumption that he came into existence at a much later date and by a more rapid process of development.*" If human evolution should prove to be comparatively rapid, "explosive" in other words, Wallace felt that his position would be vindicated, because such a rapid development of the brain would, he thought, imply a divinely directed force at work in man. In the 1870's when he wrote, however, human prehistory was largely an unknown blank. Today we can make a partial answer to Wallace's question. Since the exposure of the Piltdown hoax all of the evidence at our command—and it is considerable—points to man, in his present form, as being one of the youngest and newest of all earth's swarming inhabitants.

The Ice Age extends behind us in time for, at most, a million years. Though this may seem long to one who confines his studies to the written history of man, it is, in reality, a very short period as the student of evolution measures time. It is a period marked more by the extinction of some of the last huge land animals, like the hairy mammoth and the saber-toothed tiger, than it is by the appearance of new forms of life. To this there is only one apparent exception: the rise and spread of man over the Old World land mass.

Most of our knowledge of him—even in his massive-faced, beetle-browed stage—is now confined, since the loss of Piltdown, to the last half of the Ice Age. If we pass backward beyond this point we can find traces of crude tools, stone implements which hint that some earlier form of man was present here and there in Europe, Asia, and particularly Africa in the earlier half of Ice Age time, but to the scientist it is like peering into the mists floating over an unknown landscape. Here and there through the swirling vapor one catches a glimpse of a shambling figure, or a half-wild primordial face stares back at one from some momentary opening in the fog. Then, just as one grasps at a clue, the long gray twilight settles in and the wraiths and the half-heard voices pass away.

Nevertheless, particularly in Africa, a remarkable group of humanlike apes have been discovered: creatures with small brains and teeth of a remarkably human cast. Prominent scientists are still debating whether they are on the direct line of ascent to man or are merely near relatives of ours. Some, it is now obvious, existed too late in time to be our true ancestors, though this does not mean that their bodily characters may not tell us what the earliest anthropoids who took the human turn of the road were like.

These apes are not all similar in type or appearance. They are men and yet not men. Some are frailer-bodied, some have great, bone-cracking jaws and massive gorilloid crests atop their skulls. This fact leads us to another of Wallace's remarkable perceptions of long ago. With the rise of the truly human brain, Wallace saw that man had transferred to his machines and tools many of the alterations of parts that in animals take place through evolution of the body. Unwittingly, man had assigned to his machines the selective evolution which in the animal changes the nature of its bodily structure through the ages. Man of today, the atomic manipulator, the aeronaut who flies faster than sound, has precisely the same brain and body as his ancestors of twenty thousand years ago who painted the last Ice Age mammoths on the walls of caves in France.

To put it another way, it is man's ideas that have evolved and changed the world about him. Now, confronted by the lethal radiations of open space and the fantastic speeds of his machines, he has to invent new electronic controls that operate faster than his nerves, and he must shield his naked body against atomic radiation by the use of protective metals. Already he is physically antique in this robot world he has created. All that sustains him is that small globe of gray matter through which spin his ever-changing conceptions of the universe.

Yet, as Wallace, almost a hundred years ago, glimpsed this timeless element in man, he uttered one more prophecy. When we come to trace our history into the past, he contended, sooner or later we will come to a time when the body of man begins to differ and diverge more extravagantly in its appearance. Then, he wrote, we shall know that we stand close to the starting point of the human family. In the twilight before the dawn of the human mind, man will not have been able to protect his body from change and his remains will bear the marks of all the forces that play upon the rest of life. He will be different in his form. He will be, in other words, as variable in body as we know the South African man-apes to be.

Today, with the solution of the Piltdown enigma, we must settle the question of the time involved in human evolution in favor of Wallace, not Darwin; we need not, however, pursue the mystical aspects of Wallace's thought—since other factors yet to be examined may well account for the rise of man. The rapid fading out of archaeological evidence of tools in lower Ice Age times—along with the discovery of man-apes of human aspect but with ape-sized brains, yet possessing a diverse array of bodily characters—suggests that the evolution of the human brain was far more rapid than that conceived of in early Darwinian circles. At that time it was possible to hear the Eskimos spoken of as possible survivals of Miocene men of several million years ago. By contrast to this point of view, man and his rise now appear short in time—explosively short. There is every reason to believe that whatever the nature of the forces involved in the production of the human brain, a long slow competition of human group with human group or race with race would not have resulted in such similar mental potentialities among all peoples everywhere. Something—some other factor—has escaped our scientific attention.

There are certain strange bodily characters which mark man as being more than the product of a dog-eat-dog competition with his fellows. He possesses a peculiar larval nakedness, difficult to explain on survival principles; his periods of helpless infancy and childhood are prolonged; he has aesthetic impulses which, though they vary in intensity from individual to individual, appear in varying manifestations among all peoples. He is totally dependent, in the achievement of human status, upon the careful training he receives in human society.

Unlike a solitary species of animal, he cannot develop alone. He has suffered a major loss of precise instinctive controls of behavior. To make up for this biological lack, society and parents condition the infant, supply his motivations, and promote his long-drawn training at the difficult task of becoming a normal human being. Even today some individuals fail to make this adjustment and have to be excluded from society.

We are now in a position to see the wonder and terror of the human predicament: man is totally dependent on society. Creature of dream, he has created an invisible world of ideas, beliefs, habits, and customs which buttress him about and replace for him the precise instincts of the lower creatures. In this invisible universe he takes refuge, but just as instinct may fail an animal under some shift of environmental conditions, so man's cultural beliefs may prove inadequate to meet a new situation, or, on an individual level, the confused mind may substitute, by some terrible alchemy, cruelty for love.

The profound shock of the leap from animal to human status is echoing still in the depths of our subconscious minds. It is a transition which would seem to have demanded considerable rapidity of adjustment in order for human beings to have survived, and it also involved the growth of prolonged bonds of affection in the sub-human family, because otherwise its naked, helpless offspring would have perished.

It is not beyond the range of possibility that this strange reduction of instincts in man in some manner forced a precipitous brain growth as a compensation—something that had to be hurried for survival purposes. Man's competition, it would thus appear, may have been much less with his own kind than with the dire necessity of building about him a world of ideas to replace his lost animal environment. . . . He is a pedomorph, a creature with an extended childhood.

Modern science would go on to add that many of the characters of man, such as his lack of fur, thin skull, and globular head, suggest mysterious changes in growth rates which preserve, far into human maturity, foetal or infantile characters which hint that the forces creating man drew him fantastically out of the very childhood of his brutal forerunners. Once more the words of Wallace come back to haunt us: "We may safely infer that the savage possesses a brain capable, if cultivated and developed, of performing work of a kind and degree far beyond what he ever requires it to do."

As a modern man, I have sat in concert halls and watched huge audiences floating dazed on the voice of a great singer. Alone in the dark box I have heard far off as if ascending out of some black stairwell the guttural whisperings and bestial coughings out of which that voice arose. Again, I have sat under the slit dome of a mountain observatory and marveled, as the great wheel of the galaxy turned in all its midnight splendor, that the mind in the course of three centuries has been capable of drawing into its strange, nonspatial interior that world of infinite distance and multitudinous dimensions.

Ironically enough, science, which can show us the flints and the broken skulls of our dead fathers, has yet to explain how we have come so far so fast, nor has it any completely satisfactory answer to the question asked by Wallace long ago. Those who would revile us by pointing to an ape at the foot of our family tree grasp little of the awe with which the modern scientist now puzzles over man's lonely and supreme ascent. As one great student of paleoneurology, Dr. Tilly Edinger, recently remarked, "If man has passed through a Pithecanthropus phase, the evolution of his brain has been unique, not only in its result but also in its tempo. . . . Enlargement of the cerebral hemispheres by 50 per cent seems to have taken place, speaking geologically, within an instant, and without having been accompanied by any major increase in body size."

The true secret of Piltdown, though thought by the public to be merely the revelation of unscrupulous forgery, lies in the fact that it has forced science to reexamine carefully the history of the most remarkable creation in the world—the human brain.

G. K. CHESTERTON

G. K. Chesterton (1874–1936), born, bred, and educated in London, achieved popularity with a series of detective stories beginning with *The Innocence of Father Brown* (1911). He was already well-known, however, as a journalist and social and literary critic, with books on Charles Dickens, Bernard Shaw, and William Blake. He advocated "Distribution-

ism," the distributing of wealth, taking Bacon's epigram as his motto:
"Money is like muck, no good except it be spread." He converted to
Catholicism in 1922, yet maintained his friendship with the atheist Shaw.

SCIENCE AND THE SAVAGES

Here is the epigrammatical, coordinating mind at its best, running its
coordinates in parallel and contrasting them epigrammatically: "student
of nature" against "student of human nature," for instance. Chesterton
can also subordinate, as with "man of science" in his second paragraph,
and he constantly plays off short against long, varying the length of his
statements with the rhythm of his meaning. As you read, try to absorb
the play of his language for the joy of it, adapting something for your own.

A permanent disadvantage of the study of folk-lore and kindred subjects is that the man of science can hardly be in the nature of things
very frequently a man of the world. He is a student of nature; he is
scarcely ever a student of human nature. And even where this difficulty
is overcome, and he is in some sense a student of human nature, this is
only a very faint beginning of the painful progress towards being
human. For the study of primitive race and religion stands apart in one
important respect from all, or nearly all, the ordinary scientific studies.
A man can understand astronomy only by being an astronomer; he can
understand entomology only by being an entomologist (or, perhaps, an
insect); but he can understand a great deal of anthropology merely by
being a man. He is himself the animal which he studies. Hence arises
the fact which strikes the eye everywhere in the records of ethnology
and folk-lore—the fact that the same frigid and detached spirit which
leads to success in the study of astronomy or botany leads to disaster
in the study of mythology or human origins. It is necessary to cease to
be a man in order to do justice to a microbe; it is not necessary to cease
to be a man in order to do justice to men. That same suppression of
sympathies, that same waving away of intuitions or guess-work which
make a man preternaturally clever in dealing with the stomach of a
spider, will make him preternaturally stupid with the heart of man. He
is making himself inhuman in order to understand humanity. An ignorance of the other world is boasted by many men of science; but in this
matter their defect arises, not from ignorance of the other world, but
from ignorance of this world. For the secrets about which anthropologists concern themselves can be best learnt, not from books or voyages,
but from the ordinary commerce of man with man. The secret of why

some savage tribe worships monkeys or the moon is not to be found even by travelling among those savages and taking down their answers in a note-book, although the cleverest man may pursue this course. The answer to the riddle is in England; it is in London; nay, it is in his own heart. When a man has discovered why men in Bond Street wear black hats he will at the same moment have discovered why men in Timbuctoo wear red feathers. The mystery in the heart of some savage war-dance should not be studied in books of scientific travel; it should be studied at a subscription ball. If a man desires to find out the origins of religions, let him not go to the Sandwich Islands; let him go to church. If a man wishes to know the origin of human society, to know what society, philosophically speaking, really is, let him not go into the British Museum; let him go into society.

This total misunderstanding of the real nature of ceremonial gives rise to the most awkward and dehumanized versions of the conduct of men in rude lands or ages. The man of science, not realizing that ceremonial is essentially a thing which is done without a reason, has to find a reason for every sort of ceremonial, and, as might be supposed, the reason is generally a very absurd one—absurd because it originates not in the simple mind of the barbarian, but in the sophisticated mind of the professor. The learned man will say, for instance, "The natives of Mumbojumbo Land believe that the dead man can eat, and will require food upon his journey to the other world. This is attested by the fact that they place food in the grave, and that any family not complying with this rite is the object of the anger of the priests and the tribe." To any one acquainted with humanity this way of talking is topsy-turvy. It is like saying, "The English in the twentieth century believed that a dead man could smell. This is attested by the fact that they always covered his grave with lilies, violets, or other flowers. Some priestly and tribal terrors were evidently attached to the neglect of this action, as we have records of several old ladies who were very much disturbed in mind because their wreaths had not arrived in time for the funeral." It may be of course that savages put food with a dead man because they think that a dead man can eat, or weapons with a dead man because they think that a dead man can fight. But personally I do not believe that they think anything of the kind. I believe they put food or weapons on the dead for the same reason that we put flowers, because it is an exceedingly natural and obvious thing to do. We do not understand, it is true, the emotion which makes us think it obvious and natural; but that is because, like all the important emotions of human existence, it is essentially irrational. We do not understand the savage for the same reason that the savage does not understand himself. And the savage does not understand himself for the same reason that we do not understand ourselves either.

The obvious truth is that the moment any matter has passed through the human mind it is finally and for ever spoilt for all purposes of science. It has become a thing incurably mysterious and infinite; this mortal has put on immortality. Even what we call our material desires are spiritual, because they are human. Science can analyse a pork-chop, and say how much of it is phosphorus and how much is protein; but science cannot analyse any man's wish for a pork-chop, and say how much of it is hunger, how much custom, how much nervous fancy, how much a haunting love of the beautiful. The man's desire for the pork-chop remains literally as mystical and ethereal as his desire for heaven. All attempts, therefore, at a science of any human things, at a science of history, a science of folk-lore, a science of sociology, are by their nature not merely hopeless, but crazy. You can no more be certain in economic history that a man's desire for money was merely a desire for money than you can be certain in hagiology that a saint's desire for God was merely a desire for God. And this kind of vagueness in the primary phenomena of the study is an absolutely final blow to anything in the nature of a science. Men can construct a science with very few instruments, or with very plain instruments; but no one on earth could construct a science with unreliable instruments. A man might work out the whole of mathematics with a handful of pebbles, but not with a handful of clay which was always falling apart into new fragments, and falling together into new combinations. A man might measure heaven and earth with a reed, but not with a growing reed.

As one of the enormous follies of folk-lore, let us take the case of the transmigration of stories, and the alleged unity of their source. Story after story the scientific mythologists have cut out of its place in history, and pinned side by side with similar stories in their museum of fables. The process is industrious, it is fascinating, and the whole of it rests on one of the plainest fallacies in the world. That a story has been told all over the place at some time or other, not only does not prove that it never really happened; it does not even faintly indicate or make slightly more probable that it never happened. That a large number of fishermen have falsely asserted that they have caught a pike two feet long, does not in the least affect the question of whether any one ever really did so. That numberless journalists announce a Franco-German war merely for money is no evidence one way or the other upon the dark question of whether such a war ever occurred. Doubtless in a few hundred years the innumerable Franco-German wars that did not happen will have cleared the scientific mind of any belief in the legendary war of '70 which did. But that will be because if folk-lore students remain at all, their nature will be unchanged; and their services to folklore will be still as they are at present, greater than they know. For in truth these men do something far more godlike than studying legends; they create them.

There are two kinds of stories which the scientists say cannot be true, because everybody tells them. The first class consists of the stories which are told everywhere, because they are somewhat odd or clever; there is nothing in the world to prevent their having happened to somebody as an adventure any more than there is anything to prevent their having occurred, as they certainly did occur, to somebody as an idea. But they are not likely to have happened to many people. The second class of their "myths" consist of the stories that are told everywhere for the simple reason that they happen everywhere. Of the first class, for instance, we might take such an example as the story of William Tell, now generally ranked among legends upon the sole ground that it is found in the tales of other peoples. Now, it is obvious that this was told everywhere because whether true or fictitious it is what is called "a good story"; it is odd, exciting, and it has a climax. But to suggest that some such eccentric incident can never have happened in the whole history of archery, or that it did not happen to any particular person of whom it is told, is stark impudence. The idea of shooting at a mark attached to some valuable or beloved person is an idea doubtless that might easily occur to any boastful archer. It might be one of the fantastic caprices of some story-teller. It might equally well be one of the fantastic caprices of some tyrant. It might occur first in real life and afterwards occur in legends. Or it might just as well occur first in legends and afterwards occur in real life. If no apple has ever been shot off a boy's head from the beginning of the world, it may be done tomorrow morning, and by somebody who has never heard of William Tell.

This type of tale, indeed, may be pretty fairly paralleled with the ordinary anecdote terminating in a repartee of an Irish bull.* Such a retort as the famous "Je ne vois pas la nécessité"† we have all seen attributed to Talleyrand, to Voltaire, to Henri Quatre, to an anonymous judge, and so on. But this variety does not in any way make it more

---

* An *Irish bull* is a blunder in language.—Ed.

† In his play *Alzire* (1735), Voltaire (1694–1778) has the Conte D'Argenson (1652–1721) scold a satirist for attacking the government. The satirist replies, "Il faut que je vivre" ("I must live"). D'Argenson retorts, "Je n'en vois pas la nécessité" ("I don't see the necessity for it"). Chesterton has forgotten the "en" ("for it").—Ed.

likely that the thing was never said at all. It is highly likely that it was really said by somebody unknown. It is highly likely that it was really said by Talleyrand. In any case, it is not any more difficult to believe that the *mot* might have occurred to a man in conversation than to a man writing memoirs. It might have occurred to any of the men I have mentioned. But there is this point of distinction about it, that it is not likely to have occurred to all of them. And this is where the first class of so-called myth differs from the second to which I have previously referred. For there is a second class of incident found to be common to the stories of five or six heroes, say to Sigurd, to Hercules, to Rustem, to the Cid, and so on. And the peculiarity of this myth is that not only is it highly reasonable to imagine that it really happened to one hero, but it is highly reasonable to imagine that it really happened to all of them. Such a story, for instance, is that of a great man having his strength swayed or thwarted by the mysterious weakness of a woman. The anecdotal story, the story of William Tell, is as I have said, popular, because it is peculiar. But this kind of story, the story of Samson and Delilah, of Arthur and Guinevere, is obviously popular because it is not peculiar. It is popular as good, quiet fiction is popular, because it tells the truth about people. If the ruin of Samson by a woman, and the ruin of Hercules by a woman, have a common legendary origin, it is gratifying to know that we can also explain, as a fable, the ruin of Nelson by a woman and the ruin of Parnell by a woman. And, indeed, I have no doubt whatever that, some centuries hence, the students of folk-lore will refuse altogether to believe that Elizabeth Barrett eloped with Robert Browning, and will prove their point up to the hilt by the unquestionable fact that the whole fiction of the period was full of such elopements from end to end.

Possibly the most pathetic of all the delusions of the modern students of primitive belief is the notion they have about the thing they call anthropomorphism. They believe that primitive men attributed phenomena to a god in human form in order to explain them, because his mind in its sullen limitation could not reach any further than his own clownish existence. The thunder was called the voice of a man, the lightning the eyes of a man, because by this explanation they were made more reasonable and comfortable. The final cure for all this kind of philosophy is to walk down a lane at night. Any one who does so will discover very quickly that men pictured something semi-human at the back of all things, not because such a thought was natural, but because it was supernatural; not because it made things more comprehensible, but because it made them a hundred times more incomprehensible and mysterious. For a man walking down a lane at night can see the conspicuous fact that as long as nature keeps to her own course, she has no power with us at all. As long as a tree is a tree, it is a top-heavy monster with a hundred arms, a thousand tongues, and only one leg. But so long as a tree is a tree, it does not frighten us at all. It begins to be something alien, to be something strange, only when it looks like ourselves. When a tree really looks like a man our knees knock under us. And when the whole universe looks like a man we fall on our faces.

HENRY SEIDEL CANBY

Henry Seidel Canby (1878–1961), a leading critic of American literature at Yale, also edited the *Saturday Review of Literature* (1924–1936), among several other magazines. His many books include *Thoreau* (1939), and his edited selection of Thoreau's publications entitled *Works* (1937).

SENTENCE MAKER

This selection from Canby's *Thoreau* gets to the heart of both Thoreau and our present concern: the sentence. Sentences are where we live, in prose, and where we think. The thesis sentence shapes the essay. The topic sentence shapes the paragraph. The sentence nets our thought. As Canby suggests, the writer's sentences are the writer's very self, engaging his subject and trying to engage his general reader in it. Notice the flow and subordinating richness of Canby's own sentences as he describes those of the more epigrammatic man he admires.

Thoreau's writing was to an unusual extent a by-product of his experience. His profession was living, yet, as with all those born to be men of letters, his life seemed incomplete until he had got it described satisfactorily in words. "You . . . have the best of me in my books," he wrote to an admirer in Michigan, Calvin H. Greene, and of course he was right. Therefore, as was natural, he took his writing seriously, and was rich in self-criticism as all writers should be, but are not.

It took him most of the 1840's to get rid of Carlyle's religio-mystical view of literature, which made preachers of the young men of Thoreau's generation. When, in the fifties, his reading swung from literature toward science, he shrugged off this stale generalizing, for there was neither time nor inclination for it. It is only rarely that, after 1850, he writes about a literary masterpiece, for he was no longer studying in that school. Yet it is precisely in this last decade of his life that he makes the shrewdest comments on the art of writing—which is natural, for he had then matured his own. And here he is worth listening to, as is any first-rate writer who tries to analyze his own processes. Not the most philosophic perhaps, but certainly the most valuable, criticism we have is the occasional comment of a good writer on how to write—which means almost invariably how he writes himself.

It was a decade, as we have already seen, of crowded experiences for him with men, women, nature, and the state. There was plenty to write about, so that his Journal sometimes has sudden expansions for a day's thought and adventure which must have taken hours to set in order and express. The whole into which he hoped to fit his parts eluded his grasp, but his faith was firm that if he could reduce his observations to perfect sentences, somehow they would see the light, reach their mark, accomplish their destiny. This optimism has been justified, but only by the labor of many editors, and the enthusiasm of readers searching the trackless Journal for his best.

It was the sentence—a *sententia*—that most occupied his thought. The sentence was his medium—whatever he does and writes about, however often he rewrites or enriches, the fruit of it can be found ripened in a sentence. In the revision of *Walden* for the press, it was doubtful sentences that he threw out, then looked them over, and took back the good ones. They smelled right, as he says, using quaintly his keenest sense as if it could extend itself to words. Naturally he writes best about writing when he is writing about sentences, and these remarks have a biographical value, for they describe as no one else can do the man's mind at work. Only in those deeply impassioned pages about his Sister [the wife of his friend Emerson], so strongly felt as to be scarcely articulate, does he fail to get sentences equal to the emotional intensity or the intellectual insight of his experience. And these, of course, were not meant for publication. With Bacon, Shakespeare, Pope, Doctor Johnson, the makers of the English Bible, and Benjamin Franklin, he belongs among the great makers of the English sentence. Therefore his account of his own practice is interesting.

Two principles, especially, guided him in his writing as, sitting under a pasture oak, he set down his things seen or thought about, or, upstairs in the house on Main Street, worked his notes into his Journal. The first principle might be called intuition made articulate, a favorite idea with all the romantic Transcendentalists [a group of New England writers devoted to a philosophy stressing the importance of individual spiritual perception]:

> April 1. Sunday. 1860 . . . The fruit a thinker bears is *sentences*, —statements or opinions. He seeks to affirm something as true. I

am surprised that my affirmations or utterances come to me ready-made,—not fore-thought,—so that I occasionally awake in the night simply to let fall ripe a statement which I had never consciously considered before, and as surprising and novel and agreeable to me as anything can be. As if we only thought by sympathy with the universal mind, which thought while we were asleep. There is such a necessity [to] make a definite statement that our minds at length do it without our consciousness, just as we carry our food to our mouths. This occurred to me last night, but I was so surprised by the fact which I have just endeavored to report that I have entirely forgotten what the particular observation was.

That is the difficulty, of course, with these flashes from a mind in which the heat of long brooding turns to light—if they are not recorded on some sensitive film they are lost and gone, often irrevocably. It was Thoreau's practice to wait for the flash and then anxiously develop the impression until a sentence was made that was true to the original inspiration, yet communicable to the reader. "There is no more Herculean task than to think a thought about this life and then get it expressed." To write that way is dangerous, since the flow of thought is checked while expression is made perfect; yet it is hard not to believe that here is the secret of Thoreau's durability. The rifle is more penetrating than the shotgun; the line is remembered when the poem is forgot.

But these sudden luminosities of thought or irradiations of experience were seldom made articulate at the first trial:

> Jan. 26. 1852 ... Whatever wit has been produced on the spur of the moment will bear to be reconsidered and reformed with phlegm. The arrow had best not be loosely shot. The most transient and passing remark must be ... made sure and warranted, as if the earth had rested on its axle to back it, and all the natural forces lay behind it. The writer must direct his sentences as carefully and leisurely as the marksman his rifle. ... If you foresee that a part of your essay will topple down after the lapse of time, throw it down now yourself.

Inspiration pricking him on, he writes several such sentences as these lines describe: "I feel the spur of the moment thrust deep into my side. The present is an inexorable rider." Then, with a shift of theme: "The truest account of heaven is the fairest, and I will accept none which disappoints expectation." Here are other comments:

> Nov. 12. 1851 ... Those sentences are good and well discharged which are like so many little resiliences from the spring floor of

our life. . . . Sentences uttered with your back to the wall. . . . Sentences in which there is no strain.

Aug. 22. 1851 . . . It is the fault of some excellent writers—De Quincey's first impressions on seeing London suggest it to me—that they express themselves with too great fullness and detail. They . . . lack moderation and sententiousness. They . . . say all they mean. Their sentences are not concentrated and nutty. Sentences which suggest far more than they say, which have an atmosphere about them, which do not merely report an old, but make a new, impression . . . to frame these, that is the *art* of writing. Sentences which are expensive, towards which so many volumes, so much life, went; which lie like boulders on the page, up and down or across; which contain the seed of other sentences, not mere repetition, but creation; which a man might sell his grounds and castles to build. If De Quincey had suggested each of his pages in a sentence and passed on, it would have been far more excellent writing. His style is nowhere kinked and knotted up into something hard and significant, which you could swallow like a diamond, without digesting.

That last sentence describes the way Thoreau wrote, and the reason for reading him deliberately. To skim his pages, except in parts of *Cape Cod* or in *The Maine Woods* or in some of the *Excursions*, is like walking rapidly down a gallery of fine paintings. Even with every assistance from theme and narrative, as in *Walden*, Thoreau's work reads slowly—which is not always a virtue, but often a fault, like the faults of paradox and exaggeration, of which he accused himself. He favored his best sentences at the expense of his chapters and paragraphs. They contained the most of him.

His second principle of writing was native to a man who put the art of life ahead of the art of literature. It was, to be vital:

Sept. 2. 1851 . . . We cannot write well or truly but what we write with gusto. The body, the senses, must conspire with the mind. Expression is the act of the whole man, that our speech may be vascular. The intellect is powerless to express thought without the aid of the heart and liver and of every member.

Jan. 30. Friday. 1852 . . . It is in vain to write on chosen themes. We must wait till they have kindled a flame in our minds. There must be the copulating and generating force of love behind every effort destined to be successful. The cold resolve gives birth to, begets, nothing. . . . Obey, report.

July 14. 1852. A writer who does not speak out of a full experience uses torpid words, wooden or lifeless words, such words as "humanitary," which have a paralysis in their tails.

And finally, by way of warning, the original of Barrett Wendell's often quoted phrase, "a diarrhoea of words and constipation of thought":

> Dec. 31. 1851 . . . The . . . creative moment . . . in the case of some too easy poets . . . becomes mere diarrhoea, mud and clay relaxed. The poet must not have something pass his bowels merely; that is women's poetry. He must have something pass his brain and heart and bowels, too. . . . So he gets delivered.

The rhetorical quality that many feel, even in Thoreau's best writing, is sometimes only a tone and attitude which he sustains, like a good lecturer, through all of such a book as the *Week* or *Walden*. Yet I think that the difficulty which the modern reader finds in what seems to him the stylized writing of *Walden*, or even of the *Excursions*, has a more important source in this habit of the packed and intensely expressive sentence. Our education in science, or its derivatives, has made us more inductive in our mental processes than were our immediate ancestors. We are accustomed to the kind of writing—especially in newspapers and magazines—that assembles facts, which we call news. The packed statement, which is a deduction handed over for our thinking, is unfamiliar and inspires distrust. Our writing escapes the dogmatic by being dilute and often inconclusive. It is easy to abbreviate, as the success of such magazines as *The Reader's Digest* has shown. We write, not by sentences, not even by paragraphs, but in a stream directed at one outlet. The reading of poetry has decreased in proportion to the increase of this homeopathic way of writing, for the effectiveness of poetry is an effectiveness of charged words and lines. If it is not to have high specific gravity, it would be better to write it in prose. Thoreau suffers from this changed habit of reading, since his sentences, with their backs to the wall, and their feet on Mother Earth, differ from poetry in this respect only in a freer rhythm.

Yet there is no intentional obscurity. "I am thinking," he wrote one day, "by what long discipline and at what cost a man learns to speak simply at last." Nor was there any literary affectation in his creed, although it cannot be denied that, like his contemporaries, he let his words strut and crow now and then with the *Walden* cock. "Why, the roots of *letters*," he says aptly, "are *things*. Natural objects and phenomena are the original symbols or types which express our thoughts and feelings, and yet American scholars, having little or no root in the soil, commonly strive with all their might to confine themselves to the imported symbols alone. All the true growth and experience, the living speech, they would fain reject as 'Americanisms.' " "It is a great art in the writer to improve from day to day just that soil and fertility which he has. . . ." "Your mind must not perspire,"—which last, if said of walking out-of-doors, was surely meant for writing indoors also.

The art of writing is much broader and more complex than Thoreau's remarks on sentence-making imply. There is no doubt, however, that his particular art has a survival value much greater than any novelty in his ideas. But, inevitably, it became a perfectionist art, and so a curb upon free writing. Whoever writes by sentences writes slowly, and will often follow his own nose instead of his theme. And being perfectionist, this art made the completion of any whole exceedingly difficult, because each sentence had to be a finished production. He used the spot light instead of the flood. No wonder, then, that, as a student of nature trying to put between the covers of a book an account of that age-old Concord scene in which man had found a new home, Thoreau's work was left half done. Nevertheless, he mopped up his trenches as he crossed them, and left a noble sentence for each significant experience.

SUGGESTIONS FOR WRITING

Whatever you choose to write, try varying your sentences, with a touch from Nietzsche, and a touch from Eiseley and Chesterton.

1. Write an essay supporting, or attacking, Nietzsche's view (quotations from Popper's "Utopia and Violence" and from Schweitzer might be useful): "The Value of Waterbagging," "Overthrowing the Boundary Stones in Smith Dormitory," "New Bad Against Old Good."

2. Write an essay explaining Schweitzer's idea, illustrating it, or any part of it, with something you know from experience: charity, discrimination of groups, vegetarianism, antiwar movements, euthanasia, hunting (you may find an excellent essay in the recollection of a time you may have had to kill a mouse or a fish).

3. Write an essay on "Schweitzer Replies to Stace."

4. If you have information from other courses, or sources, write about the issues raised by Darwin and Wallace, and discussed

by Elaine Morgan, Ardrey, and Leakey. You might deal with Schweitzer's assertion that scientific research has made the mystery of life more mysterious (and perhaps Chesterton's thoughts along the same line). Somewhere in your essay try to use, as Eiseley does, an experience of your own: "As a modern man, I have sat in concert halls. . . ."

5. If you have any knowledge of experiments in human reactions, as in polls of opinion, or in psychological or sociological experimentation, attack or support Chesterton's suggestion that "the same frigid and detached spirit which leads to success in the study of astronomy or botany leads to disaster" in the study of human affairs.

6. Write an essay on a subject such as "the tribal taboos of the sophomore prom."

7. Write an essay attacking or developing Chesterton's idea that scientific investigation of things human is impossible because the basic matter, having passed through the human mind, is "incurably mysterious and infinite." Consider what he says about motives, about anthropomorphic belief. Use what you know of psychology, history, sociology, or literary criticism.

8. Try to write five sentences of the Thoreauvian kind, *sententiae* with their roots in natural objects. Sit under an oak and see what sentences your intuition can bring forth. Write with gusto, the body and senses conspiring. Try something like Thoreau's "The fruit a thinker bears is sentences" or Canby's "The rifle is more penetrating than the shotgun; the line is remembered when the poem is forgot"—sentences that lie like boulders on the page.

9. Write an essay on the following theme: "It is in vain to write on chosen themes."

10. As a final exercise in forging sentences, take Nietzsche's first sentence, which is a *compound* sentence—a series of coordinate statements (from "The strongest" to "religions and moralities")—and rewrite it as a *complex* sentence, with everything subordinated to the basic proposition that the strongest and most evil spirits have advanced humanity most. Start with "Having always rekindled . . . , having always reawakened . . . ."

11. Now see if you can write a hundred-word sentence with everything subordinated to one main statement, using any subject, the more playful the better. Here is a useful pattern:

Having (Although, After, When)——————————,
  having————————————————————,
  having————————————————————,
  having————————————————————,
     she got up
     because——————————————,
     because——————————————,
    and because——————————————.

You can use other subordinating words, of course, and you can spin out your statements by inserting still further subordinations: "because she, *who had slept for forty-eight hours, and who never got up before noon anyway,* now realized . . . ." You can place your main statement early or late, but if you let it in too soon you sometimes run out of gas.

Six
Words: The Descriptive
and Figurative Dimension

Words picture the world as we see it. They describe, but they carry the colors of our spirits. Cooley knows this, as he comments on the books he likes. If words lack character, they convey no reality. We cannot believe in anything, with nobody there. Thoreau, the sentence-smith, puts it another way, as if words were like seeds, common and unnoticed, just waiting to be awakened. But he failed to notice that his own personality was the breath of spring.

Nevertheless, he saw and enjoyed the essential energy in words. He knew how to pun, to turn common abstractions back into their original metaphors. Go through Thoreau thoroughly, with a pencil poised for puns. No other writer can teach you so well the figurative potency in common words, as well as the ways to release it with a play of mind and language that is, indeed, a kind of inspired punning.

White, too, is a master of the sentence—see his second sentence, for example—but his gift, again, comes down to words themselves. He learned from Thoreau the best that anyone can learn from him, the wonder and the simple freedom of being alive in one's own spirit; and he must also have learned something of Thoreau's craft in writing: the potency of individual words. White's pulse is different from Thoreau's, but he has much the same ability to keep his language freshened with metaphor. Both men, you will notice, imply that all language is a metaphor, a kind of perpetual *as if*, expressing the eternal idiom of nature and spirit.

Heller, too, is a figurative wordster, though quieter than Thoreau and White, and he is much less frivolous, but his words frequently glow from the same intelligent play. Underline all striking words, especially metaphors, as you read.

CHARLES HORTON COOLEY

Charles Horton Cooley (1864–1929) was professor of sociology at the University of Michigan. His books, including *Human Nature and the Social Order*, *Heredity or Environment*, and *Genius, Fame and the Comparison of Races*, were written around the turn of the century as sociology was just taking shape as a discipline. *Life and the Student*, from which these reflections are taken, appeared in 1927.

LIFE AND THE STUDENT

This selection asserts the value of individuality in writing, as it conveys the personality of a remarkable man, a pioneering sociologist wonderfully open to all life in the books and people around him. He himself, the caring person, becomes a part of his work, and the work gives evidence of his care—as did the sailboat he built, with care in every joint and line.

An intelligent reader goes slowly when he feels that each word has its peculiar and essential force. He watches the author. We *want* to make out personality, and if there is the least trace of it imagination is excited and puts forth guesses, we become clairvoyant. We want the author himself, as an explanation, a guaranty, a vehicle for the thought. And we find him in his choice of words, in the movement of his sentences, in the attitudes and habits of feeling implicit in what he says, in a hundred signs not less telling, to the sensitive reader, than the visible and audible man.

I know one who can keep children laughing with only a droll look now and then, and so there are authors who keep you amused and expectant of humor though they but rarely deliver it. We act on others not so much by what we explicitly do as by inciting their imaginations to work in a certain direction.

If a man writes thoughtfully he will not fail to impart his spirit, however slight the matter may seem. From Gissing's* sketches of travel *By*

* George Gissing (1827–1903), English novelist.

the Ionian Sea I get a deep and moving sense of his personality: just how and where it is conveyed would be hard to say. Like everything he wrote it is interfused with a fine kind of pride.

I love good books of travel, with a real atmosphere of strange places, but I find very few of them. I go to the library to find a book on Italy, and try one after another without satisfaction. The trouble is, in general, that there is nobody at home. The writer forsook himself when he wrote, he was not heartily in it, the works are perfunctory, not containing any full stream of spirit to float you away into new regions of life, thin, colorless, hardly existent.

If I think of certain academic men and ask whether they would be interesting in literature, I see that they would not. They are too anxious about being something else than simply men, not firmly enough poised. They see themselves in the light of some phase of opinion, as literary or scientific. A solid carpenter is better; he seems more human, less institutional.

I find Henry James's early letters from Europe less interesting than Mr. Dreiser's* rather crude book *A Traveler at Forty.* There is no stark personality in them; it is impersonal culture and craftsmanship; he is lost in his art.

A choice spirit defines itself in great part by what it avoids—the trite, the superfluous, the insincere, the immoderate—and may hold our attention more by this than by positive matter. The harm of a needless word is not so much in wasting the reader's attention as in impairing his confidence in the writer.

How grateful are limits! In a tale of Jane Austen you may be sure there are no social problems, no intellectual puzzles, no harrowing emotion. It is all well within your reach, clearly imagined, spirited, witty, exquisite of its kind. Second-rateness consists largely in slopping over, in not drawing a firm line around your picture, in doing poorly what you ought not to do at all.

Henry James is one of the authors that I can read with delight over and over again. He has a whole-hearted joy in his work and exhales a joyous though much rarefied atmosphere, wherein, if you can breathe it, you may recreate your mind with exploration of a subtile and enticing world. In his earlier books he has also a light ingratiating humor

* Theodore Dreiser (1871–1945), American novelist.

and a caressing flow of speech. That his range is limited, that there is no passion in him except the passion for literature, is perhaps an added charm; he invites you into an enclosed garden where nothing lives but literary grace and psychological intelligence.

I read the French moralists—de la Rochefoucauld, La Bruyère, Pascal— not so much for the value of their ideas, however great that may be, as because I like the company of men who are interested in such ideas.

Character

What is it that makes most books unsatisfying? Is it not lack of character, of reality? A certain opportunism, aiming at the market rather than at truth? The writers seem too much applicants for favor. They offer, for the most part, not solid individual contributions but voices in a chorus, each taking the key from the rest but striving to be a little louder or clearer or sharper or in some way consciously distinct, so as to be sure of being heard. What we want, apparently, is to hear voices that are *un*consciously distinct, not anxious about being heard, speaking from a quiet background of normal life and expressing without strain a natural and interesting self.

Composure is communicated by the gesture of a book, a way about it that makes one feel that the writer is in no hurry, is not trying too hard and enjoys his paragraph as he makes it. We wish him to create a world of his own, joyous and serene, and then make it our world. He must be bold and unique for us, because we are to enter into him. He should live the most satisfying life he can, so that we may see how it is done. Apology is as distasteful as it would be in an actor; it destroys our illusion.

One must be in quiet and secure possession of some sort of a homestead in order to be worthwhile in literature.

HENRY DAVID THOREAU

Henry David Thoreau (1817–1862), who was born in Concord, Massachusetts, turned to nearby Walden Pond—after Harvard and short stints at teaching, surveying, and making pencils in his father's factory—for his famous two-year experiment in living self-sufficiently in the woods (1845–1847). Failing to find a publisher for his *A Week on the Concord and Merrimack Rivers,* which he completed at Walden Pond, Thoreau finally published it in 1849 at his own expense and withheld *Walden,* rewriting it considerably until 1854. Attempts at lecturing also failed, and he returned to pencils and surveying for the rest of his life, except for work in the antislavery movement and the publication of "Civil Disobedience" (1849), which was to influence Mahatma Gandhi. Signs of tuberculosis began to appear a decade before his death. Published posthumously were *The Maine Woods* (1863), *Cape Cod* (1865), and *A Yankee in Canada* (1866).

WHERE I LIVED, AND WHAT I LIVED FOR

In this chapter from *Walden,* Thoreau explains his wish to discover and experience the essentials of life, which the routine rounds of existence always seem to carpet with comfortable trivialities or wearisome and unnecessary labors. He is the world's most famous dropout, as he tries to drop in on the vital center of being. Do you see what he means? Does he reflect impulses of your own? To enjoy his meaty power over words, underline his puns and metaphors. Note the imaginative punster at work in his opening passage as he plays with the *idea* of buying a farm, with the fact that one really possesses a thing only in one's consciousness and imagination. *Season* takes on a strong agricultural climate; *survey* means both to look over and to measure; *price* means a cost not only financial but also spiritual. Can you unravel the punning dynamics of *deed?*

At a certain season of our life we are accustomed to consider every spot as the possible site of a house. I have thus surveyed the country on every side within a dozen miles of where I live. In imagination I have bought all the farms in succession, for all were to be bought, and I knew their price. I walked over each farmer's premises, tasted his wild apples, discoursed on husbandry with him, took his farm at his price, at any price, mortgaging it to him in my mind; even put a higher price on it,— took every thing but a deed of it,—took his word for his deed, for I dearly love to talk,—cultivated it, and him too to some extent, I trust, and withdrew when I had enjoyed it long enough, leaving him to carry it on. This experience entitled me to be regarded as a sort of real-estate broker by my friends. Wherever I sat, there I might live, and the landscape radiated from me accordingly. What is a house but a *sedes,* a seat?—better if a country seat. I discovered many a site for a house not likely to be soon improved, which some might have thought too far from the village, but to my eyes the village was too far from it. Well, there I might live, I said; and there I did live, for an hour, a summer and a winter life; saw how I could let the years run off, buffet the winter through, and see the spring come in. The future inhabitants of this region, wherever they may place their houses, may be sure that they have been anticipated. An afternoon sufficed to lay out the land into orchard, woodlot, and pasture, and to decide what fine oaks or pines should be left to stand before the door, and whence each blasted tree could be seen to the best advantage; and then I let it lie, fallow perchance, for a man is rich in proportion to the number of things which he can afford to let alone.

My imagination carried me so far that I even had the refusal of several farms,—the refusal was all I wanted,—but I never got my fingers burned by actual possession. The nearest that I came to actual possession was when I bought the Hollowell place, and had begun to sort my seeds, and collected materials with which to make a wheelbarrow to carry it on or off with; but before the owner gave me a deed of it, his wife—every man has such a wife—changed her mind and wished to keep it, and he offered me ten dollars to release him. Now, to speak the truth, I had but ten cents in the world, and it surpassed my arithmetic to tell, if I was that man who had ten cents, or who had a farm, or ten dollars, or all together. However, I let him keep the ten dollars and the farm too, for I had carried it far enough; or rather, to be generous, I sold him the farm for just what I gave for it, and, as he was not a rich man, made him a present of ten dollars, and still had my ten cents, and seeds, and materials for a wheelbarrow left. I found thus that I had been a rich man without any damage to my poverty. But I retained the landscape, and I have since annually carried off what it yielded without a wheelbarrow. With respect to landscapes,—

> I am monarch of all I *survey*,
> My right there is none to dispute.

I have frequently seen a poet withdraw, having enjoyed the most valuable part of a farm, while the crusty farmer supposed that he had got a few wild apples only. Why, the owner does not know it for many years when a poet has put his farm in rhyme, the most admirable kind of invisible fence, has fairly impounded it, milked it, skimmed it, and got all the cream, and left the farmer only the skimmed milk.

The real attractions of the Hollowell farm, to me, were: its complete retirement, being about two miles from the village, half a mile from the nearest neighbor, and separated from the highway by a broad field; its bounding on the river, which the owner said protected it by its fogs from frosts in the spring, though that was nothing to me; the gray color and ruinous state of the house and barn, and the dilapidated fences, which put such an interval between me and the last occupant; the hollow and lichen-covered apple trees, gnawed by rabbits, showing what kind of neighbors I should have; but above all, the recollection I had of it from my earliest voyages up the river, when the house was concealed behind a dense grove of red maples, through which I heard the house-dog bark. I was in haste to buy it, before the proprietor finished getting out some rocks, cutting down the hollow apple trees, and grubbing up some young birches which had sprung up in the pasture, or, in short, had made any more of his improvements. To enjoy these advantages I was ready to carry it on; like Atlas, to take the world on my shoulders,—I never heard what compensation he received for that,—and do all those things which had no other motive or excuse but that I might pay for it and be unmolested in my possession of it; for I knew all the while that it would yield the most abundant crop of the kind I wanted if I could only afford to let it alone. But it turned out as I have said.

All that I could say, then, with respect to farming on a large scale (I have always cultivated a garden) was, that I had had my seeds ready. Many think that seeds improve with age. I have no doubt that time discriminates between the good and the bad; and when at last I shall plant, I shall be less likely to be disappointed. But I would say to my fellows, once for all, As long as possible live free and uncommitted. It makes but little difference whether you are committed to a farm or the county jail.

Old Cato, whose "De Re Rusticâ" is my "Cultivator," says,—and the only translation I have seen makes sheer nonsense of the passage,— "When you think of getting a farm, turn it thus in your mind, not to buy greedily; nor spare your pains to look at it, and do not think it enough to go round it once. The oftener you go there the more it will please you, if it is good." I think I shall not buy greedily, but go round and round it as long as I live, and be buried in it first, that it may please me the more at last.

The present was my next experiment of this kind, which I purpose to describe more at length, for convenience, putting the experience of two years into one. As I have said, I do not propose to write an ode to dejection, but to brag as lustily as chanticleer in the morning, standing on his roost, if only to wake my neighbors up.

When first I took up my abode in the woods, that is, began to spend my nights as well as days there, which, by accident, was on Independence day, or the fourth of July, 1845, my house was not finished for winter, but was merely a defense against the rain, without plastering or chimney, the walls being of rough, weather-stained boards, with wide chinks, which made it cool at night. The upright white hewn studs and freshly planed door and window casings gave it a clean and airy look, especially in the morning, when its timbers were saturated with dew, so that I fancied that by noon some sweet gum would exude from them. To my imagination it retained throughout the day more or less of this auroral character, reminding me of a certain house on a mountain which I had visited the year before. This was an airy and unplastered cabin, fit to entertain a travelling god, and where a goddess might trail her garments. The winds which passed over my dwelling were such as sweep over the ridges of mountains, bearing the broken strains, or celestial parts only, of terrestrial music. The morning wind forever blows, the poem of creation is uninterrupted; but few are the ears that hear it. Olympus is but the outside of the earth everywhere.

The only house I had been the owner of before, if I except a boat, was a tent, which I used occasionally when making excursions in the summer, and this is still rolled up in my garret; but the boat, after passing from hand to hand, has gone down the stream of time. With this more substantial shelter about me, I had made some progress toward settling in the world. This frame, so slightly clad, was a sort of crystallization around me, and reacted on the builder. It was suggestive somewhat as a picture in outlines. I did not need to go out-doors to take the air, for the atmosphere within had lost none of its freshness. It was not so much within-doors as behind a door where I sat, even in the rainiest weather. The Harivansa says, "An abode without birds is like a meat without seasoning." Such was not my abode, for I found myself suddenly neighbor to the birds; not by having imprisoned one, but having caged myself near them. I was not only nearer to some of those which commonly frequent the garden and the orchard, but to those wilder and more thrilling songsters of the forest which never, or rarely, serenade a villager,—the wood-thrush, the veery, the scarlet tanager, the field-sparrow, the whippoorwill, and many others.

I was seated by the shore of a small pond, about a mile and a half south of the village of Concord and somewhat higher than it, in the midst of an extensive wood between that town and Lincoln, and about two miles south of that our only field known to fame, Concord Battle Ground; but I was so low in the woods that the opposite shore, half a mile off, like the rest, covered with wood, was my most distant horizon. For the first week, whenever I looked out on the pond it impressed me like a tarn high up on the side of a mountain, its bottom far above the surface of other lakes, and, as the sun arose, I saw it throwing off its nightly clothing of mist, and here and there, by degrees, its soft ripples or its smooth reflecting surface was revealed, while the mists, like ghosts, were stealthily withdrawing in every direction into the woods, as at the breaking up of some nocturnal conventicle. The very dew seemed to hang upon the trees later into the day than usual, as on the sides of mountains.

This small lake was of most value as a neighbor in the intervals of a gentle rain storm in August, when, both air and water being perfectly still, but the sky overcast, mid-afternoon had all the serenity of evening, and the wood-thrush sang around, and was heard from shore to shore. A lake like this is never smoother than at such a time; and the clear portion of the air above it being shallow and darkened by clouds, the water, full of light and reflections, becomes a lower heaven itself so much the more important. From a hill top near by, where the wood had been recently cut off, there was a pleasing vista southward across the pond, through a wide indentation in the hills which form the shore there, where their opposite sides sloping toward each other suggested a stream flowing out in that direction through a wooded valley, but stream there was none. That way I looked between and over the near green hills to some distant and higher ones in the horizon, tinged with blue. Indeed, by standing on tiptoe I could catch a glimpse of some of the peaks of the still bluer and more distant mountain ranges in the north-west, those true-blue coins from heaven's own mint, and also of some portion of the village. But in other directions, even from this point, I could not see over or beyond the woods which surrounded me. It is well to have some water in your neighborhood, to give buoyancy to and float the earth. One value even of the smallest well is, that when you look into it you see that earth is not continent but insular. This is as important as that it keeps butter cool. When I looked across the pond from this peak toward the Sudbury meadows, which in time of flood I distinguished elevated perhaps by a mirage in their seething valley, like a coin in a basin, all the earth beyond the pond appeared like a thin crust insulated and floated even by this small sheet of intervening water, and I was reminded that this on which I dwelt was but *dry land*.

Though the view from my door was still more contracted, I did not feel crowded or confined in the least. There was pasture enough for my imagination. The low shrub-oak plateau to which the opposite shore arose, stretched away toward the prairies of the West and the steppes of Tartary, affording ample room for all the roving families of men. "There are none happy in the world but beings who enjoy freely a vast horizon,"—said Damodara, when his herds required new and larger pastures.

Both place and time were changed, and I dwelt nearer to those parts of the universe and to those eras in history which had most attracted me. Where I lived was as far off as many a region viewed nightly by astronomers. We are wont to imagine rare and delectable places in some remote and more celestial corner of the system, behind the constellation of Cassiopeia's Chair, far from noise and disturbance. I discovered that my house actually had its site in such a withdrawn, but forever new and unprofaned, part of the universe. If it were worth the while to settle in those parts near to the Pleiades or the Hyades, to Aldebaran or Altair, then I was really there, or at an equal remoteness from the life which I had left behind, dwindled and twinkling with as fine a ray to my nearest neighbor, and to be seen only in moonless nights by him. Such was that part of creation where I had squatted;—

> There was a shepherd that did live,
> And held his thoughts as high
> As were the mounts whereon his flocks
> Did hourly feed him by.

What should we think of the shepherd's life if his flocks always wandered to higher pastures than his thoughts?

Every morning was a cheerful invitation to make my life of equal simplicity, and I may say innocence, with Nature herself. I have been as sincere a worshiper of Aurora as the Greeks. I got up early and bathed in the pond; that was a religious exercise, and one of the best things which I did. They say that characters were engraven on the bathing tub of king Tching-thang to this effect: "Renew thyself completely each day; do it again, and again, and forever again." I can understand that. Morning brings back the heroic ages. I was as much affected by the faint hum of a mosquito making its invisible and unimaginable tour through my apartment at earliest dawn, when I was sitting with door and windows open, as I could be by any trumpet that ever sang of fame. It was Homer's requiem; itself an Iliad and Odyssey in the air, singing its own wrath and wanderings. There was something cosmical about it; a standing advertisement, till forbidden, of the everlasting vigor and fertility of the world. The morning, which is the most memorable season of the day, is the awakening hour. Then there is least somnolence in us; and for an hour, at least, some part of us awakes which slumbers all the rest of the day and night. Little is to be expected of that day, if it can be called a day, to which we are not awakened by our Genius, but by the mechanical nudgings of some servitor, are not awakened by our newly-acquired force and aspirations from within, accompanied by the undulations of celestial music, instead of factory bells, and a fragrance filling the air—to a higher life than we fell asleep from; and thus the darkness bear its fruit, and prove itself to be good, no less than the light. That man who does not believe that each day contains an earlier, more sacred, and auroral hour than he has yet profaned, has despaired of life, and is pursuing a descending and darkening way. After a partial cessation of his sensuous life, the soul of man, or its organs rather, are reinvigorated each day, and his Genius tries again what noble life it can make. All memorable events, I should say, transpire in morning time and in a morning atmosphere. The Vedas say, "All intelligences awake with the morning." Poetry and art, and the fairest and most memorable of the actions of men, date from such an hour. All poets and heroes, like Memnon, are the children of Aurora, and emit their music at sunrise. To him whose elastic and vigorous thought keeps pace with the sun, the day is a perpetual morning. It matters not what the clocks say or the attitudes and labors of men. Morning is when I am awake and there is a dawn in me. Moral reform is the effort to throw off sleep. Why is it that men give so poor an account of their day if they have not been slumbering? They are not such poor calculators. If they had not been overcome with drowsiness they would have performed something. The millions are awake enough for physical labor; but only one in a million is awake enough for effective intellectual exertion, only one in a hundred millions to a poetic or divine life. To be awake is to be alive. I have never yet met a man who was quite awake. How could I have looked him in the face?

We must learn to reawaken and keep ourselves awake, not by mechanical aids, but by an infinite expectation of the dawn, which does not forsake us in our soundest sleep. I know of no more encouraging fact than the unquestionable ability of man to elevate his life by a conscious endeavor. It is something to be able to paint a particular picture, or to carve a statue, and so to make a few objects beautiful; but it is far more glorious to carve and paint the very atmosphere and medium through which we look, which morally we can do. To affect the quality of the day, that is the highest of arts. Every man is tasked to make his life, even in its details, worthy of the contemplation of his most elevated and critical hour. If we refused, or rather used up, such paltry information as we get, the oracles would distinctly inform us how this might be done.

I went to the woods because I wished to live deliberately, to front only the essential facts of life, and see if I could not learn what it had to teach, and not, when I came to die, discover that I had not lived. I did not wish to live what was not life, living is so dear; nor did I wish to practice resignation, unless it was quite necessary. I wanted to live deep and suck out all the marrow of life, to live so sturdily and Spartan-like as to put to rout all that was not life, to cut a broad swath and shave close, to drive life into a corner, and reduce it to its lowest terms, and, if it proved to be mean, why then to get the whole and genuine meanness of it, and publish its meanness to the world; or if it were sublime, to know it by experience, and be able to give a true account of it in my next excursion. For most men, it appears to me, are in a strange uncertainty about it, whether it is of the devil or of God, and have *somewhat hastily* concluded that it is the chief end of man here to "glorify God and enjoy him forever."

Still we live meanly, like ants; though the fable tells us that we were long ago changed into men; like pygmies we fight with cranes; it is error upon error, and clout upon clout, and our best virtue has for its occasion a superfluous and evitable wretchedness. Our life is frittered away by detail. An honest man has hardly need to count more than his ten fingers, or in extreme cases he may add his ten toes, and lump the rest. Simplicity, simplicity, simplicity! I say, let your affairs be as two or three, and not a hundred or a thousand; instead of a million count half a dozen, and keep your accounts on your thumb nail. In the midst of this chopping sea of civilized life, such are the clouds and storms and quicksands and thousand-and-one items to be allowed for, that a man has to live, if he would not founder and go to the bottom and not make his port at all, by dead reckoning, and he must be a great calculator indeed who succeeds. Simplify, simplify. Instead of three meals a day, if it be necessary eat but one; instead of a hundred dishes, five; and reduce other things in proportion. Our life is like a German Confederacy, made up of petty states, with its boundary forever fluctuating, so that even a German cannot tell you how it is bounded at any moment. The nation itself, with all its so-called internal improvements, which, by the way, are all external and superficial, is just such an unwieldy and overgrown establishment, cluttered with furniture and tripped up by its own traps, ruined by luxury and heedless expense, by want of calculation and a worthy aim, as the million households in the land; and the only cure for it as for them is in a rigid economy, stern and more than Spartan simplicity of life and elevation of purpose. It lives too fast. Men think that it is essential that the *Nation* have commerce, and export ice, and talk through a telegraph, and ride thirty miles an hour, without a doubt, whether *they* do or not; but whether we should live like baboons or like men, is a little uncertain. If we do not get our sleepers, and forge rails, and devote days and nights to the work, but go to tinkering upon our *lives* to improve *them*, who will build railroads? And if railroads are not built, how shall we get to heaven in season? But if we stay at home and mind our business, who will want railroads? We do not ride on the railroad; it rides upon us. Did you ever think what those sleepers are that underlie the railroad? Each one is a man, an Irishman, or a Yankee man. The rails are laid on them, and they are covered with sand, and the cars run smoothly over them. They are sound sleepers, I assure you. And every few years a new lot is laid down and run over; so that, if some have the pleasure of riding on a rail, others have the misfortune to be ridden upon. And when they run over a man that is walking in his sleep, a supernumerary sleeper in the wrong position, and wake him up, they suddenly stop the cars, and make a hue and cry about it, as if this were an exception. I am glad to know that it takes a gang of men for every five miles to keep the sleepers down and level in their beds as it is, for this is a sign that they may sometime get up again.

Why should we live with such hurry and waste of life? We are determined to be starved before we are hungry. Men say that a stitch in time saves nine, and so they take a thousand stitches to-day to save nine tomorrow. As for *work*, we haven't any of any consequence. We have the Saint Vitus' dance, and cannot possibly keep our heads still. If I should only give a few pulls at the parish bellrope, as for a fire, that is, without setting the bell, there is hardly a man on his farm in the outskirts of Concord, notwithstanding that press of engagements which was his excuse so many times this morning, nor a boy, nor a woman, I might almost say, but would forsake all and follow that sound, not mainly to save property from the flames, but, if we will confess the truth, much more to see it burn, since burn it must, and we, be it known, did not set it on fire,—or to see it put out, and have a hand in it, if that is done as handsomely; yes, even if it were the parish church itself. Hardly a man takes a half hour's nap after dinner, but when he wakes he holds up his head and asks. "What's the news?" as if the rest of mankind had stood his sentinels. Some give directions to be waked every half hour, doubtless for no other purpose; and then, to pay for it, they tell what they have dreamed. After a night's sleep the news is as indispensable as the breakfast. "Pray tell me any thing new that has happened to a man anywhere on this globe,"—and he reads it over his coffee and rolls, that a man has had his eyes gouged out this morning on the Wachito River; never dreaming the while that he lives in the dark unfathomed mammoth cave of this world, and has but the rudiment of an eye himself.

For my part, I could easily do without the post-office. I think that there are very few important communications made through it. To speak critically, I never received more than one or two letters in my life—I wrote this some years ago—that were worth the postage. The penny-post is, commonly, an institution through which you seriously offer a man that penny for his thoughts which is so often safely offered in jest. And I am sure that I never read any memorable news in a news-paper. If we read of one man robbed, or murdered, or killed by accident, or one house burned, or one vessel wrecked, or one steamboat blown up, or one cow run over on the Western Railroad, or one mad dog killed, or one lot of grasshoppers in the winter,—we never need read of another. One is enough. If you are acquainted with the principle, what do you care for myriad instances and applications? To a philosopher all *news*, as it is called, is gossip, and they who edit and read it are old women over their tea. Yet not a few are greedy after this gossip. There was such a rush, as I hear, the other day at one of the offices to learn the foreign news by the last arrival, that several large squares of plate glass belonging to the establishment were broken by the pressure,—news which I seriously think a ready wit might write a twelve-month or twelve years beforehand with sufficient accuracy. As for Spain, for instance, if you know how to throw in Don Carlos and the Infanta, and Don Pedro and Seville and Granada, from time to time in the right proportions,—they may have changed the names a little since I saw the papers,—and serve up a bull-fight when other entertainments fail, it will be true to the letter, and give us as good an idea of the exact state or ruin of things in Spain as the most succinct and lucid reports under this head in the newspapers: and as for England, almost the last significant scrap of news from that quarter was the revolution of 1649; and if you have learned the history of her crops for an average year, you never need attend to that thing again, unless your speculations are of a merely pecuniary character. If one may judge who rarely looks into the newspapers, nothing new does ever happen in foreign parts, a French revolution not excepted.

What news! how much more important to know what that is which was never old! "Kieou-he-yu (great dignitary of the state of Wei) sent a man to Khoung-tseu to know his news. Khoung-tseu caused the messenger to be seated near him, and questioned him in these terms: What is your master doing? The messenger answered with respect: My master desires to diminish the number of his faults, but he cannot come to the end of them. The messenger being gone, the philosopher remarked: What a worthy messenger! What a worthy messenger!" The preacher, instead of vexing the ears of drowsy farmers on their day of rest at the end of the week,—for Sunday is the fit conclusion of an ill-spent week, and not the fresh and brave beginning of a new one,—with this one other draggle-tail of a sermon, should shout with thundering voice,— "Pause! Avast! Why so seeming fast, but deadly slow?"

Shams and delusions are esteemed for soundest truths, while reality is fabulous. If men would steadily observe realities only, and not allow themselves to be deluded, life, to compare it with such things as we know, would be like a fairy tale and the Arabian Nights' Entertainments. If we respected only what is inevitable and has a right to be, music and poetry would resound along the streets. When we are unhurried and wise, we perceive that only great and worthy things have any permanent and absolute existence,—that petty fears and petty pleasures are but the shadow of the reality. This is always exhilarating and sublime. By closing the eyes and slumbering, and consenting to be deceived by shows, men establish and confirm their daily life of routine and habit everywhere, which still is built on purely illusory foundations. Children, who play life, discern its true law and relations more clearly than men, who fail to live it worthily, but who think that they are wiser by experience, that is, by failure. I have read in a Hindoo book, that "there was a king's son, who, being expelled in infancy from his native city, was brought up by a forester, and, growing up to maturity in that state, imagined himself to belong to the barbarous race with which he lived. One of his father's ministers having discovered him, revealed to him what he was, and the misconception of his character was removed, and he knew himself to be a prince. So soul," continues the Hindoo philosopher, "from the circumstances in which it is placed, mistakes its own character, until the truth is revealed to it by some holy teacher, and then it knows itself to be *Brahme*." I perceive that we inhabitants of New England live this mean life that we do because our vision does not penetrate the surface of things. We think that that *is* which *appears* to be. If a man should walk through this town and see only the reality, where, think you, would the "Mill-dam" go to? If he should give us an account of the realities he beheld there, we should not recognize the place in his description. Look at a meetinghouse, or a courthouse, or a jail, or a shop, or a dwelling-house, and say what that thing really is before a true gaze, and they would all go to pieces in your account of them. Men esteem truth remote, in the outskirts of the system, behind the farthest star, before Adam and after the last man. In eternity there is indeed something true and sublime. But all these times and places and occasions are now and here. God himself culminates in the present moment, and will never be more divine in the lapse of all the ages. And we are enabled to apprehend at all what is sublime and noble only by the perpetual instilling and drenching of the reality that surrounds us. The universe constantly and obediently answers to our conceptions; whether we travel fast or slow, the track is laid for us. Let us spend our lives in conceiving then. The poet or the artist never yet had so fair and noble a design but some of his posterity at least could accomplish it.

Let us spend one day as deliberately as Nature, and not be thrown off the track by every nutshell and mosquito's wing that falls on the rails. Let us rise early and fast, or break fast, gently and without perturbation; let company come and let company go, let the bells ring and the children cry,—determined to make a day of it. Why should we knock under and go with the stream? Let us not be upset and overwhelmed in that terrible rapid and whirlpool called a dinner, situated in the meridian shallows. Weather this danger and you are safe, for the rest of the way is down hill. With unrelaxed nerves, with morning vigor, sail by it, looking another way, tied to the mast like Ulysses. If the engine whistles, let it whistle till it is hoarse for its pains. If the bell rings, why should we run? We will consider what kind of music they are like. Let us settle ourselves, and work and wedge our feet downward through the mud and slush of opinion, and prejudice, and tradition, and delusion, and appearance, that alluvion which covers the globe, through Paris and London, through New York and Boston and Concord, through church and state, through poetry and philosophy and religion, till we come to a hard bottom and rocks in place, which we can call *reality*, and say, This is, and no mistake; and then begin, having a *point d'appui*, below freshet and frost and fire, a place where you might found a wall or a state, or set a lamp-post safely, or perhaps a gauge, not a Nilometer, but a Realometer, that future ages might know how deep a freshet of shams and appearances had gathered from time to time. If you stand right fronting and face to face to a fact, you will see the sun glimmer on both its surfaces, as if it were a cimeter, and feel its sweet edge dividing you through the heart and marrow, and so you will happily conclude your mortal career. Be it life or death, we crave only reality. If we are really dying, let us hear the rattle in our throats and feel cold in the extremities; if we are alive, let us go about our business.

Time is but the stream I go a-fishing in. I drink at it; but while I drink I see the sandy bottom and detect how shallow it is. Its thin current slides away, but eternity remains. I would drink deeper; fish in the sky, whose bottom is pebbly with stars. I cannot count one. I know not the first letter of the alphabet. I have always been regretting that I was not as wise as the day was born. The intellect is a cleaver; it discerns and rifts its way into the secret of things. I do not wish to be any more busy with my hands than is necessary. My head is hands and feet. I feel all my best faculties concentrated in it. My instinct tells me that my head is an organ for burrowing, as some creatures use their snout and fore-paws, and with it I would mine and burrow my way through these hills. I think that the richest vein is somewhere

hereabouts; so by the divining rod and thin vapors I judge; and here
I will begin to mine.

E. B. WHITE

Elwyn Brooks White (1899–) has written for *The New Yorker* almost from
its launching in 1925, and, perhaps, more than anyone, has shaped its
style, its diffident serio-comic tone. His revision of William Strunk, Jr.'s,
The Elements of Style, the text he used as a freshman at Cornell, is still
a best-seller, as are his children's books, *Stuart Little* (1945) and *Charlotte's
Web* (1952). *One Man's Meat* (1949) and *The Second Tree from the Corner*
(1954) are his best-known books of essays.

A SLIGHT SOUND AT EVENING

In White's admiration of Thoreau, we can see one source of his own
quiet magic: a love of words and their wily ways in catching at the
simple wonders of life, together with a protective humor to keep from
going overboard. Like Thoreau, White is a playful alluder, slipping in
phrases from other writers on the assumption that his readers are so
knowledgeable they will recognize and enjoy them. As you read, mark
White's allusions, especially those echoes from Thoreau's piece. Notice
his coupling of complex words with the commonplace—*inspirational
puffballs*—his admixture of slangy words—*Nature Boy, whack, show-off,
ruckus*—and his phrases from commercial America—*vitamin-enriched,
in-town location.*

In his journal for July 10–12, 1841, Thoreau wrote: "A slight sound
at evening lifts me up by the ears, and makes life seem inexpressibly
serene and grand. It may be in Uranus, or it may be in the shutter."
The book into which he later managed to pack both Uranus and the
shutter was published in 1854, and now, a hundred years having gone
by, *Walden*, its serenity and grandeur unimpaired, still lifts us up by
the ears, still translates for us that language we are in danger of forgetting, "which all things and events speak without metaphor, which
alone is copious and standard."

Walden is an oddity in American letters. It may very well be the
oddest of our distinguished oddities. For many it is a great deal too
odd, and for many it is a particular bore. I have not found it to be a
well-liked book among my acquaintances, although usually spoken of
with respect, and one literary critic for whom I have the highest regard
can find no reason why anyone gives *Walden* a second thought. To

admire the book is, in fact, something of an embarrassment, for the mass of men have an indistinct notion that its author was a sort of Nature Boy.

I think it is of some advantage to encounter the book at a period in one's life when the normal anxieties and enthusiasms and rebellions of youth closely resemble those of Thoreau in that spring of 1845 when he borrowed an axe, went out to the woods, and began to whack down some trees for timber. Received at such a juncture, the book is like an invitation to life's dance, assuring the troubled recipient that no matter what befalls him in the way of success or failure he will always be welcome at the party—that the music is played for him, too, if he will but listen and move his feet. In effect, that is what the book is—an invitation, unengraved; and it stirs one as a young girl is stirred by her first big party bid. Many think it a sermon; many set it down as an attempt to rearrange society; some think it an exercise in nature-loving; some find it a rather irritating collection of inspirational puffballs by an eccentric show-off. I think it none of these. It still seems to me the best youth's companion yet written by an American, for it carries a solemn warning against the loss of one's valuables, it advances a good argument for traveling light and trying new adventures, it rings with the power of positive adoration, it contains religious feeling without religious images, and it steadfastly refuses to record bad news. Even its pantheistic note is so pure as to be noncorrupting—pure as the flute-note blown across the pond on those faraway summer nights. If our colleges and universities were alert, they would present a cheap pocket edition of the book to every senior upon graduating, along with his sheepskin, or instead of it. Even if some senior were to take it literally and start felling trees, there could be worse mishaps: the axe is older than the Dictaphone and it is just as well for a young man to see what kind of chips he leaves before listening to the sound of his own voice. And even if some were to get no farther than the table of contents, they would learn how to name eighteen chapters by the use of only thirty-nine words and would see how sweet are the uses of brevity.

If Thoreau had merely left us an account of a man's life in the woods, or if he had simply retreated to the woods and there recorded his complaints about society, or even if he had contrived to include both records in one essay, *Walden* would probably not have lived a hundred years. As things turned out, Thoreau, very likely without knowing quite what he was up to, took man's relation to nature and man's dilemma in society and man's capacity for elevating his spirit and he beat all these matters together, in a wild free interval of self-justification and delight, and produced an original omelette from which people can draw nourishment on a hungry day. *Walden* is one of the first of the vitamin-enriched American dishes. If it were a little less good than it is, or even a little less queer, it would be an abominable book. Even as it is, it will continue to baffle and annoy the literal mind and all those who are unable to stomach its caprices and imbibe its theme. Certainly the plodding economist will continue to have rough going if he hopes to emerge from the book with a clear system of economic thought. Thoreau's assault on the Concord society of the mid-nineteenth century has the quality of a modern Western: he rides into the subject at top speed, shooting in all directions. Many of his shots ricochet and nick him on the rebound, and throughout the melee there is a horrendous cloud of inconsistencies and contradictions, and when the shooting dies down and the air clears, one is impressed chiefly by the courage of the rider and by how splendid it was that somebody should have ridden in there and raised all that ruckus.

When he went to the pond, Thoreau struck an attitude and did so deliberately, but his posturing was not to draw the attention of others to him but rather to draw his own attention more closely to himself. "I learned this at least by my experiment: that if one advances confidently in the direction of his dreams, and endeavors to live the life which he has imagined, he will meet with a success unexpected in common hours." The sentence has the power to resuscitate the youth drowning in his sea of doubt. I recall my exhilaration upon reading it, many years ago, in a time of hesitation and despair. It restored me to health. And now in 1954 when I salute Henry Thoreau on the hundredth birthday of his book, I am merely paying off an old score—or an installment on it.

In his journal for May 3-4, 1838—Boston to Portland—he wrote: "Midnight—head over the boat's side—between sleeping and waking—with glimpses of one or more lights in the vicinity of Cape Ann. Bright moonlight—the effect heightened by seasickness." The entry illuminates the man, as the moon the sea on that night in May. In Thoreau the natural scene was heightened, not depressed, by a disturbance of the stomach, and nausea met its match at last. There was a steadiness in at least one passenger if there was none in the boat. Such steadiness (which in some would be called intoxication) is at the heart of *Walden*— confidence, faith, the discipline of looking always at what is to be seen, undeviating gratitude for the life-everlasting that he found growing in his front yard. "There is nowhere recorded a simple and irrepressible satisfaction with the gift of life, any memorable praise of God." He worked to correct that deficiency. *Walden* is his acknowledgment of the gift of life. It is the testament of a man in a high state of indignation because (it seemed to him) so few ears heard the uninterrupted poem of creation, the morning wind that forever blows. If the man sometimes wrote as though all his readers were male, unmarried, and well-connected, it is because he gave his testimony during the callow years, and, for that matter, never really grew up. To reject the book because of the immaturity of the author and the bugs in the logic is to throw away a bottle of good wine because it contains bits of the cork.

Thoreau said he required of every writer, first and last, a simple and sincere account of his own life. Having delivered himself of this chesty dictum, he proceeded to ignore it. In his books and even in his enormous journal, he withheld or disguised most of the fact from which an understanding of his life could be drawn. *Walden*, subtitled "Life in the Woods," is not a simple and sincere account of a man's life, either in or out of the woods; it is an account of a man's journey into the mind, a toot on the trumpet to alert the neighbors. Thoreau was well aware that no one can alert his neighbors who is not wide awake himself, and he went to the woods (among other reasons) to make sure that he would stay awake during his broadcast. What actually took place during the years 1845–47 is largely unrecorded, and the reader is excluded from the private life of the author, who supplies almost no gossip about himself, a great deal about his neighbors and about the universe.

As for me, I cannot in this short ramble give a simple and sincere account of my own life, but I think Thoreau might find it instructive to know that this memorial essay is being written in a house that, through no intent on my part, is the same size and shape as his own domicile on the pond—about ten by fifteen, tight, plainly finished, and at a little distance from my Concord. The house in which I sit this morning was built to accommodate a boat, not a man, but by long experience I have learned that in most respects it shelters me better than the larger dwelling where my bed is, and which, by design, is a man-house not a boathouse. Here in the boathouse I am a wilder and, it would appear, a healthier man, by a safe margin. I have a chair, a bench, a table, and I can walk into the water if I tire of the land. My house fronts a cove. Two fishermen have just arrived to spot fish from the air—an osprey and a man in a small yellow plane who works for the fish company. The man, I have noticed, is less well equipped than the hawk, who can dive directly on his fish and carry it away, without telephoning. A mouse and a squirrel share the house with me. The building is, in fact, a multiple dwelling, a semidetached affair. It is because I am semidetached while here that I find it possible to transact this private business with the fewest obstacles.

There is also a woodchuck here, living forty feet away under the wharf. When the wind is right, he can smell my house; and when the wind is contrary, I can smell his. We both use the wharf for sunning, taking turns, each adjusting his schedule to the other's convenience. Thoreau once ate a woodchuck. I think he felt he owed it to his readers, and that it was little enough, considering the indignities they were suffering at his hands and the dressing-down they were taking. (Parts of *Walden* are pure scold.) Or perhaps he ate the woodchuck because he believed every man should acquire strict business habits, and the woodchuck was destroying his market beans. I do not know. Thoreau had a strong experimental streak in him. It is probably no harder to eat a woodchuck than to construct a sentence that lasts a hundred years. At any rate, Thoreau is the only writer I know who prepared himself for his great ordeal by eating a woodchuck; also the only one who got a hangover from drinking too much water. (He was drunk the whole time, though he seldom touched wine or coffee or tea.)

Here in this compact house where I would spend one day as deliberately as Nature if I were not being pressed by *The Yale Review*, and with a woodchuck (as yet uneaten) for neighbor, I can feel the companionship of the occupant of the pondside cabin in Walden woods, a mile from the village, near the Fitchburg right of way. Even my immediate business is no barrier between us: Thoreau occasionally batted out a magazine piece, but was always suspicious of any sort of purposeful work that cut into his time. A man, he said, should take care not to be thrown off the track by every nutshell and mosquito's wing that falls on the rails.

There has been much guessing as to why he went to the pond. To set it down to escapism is, of course, to misconstrue what happened. Henry went forth to battle when he took to the woods, and *Walden* is the report of a man torn by two powerful and opposing drives— the desire to enjoy the world (and not be derailed by a mosquito wing) and the urge to set the world straight. One cannot join these two successfully, but sometimes, in rare cases, something good or even great results from the attempt of the tormented spirit to reconcile them. Henry went forth to battle, and if he set the stage himself, if he fought on his own terms and with his own weapons, it was because it was his nature to do things differently from most men, and to act in a cocky fashion. If the pond and the woods seemed a more plausible site for a house than an in-town location, it was because a cowbell made for him a sweeter sound than a churchbell. *Walden*, the book, makes the sound of the cowbell, more than a churchbell, and proves the point, although both sounds are in it, and both remarkably clear and sweet. He simply preferred his churchbell at a little distance.

I think one reason he went to the woods was a perfectly simple and commonplace one—and apparently he thought so, too. "At a certain season of our life," he wrote, "we are accustomed to consider every spot as the possible site of a house." There spoke the young man, a few years out of college, who had not yet broken away from home. He hadn't married, and he had found no job that measured up to his rigid standards of employment, and like any young man, or young animal, he felt uneasy and on the defensive until he had fixed himself a den. Most young men, of course, casting about for a site, are content merely to draw apart from their kinfolks. Thoreau, convinced that the greater part of what his neighbors called good was bad, withdrew from a great deal more than family: he pulled out of everything for a while, to serve everybody right for being so stuffy, and to try his own prejudices on the dog.

The house-hunting sentence above, which starts the Chapter called "Where I Lived, and What I Lived For," is followed by another passage that is worth quoting here because it so beautifully illustrates the offbeat prose that Thoreau was master of, a prose at once strictly disciplined and wildly abandoned. "I have surveyed the country on every side within a dozen miles of where I live," continued this delirious young man. "In imagination I have bought all the farms in succession, for all were to be bought, and I knew their price. I walked over each farmer's premises, tasted his wild apples, discoursed on husbandry with him, took his farm at his price, at any price, mortgaging it to him in my mind; even put a higher price on it—took everything but a deed of it—took his word for his deed, for I dearly love to talk—cultivated it, and him too to some extent, I trust, and withdrew when I had enjoyed it long enough, leaving him to carry it on." A copydesk man would get a double hernia trying to clean up that sentence for the management, but the sentence needs no fixing, for it perfectly captures the meaning of the writer and the quality of the ramble.

"Wherever I sat, there might I live, and the landscape radiated from me accordingly." Thoreau, the home-seeker, sitting on his hummock with the entire State of Massachusetts radiating from him, is to me the most humorous of the New England figures, and *Walden* the most humorous of the books, though its humor is almost continuously subsurface and there is nothing funny anywhere, except a few weak jokes and bad puns that rise to the surface like a perch in the pond that rose to the sound of the maestro's flute. Thoreau tended to write in sentences, a feat not every writer is capable of, and *Walden* is, rhetorically speaking, a collection of certified sentences, some of them, it would now appear, as indestructible as they are errant. The book is distilled from the vast journals, and this accounts for its intensity: he picked out bright particles that pleased his eye, whirled them in the kaleidoscope of his content, and produced the pattern that has endured—the color, the form, the light.

On this its hundredth birthday, Thoreau's *Walden* is pertinent and timely. In our uneasy season, when all men unconsciously seek a retreat from a world that has got almost completely out of hand, his house in the Concord woods is a haven. In our culture of gadgetry and the multiplicity of convenience, his cry "Simplicity, simplicity, simplicity!" has the insistence of a fire alarm. In the brooding atmosphere of war and the gathering radioactive storm, the innocence and serenity of his summer afternoons are enough to burst the remembering heart, and one gazes back upon that pleasing interlude—its confidence, its purity, its deliberateness—with awe and wonder, as one would look upon the the face of a child asleep.

"This small lake was of most value as a neighbor in the intervals of a gentle rain-storm in August, when, both air and water being perfectly still, but the sky overcast, midafternoon had all the serenity of evening, and the wood-thrush sang around, and was heard from shore to shore." Now, in the perpetual overcast in which our days are spent, we hear with extra perception and deep gratitude that song, tying century to century.

I sometimes amuse myself by bringing Henry Thoreau back to life and showing him the sights. I escort him into a phone booth and let him dial Weather. "This is a delicious evening," the girl's voice says, "when the whole body is one sense, and imbibes delight through every pore." I show him the spot in the Pacific where an island used to be, before some magician made it vanish. "We know not where we are," I murmur. "The light which puts out our eyes is darkness to us. Only that day dawns to which we are awake." I thumb through the latest copy of *Vogue* with him. "Of two patterns which differ only by a few threads more or less of a particular color," I read, "the one will be sold readily, the other lie on the shelf, though it frequently happens that, after the lapse of a season, the latter becomes the most fashionable." Together we go out-boarding on the Assabet, looking for what we've lost—a hound, a bay horse, a turtledove. I show him a distracted farmer who is trying to repair a hay baler before the thunder shower breaks. "This farmer," I remark, "is endeavoring to solve the problem of a livelihood by a formula more complicated than the problem itself. To get his shoe strings he speculates in herds of cattle."

I take the celebrated author to Twenty-One for lunch, so the waiters may study his shoes. The proprietor welcomes us. "The gross feeder," remarks the proprietor, sweeping the room with his arm, "is a man in the larva stage." After lunch we visit a classroom in one of those schools conducted by big corporations to teach their superannuated executives how to retire from business without serious injury to their health. (The shock to men's systems these days when relieved of the exacting routine of amassing wealth is very great and must be cushioned.) "It is not necessary," says the teacher to his pupils, "that a man should earn his living by the sweat of his brow, unless he sweats easier than I do. We are determined to be starved before we are hungry."

I turn on the radio and let Thoreau hear Winchell beat the red hand around the clock. "Time is but the stream I go a-fishing in," shouts Mr. Winchell, rattling his telegraph key. "Hardly a man takes a half hour's nap after dinner, but when he wakes he holds up his head and asks, 'What's the news?' If we read of one man robbed, or murdered, or killed by accident, or one house burned, or one vessel wrecked, or one steamboat blown up, or one cow run over on the Western Railroad, or one mad dog killed, or one lot of grasshoppers in the winter—we need never read of another. One is enough."

I doubt that Thoreau would be thrown off balance by the fantastic sights and sounds of the twentieth century. "The Concord nights," he once wrote, "are stranger than the Arabian nights." A four-engined air liner would merely serve to confirm his early views on travel. Everywhere he would observe, in new shapes and sizes, the old predicaments and follies of men—the desperation, the impedimenta, the meanness— along with the visible capacity for elevation of the mind and soul. "This curious world which we inhabit is more wonderful than it is convenient; more beautiful than it is useful; it is more to be admired and enjoyed than used." He would see that today ten thousand engineers are busy making sure that the world shall be convenient if they bust doing it, and others are determined to increase its usefulness even though its beauty is lost somewhere along the way.

At any rate, I'd like to stroll about the countryside in Thoreau's company for a day, observing the modern scene, inspecting today's snowstorm, pointing out the sights, and offering belated apologies for my sins. Thoreau is unique among writers in that those who admire him find him uncomfortable to live with—a regular hairshirt of a man. A little band of dedicated Thoreauvians would be a sorry sight indeed: fellows who hate compromise and have compromised, fellows who love wildness and have lived tamely, and at their side, censuring them and chiding them, the ghostly figure of this upright man, who long ago gave corroboration to impulses they perceived were right and issued warnings against the things they instinctively knew to be their enemies. I should hate to be called a Thoreauvian, yet I wince every time I walk into the barn I'm pushing before me, seventy-five feet by forty, and the author of *Walden* has served as my conscience through the long stretches of my trivial days.

Hairshirt or no, he is a better companion than most, and I would not swap him for a soberer or more reasonable friend even if I could. I can reread his famous invitation with undiminished excitement. The sad thing is that not more acceptances have been received, that so many decline for one reason or another, pleading some previous engagement or ill health. But the invitation stands. It will beckon as long as this remarkable book stays in print—which will be as long as there are August afternoons in the intervals of a gentle rainstorm, as long as there are ears to catch the faint sounds of the orchestra. I find it agreeable to sit here this morning, in a house of correct proportions, and hear across a century of time his flute, his frogs, and his seductive summons to the wildest revels of them all.

ERICH HELLER

Erich Heller (1911–) was born in Bohemia. A Doctor of Law and German Literature from Charles University in Prague, a Ph.D. in English literature from Cambridge, he now is Avalon Professor of Humanities at Northwestern University. He has written widely on modern German and European literature, notably in *The Disinherited Mind: Essays in Modern German Literature and Thought* (1952), *The Ironic German: A Study of Thomas Mann* (1958), *The Artist's Journey into the Interior and Other Essays* (1965), and *Franz Kafka* (1974).

THE IMPORTANCE OF NIETZSCHE

This essay explains one of the modern world's most startling and influential thinkers, a man frequently misunderstood, particularly as the unwitting Frankenstein of Hitler's monstrous Superman. This piece speaks to one of the main themes of both Stace and Bigelow. Heller insists on the "center of sanity" in Nietzsche's paradoxes, in his "fever-chart" for a world gone sick. Notice the figurative edges to Heller's words, as he puts them in new contexts—*inspired diatribe* or *national heretic*, for instance. He will assert, to our surprise, that the modern mind "speaks German" (perhaps echoing Sapir) and will then show us exactly the surprising truth in that figuratively extreme statement. Heller seems to have acquired a certain metaphorical boldness from the man he interprets and and translates for us, as in Nietzsche's own astonishing metaphors: "Who gave us the sponge with which to wipe out the whole horizon? How did we set about unchaining our earth from her sun?" Notice Nietzsche's remarkable passage about "the Guest of Stone" on p. 237.

1

In 1873, two years after Bismarck's Prussia had defeated France, a young German who happened to live in Switzerland and taught classical philology in the University of Basel, wrote a treatise concerned with "the German mind." It was an inspired diatribe against, above all, the German notion of *Kultur* and against the philistine readiness to believe that military victory proved cultural superiority. This was, he said, a disastrous superstition, symptomatic in itself of the absence of any true culture. According to him, the opposite was true: the civilization of the vanquished French was bound more and more to dominate the victorious German people that had wasted its spirit upon the chimera of political power.*

This national heretic's name, rather obscure at the time, was Friedrich Nietzsche. What, almost a century ago, he wrote about the perverse relationship between military success and intellectual dominance proved true: not then, perhaps, but now. Defeated in two wars, Germany appears to have invaded vast territories of the world's mind, with Nietzsche himself as no mean conqueror. For his was the vision of things to come. Among all the thinkers of the nineteenth century he is, with the possible exceptions of Dostoevsky and Kierkegaard, the only one who would not be too amazed by the amazing scene upon which we now move in sad, pathetic, heroic, stoic, or ludicrous bewilderment. Much, too much, would strike him as *déjà vu*: yes, he had foreseen it; and he would understand: for the "Modern Mind" speaks German, not always good German, but fluent German nonetheless. It was, alas, forced to learn the idiom of Karl Marx, and was delighted to be introduced to itself in the language of Sigmund Freud; taught by Ranke and, later, Max Weber, it acquired its historical and sociological self-consciousness, moved out of its tidy Newtonian universe on the instruction of Einstein, and followed a design of Oswald Spengler's in sending from the depth of its spiritual depression most ingeniously engineered objects higher than the moon. Whether it discovers, with Heidegger, the true habitation of its *Existenz* on the frontiers of Nothing, or meditates, with Sartre and Camus, *le Néant* or the Absurd; whether—to pass to its less serious moods—it is nihilistically young and profitably angry in London or rebelliously debauched and buddhistic in San Francisco—*man spricht deutsch*. It is all part of a story told by Nietzsche.

As for modern German literature and thought, it is hardly an exaggeration to say that they would not be what they are if Nietzsche had never

* I have omitted Heller's footnotes, which merely cite the German sources.—Ed.

lived. Name almost any poet, man of letters, philosopher, who wrote in German during the twentieth century and attained to stature and influence—Rilke, George, Kafka, Thomas Mann, Ernst Jünger, Musil, Benn, Heidegger, or Jaspers—and you name at the same time Friedrich Nietzsche. He is to them all—whether or not they know and acknowledge it (and most of them do)—what St. Thomas Aquinas was to Dante: the categorical interpreter of a world which they contemplate poetically or philosophically without ever radically upsetting its Nietzschean structure.

Nietzsche died in 1900, after twelve years of a total eclipse of his intellect, insane—and on the threshold of this century. Thinking and writing to the very edge of insanity, and with some of his last pages even going over it, he read and interpreted the temperatures of his own mind; but by doing so, he has drawn the fever-chart of an epoch. Indeed, much of his work reads like the self-diagnosis of a desperate physician who, suffering the disease on our behalf, comes to prescribe as a cure that we should form a new idea of health, and live by it.

He was convinced that it would take at least fifty years before a few men would understand what he had accomplished; and he feared that even then his teaching would be misinterpreted and misapplied. "I am terrified," he wrote, "by the thought of the sort of people who may one day invoke my authority." But is this not, he added, the anguish of every great teacher? He knows that he may prove a disaster as much as a blessing. The conviction that he was a great teacher never left him after he had passed through that period of sustained inspiration in which he wrote the first part of *Zarathustra*. After this, all his utterances convey the disquieting self-confidence and the terror of a man who has reached the culmination of that paradox which he embodies, a paradox which we shall try to name and which ever since has cast its dangerous spell over some of the finest and some of the coarsest minds.

Are we then, at the remove of two generations, in a better position to probe Nietzsche's mind and to avoid, as he hoped some might, the misunderstanding that he was merely concerned with the religious, philosophical, or political controversies fashionable in his day? And if this be a misinterpretation, can we put anything more valid in its place? What is the knowledge which he claims to have, raising him in his own opinion far above the contemporary level of thought? What is the discovery which serves him as a lever to unhinge the whole fabric of traditional values?

It is the knowledge that God is dead.

The death of God he calls the greatest event in modern history and the cause of extreme danger. Note well the paradox contained in these words. He never said that there was no God, but that the Eternal had been vanquished by Time and that the Immortal suffered death at the hands of mortals: God is dead. It is like a cry mingled of despair and triumph, reducing, by comparison, the whole story of atheism and agnosticism before and after him to the level of respectable mediocrity and making it sound like a collection of announcements by bankers who regret they are unable to invest in an unsafe proposition. Nietzsche, for the nineteenth century, brings to its *perverse* conclusion a line of religious thought and experience linked with the names of St. Paul, St. Augustine, Pascal, Kierkegaard, and Dostoevsky, minds for whom God was not simply the creator of an order of nature within which man has his clearly defined place, but to whom He came rather in order to challenge their natural being, making demands which appeared absurd in the light of natural reason. These men are of the family of Jacob: having wrestled with God for His blessing, they ever after limp through life with the framework of Nature incurably out of joint. Nietzsche is just such a wrestler; except that in him the shadow of Jacob merges with the shadow of Prometheus. Like Jacob, Nietzsche too believed that he prevailed against God in that struggle, and won a new name for himself, the name of Zarathustra. But the words *he* spoke on his mountain to the angel of the Lord were: "I will not let thee go, except thou curse me." Or, in words which Nietzsche did in fact speak: "I have on purpose devoted my life to exploring the whole contrast to a truly religious nature. I know the Devil and all his visions of God."

"God is dead"—this is the very core of Nietzsche's spiritual existence, and what follows is despair, *and* hope in a new greatness of man, visions of catastrophe *and* glory, the icy brilliance of analytical reason, fathoming with affected irreverence those depths hitherto hidden by awe and fear, and, side-by-side with it, the ecstatic invocations of a ritual healer. Probably inspired by Hölderlin's dramatic poem *Empedocles*, the young Nietzsche, who loved what he knew of Hölderlin's poetry, at the age of twenty planned to write a drama with Empedocles as its hero. His notes show that he saw the Greek philosopher as the tragic personification of his age, as a man in whom the latent conflicts of his epoch attained to consciousness, as one who suffered and died as the victim of an unresolvable tension: born with the soul of a *homo religiosus*, a seer, a prophet, and poet, he yet had the mind of a radical skeptic; and defending his soul against his mind and, in turn, his mind against his soul, he made his soul lose its spontaneity, and finally his mind its rationality. Had Nietzsche ever written the drama *Empedocles*, it might have become, in uncanny anticipation, his *own* tragedy.

It is a passage from Nietzsche's *Gaya Scienza*, his *Cheerful Science*, which conveys best the substance and quality of the mind, indeed the whole spiritual situation, from which the pronouncement of the death of God sprang. The passage is prophetically entitled "The Madman" and might have been called "The New Diogenes." Here is a brief extract from it:

Have you not heard of that madman who, in the broad light of the forenoon, lit a lantern and ran into the market-place, crying incessantly: "I am looking for God!" . . . As it happened, many were standing there who did not believe in God, and so he aroused great laughter . . . The madman leapt right among them . . . "Where is God?" he cried, "Well, I will tell you. *We have murdered him*—you and I . . . But how did we do this deed? . . . Who gave us the sponge with which to wipe out the whole horizon? How did we set about unchaining our earth from her sun? Whither is it moving now? Whither are we moving? . . . Are we not falling incessantly? . . . Is night not approaching, and more and more night? Must we not light lanterns in the forenoon? Behold the noise of the grave-diggers, busy to bury God . . . And we have killed him! What possible comfort is there for us? . . . Is not the greatness of this deed too great for us? To appear worthy of it, must not we ourselves become gods?"—At this point the madman fell silent and looked once more at those around him: "Oh," he said, "I am too early. My time has not yet come. The news of this tremendous event is still on its way . . . Lightning and thunder take time, the light of the stars takes time to get to us, deeds take time to be seen and heard . . . and *this* deed is still farther from them than the farthest stars—*and yet it was they themselves who did it!*"

And elsewhere, in a more prosaic mood, Nietzsche says: "People have no notion yet that from now onwards they exist on the mere pittance of inherited and decaying values"—soon to be overtaken by an enormous bankruptcy.

The story of the Madman, written two years before *Zarathustra* and containing *in nuce* the whole message of the Superman, shows the distance that divides Nietzsche from the conventional attitudes of atheism. He is the madman, breaking with his sinister news into the marketplace complacency of the pharisees of unbelief. They have done away with God, and yet the report of their own deed has not yet reached them. They know not what they have done, but He who could forgive them is no more. Much of Nietzsche's work ever after is the prophecy of their fate: "The story I have to tell is the history of the next two centuries. . . . For a long time now our whole civilization has been driving, with a tortured intensity growing from decade to decade, as if towards a catastrophe: restlessly, violently, tempestuously, like a mighty river desiring the end of its journey, without pausing to reflect, indeed fearful of reflection. . . . Where we live, soon nobody will be able to exist." For men become enemies, and each his own enemy. From now onward they will *hate*, Nietzsche believes, however many *comforts* they will lavish upon themselves, and hate *themselves* with a new hatred, unconsciously at work in the depths of their souls. True, there will be ever better reformers of society, ever better socialists, and ever better hospitals, and an ever increasing intolerance of pain and poverty and suffering and death, and an ever more fanatical craving for the greatest happiness of the greatest numbers. Yet the deepest impulse informing their striving will not be love and will not be compassion. Its true source will be the panic-struck determination not to have to ask the question "What is the meaning of our lives?"—the question which will remind them of the death of God, the uncomfortable question inscribed on the features of those who are uncomfortable, and asked above all by pain and poverty and suffering and death. Rather than allowing that question to be asked, they will do everything to smooth it away from the face of humanity. For they cannot endure it. And yet they will despise themselves for not enduring it, and for their guilt-ridden inability to answer it; and their self-hatred will betray them behind the back of their apparent charity and humanitarian concern. For *there* they will assiduously construct the tools for the annihilation of human kind. "There will be wars," Nietzsche writes, "such as have never been waged on earth." And he says: "I foresee something terrible. Chaos everywhere. Nothing left which is of any value; nothing which commands: Thou shalt!" This would have been the inspiration of the final work which Nietzsche often said he would write and never wrote: *The Will to Power*, or as he sometimes wanted to call it, *The Transvaluation of All Values. It might have given his full diagnosis of what he termed nihilism, the state of human beings and societies faced with a total eclipse of all values.

It is in defining and examining the (for him *historical*) phenomenon of nihilism that Nietzsche's attack on Christianity sets in (and it has remained the only truly subtle point which, within the whole range of his more and more unrestrained argumentativeness, this Antichrist makes against Christianity). For it is at this point that Nietzsche asks (and asks the same question in countless variations throughout his works): What are the *specific* qualities which the Christian tradition has instilled and cultivated in the minds of men? They are, he thinks, twofold: on the one hand, a more refined sense of truth than any other civilization has known, an almost uncontrollable desire for absolute spiritual and intellectual certainties; and, on the other hand, the ever-present suspicion that life on this earth is not in itself a supreme value, but in need of a higher, a transcendental justification. This, Nietzsche believes, is a destructive, and even self-destructive alliance, which is bound finally to corrode the very Christian beliefs on which it rests. For the mind, exercised and guided in its search for knowledge by the most sophisticated and comprehensive theology the world has ever known— a theology which through St. Thomas Aquinas has assimilated into its grand system the genius of Aristotle—was at the same time fashioned and directed by the indelible Christian distrust of the ways of the world. Thus it had to follow, with the utmost logical precision and determination, a course of systematically "devaluing" the knowably real. This mind, Nietzsche predicts, will eventually, in a frenzy of intellectual honesty, unmask as humbug and "meaningless" that which it began by regarding as the finer things in life. The boundless faith in truth, the joint legacy of Christ and Greek, will in the end dislodge every possible belief in the truth of any faith. Souls, long disciplined in a school of unworldliness and humility, will insist upon knowing the worst about themselves, indeed will only be able to grasp what is humiliating. Psychology will denigrate the creations of beauty, laying bare the tangle of unworthy desires of which they are "mere" sublimations. History will undermine the accumulated reputation of the human race by exhuming from beneath the splendid monuments the dead body of the past, revealing everywhere the spuriousness of motives, the human, all-too-human. And science itself will rejoice in exposing this long-suspected world as a mechanical contraption of calculable pulls and pushes, as a self-sufficient agglomeration of senseless energy, until finally, in a surfeit of knowledge, the scientific mind will perform the somersault of self-annihilation. "The nihilistic consequences of our natural sciences"—this is one of Nietzsche's fragmentary jottings—"from its pursuits there follows ultimately a self-decomposition, a turning against itself," which—and this is one of his most amazingly precise predictions—would first show itself in the impossibility, within science itself, of comprehending the very object of its inquiry within *one* logically coherent system, and would lead to extreme scientific pessimism, to an inclination to embrace a kind of analytical, abstract mysticism by which man would shift himself and his world to where, Nietzsche thinks, they were driving "ever since Copernicus: from the center towards an unknown X."

2

It is the tremendous paradox of Nietzsche that he himself follows, and indeed consciously wishes to hasten, this course of "devaluation"— particularly as a psychologist: and at the onset of megalomania he called himself the first psychologist in the world—"there was no psychology before me," a self-compliment which Sigmund Freud all but endorsed when, surprisingly late in his life, he came to know Nietzsche's writings. He had good reason to do so. Consider, for instance, the following passage from Nietzsche's *Beyond Good and Evil:*

> The world of historical values is dominated by forgery. These great poets, like Byron, Musset, Poe, Leopardi, Kleist, Gogol (I dare not mention greater names, but I mean them)—all endowed with souls wishing to conceal a break; often avenging themselves with their works upon some inner desecration, often seeking oblivion in their lofty flights from their all-too-faithful memories, often lost in mud and almost in love with it until they become like will-o-the-wisps of the morasses and simulate the stars . . . oh what a torture are all these great artists and altogether these higher beings, what a torture to him who has guessed their true nature.

This does indeed anticipate many a more recent speculation on traumata and compensations, on lusts and sublimations, on wounds and bows. Yet the extraordinary Nietzsche—incomprehensible in his contradictions except as the common strategist of two opposing armies who plans for the victory of a mysterious third—a few pages later takes back the guessing, not without insulting himself in the process: "From which it follows that it is the sign of a finer humanity to respect 'the mask' and not, in the wrong places, indulge in psychology and psychological curiosity." And furthermore: "He who does not *wish* to see what is great in a man, has the sharpest eye for that which is low and superficial in him, and so gives away—himself."

If Nietzsche is not the first psychologist of Europe, he is certainly a great psychologist—and perhaps really the first who comprehended what his more methodical successors, "strictly scientific" in their approach, did not see: *the psychology and the ethics of knowledge itself;* and both the psychology and the ethics of knowledge are of particular relevance when the knowledge in question purports to be knowledge of the human psyche. It was, strangely enough, Nietzsche's amoral metaphysics, his doubtful but immensely fruitful intuition of the Will to Power as being the ultimate reality of the world, that made him into the first *moralist of knowledge* in his century and long after. While all his scientific and scholarly contemporaries throve on the comfortable assumptions that, firstly, there was such a thing as "objective," and therefore morally neutral, knowledge, and that, secondly, everything that *can* be known "objectively" is therefore also *worth knowing*, he realized that knowledge, or at least the mode of knowledge predominant

at his time and ours, is the subtlest guise of the Will to Power; and that
as a manifestation of the will it is liable to be judged morally. For him,
there can be no knowledge without a compelling urge to acquire it; and
he knew that the knowledge thus acquired invariably reflects the nature
of the impulse by which the mind was prompted. It is this impulse
which *creatively* partakes in the making of the knowledge, and its share
in it is truly immeasurable when the knowledge is about the very source
of the impulse: the soul. This is why all interpretations of the soul must
to a high degree be self-interpretations: the sick interpret the sick, and
the dreamers interpret dreams. Or, as the Viennese satirist Karl Kraus—
with that calculated injustice which is the prerogative of satire—once
said of a certain psychological theory: "Psychoanalysis is the disease of
which it pretends to be the cure."

Psychology is bad psychology if it disregards its own psychology.
Nietzsche knew this. He was, as we have seen from his passage about
"those great men," a most suspicious psychologist, but he was at the
same time suspicious of the suspicion which was the father of his
thought. Homer, to be sure, did not suspect his heroes, but Stendhal did.
Does this mean that Homer knew less about the heroic than Stendhal?
Does it make sense to say that Flaubert's Emma Bovary is the product
of an imagination more profoundly initiated into the psychology of
women than that which created Dante's Beatrice? Is Benjamin Constant,
who created the dubious lover Adolphe, on more intimate terms with
the nature of a young man's erotic passion than is Shakespeare, the
begetter of Romeo? Certainly, Homer's Achilles and Stendhal's Julien
Sorel are different heroes, Dante's Beatrice and Flaubert's Emma Bovary
are different women, Shakespeare's Romeo and Constant's Adolphe are
different lovers, but it would be naïve to believe that they simply differ
"in actual fact." Actual facts hardly exist in either art or psychology:
both interpret and both claim universality for the meticulously presented particular. Those creatures made by creative imaginations can
indeed not be compared; yet if they differ as, in life, one person differs
from another, at the same time, because they have their existence not
"in life" but in art, they are incommensurable above all by virtue of
their author's incommensurable *wills* to know the human person, to
know the hero, the woman, the lover. It is not better and more knowing
minds that have created the suspect hero, the unlovable woman, the
disingenuous lover, but minds possessed by different desires for a different knowledge, a knowledge uninformed with the wonder and pride that
know Achilles, the love that knows Beatrice, the passion and compassion that know Romeo. When Hamlet has come to know the frailty of
woman, he knows Ophelia not better than when he was "unknowingly"

in love with her; he only knows her differently and he knows her worse.

All *new* knowledge about the soul is knowledge about a *different* soul. For can it ever happen that the freely discovering mind says to the soul: "This is what you are!"? Is it not rather as if the mind said to the soul: "This is how I *wish* you to see yourself! This is the image after which I create you! This is my secret about you: I shock you with it and, shockingly, at once wrest it from you"? And worse: having thus received *and* revealed its secret, the soul is no longer what it was when it lived in secrecy. For there are secrets which are *created* in the process of their revelation. And worse still: having been told its secrets, the soul may cease to be a soul. The step from modern psychology to soullessness is as imperceptible as that from modern physics to the dissolution of the concept "matter."

It is this disturbing state of affairs which made Nietzsche deplore "the torture" of psychologically "guessing the true nature of those higher beings" and, at the same time, recommend "respect for the mask" as a condition of "finer humanity." (A great pity he never wrote what, if we are to trust his notes, he planned to say in the abortive *Will to Power* about the literature of the nineteenth century. For no literary critic of the age has had a more penetrating insight into the "nihilistic" character of that "absolute aestheticism" that, from Baudelaire onward, has been the dominant inspiration of European poetry. Respectfully, and sometimes not so respectfully, Nietzsche recognized that behind the aesthetic "mask" there was a face distorted by the loathing of "reality." And it was the realistic and psychological novel that revealed to him that epoch's utterly pessimistic idea of its world. How intimately he knew those aesthetic Furies, or furious Muses, that haunted the mind of Flaubert, inspiring him to produce an *oeuvre* in which absolute pessimism, radical psychology, and extreme aestheticism are so intriguingly fused.)

For Nietzsche, however, *all* the activities of human consciousness share the predicament of psychology. There can be, for him, no "pure" knowledge, only satisfactions, however sophisticated, of the ever-varying intellectual needs of the *will to know*. He therefore demands that man should accept *moral responsibility* for the kind of questions he asks, and that he should realize what *values* are implied in the answers he seeks— and in this he was more Christian than all our post-Faustian Fausts of truth and scholarship. "The desire for truth," he says, "is itself in need of critique. Let this be the definition of my philosophical task. By way of experiment, I shall question for once the value of truth." And does he not! And he protests that, in an age which is as uncertain of its values

as is his and ours, the search for truth will issue in either trivialities or—
catastrophe. We may well wonder how he would react to the pious hopes
of our day that the intelligence and moral conscience of politicians will
save the world from the disastrous products of our scientific explorations
and engineering skills. It is perhaps not too difficult to guess; for he
knew that there was a fatal link between the moral resolution of scientists to follow the scientific search *wherever*, by its own momentum, it
will take us, and the moral debility of societies not altogether disinclined
to "apply" the results, however catastrophic. Believing that there was a
hidden identity between *all* the expressions of the Will to Power, he saw
the element of moral nihilism in the ethics of our science: its determination not to let "higher values" interfere with its highest value—Truth
(as it conceives it). Thus he said that the goal of knowledge pursued by
the natural sciences means perdition.

3

"God is dead"—and man, in his heart of hearts, is incapable of forgiv-
ing himself for having done away with Him: he is bent upon punishing
himself for this, his "greatest deed." For the time being, however, he will
take refuge in many an evasive action. With the instinct of a born hunter,
Nietzsche pursues him into all his hiding places, cornering him in each
of them. Morality without religion? Indeed not: "All purely moral demands without their religious basis," he says, "must needs end in
nihilism." What is there left? Intoxication. "Intoxication with music, with
cruelty, with hero-worship, or with hatred . . . Some sort of mysticism . . .
Art for Art's sake, Truth for Truth's sake, as a narcotic against self-
disgust; some kind of routine, *any* silly little fanaticism. . . ." But none
of these drugs can have any lasting effect. The time, Nietzsche predicts,
is fast approaching when secular crusaders, tools of man's collective
suicide, will devastate the world with their rival claims to compensate
for the lost Kingdom of Heaven by setting up on earth the ideological
rules of Love and Justice which, by the very force of the spiritual de-
rangement involved, will lead to the rules of cruelty and slavery; and he
prophesies that the war for global domination will be fought on behalf
of philosophical doctrines.

In one of his notes written at the time of *Zarathustra* Nietzsche says:
"He who no longer finds what is great in God, will find it nowhere. He
must either deny or create it." These words take us to the heart of that
paradox that enwraps Nietzsche's whole existence. He is, by the very
texture of his soul and mind, one of the most radically religious natures

that the nineteenth century brought forth, but is endowed with an intellect which guards, with the aggressive jealousy of a watchdog, all the approaches to the temple. For such a man, what, after the *denial* of God, is there left to *create*? Souls, not only strong enough to endure Hell, but to transmute its agonies into superhuman delight—in fact: the Superman. Nothing short of the transvaluation of all values can save us. Man has to be made immune from the effects of his second Fall and final separation from God: he must learn to see in his second expulsion the promise of a new paradise. For "the Devil may become envious of him who suffers so deeply, and throw him out—into Heaven."

Is there, then, any cure? Yes, says Nietzsche: a new kind of psychic health. And what is Nietzsche's conception of it? How is it to be brought about? By perfect self-knowledge *and* perfect self-transcendence. But to explain this, we should have to adopt an idiom disturbingly compounded of the language of Freudian psychology and tragic heroism. For the self-knowledge which Nietzsche expects all but requires a course in depth-analysis; but the self-transcendence he means lies not in the practice of virtue as a sublimation of natural meanness; it can only be found in a kind of unconditional and almost supranatural sublimity. If there were a Christian virtue, be it goodness, innocence, chastity, saintliness, or self-sacrifice, that could not, however much he tried, be interpreted as a compensatory maneuver of the mind to "transvalue" weakness and frustration, Nietzsche might affirm it (as he is constantly tempted to praise Pascal). The trouble is that there cannot be such a virtue. For virtues are reflected upon by minds; and even the purest virtue will be suspect to a mind filled with suspicion. To think thoughts so immaculate that they must command the trust of even the most untrusting imagination, and to act from motives so pure that they are out of reach of even the most cunning psychology, this is the unattainable ideal, it would seem, of this first psychologist of Europe. "Caesar—with the heart of Christ!" he once exclaimed in the secrecy of his notebook. Was this perhaps a definition of the Superman, this darling child of his imagination? It may well be; but this lofty idea meant, alas, that he had to think the meanest thought: he saw in the real Christ an illegitimate son of the Will to Power, a frustrated rabbi who set out to save himself and the underdog humanity from the intolerable strain of impotently resenting the Caesars: *not* to be Caesar was now proclaimed a spiritual distinction—a newly invented form of power, the power of the powerless.

Nietzsche had to fail, and fail tragically, in his determination to create a new man from the clay of negation. Almost with the same breath with which he gave the life of his imagination to the Superman, he blew the flame out again. For Zarathustra who preaches the Superman also teaches the doctrine of the Eternal Recurrence of All Things; and according to this doctrine nothing can ever come into being that had not existed at some time before—and, Zarathustra says, "never yet has there been a Superman." Thus the expectation of the Superman, this majestic new departure of life, indeed the possibility of any novel development, seems frustrated from the outset, and the world, caught forever in a cycle of gloomily repeated constellations of energy, stands condemned to a most dismal eternity.

Yet the metaphysical nonsense of these contradictory doctrines is not entirely lacking in poetic and didactic method. The Eternal Recurrence of All Things is Nietzsche's mythic formula of a meaningless world, the universe of nihilism, and the Superman stands for its transcendence, for the miraculous resurrection of meaning from its total negation. All Nietzsche's miracles are paradoxes designed to jerk man out of his false beliefs—in time before they bring about his spiritual destruction in an ecstasy of disillusionment and frustration. The Eternal Recurrence is the high school meant to teach strength through despair. The Superman graduates from it *summa cum laude et gloria*. He is the prototype of health, the man who has learned to live without belief and without truth, and, superhumanly delighting in life "as such," actually *wills* the Eternal Recurrence: Live in such a way that you desire nothing more than to live this very same life again and again! The Superman, having attained to this manner of existence which is exemplary and alluring into all eternity, despises his former self for craving moral sanctions, for satisfying his will to power in neurotic sublimation, for deceiving himself about the "meaning" of life. What will he be then, this man who at last knows what life *really* is? Recalling Nietzsche's own accounts of all-too-human nature, and his analysis of the threadbare fabric of traditional values and truths, may he not be the very monster of nihilism, a barbarian, not necessarily blond, but perhaps a conqueror of the world, shrieking bad German from under his dark mustache? Yes, Nietzsche feared his approach in history: the vulgar caricature of the Superman. And because he also feared that the liberally decadent and agnostically disbelieving heirs to Christian morality would be too feeble to meet the challenge, having enfeebled the idea of civilized existence and rendered powerless the good, he sent forth from his imagination the Superman to defeat the defeat of man.

Did Nietzsche himself *believe* in the truth of his doctrines of the Superman and the Eternal Recurrence? In one of his posthumously published notes he says of the Eternal Recurrence: "We have produced the hardest possible thought—the Eternal Recurrence of All Things— now let us create the creature who will accept it lightheartedly and joy-

fully!" Clearly, there must have been times when he thought of the Eternal Recurrence not as a "Truth" but as a kind of spiritual Darwinian test to select for survival the spiritually fittest. There is a note of his which suggests precisely this: "I perform the great experiment: Who can bear the idea of the Eternal Recurrence?" This is a measure of Nietzsche's own unhappiness: the nightmare of nightmares was to him the idea that he might have to live his identical life again and again and again; and an ever deeper insight into the anatomy of despair we gain from this note: "Let us consider this idea in its most terrifying form: existence, as it is, without meaning or goal, but inescapably recurrent, without a final into nothingness. . . . Those who cannot bear the sentence, There is no salvation, _ought_ to perish!" Indeed, Nietzsche's Superman is the creature strong enough to live forever a cursed existence and even to transmute it into the Dionysian rapture of tragic acceptance. Schopenhauer called man the _animal metaphysicum_. It is certainly true of Nietzsche, the renegade _hom religiosus_. Therefore, if God was dead, then for Nietzsche man was an eternally created misfit, the diseased animal, as he called him, plagued by a metaphysical hunger which it was now impossible to feed even if all the Heavens were to be ransacked. Such a creature was doomed: he had to die out, giving way to the Superman who would miraculously feed on barren fields and finally conquer the metaphysical hunger itself without any detriment to the glory of life.

Did Nietzsche himself _believe_ in the Superman? In the manner in which a poet believes in the truth of his creations. Did Nietzsche believe in the truth of poetic creations? Once upon a time when, as a young man, he wrote _The Birth of Tragedy_, Nietzsche did believe in the power of art to transfigure life by creating lasting images of true beauty out of the meaningless chaos. It had seemed credible enough as long as his gaze was enraptured by the distant prospect of classical Greece and the enthusiastic vicinity of Richard Wagner's Tribschen. Soon, however, his deeply Romantic belief in art turned to skepticism and scorn; and his unphilosophical anger was provoked by those "metaphysical counterfeiters," as he called them, who enthroned the trinity of beauty, goodness, and truth. "One should beat them," he said. Poetic beauty _and_ truth? No, "we have _Art_ in order not to perish of Truth"; and, says Zarathustra, "poets lie too much"—and adds dejectedly: "But Zarathustra too is a poet . . . _We_ lie too much." And he did: while Zarathustra preached the Eternal Recurrence, his author confided to his diary: "I do not wish to live _again_. How have I borne life? By creating. What has made me endure? The vision of the Superman who affirms life. I have tried to affirm life _myself_ —but ah!"

Was he, having lost God, capable of truly believing in anything? "He who no longer finds what is great in God will find it nowhere—he must either deny it or create it." Only the "either-or" does not apply. All his life Nietzsche tried to do both. He had the passion for truth and no belief in it. He had the love of life and despaired of it. This is the stuff from which demons are made—perhaps the most powerful secret demon eating the heart out of the modern mind. To have written and enacted the extremist story of his mind is Nietzsche's true claim to greatness. "The Don Juan of the Mind" he once called, in a "fable" he wrote, a figure whose identity is hardly in doubt:

> The Don Juan of the Mind: no philosopher or poet has yet discovered him. What he lacks is the love of the things he knows, what he possesses is *esprit*, the itch and delight in the chase and intrigue of knowledge—knowledge as far and high as the most distant stars. Until in the end there is nothing left for him to chase except the knowledge which hurts most, just as a drunkard in the end drinks absinthe and methylated spirits. And in the very end he craves for Hell—it is the only knowledge which can still seduce him. Perhaps it too will disappoint, as everything that he knows. And if so, he will have to stand transfixed through all eternity, nailed to disillusion, having himself become the Guest of Stone, longing for a last supper of knowledge which he will never receive. For in the whole world of things there is nothing left to feed his hunger.

It is a German Don Juan, this Don Juan of the Mind; and it is amazing that Nietzsche should not have recognized his features: the features of Goethe's Faust at the point at which he has succeeded at last in defeating the plan of salvation.

And yet Nietzsche's work, wrapped in paradox after paradox, taking us to the limits of what is still comprehensible and often beyond, carries elements which issue from a center of sanity. No doubt, this core is in perpetual danger of being crushed, and was in fact destroyed in the end. But it is there, and is made of the stuff of which goodness is made. A few years before he went mad, he wrote: "My life is now comprised in the wish that the truth about all things be different from my way of seeing it: if only someone would convince me of the improbability of my truths!" And he said: "Lonely and deeply suspicious of myself as I was, I took, not without secret spite, sides *against* myself and *for* anything that happened to hurt me and was hard for me." Why? Because he was terrified by the prospect that all the better things in life, all honesty of mind, integrity of character, generosity of heart, fineness of aesthetic perception, would be corrupted and finally cast away by the new barbarians, unless the mildest and gentlest hardened themselves for the war which was about to be waged against them: "Caesar—with the heart of Christ!"

Time and again we come to a point in Nietzsche's writings where the shrill tones of the rebel are hushed by the still voice of the autumn of a world waiting in calm serenity for the storms to break. Then this tormented mind relaxes in what he once called the *Rosengeruch des Unwiederbringlichen*—an untranslatably beautiful lyricism of which the closest equivalent in English is perhaps Yeats' lines:

> Man is in love and loves what vanishes.
> What more is there to say?

In such moments the music of Bach brings tears to his eyes and he brushes aside the noise and turmoil of Wagner; or he is, having deserted Zarathustra's cave in the mountains, enchanted by the gentle grace of a Mediterranean coastline. Rejoicing in the quiet lucidity of Claude Lorrain, or seeking the company of Goethe in conversation with Eckermann, or comforted by the composure of Stifter's *Nachsommer*, a Nietzsche emerges, very different from the one who used to inhabit the fancies of Teutonic schoolboys, and, alas, schoolmasters, a Nietzsche who is a traditionalist at heart, a desperate lover who castigates what he loves because he knows it will abandon him and the world. It is the Nietzsche who can with one sentence cross out all the dissonances of his apocalyptic voices: "I once saw a storm raging over the sea, and a clear blue sky above it; it was then that I came to dislike all sunless, cloudy passions which know no light, except the lightning." And this was written by the same man who said that his tool for philosophizing was the hammer, and of himself that he was not human but dynamite.

In these regions of his mind dwells the terror that he may have helped to bring about the very opposite of what he desired. When this terror comes to the fore, he is much afraid of the consequences of his teaching. Perhaps the best will be driven to despair by it, the very worst accept it? And once he put into the mouth of some imaginary titanic genius what is his most terrible prophetic utterance: "Oh grant madness, you heavenly powers! Madness that at last I may believe in myself . . . I am consumed by doubts, for I have killed the Law. . . . If I am not more than the Law, then I am the most abject of all men."

What, then, is the final importance of Nietzsche? For one of his readers it lies in his example which is so strange, profound, confounded, alluring, and forbidding that it can hardly be looked upon as exemplary.

But it cannot be ignored either. For it has something to do with living lucidly in the dark age of which he so creatively despaired.

SUGGESTIONS FOR WRITING

1. Write five or six sentences, each containing a pun that awakens a sleeping metaphor, as Thoreau does with "throw off the track." Try something like "The apple of Jones's eye seemed a little over-ripe," or "And there she planted her feet: you could almost see them take root."

2. To familiarize yourself with figurative writing, take several of Thoreau's figures of speech and analyze each one according to the three principal levels of figurative subtlety: the simile, the meta-phor, the implied metaphor. The *simile* makes its figurative com-parison openly, using *like, as,* or *as if*:

    > He was *like* a lion.
    > He roared *as* a lion roars.
    > He roared *as if* he were a lion.

    The *metaphor* exaggerates further by pretending that "he *is* a lion." (In other words, drop the *like* from a simile and you have a meta-phor.) The *implied metaphor* hints at the pretended identity with-out naming it, implying "lion" by using only a lionish attribute or two: "He shook his yellow mane as if he were king of the jungle."
    Now, pick up one of your selections from Thoreau's figures of speech, put it in whichever of the three levels it belongs, and fill in the other two levels, rephrasing the figure to suit them. For instance, the following figure of Thoreau's is an implied metaphor: "a poet has put his farm in rhyme, . . . milked it, skimmed it, and got all the cream." Now, what would the figure be, stated plainly as a simile and as a metaphor? Your answer would look like this:

    SIMILE: The farm is like a cow.
    METAPHOR: The farm is a cow.
    IMPLIED METAPHOR: (Thoreau) "a poet . . . milked it, skimmed it, and got all the cream."

    Here is another example, with Thoreau giving the metaphor, leaving you to make the simile and implied metaphor:

    SIMILE: The distant mountain ranges are like coins.

> METAPHOR: (Thoreau) "distant mountain ranges . . . , those true-blue coins from heaven's own mint."
>
> IMPLIED METAPHOR: The distant mountain ranges seemed fresh and newly minted.

3. Write five phrases that mix formal and informal diction, as in the following examples from E. B. White: "The immaturity of the author and the *bugs* in the logic"; "so beautifully illustrates the *offbeat* prose"; "It was his nature to do things differently from most men, and to act in a *cocky* fashion"; "perfectly captures the meaning of the writer and the quality of the *ramble*."

4. From your own experience write an essay illustrating one of Thoreau's assertions: "A man is rich in proportion to the number of things he can afford to let alone"; "To be awake is to be alive"; "Let us spend one day as deliberately as Nature" (the last might be a wonderful opening for humor, the shoes full of water, the sandwiches full of ants).

5. Illustrate from your own experience, and with references and allusions to Thoreau, the Thoreauvian satisfaction in building a tree house, spending a night in the woods, planting a watermelon patch, turning a boathouse (just the size of Thoreau's cabin) into a studio for rumination, or knowing a woodchuck (as yet uneaten).

6. Write about some book that has changed the direction of your life, quoting something from Cooley to help you describe the book's quality: "A choice spirit defines itself in great part by what it avoids"; "He has a whole-hearted joy in his work"; "expressing without a strain a natural and interesting self."

7. Try a passage in parody or imitation of Thoreau. Now try one imitating White, attempting to catch a prose that can echo Shakespeare's "Sweet are the uses of adversity," that can add an egg-beater and a Western, that can follow a *plodding economist* with a *rough going*, and that still can pay a hairshirt of a man a praise so high it almost bursts the remembering heart.

8. Write five combinations of words not usually found together, as in Heller's *inspired diatribe* (this is known as *oxymoron*—a "pointed stupidity," *oxy* meaning "point" and *moron* meaning what it says), where the apparent contradiction of the terms sharpens the underlying point: *mad genius, beautifully ugly, a wicked virtue,* and so forth. Write another five in which the two words come from different areas of activity or thought, as when Heller transplants

heretic from the religious to the political arena by adding *national,* calling Nietzsche a *national heretic.* Try something like *political wallflower, academic shortstop, athletic thinker,* and so forth.

9. Write a metaphor that extends through several sentences, as in Heller's extension of "he read and interpreted the temperatures of his own mind."

10. Try three or four Nietzschean paradoxes, attained by playing on different forms of the same word: "Nothing short of the *transvaluation* of all *values* can save us"—"even the purest virtue will be *suspect* to a mind filled with *suspicion*"—"the *power* of the *powerless.*"

Seven
The Personal Essay

Here is an opportunity to limber and freshen your prose by telling a story about yourself, or someone else, as the body of your essay, the complete evidence. Each of the writers in this section has done this in one way or another, building on the anecdote, making a point about something that happened. These essays are really just anecdotes—what we would tell about ourselves, or someone else, in casual conversation—elaborated, fleshed out into fuller detail and clarity. Here is your opportunity for fully colloquial language, for "he said" and "she said," for colorful and explicit description. After you read each piece, see (once again) if you can put its point—its thesis—into one sentence.

GEORGE ORWELL

We have already met George Orwell—Eric Arthur Blair—in "Politics and the English Language" in Chapter 4.

SHOOTING AN ELEPHANT

This may be the best personal essay ever written. It has certainly become a classic, and almost instantaneously, since it appeared in 1950 heading the posthumous collection of Orwell's essays, which bears the name *Shooting an Elephant and Other Essays* and contains "Politics and the English Language." It demonstrates superbly how a personal anecdote can illustrate a general expository point—imperialism is evil—a thesis that might have been developed at length in a conventional essay, with illustrations from history and testimony from other observers. As you read, notice how Orwell's language keeps the picture before your eyes, and how, when his impressions grow vivid, he moves into metaphor to tell more clearly how it was—"as neatly as one skins a rabbit." Ask yourself what the difference in force is between the simile and the metaphor, "like a huge rock toppling" and "grandmotherly air." Notice also how Orwell's stringent honesty about his feelings enforces his thesis, that which he knows to be right.

In Moulmein, in Lower Burma, I was hated by large numbers of people —the only time in my life that I have been important enough for this to happen to me. I was sub-divisional police officer of the town, and in an aimless, petty kind of way anti-European feeling was very bitter. No one had the guts to raise a riot, but if a European woman went through the bazaars alone somebody would probably spit betel juice over her dress. As a police officer I was an obvious target and was baited whenever it seemed safe to do so. When a nimble Burman tripped me up on the football field and the referee (another Burman) looked the other way, the crowd yelled with hideous laughter. This happened more than once. In the end the sneering yellow faces of young men that met me everywhere, the insults hooted after me when I was at a safe distance, got badly on my nerves. The young Buddhist priests were the worst of all. There were several thousands of them in the town and none of them seemed to have anything to do except stand on street corners and jeer at Europeans.

All this was perplexing and upsetting. For at that time I had already made up my mind that imperialism was an evil thing and the sooner I chucked up my job and got out of it the better. Theoretically—and secretly, of course—I was all for the Burmese and all against their oppressors, the British. As for the job I was doing, I hated it more bitterly than I can perhaps make clear. In a job like that you see the dirty work of Empire at close quarters. The wretched prisoners huddling in the stinking cages of the lockups, the grey, cowed faces of the long-term convicts, the scarred buttocks of the men who had been flogged with bamboos—all these oppressed me with an intolerable sense of guilt. But I could get nothing into perspective. I was young and ill-educated and I had had to think out my problems in the utter silence that is imposed on every Englishman in the East. I did not even know that the British Empire is dying, still less did I know that it is a great deal better than the younger empires that are going to supplant it. All I knew was that I was stuck between my hatred of the empire I served and my rage against the evil-spirited little beasts who tried to make my job impossible. With one part of my mind I thought of the British Raj as an unbreakable tyranny, as something clamped down, in *saecula saeculorum*, upon the will of prostrate peoples; with another part I thought that the greatest joy in the world would be to drive a bayonet into a Buddhist priest's guts. Feelings like these are the normal by-products of imperialism; ask any Anglo-Indian official, if you can catch him off duty.

One day something happened which in a roundabout way was enlightening. It was a tiny incident in itself, but it gave me a better glimpse than I had had before of the real nature of imperialism—the real motives for which despotic governments act. Early one morning the sub-inspector at a police station the other end of the town rang me up on the 'phone and said that an elephant was ravaging the bazaar. Would I please come and do something about it? I did not know what I could do, but I wanted to see what was happening and I got on to a pony and started out. I took my rifle, an old .44 Winchester and much too small to kill an elephant, but I though the noise might be useful *in terrorem*. Various Burmans stopped me on the way and told me about the elephant's doings. It was not, of course, a wild elephant, but a tame one which had gone "must." It had been chained up, as tame elephants always are when their attack of "must" is due, but on the previous night it had broken its chain and escaped. Its mahout, the only person who could manage it when it was in that state, had set out in pursuit, but had taken the wrong direction and was now twelve hours' journey away, and in the morning the elephant had suddenly reappeared in the town. The Burmese population had no weapons and were quite helpless against it. It had already destroyed somebody's bamboo hut, killed a cow and raided some fruit-stalls and devoured the stock; also it had met the municipal rubbish van and, when the driver jumped out and took to his heels, had turned the van over and inflicted violences upon it.

The Burmese sub-inspector and some Indian constables were waiting for me in the quarter where the elephant had been seen. It was a very poor quarter, a labyrinth of squalid bamboo huts, thatched with palm-leaf, winding all over a steep hillside. I remember that it was a cloudy, stuffy morning at the beginning of the rains. We began questioning the people as to where the elephant had gone and, as usual, failed to get any definite information. That is invariably the case in the East; a story always sounds clear enough at a distance, but the nearer you get to the scene of events the vaguer it becomes. Some of the people said that the elephant had gone in one direction, some said that he had gone in another, some professed not even to have heard of any elephant. I had almost made up my mind that the whole story was a pack of lies, when we heard yells a little distance away. There was a loud, scandalized cry of "Go away, child! Go away this instant!" and an old woman with a switch in her hand came round the corner of a hut, violently shooing away a crowd of naked children. Some more women followed, clicking their tongues and exclaiming; evidently there was something that the children ought not to have seen. I rounded the hut and saw a man's dead body sprawling in the mud. He was an Indian, a black Dravidian coolie, almost naked, and he could not have been dead many minutes. The people said that the elephant had come suddenly upon him round the corner of the hut, caught him with its trunk, put its foot on his back and ground him into the earth. This was the rainy season and the ground was soft, and his face had scored a trench a foot deep and a couple of yards long. He was lying on his belly with arms crucified and head sharply twisted to one side. His face was coated with mud, the eyes wide open, the teeth bared and grinning with an expression of unendurable agony. (Never tell me, by the way, that the dead look peaceful. Most of the corpses I have seen looked devilish.) The friction of the great beast's foot had stripped the skin from his back as neatly as one skins a rabbit. As soon as I saw the dead man I sent an orderly to a friend's house nearby to borrow an elephant rifle. I had already sent back the pony, not wanting it to go mad with fright and throw me if it smelt the elephant.

The orderly came back in a few minutes with a rifle and five cartridges, and meanwhile some Burmans had arrived and told us that the elephant was in the paddy fields below, only a few hundred yards away. As I started forward practically the whole population of the quarter flocked out of the houses and followed me. They had seen the rifle and were all shouting excitedly that I was going to shoot the elephant. They had not shown much interest in the elephant when he was merely ravaging their homes, but it was different now that he was going to be shot. It was a bit of fun to them, as it would be to an English crowd; besides they wanted the meat. It made me vaguely uneasy. I had no intention of shooting the elephant—I had merely sent for the rifle to defend myself if necessary—and it is always unnerving to have a crowd following you. I marched down the hill, looking and feeling a fool, with the rifle over my shoulder and an ever-growing army of people jostling at my heels. At the bottom, when you got away from the huts, there was a metalled road and beyond that a miry waste of paddy fields a thousand yards across, not yet ploughed but soggy from the first rains and dotted with coarse grass. The elephant was standing [eighty]* yards from the road, his left side towards us. He took not the slightest notice of the crowd's approach. He was tearing up bunches of grass, beating them against his knees to clean them and stuffing them into his mouth.

I had halted on the road. As soon as I saw the elephant I knew with perfect certainty that I ought not to shoot him. It is a serious matter to shoot a working elephant—it is comparable to destroying a huge and costly piece of machinery—and obviously one ought not to do it if it can possible be avoided. And at that distance, peacefully eating, the elephant looked no more dangerous than a cow. I thought then and I think now that his attack of "must" was already passing off; in which case he would merely wander harmlessly about until the mahout came back and caught him. Moreover, I did not in the least want to shoot him. I decided that I would watch him for a little while to make sure that he did not turn savage again, and then go home.

But at that moment I glanced round at the crowd that had followed me. It was an immense crowd, two thousand at the least and growing every minute. It blocked the road for a long distance on either side. I looked at the sea of yellow faces above the garish clothes—faces all happy and excited over this bit of fun, all certain that the elephant was going to be shot. They were watching me as they would watch a conjurer about to perform a trick. They did not like me, but with the magical rifle in my hands I was momentarily worth watching. And suddenly I realized that I should have to shoot the elephant after all. The people expected it of me and I had got to do it; I could feel their two thousand wills pressing me forward, irresistibly. And it was at this moment, as I stood there with the rifle in my hands, that I first grasped the hollowness, the futility of the white man's dominion in the East. Here was I, the white man with his gun, standing in front of the unarmed native crowd—seemingly the leading actor of the piece; but in reality I was only an absurd puppet pushed to and fro by the will of those yellow faces behind. I perceived in this moment that when the white man turns tyrant it is his own freedom that he destroys. He becomes a sort of hollow, posing dummy, the conventionalized figure of a sahib. For it is the condition of his rule that he shall spend his life in trying to impress the "natives," and so in every crisis he has got to do what the "natives" expect of him. He wears a mask, and his face grows to fit it. I had got to

---

* Original and all reprints say "eight," an obvious error.—Ed.

shoot the elephant. I had committed myself to doing it when I sent for the rifle. A sahib has got to act like a sahib; he has got to appear resolute, to know his own mind and do definite things. To come all that way, rifle in hand, with two thousand people marching at my heels, and then to trail feebly away, having done nothing—no, that was impossible. The crowd would laugh at me. And my whole life, every white man's life in the East, was one long struggle not to be laughed at.

But I did not want to shoot the elephant. I watched him beating the bunch of grass against his knees, with that preoccupied grandmotherly air that elephants have. It seemed to me that it would be murder to shoot him. At that age I was not squeamish about killing animals, but I had never shot an elephant and never wanted to. (Somehow it always seems worse to kill a *large* animal.) Besides, there was the beast's owner to be considered. Alive, the elephant was worth at least a hundred pounds; dead, he would only be worth the value of his tusks, five pounds, possibly. But I had got to act quickly. I turned to some experienced-looking Burmans who had been there when we arrived, and asked them how the elephant had been behaving. They all said the same thing: he took no notice of you if you left him alone, but he might charge if you went too close to him.

It was perfectly clear to me what I ought to do. I ought to walk up to within, say, twenty-five yards of the elephant and test his behavior. If he charged, I could shoot; if he took no notice of me, it would be safe to leave him until the mahout came back. But also I knew that I was going to do no such thing. I was a poor shot with a rifle and the ground was soft mud into which one would sink at every step. If the elephant charged and I missed him, I should have about as much chance as a toad under a steamroller. But even then I was not thinking particularly of my own skin, only of the watchful yellow faces behind. For at that moment, with the crowd watching me, I was not afraid in the ordinary sense, as I would have been if I had been alone. A white man mustn't be frightened in front of "natives"; and so, in general, he isn't frightened. The sole thought in my mind was that if anything went wrong those two thousand Burmans would see me pursued, caught, trampled on and reduced to a grinning corpse like that Indian up the hill. And if that happened it was quite probable that some of them would laugh. That would never do. There was only one alternative. I shoved the cartridges into the magazine and lay down on the road to get a better aim.

The crowd grew very still, and a deep, low, happy sigh, as of people who see the theatre curtain go up at last, breathed from innumerable throats. They were going to have their bit of fun after all. The rifle was a beautiful German thing with cross-hair sights. I did not then know that in shooting an elephant one would shoot to cut an imaginary bar running from ear-hole to ear-hole. I ought therefore, as the elephant was sideways on, to have aimed straight at his ear-hole; actually I aimed several inches in front of this, thinking the brain would be further forward.

When I pulled the trigger I did not hear the bang or feel the kick— one never does when a shot goes home—but I heard the devilish roar of glee that went up from the crowd. In that instant, in too short a time, one would have thought, even for the bullet to get there, a mysterious terrible change had come over the elephant. He neither stirred nor fell, but every line of his body had altered. He looked suddenly stricken, shrunken, immensely old, as though the frightful impact of the bullet had paralysed him without knocking him down. At last, after what seemed a long time—it might have been five seconds, I dare say—he sagged flabbily to his knees. His mouth slobbered. An enormous senility seemed to have settled upon him. One could have imagined him thousands of years old. I fired again into the same spot. At the second shot he did not collapse but climbed with desperate slowness to his feet and stood weakly upright, with legs sagging and head drooping. I fired a third time. That was the shot that did for him. You could see the agony of it jolt his whole body and knock the last remnant of strength from his legs. But in falling he seemed for a moment to rise, for as his hind legs collapsed beneath him he seemed to tower upwards like a huge rock toppling, his trunk reaching skywards like a tree. He trumpeted, for the first and only time. And then down he came, his belly towards me, with a crash that seemed to shake the ground even where I lay.

I got up. The Burmans were already racing past me across the mud. It was obvious that the elephant would never rise again, but he was not dead. He was breathing very rhythmically with long rattling gasps, his great mound of a side painfully rising and falling. His mouth was wide open—I could see far down into caverns of pale pink throat. I waited a long time for him to die, but his breathing did not weaken. Finally I fired my two remaining shots into the spot where I thought his heart must be. The thick blood welled out of him like red velvet, but still he did not die. His body did not even jerk when the shots hit him, the tortured breathing continued without a pause. He was dying, very slowly and in great agony, but in some world remote from me where not even a bullet could damage him further. I felt that I had got to put an end to that dreadful noise. It seemed dreadful to see the great beast lying there, powerless to move and yet powerless to die, and not even to be able to finish him. I sent back for my small rifle and poured shot after shot into his heart and down his throat. They seemed to make no impression. The tortured gasps continued as steadily as the ticking of a clock. In the end I could not stand it any longer and went away. I heard later that it took him half an hour to die. Burmans were bringing dahs and baskets even before I left, and I was told they had stripped his body almost to the bones by the afternoon.

Afterwards, of course, there were endless discussions about the shooting of the elephant. The owner was furious, but he was only an Indian and could do nothing. Besides, legally I had done the right thing, for a mad elephant has to be killed, like a mad dog, if its owner fails to control it. Among the Europeans opinion was divided. The older men said I was right, the young men said it was a damn shame to shoot an elephant for killing a coolie, because an elephant was worth more than any damn Coringhee coolie. And afterwards I was very glad that the coolie had been killed; it put me legally in the right and it gave me a sufficient pretext for shooting the elephant. I often wondered whether any of the others grasped that I had done it solely to avoid looking a fool.

JAMES BALDWIN

James Baldwin (1924–), born in Harlem, began writing in junior high school, where Countee Cullen, a prominent poet in the Harlem Renaissance of the 1920's, was his teacher. Later, under the encouragement of Richard Wright, he won several fellowships, including a Guggenheim. But he bought a one-way ticket to France in 1948, intending never to return. His first novel, *Go Tell It on the Mountain,* appeared in 1953. After a decade of living in Europe, he returned to the United States, where he now spends most of his time.

FIFTH AVENUE UPTOWN: A LETTER FROM HARLEM

This essay describes how Jim Crow moved north and into a segregation the more depressing because it was complacently overlooked. Notice how, to underline his point, Baldwin combines impressions from childhood with observations of the man returned to the scene. Mark his telling details: the shoemaker *head down,* the bursts of metaphorical *fishhooks* and *barbed wire.*

There is a housing project standing now where the house in which we grew up once stood, and one of those stunted city trees is snarling where our doorway use to be. This is on the rehabilitated side of the avenue. The other side of the avenue—for progress takes time—has not been rehabilitated yet and it looks exactly as it looked in the days when we sat with our noses pressed against the windowpane, longing to be allowed to go "across the sreet." The grocery store which gave us credit is still there, and there can be no doubt that it is still giving credit. The people in the project certainly need it—far more, indeed, than they ever needed the project. The last time I passed by, the Jewish proprietor was still standing among his shelves, looking sadder and heavier but scarcely any older. Farther down the block stands the shoe-repair store in which our shoes were repaired until reparation became impossible and in which, then, we bought all our "new" ones. The Negro proprietor is still in the window, head down, working at the leather.

These two, I imagine, could tell a long tale if they would (perhaps they would be glad to if they could), having watched so many, for so long, struggling in the fishhooks, the barbed wire, of this avenue.

The avenue is elsewhere the renowned and elegant Fifth. The area I am describing, which, in today's gang parlance, would be called "the turf," is bounded by Lenox Avenue on the west, the Harlem River on the east, 135th Street on the north, and 130th Street on the south. We never lived beyond these boundaries; this is where we grew up. Walking along 145th Street—for example—familiar as it is, and similar, does not have the same impact because I do not know any of the people on the block. But when I turn east on 131st Street and Lenox Avenue, there is first a soda-pop joint, then a shoeshine "parlor," then a grocery store, then a dry cleaners', then the houses. All along the street there are people who watched me grow up, people who grew up with me, people I watched grow up along with my brothers and sisters; and, sometimes in my arms, sometimes underfcot, sometimes at my shoulder—or on it— their children, a riot, a forest of children, who include my nieces and nephews.

When we reach the end of this long block, we find ourselves on wide, filthy, hostile Fifth Avenue, facing that project which hangs over the avenue like a monument to the folly, and the cowardice, of good intentions. All along the block, for anyone who knows it, are immense human gaps, like craters. These gaps are not created merely by those who have moved away, inevitably into some other ghetto; or by those who have risen, almost always into a greater capacity for self-loathing and self-delusion; or yet by those who, by whatever means—World War II, the Korean war, a policeman's gun or billy, a gang war, a brawl, madness, an overdose of heroin, or, simply, unnatural exhaustion—are dead. I am talking about those who are left, and I am talking principally about the young. What are they doing? Well, some, a minority, are fanatical churchgoers, members of the more extreme of the Holy Roller sects.

Many, many more are "moslems," by affiliation or sympathy, that is to say that they are united by nothing more—and nothing less—than a hatred of the white world and all its work. They are present, for example, at every Buy Black street-corner meeting—meetings in which the speaker urges his hearers to cease trading with white men and establish a separate economy. Neither the speaker nor his hearers can possibly do this, of course, since Negroes do not own General Motors or RCA or the A & P, nor, indeed, do they own more than a wholly insufficient fraction of anything else in Harlem (those who *do* own anything are more interested in their profits than in their fellows). But these meetings nevertheless keep alive in the participators a certain pride of bitterness without which, however futile this bitterness may be, they could scarcely remain alive at all. Many have given up. They stay home and watch the TV screen, living on the earnings of their parents, cousins, brothers, or uncles, and only leave the house to go to the nearest bar. "How're you making it?" one may ask, running into them along the block, or in the bar. "Oh, I'm TV-ing it"; with the saddest, sweetest, most shamefaced of smiles, and from a great distance. This distance one is compelled to respect; anyone who has traveled so far will not easily be dragged again into the world. There are further retreats, of course, than the TV screen or the bar. There are those who are simply sitting on their stoops, "stoned," animated for a moment only, and hideously, by the approach of someone who may lend them the money for a "fix." Or by the approach of someone from whom they can purchase it, one of the shrewd ones, on the way to prison or just coming out.

And the others, who have avoided all of these deaths, get up in the morning and go downtown to meet "the man." They work in the white man's world all day and come home in the evening to this fetid block. They struggle to instill in their children some private sense of honor or dignity which will help the child to survive. This means, of course, that they must struggle, stolidly, incessantly, to keep this sense alive in themselves, in spite of the insults, the indifference, and the cruelty they are certain to encounter in their working day. They patiently browbeat the landlord into fixing the heat, the plaster, the plumbing; this demands prodigious patience; nor is patience usually enough. In trying to make their hovels habitable, they are perpetually throwing good money after bad. Such frustration, so long endured, is driving many strong, admirable men and women whose only crime is color to the very gates of paranoia.

One remembers them from another time—playing handball in the playground, going to church, wondering if they were going to be promoted at school. One remembers them going off to war—gladly, to escape this block. One remembers their return. Perhaps one remembers their wedding day. And one sees where the girl is now—vainly looking for salvation from some other embittered, trussed, and struggling boy—and sees the all-but-abandoned children in the streets.

Now I am perfectly aware that there are other slums in which white men are fighting for their lives, and mainly losing. I know that blood is also flowing through those streets and that the human damage there is incalculable. People are continually pointing out to me the wretchedness of white people in order to console me for the wretchedness of blacks. But an itemized account of the American failure does not console me and it should not console anyone else. That hundreds of thousands of white people are living, in effect, no better than the "niggers" is not a fact to be regarded with complacency. The social and moral bankruptcy suggested by this fact is of the bitterest, most terrifying kind.

The people, however, who believe that this democratic anguish has some consoling value are always pointing out that So-and-So, white, and So-and-So, black, rose from the slums into the big time. The existence—the public existence—of, say, Frank Sinatra and Sammy Davis, Jr., proves to them that America is still the land of opportunity and that inequalities vanish before the determined will. It proves nothing of the sort. The determined will is rare—at the moment, in this country, it is unspeakably rare—and the inequalities suffered by the many are in no way justified by the rise of a few. A few have always risen—in every country, every era, and in the teeth of regimes which can by no stretch of the imagination be thought of as free. Not all of these people, it is worth remembering, left the world better than they found it. The determined will is rare, but it is not invariably benevolent. Furthermore, the American equation of success with the big time reveals an awful disrespect for human life and human achievement. This equation has placed our cities among the most dangerous in the world and has placed our youth among the most empty and most bewildered. The situation of our youth is not mysterious. Children have never been very good at listening to their elders, but they have never failed to imitate them. They must, they have no other models. That is exactly what our children are doing. They are imitating our immorality, our disrespect for the pain of others.

All other slum dwellers, when the bank account permits it, can move out of the slum and vanish altogether from the eye of persecution. No Negro in this country has ever made that much money and it will be a long time before any Negro does. The Negroes in Harlem, who have no money, spend what they have on such gimcracks as they are sold. These include "wider" TV screens, more "faithful" hi-fi sets, more "powerful" cars, all of which, of course, are obsolete long before they are paid for. Anyone who has ever struggled with poverty knows how extremely expensive it is to be poor; and if one is a member of a captive population, economically speaking, one's feet have simply been placed on the treadmill forever. One is victimized, economically, in a thousand ways—rent, for example, or car insurance. Go shopping one day in Harlem—for anything and compare Harlem prices and quality with those downtown.

The people who have managed to get off this block have only got as far as a more respectable ghetto. This respectable ghetto does not even have the advantages of the disreputable one—friends, neighbors, a familiar church, and friendly tradesmen; and it is not, moreover, in the nature of any ghetto to remain respectable long. Every Sunday, people who have left the block take the lonely ride back, dragging their increasingly discontented children with them. They spend the day talking, not always with words, about the trouble they've seen and the trouble —one must watch their children—they are only too likely to see. For children do not like ghettos. It takes them nearly no time to discover exactly why they are there.

The projects in Harlem are hated. They are hated almost as much as policemen, and this is saying a great deal. And they are hated for the same reason: both reveal, unbearably, the real attitude of the white world, no matter how many liberal speeches are made, no matter how many lofty editorials are written, no matter how many civil-rights commissions are set up.

The projects are hideous, of course, there being a law, apparently respected throughout the world, that popular housing shall be as cheerless as a prison. They are lumped all over Harlem, colorless, bleak, high, and revolting. The wide windows look out on Harlem's invincible and indescribable squalor: the Park Avenue railroad tracks, around which, about forty years ago, the present dark community began; the unrehabilitated houses, bowed down, it would seem, under the great weight of frustration and bitterness they contain; the dark, the ominous schoolhouses from which the child may emerge maimed, blinded, hooked, or enraged for life; and the churches, churches, block upon block of churches, niched in the walls like cannon in the walls of a fortress. Even if the administration of the projects were not so insanely humiliating (for example: one must report raises in salary to the management, which will then eat up the profit by raising one's rent; the management has the right to know who is staying in your apartment; the management can ask you to leave, at their discretion), the projects would still be hated because they are an insult to the meanest intelligence.

Harlem got its first private project, Riverton*—which is now, naturally, a slum—about twelve years ago because at that time Negroes were not allowed to live in Stuyvesant Town. Harlem watched Riverton go up, therefore, in the most violent bitterness of spirit, and hated it long before the builders arrived. They began hating it at about the time people began moving out of their condemned houses to make room for this additional proof of how thoroughly the white world despised them. And they had scarcely moved in, naturally, before they began smashing windows, defacing walls, urinating in the elevators, and fornicating in the playgrounds. Liberals, both white and black, were appalled at the spectacle. I was appalled by the liberal innocence—or cynicism, which comes out in practice as much the same thing. Other people were delighted to be able to point to proof positive that nothing could be done to better the lot of the colored people. They were, and are, right in one respect: that nothing can be done as long as they are treated like colored people. The people in Harlem know they are living there because white people do not think they are good enough to live anywhere else. No amount of "improvement" can sweeten this fact. Whatever money is now being earmarked to improve this, or any other ghetto, might as well be burnt. A ghetto can be improved in one way only: out of existence.

Similarly, the only way to police a ghetto is to be oppressive. None of the Police Commissioner's men, even with the best will in the world, have any way of understanding the lives led by the people they swagger about in twos and threes controlling. Their very presence is an insult, and it would be, even if they spent their entire day feeding gumdrops to children. They represent the force of the white world, and the world's real intentions are, simply, for that world's criminal profit and ease, to keep the black man corraled up here, in his place. The badge, the gun in the holster, and the swinging club make vivid what will happen should his rebellion become overt. Rare, indeed, is the Harlem citizen, from the most circumspect church member to the most shiftless adoles-

---

* The inhabitants of Riverton were much embittered by this description; they have, apparently, forgotten how their project came into being; and have repeatedly informed me that I cannot possibly be referring to Riverton, but to another housing project which is directly across the street. It is quite clear, I think, that I have no interest in accusing any individuals or families of the depredations herein described: but neither can I deny the evidence of my own eyes. Nor do I blame anyone in Harlem for making the best of a dreadful bargain. But anyone who lives in Harlem and imagines that he has not struck this bargain, or that what he takes to be his status (in whose eyes?) protects him against the common pain, demoralization, and danger, is simply self-deluded.

cent, who does not have a long tale to tell of police incompetence, injustice, or brutality. I myself have witnessed and endured it more than
once. The businessmen and racketeers also have a story. And so do the
prostitutes. (And this is not, perhaps, the place to discuss Harlem's very
complex attitude toward black policemen, nor the reasons, according to
Harlem, that they are nearly all downtown.)

It is hard, on the other hand, to blame the policeman, blank, good-
natured, thoughtless, and insuperably innocent, for being such a perfect
representative of the people he serves. He, too, believes in good intentions and is astounded and offended when they are not taken for the
deed. He has never, himself, done anything for which to be hated—
which of us has?—and yet he is facing, daily and nightly, people who
would gladly see him dead, and he knows it. There is no way for him
not to know it: there are few things under heaven more unnerving than
the silent, accumulating contempt and hatred of a people. He moves
through Harlem, therefore, like an occupying soldier in a bitterly hostile
country; which is precisely what, and where, he is, and is the reason he
walks in twos and threes. And he is not the only one who knows why
he is always in company: the people who are watching him know why,
too. Any street meeting, sacred or secular, which he and his colleagues
uneasily cover has as its explicit or implicit burden the cruelty and injustice of the white domination. And these days, of course, in terms
increasingly vivid and jubilant, it speaks of the end of that domination.
The white policeman standing on a Harlem street corner finds himself
at the very center of the revolution now occurring in the world. He is
not prepared for it—naturally, nobody is—and, what is possibly much
more to the point, he is exposed, as few white people are, to the anguish
of the black people around him. Even if he is gifted with the merest
mustard grain of imagination, something must seep in. He cannot avoid
observing that some of the children, in spite of their color, remind him
of children he has known and loved, perhaps even of his own children.
He knows that he certainly does not want *his* children living this way.
He can retreat from his uneasiness in only one direction: into a callous-
ness which very shortly becomes second nature. He becomes more cal-
lous, the population becomes more hostile, the situation grows more
tense, and the police force is increased. One day, to everyone's astonishment, someone drops a match in the powder keg and everything blows
up. Before the dust has settled or the blood congealed, editorials,
speeches, and civil-rights commissions are loud in the land, demanding
to know what happened. What happened is that Negroes want to be
treated like men.

Negroes want to be treated like men: a perfectly straightforward statement, containing only seven words. People who have mastered Kant, Hegel, Shakespeare, Marx, Freud, and the Bible find this statement utterly impenetrable. The idea seems to threaten profound, barely conscious assumptions. A kind of panic paralyzes their features, as though they found themselves trapped on the edge of a steep place. I once tried to describe to a very well-known American intellectual the conditions among Negroes in the South. My recital disturbed him and made him indignant; and he asked me in perfect innocence, "Why don't all the Negroes in the South move North?" I tried to explain what *has* happened, unfailingly, whenever a significant body of Negroes move North. They do not escape Jim Crow: they merely encounter another, not-less-deadly variety. They do not move to Chicago, they move to the South Side; they do not move to New York, they move to Harlem. The pressure within the ghetto causes the ghetto walls to expand, and this expansion is always violent. White people hold the line as long as they can, and in as many ways as they can, from verbal intimidation to physical violence. But inevitably the border which has divided the ghetto from the rest of the world falls into the hands of the ghetto. The white people fall back bitterly before the black horde; the landlords make a tidy profit by raising the rent, chopping up the rooms, and all but dispensing with the upkeep; and what has once been a neighborhood turns into a "turf." This is precisely what happened when the Puerto Ricans arrived in their thousands—and the bitterness thus caused is, as I write, being fought out all up and down those streets.

Northerners indulge in an extremely dangerous luxury. They seem to feel that because they fought on the right side during the Civil War, and won, they have earned the right merely to deplore what is going on in the South, without taking any responsibility for it; and that they can ignore what is happening in Northern cities because what is happening in Little Rock or Birmingham is worse. Well, in the first place, it is not possible for anyone who has not endured both to know which is "worse." I know Negroes who prefer the South and white Southerners, because "At least there, you haven't got to play any guessing games!" The guessing games referred to have driven more than one Negro into the narcotics ward, the madhouse, or the river. I know another Negro, a man very dear to me, who says, with conviction and with truth, "The spirit of the South is the spirit of America." He was born in the North and did his military training in the South. He did not, as far as I can gather, find the South "worse"; he found it, if anything, all too familiar. In the second place, though, even if Birmingham *is* worse, no doubt

Johannesburg, South Africa, beats it by several miles, and Buchenwald was one of the worst things that ever happened in the entire history of the world. The world has never lacked for horrifying examples; but I do not believe that these examples are meant to be used as justification for our own crimes. This perpetual justification empties the heart of all human feeling. The emptier our hearts become, the greater will be our crimes. Thirdly, the South is not merely an embarrassingly backward region, but a part of this country, and what happens there concerns every one of us.

As far as the color problem is concerned, there is but one great difference between the Southern white and the Northerner: the Southerner remembers, historically and in his own psyche, a kind of Eden in which he loved black people and they loved him. Historically, the flaming sword laid across this Eden is the Civil War. Personally, it is the Southerner's sexual coming of age, when, without any warning, unbreakable taboos are set up between himself and his past. Everything, thereafter, is permitted him except the love he remembers and has never ceased to need. The resulting, indescribable torment affects every Southern mind and is the basis of the Southern hysteria.

None of this is true for the Northerner. Negroes represent nothing to him personally, except, perhaps, the dangers of carnality. He never sees Negroes. Southerners see them all the time. Northerners never think about them whereas Southerners are never really thinking of anything else. Negroes are, therefore, ignored in the North and are under surveillance in the South, and suffer hideously in both places. Neither the Southerner nor the Northerner is able to look on the Negro simply as a man. It seems to be indispensable to the national self-esteem that the Negro be considered either as a kind of ward (in which case we are told how many Negroes, comparatively, bought Cadillacs last year and how few, comparatively, were lynched), or as a victim (in which case we are promised that he will never vote in our assemblies or go to school with our kids). They are two sides of the same coin and the South will not change—*cannot* change—until the North changes. The country will not change until it reexamines itself and discovers what it really means by freedom. In the meantime, generations keep being born, bitterness is increased by incompetence, pride, and folly, and the world shrinks around us.

It is a terrible, an inexorable, law that one cannot deny the humanity of another without diminishing one's own: in the face of one's victim, one sees oneself. Walk through the streets of Harlem and see what we, this nation, have become.

ALEX HALEY

Alex Haley (1921–), born in Ithaca, N.Y., began writing as an enlisted man in the Coast Guard during World War II, from which he retired in 1959 after twenty years of service. He was the ghost-writer of *The Autobiography of Malcolm X* (1964). He had proposed an article to *The Reader's Digest* on the emerging Black Muslim movement—his first step as a free-lance professional—and met an initially hostile Malcolm X, the movement's young chief of staff. His "Mr. Muhammad Speaks" appeared in *The Reader's Digest* in 1960 as the first featured article on the Muslims in any magazine. An article in *The Saturday Evening Post* and a long interview with Malcolm X in *Playboy* followed, all leading to an invitation from the Grove Press to see if he could persuade Malcolm X to cooperate in writing an autobiography. Haley has also published his own autobiographical account of his search for his own roots in several versions. He also founded the Kinte Foundation, a library of black history, in Washington, D.C.

MY SEARCH FOR ROOTS

The story of this unusual search through the mists of history for lineage and identity tells itself. What does it do to adjust our focus? Compare Haley's attitude toward the "old-timey stuff" with his mother's. What were his immediate motives, and what was the result?

My earliest memory is of Grandma, Cousin Georgia, Aunt Plus, Aunt Liz and Aunt Till talking on our front porch in Henning, Tenn. At dusk, these wrinkled, graying old ladies would sit in rocking chairs and talk, about slaves and massas and plantations—pieces and patches of family history, passed down across the generations by word of mouth. "Old-timey stuff," Mamma would exclaim. She wanted no part of it.

The furthest-back person Grandma and the others ever mentioned was "the African." They would tell how he was brought here on a ship to a place called "Naplis" and sold as a slave in Virginia. There he mated with another slave, and had a little girl named Kizzy.

When Kizzy became four or five, the old ladies said, her father would point out to her various objects and name them in his native tongue. For example, he would point to a guitar and make a single-syllable sound, *ko*. Pointing to a river that ran near the plantation, he'd say "Kamby Bolongo." And when other slaves addressed him as Toby—the name given him by his massa—the African would strenuously reject it, insisting that his name was "Kin-tay."

Kin-tay often told Kizzy stories about himself. He said that he had been near his village in Africa, chopping wood to make a drum, when he had been set upon by four men, overwhelmed, and kidnapped into slavery. When Kizzy grew up and became a mother, she told her son these stories, and he in turn would tell *his* children. His granddaughter became my grandmother, and she pumped that saga into me as if it were plasma, until I knew by rote the story of the African, and the subsequent generational wending of our family through cotton and tobacco plantations into the Civil War and then freedom.

At 17, during World War II, I enlisted in the Coast Guard, and found myself a messboy on a ship in the Southwest Pacific. To fight boredom, I began to teach myself to become a writer. I stayed on in the service after the war, writing every single night, seven nights a week, for eight years before I sold a story to a magazine. My first story in the Digest was published in June 1954: "The Harlem Nobody Knows." At age 37, I retired from military service, determined to be a full-time writer. Working with the famous Black Muslim spokesman, I did the actual writing for the book *The Autobiography of Malcolm X*.

I remembered still the vivid highlights of my family's story. Could this account possibly be documented for a book? During 1962, between other assignments, I began following the story's trail. In plantation records, wills, census records, I documented bits here, shreds there. By now, Grandma was dead; repeatedly I visited other close sources, most notably our encyclopedic matriarch, "Cousin Georgia" Anderson in Kansas City, Kansas. I went as often as I could to the National Archives in Washington, and the Library of Congress, and the Daughters of the American Revolution Library.

By 1967 I felt I had the seven generations of the U.S. side documented. But the unknown quotient in the riddle of the past continued to be those strange, sharp, angular sounds spoken by the African himself. Since I lived in New York City, I began going to the United Nations lobby, stopping Africans and asking if they recognized the sounds. Every one of them listened to me, then quickly took off. I can well understand: me with a Tennessee accent, trying to imitate African sounds!

Finally, I sought out a linguistics expert who specialized in African languages. To him I repeated the phrases. The sound "Kin-tay," he said, was a Mandinka tribe surname. And "Kamby Bolongo" was probably the Gambia River in Mandinka dialect. Three days later, I was in Africa.

In Banjul, the capital of Gambia, I met with a group of Gambians. They told me how for centuries the history of Africa has been preserved.

In the older villages of the back country there are old men, called *griots*, who are in effect living archives. Such men know and, on special occasions, tell the cumulative histories of clans, or families, or villages, as those histories have long been told. Since my forefather had said his name was Kin-tay (properly spelled Kinte), and since the Kinte clan was known in Gambia, they would see what they could do to help me.

I was back in New York when a registered letter came from Gambia. Word had been passed in the back country, and a *griot* of the Kinte clan had, indeed, been found. His name, the letter said, was Kebba Kanga Fofana. I returned to Gambia and organized a safari to locate him.

There is an expression called "the peak experience," a moment which, emotionally, can never again be equaled in your life. I had mine, that first day in the village of Juffure, in the back country in black West Africa.

When our 14-man safari arrived within sight of the village, the people came flocking out of their circular mud huts. From a distance I could see a small, old man with a pillbox hat, an off-white robe and an aura of "somebodiness" about him. The people quickly gathered around me in a kind of horseshoe pattern. The old man looked piercingly into my eyes, and he spoke in Mandinka. Translation came from the interpreters I had brought with me.

"Yes, we have been told by the forefathers that there are many of us from this place who are in exile in that place called America."

Then the old man, who was 73 rains of age—the Gambian way of saying 73 years old, based upon the one rainy season per year—began to tell me the lengthy ancestral history of the Kinte clan. It was clearly a formal occasion for the villagers. They had grown mouse-quiet, and stood rigidly.

Out of the *griot's* head came spilling lineage details incredible to hear. He recited who married whom, two or even three centuries back. I was struck not only by the profusion of details, but also by the Biblical pattern of the way he was speaking. It was something like, "—and so-and-so took as a wife so-and-so, and begat so-and-so. . . ."

The *griot* had talked for some hours, and had got to about 1750 in our calendar. Now he said, through an interpreter, "About the time the king's soldiers came, the eldest of Omoro's four sons, Kunta, went away from this village to chop wood—and he was never seen again. . . ."

Goose pimples came out on me the size of marbles. He just had no way in the world of knowing that what he told me meshed with what I'd heard from the old ladies on the front porch in Henning, Tenn. I got out my notebook, which had in it what Grandma had said about the

African. One of the interpreters showed it to the others, and they went to the *griot*, and they all got agitated. Then the *griot* went to the people, and *they* all got agitated.

I don't remember anyone giving an order, but those 70-odd people formed a ring around me, moving counterclockwise, chanting, their bodies close together. I can't begin to describe how I felt. A woman broke from the circle, a scowl on her jet-black face, and came charging toward me. She took her baby and almost roughly thrust it out at me. The gesture meant "Take it!" and I did, clasping the baby to me. Whereupon the woman all but snatched the baby away. Another woman did the same with her baby, then another, and another.

A year later, a famous professor at Harvard would tell me: "You were participating in one of the oldest ceremonies of humankind, called 'the laying on of hands.' In their way, these tribespeople were saying to you, 'Through this flesh, which is us, we are you and you are us.' "

Later, as we drove out over the back-country road, I heard the staccato sound of drums. When we approached the next village, people were packed alongside the dusty road, waving, and the din from them welled louder as we came closer. As I stood up in the Land Rover, I finally realized what it was they were all shouting: "Meester Kinte! Meester Kinte!" In their eyes I was the symbol of all black people in the United States whose forefathers had been torn out of Africa while theirs remained.

Hands before my face, I began crying—crying as I have never cried in my life. Right at that time, crying was all I could do.

I went then to London. I searched and searched, and finally in the British Parliamentary records I found that the "king's soldiers" mentioned by the *griot* refered to a group called "Colonel O'Hare's forces," which had been sent up the Gambia River in 1767 to guard the then British-operated James Fort, a slave fort.

I next went to Lloyds of London, where doors were opened for me to research among all kinds of old maritime records. I pored through the records of slave ships that had sailed from Africa. Volumes upon volumes of these records exist. One afternoon about 2:30, during the seventh week of searching, I was going through my 1023rd set of ship records. I picked up a sheet that had on it the reported movements of 30 slave ships, my eyes stopped at No. 18, and my glance swept across the column entries. This vessel had sailed directly from the Gambia River to America in 1767; her name was the *Lord Ligonier*; and she had arrived at Annapolis (Naplis) the morning of September 29, 1767.

Exactly 200 years later, on September 29, 1967, there was nowhere in the world for me to be except standing on a pier at Annapolis, staring sea-ward across those waters over which my great-great-great-great-grandfather had been brought. And there in Annapolis I inspected the microfilmed records of the *Maryland Gazette*. In the issue of October 1, 1767, on page 3, I found an advertisement informing readers that the *Lord Ligonier* had just arrived from the River Gambia, with "a cargo of choice, healthy SLAVES" to be sold at auction the following Wednesday.

In the years since, I have done extensive research in 50 or so libraries, archives and repositories on three continents. I spent a year combing through countless documents to learn about the culture of Gambia's villages in the 18th and 19th centuries. Desiring to sail over the same waters navigated by the *Lord Ligonier*, I flew to Africa and boarded the freighter *African Star*. I forced myself to spend the ten nights of the crossing in the cold, dark cargo hold, stripped to my underwear, lying on my back on a rough, bare plank. But this was sheer luxury compared to the inhuman ordeal suffered by those millions who, chained and shackled, lay in terror and in their own filth in the stinking darkness through voyages averaging 60 to 70 days.

STANLEY VESTAL

Stanley Vestal is the pseudonym of Walter S. Campbell (1887–1957). He wrote several books dealing with the American West. His subjects include the Missouri River, Kit Carson, Jim Bridger, and Sitting Bull. Under his own name, he wrote two books about the craft of writing nonfiction.

THE MAN WHO KILLED CUSTER

The young Sioux who killed Custer relives the battle in his eighties. How does his story readjust your assumptions? Does White Bull's view of the battle differ from Vestal's? from yours?

Soon after the allied tribes defeated General George Crook at the Battle of the Rosebud, June 17, 1876, they pitched their camps on the prairies just west of the winding Little Big Horn River.* As White Bull related it to me, each tribe had its own camp circle, each band in its own segment, each tepee in its proper place. The Cheyenne camp circle lay farthest north, with the four Sioux circles—Sans Arc, Ogalalla, Minniconjou, Hunkpapa—upstream. Chief White Bull's tepee stood in the

* In southeastern Montana.

Sans Arc circle, since his wife of that time was a Sans Arc woman. That morning he was out with his grazing ponies about a thousand yards from the river, trying to keep them together. As usual, he carried his seventeen-shot Winchester and wore two filled cartridge belts. It was very dry and dusty with little wind, and his horses were restless, for the flies were a plague on the Little Big Horn that summer.

It was not yet time for the midday watering when White Bull heard a man yelling the alarm. Immediately he jumped on his best running horse, a fast bay, and ran his ponies back to camp. By that time he could see the column of dust to the south. First of all White Bull saw his own family mounted and sent on to safety. Then he rode as hard as he could the three miles to the camp of his uncle, Sitting Bull, the Hunkpapa circle, which Reno's troopers were approaching. By the time he reached it, the women and children had fled and nearly a thousand warriors had gathered to resist the troops. Already some Sioux had been shot down, and Major Reno's Indian scouts were running off the Sioux ponies.

Before White Bull could take any effective part in the fight, the soldiers fell back to the timber along the river, and soon after climbed into their saddles and raced away up the river looking for places to cross.

Said White Bull, "Then the Indians charged them. They used war clubs and gun barrels, shooting arrows into them, riding them down. It was like a buffalo hunt. The soldiers offered no resistance. I saw one soldier on a gray horse, aimed at him and fired, but missed. Just then I heard someone behind me yelling that soldiers were coming from the east [Custer's force] to attack the north end of the camp where I had left my ponies. We all raced downstream together. Some rode through the camps and crossed the river north of them, but I and many others crossed and rode up a gully to strike the soldiers on the flank. After a while I could see five bunches of soldiers trotting along the bluffs. I knew it would be a big fight. I stopped, unsaddled my horse, and stripped off my leggings, so that I could fight better. By the time I was near enough to shoot at the soldiers, they seemed to form four groups, heading northwest along the ridge.

All the Indians were shooting. I saw two soldiers fall from their horses. The soldiers fired back at us from the saddle. They shot so well that some of us retreated to the south, driven out of the ravine. Soon after, the soldiers halted and some got off their horses. By that time the Indians were all around the soldiers, but most of them were between the soldiers and the river, trying to defend the camp and the ford. Several little bunches of Indians took cover where they could, and kept firing at the white men.

When they ran me out of the ravine I rode south and worked my way over to the east of the mounted bunch of soldiers. Crazy Horse was there with a party of warriors and I joined them. The Indians kept gathering, more and more, around this last bunch of soldiers. These mounted soldiers kept falling back along the ridge, trying to reach the rest of the soldiers who were fighting on foot.

When I saw the soldiers retreating, I whipped up my pony, and hugging his neck, dashed across between the two troops. The soldiers shot at me but missed me. I circled back to my friends. I thought I would do it again. I yelled, 'This time I will not turn back,' and charged at a run the soldiers of the last company. Many of the Sioux joined my charge and this seemed to break the courage of those soldiers. They all ran, every man for himself, some afoot and some on horseback, to reach their comrades on the other side. All the Indians were shooting."

Such fighting, though necessary in defending the camp and killing enemies, was to the Indians "just shooting." For, to the Sioux warrior, the striking of a blow or "coup" upon an enemy's person with the hand or something held in the hand was the most glorious deed a warrior could perform, and his rating depended upon the number of such coups he could gather. Among the Sioux, four men might count a coup upon the same enemy in the same fight, and on that occasion ranked in the order of their striking him. To strike first was the greatest honor possible and the man who had done that could wear the Indian's medal of honor—an eagle's tail feather—upright in his back hair. To shoot or scalp an enemy, to capture his gun or his horse, were creditable, but none of these compared as war honors with the coup.

White Bull said, "I saw a mounted soldier waver in his saddle. I quirted my pony and raced up to strike him and count the first coup on this enemy. Before I could reach him, he fell dying from his saddle. I reined up my pony, jumped down and struck the body with my quirt. I yelled, 'Onhey! I have overcome this one.' I took the man's revolver and cartridge belt.

Did-Not-Go-Home struck this enemy right after me; he counted the second coup. I jumped on my horse and hurried on to join the charge through the dust and smoke drifting down the hill.

I saw a soldier on horseback left behind; his horse had played out. I charged him, Crazy Horse following. The soldier heard me coming and tried to turn in his saddle and aim his carbine at me. But before he could shoot, I was alongside. I grabbed him by the shoulders of his blue coat and jerked hard to throw him off his horse. He fired in the air, screamed, and fell from his horse. This was another first coup for me. Crazy Horse struck this man second.

Other soldiers were left afoot. I saw one with Indians all around him, turning from side to side, threatening them with his carbine to keep them at a distance. I rode straight at him. When I got close, he fired, but I dodged and he missed me. Then I rode him down. Bear Lice counted the second coup. The survivors of these two bunches of soldiers moved up and joined those to the north and west, about where the monument stands now. Another bunch of soldiers was down the hill nearer the river. The air was full of dust and smoke.

Here and there through the fog you could see a wounded man left behind afoot. I saw one bleeding from a wound in his left thigh. He had a revolver in one hand and a carbine in the other. He stood all alone shooting at the Indians. They could not get at him. I rode at his back. He did not see me coming. I rode him down, counting the first coup. Brave Crow counted the second coup on this enemy. By this time, all the soldiers up the hill had let their horses go. They lay down and kept shooting.

The horses turned loose by the soldiers, bays, sorrels and grays— were running in all directions. Lots of Indians stopped shooting to capture these horses. I tried to head some off, but other Indians were ahead of me. I caught just one sorrel.

Now that the soldiers were all dismounted their firing was very fierce. All at once, my horse went down, and I was left afoot. For a while the Indians all took cover and kept shooting at the soldiers."

This fight, known to white men as the Battle of the Little Big Horn or Custer's Last Stand, is known to the Sioux as *Pe-hin* (Head-hair) *Hanska* (Long) *Ktepi* (Killed), for on the frontier Custer usually wore his hair long and was called "Long Hair" by the Indians. The battle, therefore, was "the fight in which Long Hair was killed."

On the day of his death Custer was considered the most dashing and successful cavalry officer in the Army. During the Civil War he had distinguished himself repeatedly, and his division had led the van in the pursuit of General Lee's forces. It was to him that the Confederates brought their white flag just before Lee's surrender. General Sheridan reported, "I know of no one whose efforts have contributed more to this happy result than those of Custer." To Custer was given the table on which Grant wrote the terms of surrender. He was celebrated as "the boy general" who had never lost a gun or color, and "Custer's luck" was a proverb in the Army.

He had been the second strongest man in his class at West Point and remained to the end a man of extraordinary vigor. Lithe, slender, with broad shoulders, he was a fine horseman and good shot, standing six feet in his boots and weighing about 165 pounds. He could ride all

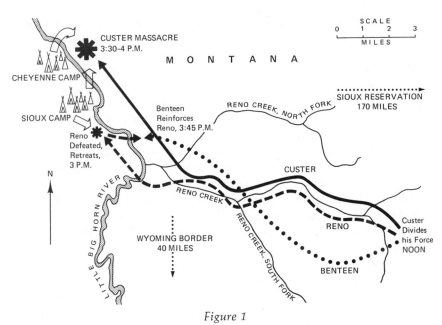

Figure 1

This map shows in somewhat simplified form the Battle of the Little Big Horn, June 25, 1876. Due to variations of opinion, Custer's route after he left Reno and the times given for the actions can be only approximations. But one key factor in the 7th Cavalry's defeat is clear: each of the three commands had only the faintest inkling of what was happening to the others during that hot, bloody afternoon.

day, carry on his duties until midnight, then scribble long letters to his wife—one of them running to eighty pages—and still be raring to go in the morning.

At this time Custer was in disfavor with President Grant. He had been nursing a grudge against Grant's secretary of war, W. W. Belknap, and early in 1876, when Belknap was hauled before a congressional committee on charges of sharing illegally in the profits of post traders, Custer went to Washington to testify against him. His evidence was largely hearsay, and he defamed Belknap's character and that of Grant's younger brother—thus maligning the President himself. When Custer came to his senses, he tried to explain his position to Grant. But the President refused to see him, and to punish the hothead further, removed him from command of the crack 7th Cavalry.

Yet there was no one who could match Custer as an Indian fighter. General Terry knew this as well as anyone, and in May, Terry persuaded Grant to reinstate Custer on grounds that his services were indispensable in the campaign against the Sioux and Northern Cheyenne. But for this chance, the Battle of the Little Big Horn might never have happened.

White Bull, although only 26 years old, had already taken part in nineteen engagements. Ten of these were with white men, one with government Indian scouts, and the rest with Indian enemies. He had counted seven coups, six of them "firsts," had taken two scalps, killed three enemies, wounded one, shot three enemy horses, rescued six wounded comrades, and recovered one dead body under fire. He had captured and spared an enemy Assiniboin woman and her husband, had stolen 45 enemy horses, had been hit twice in battle by bullets, and had had a horse shot from under him. Three different warrior societies had invited him to become a member, and on two occasions he had undergone the voluntary tortures of the Sun Dance. He had thrice been given a new name because of brave deeds.

Custer was stronger than White Bull, but the Indian had far more experience in hand-to-hand fighting than the officer. Such it would be now as the Indians closed in on the few remaining troopers. Here is how White Bull described it:

"I charged in. A tall, well-built soldier with yellow hair and mustache saw me coming and tried to bluff me, aiming his rifle at me. But when I rushed him, he threw his rifle at me without shooting. I dodged it. We grabbed each other and wrestled there in the dust and smoke. It was like fighting in a fog. This soldier was very strong and brave. He tried to wrench my rifle from me. I lashed him across the face with my quirt, striking the coup. He let go, then grabbed my gun with both hands until I struck him again.

But the tall soldier fought hard. He was desperate. He hit me with his fists on the jaw and shoulders, then grabbed my long braids with both hands, pulled my face close and tried to bite my nose off. I yelled for help: 'Hey, hey, come over and help me!' I thought that soldier would kill me.

Bear Lice and Crow Boy heard me call and came running. These friends tried to hit the soldier. But we were whirling around, back and forth, so that most of their blows hit me. They knocked me dizzy. I yelled as loud as I could to scare my enemy, but he would not let go. Finally I broke free.

He drew his pistol. I wrenched it out of his hand and struck him with it three or four times on the head, knocked him over, shot him in the head, and fired at his heart. I took his pistol and cartridge belt. Hawk-Stays-Up struck second on his body.

Ho hechetu! That was a fight, a hard fight. But it was a glorious battle, I enjoyed it. I was picking up head-feathers right and left that day.

Now I was between the river and the soldiers on the hill. I started up the hill. Suddenly I stumbled and fell. My leg was numb, I saw that my ankle was swollen. The skin was not broken, only bruised. I must have been hit by a spent bullet. I crawled into a ditch and lay there till all the soldiers were killed. At the time I stopped fighting, only ten soldiers were on their feet. They were the last ones alive."

White Bull scoffed at the yarns about the soldiers committing mass suicide. Said he: "The soldiers looked tired, but they fought to the end. There were few cartridges left in the belts I took off the soldiers.

I waited where I was until my friend With Horns came along and found me. He put me on his horse and led it back across the river. The people were some distance west on the flat; they had not had time to move their tepees."

After resting, eating, and having the wound dressed, White Bull mounted his horse and forded the river to get his leggings and saddle. He then rode over the battleground to see the dead. Most of the bodies were naked. He did not see anyone mutilating the dead.

"On the hill top, I met my relative Bad Soup. He had been around Fort Abraham Lincoln and knew Long Hair by sight. When we came to the tall soldier lying on his back naked, Bad Soup pointed him out and said, 'Long Hair thought he was the greatest man in the world. Now he lies there.'

'Well,' I said, 'if that is Long Hair, I am the man who killed him.' Nobody scalped Long Hair, because his hair was cut short."

Of course, Bad Soup was not the only Indian who had seen Custer, and others may have recognized his body. At any rate, I have never met an old-time Sioux who took part in that fight who had any doubt that White Bull killed Custer. But White Bull declared to me: "They say that I killed Long Hair, but I never saw him to know him before the battle. I do not think my cousin, Bad Soup, would have lied to me."

White Bull did not know what became of Custer's pistol, as after he was hit he could not go back to gather up his trophies. By the time he rode out to inspect the battlefield other Indians had carried them off. (According to the authority General Edward S. Godfrey, "Custer carried a Remington Sporting rifle, octagon barrel; two Bulldog self-cocking, English white-handled pistols, with a ring in the butt for a lanyard; a hunting knife, in a beaded fringed scabbard; and a canvas cartridge belt.")

When the celebration of the fiftieth anniversary of Custer's Last Stand was held on the battlefield, White Bull and many other Indian veterans of the fight were invited to take part. Some, fearing reprisals, refused to go. But White Bull said, "I am not afraid," and attended. There General Godfrey led the 7th Cavalry over Custer's trail to the monument which was erected where he fell. Hundreds of mounted Indians in full war dress, preceded by eighty Sioux and Cheyenne survivors of the fight, followed Chief White Bull to meet the troops. They met near the monument. White Bull raised his palm, the sign for peace, and the General sheathed his sword. They shook hands, and the Chief gave the General a fine blanket; Godfrey gave the Chief a large American flag. After the ceremony, the Indians and soldiers paired off and rode back to camp. Nobody who knows Plains Indians can doubt that the man who killed Custer, if living, would be named to lead that Indian column.

Major Alson B. Ostrander, formerly of the 18th Infantry, had heard how Bad Soup had pointed out the body of Custer to Chief White Bull on the day of the battle. The Major asked White Bull to point out the spot where he saw Custer lying naked on his back that day. White Bull immediately complied. The Major nodded and said, "That is the spot."

The Major asked White Bull, "Are you the man who killed Custer?" White Bull answered, "Maybe." He tried to find out where Custer was wounded, but none of the white officers seemed to know.

He asked me about this. "Where do the white men say Custer was wounded?"

I replied, "In the left temple and in the left side near the heart." Much gratified, he nodded. "That is right," he said.

Naturally enough, Chief White Bull was curious about Custer and why the troops came to attack the Sioux in violation of the existing treaty. He listened attentively all one afternoon while I told him all I knew of such matters, particularly all about Custer's own fame, achievements, character, and motives. But when he learned that on the night before the battle, Custer, trying to encourage his fearful Indian government scouts, had told them that if he whipped the Sioux, he would become the Grandfather—President of the United States—and would look after their people, White Bull's old eyes gleamed. The thought that he had killed Custer had warmed his heart for years. But now to think that the man he killed might have been President was a greater glory than any Sioux had ever dreamed of. Seeing him gloat, I had no doubt that he knew well enough who had killed Custer.

The Cheyenne also say that White Bull killed Long Hair, though some of them confuse the Sioux chief with a leader of their own with the same name.

Shortly after Chief White Bull's surrender to government forces in 1876, a missionary taught him to write in the Sioux language. He then obtained a ledger and in it recorded his military history, illustrating it with pictures in the old Indian style, like those originally painted on hides. At my request, he drew a set of these on separate sheets for me, signing them with his name in Sioux and English, describing the exploit briefly in Sioux, adding his age at the time of the exploit, and the date on which the picture was made. . . .

His description of the fight is in Sioux: *Kici-ecamu-Welo* (I had a fight with him), *le Wokte* (I killed him). To further identify the soldier killed and to cite a witness to attest his exploit, White Bull added *Cetan-wan-Kol-un oki-he-kte* (Hawk-Stays-Up killed him [i.e. struck him] second). This is followed by a repetition of the first Sioux phrase. Hawk-Stays-Up, of course, testified to White Bull's coup on this soldier at what one may call the Court of Honor held after the battle, at which such honors were awarded.

Because of the hostility shown towards White Bull by his white neighbors, I was unwilling to publish these facts while the Chief and his immediate connections were still alive. If those who knew him felt so strongly, I feared that if this story were published in my biography of the Chief (*Warpath, The True Story of the Fighting Sioux*, 1934) some hothead might harm the old man. Now it can be told.

A. ALVAREZ

An English poet and critic, A. Alvarez (1929–) recently wrote *The Savage God: A Study of Suicide* (1972), in which this study appeared. A collection of essays, *Beyond All This Fiddle*, appeared in 1968.

SYLVIA PLATH: A MEMOIR

This account of a young poet's struggle to find herself has broad implications for life today: the competitive strain between professional husbands and wives, between motherhood and career, between self and parentage, self and a world of indistinct values. See where you fit in this scheme of things.

As I remember it, I met Sylvia and her husband in London in the spring of 1960. . . .

In those days Sylvia seemed effaced; the poet taking a back seat to the young mother and housewife. She had a long, rather flat body, a longish face, not pretty but alert and full of feeling with a lively mouth and fine brown eyes. Her brownish hair was scraped severely into a bun. She wore jeans and a neat shirt, briskly American: bright, clean, competent, like a young woman in a cookery advertisement, friendly and yet rather distant.

Her background, of which I knew nothing then, belied her house-wifely air: she had been a child prodigy—her first poem was published when she was eight—and then a brilliant student, winning every prize to be had, first at Wellesley High School, then at Smith College: scholarships all the way, straight A's, Phi Beta Kappa, president of this and that college society, and prizes for everything. A New York glossy magazine, *Mademoiselle*, had picked her as an outstanding possibility and wined her, dined her, and photographed her all over Manhattan. Then, almost inevitably, she had won a Fulbright to Cambridge, where she met Ted Hughes. They were married in 1956, on Bloomsday. Behind Sylvia was a self-sacrificing, widowed mother, a schoolteacher who had worked herself into the ground so that her two children might flourish. Sylvia's father—ornithologist, entomologist, ichthyologist, international authority on bumblebees, and professor of biology at Boston University—had died when she was nine. Both parents were of German stock and were German-speaking, academic, and intellectual. When she and Ted went to the States after Cambridge, a glittering university career seemed both natural and assured.

On the surface it was a typical success story: the brilliant examination-passer driving forward so fast and relentlessly that nothing could ever catch up with her. And it can last a lifetime, provided nothing checks the momentum, and the vehicle of all those triumphs doesn't disintegrate into sharp fragments from sheer speed and pressure. But already her progress had twice lurched to a halt. Between her month on *Mademoiselle* and her last year in college she had had the nervous breakdown and suicide attempt which became the theme of her novel, *The Bell Jar*. Then, once reestablished at Smith—"an outstanding teacher," said her colleagues—the academic prizes no longer seemed worth the effort. So in 1958 she had thrown over university life—Ted had never seriously contemplated it—and gone free-lance, trusting her luck and talent as a poet. All this I learned much later. Now Sylvia had simply slowed down; she was subdued, absorbed in her new baby daughter, and friendly only in that rather formal, shallow, transatlantic way that keeps you at your distance. . . .

After that I saw Ted occasionally, Sylvia more rarely. He and I would meet for a beer in one of the pubs near Primrose Hill or the Heath, and sometimes we would walk our children together. We almost never talked shop; without mentioning it, we wanted to keep things unprofes-

sional. At some point during the summer Ted and I did a broadcast together. Afterward we collected Sylvia from the flat and went across to
their local. The recording had been a success and we stood outside the
pub, around the baby's pram, drinking our beers and pleased with ourselves. Sylvia, too, seemed easier, wittier, less constrained than I had
seen her before. For the first time I understood something of the real
charm and speed of the girl. . . .

I didn't see her again until June, 1962, when I dropped in on them
on my way down to Cornwall for the long Whitsun weekend. They
were living a few miles north of Exeter. By Devon standards it wasn't
a pretty village: more gray stone and gloom than timber, thatch, and
flowers. Where the most perfect English villages give the impression of
never having been properly awakened, theirs seemed to have retired
into sleep. Once it might have been a center for the surrounding countryside, a place of some presence where things happened. But not any
more. Exeter had taken over, and the life of this village had drained
slowly away, like a family that has come down in the world.

The Hughes' house had once been the local manor. It was set slightly
above the rest of the village, up a steep lane next to a twelfth-century
church, and seemed important. It was large and thatched, the walls and
passages were stone, the rooms gleamed with new paint. We sat out
in the big wild garden drinking tea while little Frieda, now aged two,
teetered among the flowers. There was a small army of apple and cherry
trees, a vivid laburnum swaying with blossom, a vegetable patch, and,
off to one side, a little hillock. It turned out to be a prehistoric burial
mound. Given the Hughes' flair and tastes, it could hardly have been
anything else. Flowers glowed everywhere, the grass was long and unkempt, and the whole luxuriant place seemed to be overflowing with
summer.

They had had a new baby in January, a boy, and Sylvia had changed.
No longer quiet and withheld, a housewifely appendage to a powerful
husband, she seemed made solid and complete, her own woman again.
Perhaps the birth of a son had something to do with this new confident
air. But there was a sharpness and clarity about her that seemed to go
beyond that. It was she who showed me round the house and the garden; the electric gadgets, the freshly painted rooms, the orchard and
the burial mound—above all, the burial mound, "the wall of old corpses,"
she called it later in a poem—were *her* property. Ted, meanwhile, seemed
content to sit back and play with little Frieda, who clung to him depen-
dently. Since it was a strong, close marriage, he seemed unconcerned that
the balance of power had shifted for the time being to her.

I understood why as I was leaving, "I'm writing again," she said. "Really writing. I'd like you to see some of the new poems." Her manner was warm and open, as though she had decided I could be trusted.

Some time before, *The Observer* had accepted a poem by her called "Finisterre." We finally published it that August. In the meantime she sent a beautiful short poem, "Crossing the Water," which is not in *Ariel*, although it is as good as many that are. It arrived with a formal note and a meticulously stamped, self-addressed envelope. She seemed to be functioning as efficiently as ever. Yet when I saw Ted sometime later in London, he was tense and preoccupied. Driving on her own, Sylvia had had an accident, hurting herself and smashing up their old Morris station wagon. It could have meant anything but I judged it was serious, if only from the way his dark presence, as he spoke, darkened an even deeper shade of gloom.

When August came I went abroad for a few weeks, and by the time I got back autumn had already started. Although it was not yet mid-September, the leaves had begun to blow about the streets and the rain came down. That first morning, when I woke up to a drowning London sky, summer seemed as far away as the Mediterranean itself. Automatically, I found myself huddling into my clothes: the London crouch. We were in for a long winter.

At the end of September *The Observer* published "Crossing the Water." One afternoon soon after, when I was working and the charlady was banging around upstairs, the bell rang. It was Sylvia, smartly dressed, determinedly bright and cheerful.

"I was just passing, so I thought I'd drop in," she said. With her formal town clothes and prim bun of hair, she had the air of an Edwardian lady performing a delicate but necessary social duty.

The little studio I rented had been converted from an old stable. It lay down a long passage, behind a garage, and was beautiful, in its crumbling way, but uncomfortable: there was nothing to lounge on— only spidery Windsor chairs and a couple of rugs on the blood-red uncarpeted lino. I poured her a drink and she settled in front of the coal stove on one of the rugs, like a student, very much at her ease, sipping whiskey and making the ice clink in her glass.

"That sound makes me homesick for the States," she said. "It's the only thing that does."

We talked about her poem in *The Observer*, then chatted about nothing in particular. Finally, I asked her why she was in town. She replied, with a kind of polished cheerfulness, that she was flat-hunting, and then added casually that she and the children were living on their own for the time being. I remembered the last time I had seen her, in that overflowing Devon garden, and it seemed impossible that anything could have disrupted the idyll. But I asked no questions and she offered no explanations. Instead, she began to talk about the new drive to write that was upon her. At least a poem a day, she said, and often more. She made it sound like demonic possession. And it occurred to me that maybe this was why she and her husband had, however temporarily, parted: it was a question not of differences but of intolerable similarities. When two genuinely original, ambitious, full-time poets join in one marriage, and both are productive, every poem one writes must feel to the other as though it had been dug out of his, or her, own skull. At a certain pitch of creative intensity it must be more unbearable for the Muse to be unfaithful to you with your partner than for him, or her, to betray you with a whole army of seducers.

"I'd like to read you some of the new poems," she said, and pulled a sheaf of typescripts from her shoulder-bag on the floor beside her.

"Gladly," I said, reaching over for them. "Let's see."

She shook her head: "No. I don't want you to read them to yourself. They've got to be read out loud. I want you to *hear* them."

So, sitting cross-legged on the uncomfortable floor, with the charlady clanking away upstairs, she read me "Berck-Plage":

This is the sea, then, this great abeyance . . .

She read fast, in a hard, slightly nasal accent, rapping it out as though she were angry. Even now I find it a difficult poem to follow, the development indirect, the images concentrated and eliding thickly together. I had a vague impression of something injurious and faintly obscene, but I don't think I understood much. So when she finished I asked her to read it again. This time I heard it a little more clearly and could make some remarks about details. In some way, this seemed to satisfy her. We argued a bit and she read me more poems: one of them was "The Moon and the Yew Tree"; "Elm," I think, was another; there were six or eight in all. She would let me read none to myself, so I didn't get much, if anything, of their subtlety. But I did at least recognize that I was hearing something strong and new and hard to come to terms with. I suppose I picked on whatever details and slight signs of weakness I could as a kind of protection. She, in her turn, seemed happy to read, argue, and be heard sympathetically.

"She's a poet, isn't she?" asked my charlady the next day.

"Yes."

"I thought so," she said with grim satisfaction.

After that, Sylvia dropped in fairly often on her visits to London, always with a batch of new poems to read. This way I first heard, among others, the "Bee" poems, "A Birthday Present," "The Applicant," "Getting There," "Fever 103°," "Letter in November," and "Ariel," which I thought extraordinary. I told her it was the best thing she had done, and a few days later she sent me a fair copy of it, carefully written out in her heavy, rounded script, and illuminated like a medieval manuscript with flowers and ornamental squiggles.

One day—I'm not sure when—she read me what she called "some light verse." She meant "Daddy" and "Lady Lazarus." Her voice, as she read them, was hot and full of venom. By this time I could hear the poetry fairly clearly, without too great a time-lag and sense of inadequacy. I was appalled; at first hearing, the things seemed to be not so much poetry as assault and battery. And because I now knew something about her life, there was no avoiding how much she was part of the action. But to have commented on that would have been to imply that the poems had failed as poetry, which they clearly had not. As always, my defense was to nag her about details. There was one line I picked on in particular:

> Gentlemen, ladies
>
> These are my hands
> My knees.
>
> I may be skin and bone,
> *I may be Japanese* . . .

"Why *Japanese*?" I niggled away at her, "Do you just need the rhyme? Or are you trying to hitch an easy lift by dragging in the atomic victims? If you're going to use this kind of violent material, you've got to play it cool. . . ." She argued back sharply but later, when the poem was finally published after her death, the line had gone. And that, I think, is a pity: she did need the rhyme; the tone is quite controlled enough to support the apparently not quite relevant allusion; and I was overreacting to the initial brutality of the verse without understanding its weird elegance.

Throughout this time the evidence of the poems and the evidence of the person were utterly different. There was no trace of the poetry's despair and unforgiving destructiveness in her social manner. She remained remorselessly bright and energetic: busy with her children and her beekeeping in Devon, busy flat-hunting in London, busy seeing *The Bell Jar* through the press, busy typing and sending off her poems to largely unreceptive editors (just before she died she sent a sheaf of her best poems, most of them now classics, to one of the national British weeklies; none was accepted). She had also taken up horse-riding again, teaching herself to ride on a powerful stallion called Ariel, and was elated by this new excitement.

Cross-legged on the red floor, after reading her poems, she would talk about her riding in her twanging New England voice. And perhaps because I was also a member of the club, she talked, too, about suicide in much the same way: about her attempt ten years before which, I suppose, must have been very much on her mind as she corrected the proofs of her novel, and about her recent car crash. It had been no accident; she had gone off the road deliberately, seriously, wanting to die. But she hadn't, and all that was now in the past. For this reason I am convinced that at this time she was not contemplating suicide. On the contrary, she was able to write about the act so freely because it was already behind her. The car crash was a death she had survived, the death she sardonically felt herself fated to undergo once every decade:

> I have done it again.
> One year in every ten
> I manage it—
>
> A sort of walking miracle . . .
> I am only thirty.
> And like the cat I have nine times to die.
>
> This is Number Three . . .

In life, as in the poem, there was neither hysteria in her voice, nor any appeal for sympathy. She talked about suicide in much the same tone as she talked about any other risky, testing activity: urgently, even fiercely, but altogether without self-pity. She seemed to view death as a physical challenge she had, once again, overcome. It was an experience of much the same quality as riding Ariel or mastering a bolting horse—which she had done as a Cambridge undergraduate—or careening down a dangerous snow slope without properly knowing how to ski—an incident, also from life, which is one of the best things in *The Bell Jar*. Suicide, in short, was not a swoon into death, an attempt "to cease upon the midnight with no pain"; it was something to be felt in the nerve-ends and fought against, an initiation rite qualifying her for a *life* of her own.

God knows what wound the death of her father had inflicted on her in her childhood, but over the years this had been transformed into the conviction that to be an adult meant to be a survivor. So, for her, death was a debt to be met once every decade: in order to stay alive as a grown woman, a mother, and a poet, she had to pay—in some partial, magical way—with her life. But because this impossible payment involved also the fantasy of joining or regaining her beloved dead father, it was a passionate act, instinct as much with love as with hatred and despair. Thus in that strange, upsetting poem "The Bee Meeting," the detailed, doubtless accurate description of a gathering of local bee-keepers in her Devon village gradually becomes an invocation of some deadly ritual in which she is the sacrificial virgin whose coffin, finally, waits in the sacred grove. Why this should happen becomes, perhaps, slightly less mysterious when you remember that her father was an authority on bees; so her beekeeping becomes a way of symbolically allying herself to him, and reclaiming him from the dead.

The tone of all these late poems is hard, factual, and, despite the intensity, understated. In some strange way, I suspect she thought of herself as a realist: the deaths and resurrections of "Lady Lazarus," the nightmares of "Daddy" and the rest had all been proved on her pulses. That she brought to them an extraordinary inner wealth of imagery and associations was almost beside the point, however essential it is for the poetry itself. Because she felt she was simply describing the facts as they had happened, she was able to tap in the coolest possible way all her large reserves of skill: those subtle rhymes and half-rhymes, the flexible, echoing rhythms and offhand colloquialism by which she preserved, even in her most anguished probing, complete artistic control. Her internal horrors were as factual and precisely sensed as the barely controllable stallion on which she was learning to ride or the car she had smashed up.

So she spoke of suicide with a wry detachment, and without any mention of the suffering or drama of the act. It was obviously a matter of self-respect that her first attempt had been serious and nearly successful, instead of a mere hysterical gesture. That seemed to entitle her to speak of suicide as a subject, not as an obsession. It was an act she felt she had a right to as a grown woman and a free agent, in the same way as she felt it to be necessary to her development, given her queer conception of the adult as survivor, an imaginary Jew from the concentration camps of the mind. Because of this there was never any question of motives: you do it because you do it, just as an artist always knows what he knows.

Perhaps this is why she scarcely mentioned her father, however clearly and deeply her fantasies of death were involved with him. The autobiographical heroine of *The Bell Jar* goes to weep at her father's grave immediately before she holes up in a cellar and swallows fifty sleeping pills. In "Daddy," describing the same episode, she hammers home her reasons with repetitions:

> At twenty I tried to die
> And get back, back, back to you.
> I thought even the bones would do.

I suspect that finding herself alone again now, however temporarily and voluntarily, all the anguish she had experienced at her father's death was reactivated: despite herself, she felt abandoned, injured, enraged, and bereaved as purely and defenselessly as she had as a child twenty years before. As a result, the pain that had built up steadily inside her all that time came flooding out. There was no need to discuss motives because the poems did that for her.

These months were an amazingly creative period, comparable, I think, to the "marvellous year" in which Keats produced nearly all the poetry on which his reputation finally rests. Earlier she had written carefully, more or less painfully, with much rewriting, and according to her husband, with constant recourse to *Roget's Thesaurus*. Now, although she abandoned none of her hard-earned skills and discipline, and still rewrote and rewrote, the poems flowed effortlessly, until, at the end, she occasionally produced as many as three a day. She also told me that she was deep into a new novel. *The Bell Jar* was finished, proofread and with her publishers, she spoke of it with some embarrassment as an autobiographical apprentice-work which she had to write in order to free herself from the past. But this new book, she implied, was the genuine article.

Considering the conditions in which she worked, her productivity was phenomenal. She was a full-time mother with a two-year-old daughter, a baby of ten months, and a house to look after. By the time the children were in bed at night she was too tired for anything more strenuous than "music and brandy and water." So she got up very early each morning and worked until the children woke. "These new poems of mine have one thing in common," she wrote in a note for a reading she prepared, but never broadcast, for the BBC, "they were all written at about four in the morning—that still blue, almost eternal hour before the baby's cry, before the glassy music of the milkman, settling his bottles." In those dead hours between night and day, she was able to gather herself into herself in silence and isolation, almost as though she were reclaiming some past innocence and freedom before life got a grip on her. Then she could write. For the rest of the day she was shared among the children, the housework, the shopping, efficient, bustling, harassed, like every other housewife. . . .

Yet lonely she was, touchingly and without much disguise, despite her buoyant manner. Despite, too, the energy of her poems, which are, by any standards, subtly ambiguous performances. In them she faced her private horrors steadily and without looking aside, but the effort and risk involved in doing so acted on her like a stimulant: the worse things got and the more directly she wrote about them, the more fertile her imagination became. Just as disaster, when it finally arrives, is never as bad as it seems in expectation, so she now wrote almost with relief, swiftly as though to forestall further horrors. In a way, this is what she had been waiting for all her life, and now it had come she knew she must use it. "The passion for destruction is also a creative passion," said Michael Bakunin, and for Sylvia also this was true. She turned anger, implacability, and her roused, needle-sharp sense of trouble into a kind of celebration.

I have suggested that her cool tone depends a great deal on her realism, her sense of fact. As the months went by and her poetry became progressively more extreme, this gift of transforming every detail grew steadily until, in the last weeks, each trivial event became the occasion for poetry: a cut finger, a fever, a bruise. Her drab domestic life fused with her imagination richly and without hesitation. Around this time, for example, her husband produced a strange radio play in which the hero, driving to town, runs over a hare, sells the dead animal for five shillings, and with the blood money buys two roses. Sylvia pounced on this, isolating its core, interpreting and adjusting it according to her own needs. The result was the poem "Kindness," which ends:

> The blood jet is poetry,
> There is no stopping it.
> You hand me two children, two roses.

There was, indeed, no stopping it. Her poetry acted as a strange, powerful lens through which her ordinary life was filtered and refigured with extraordinary intensity. Perhaps the elation that comes of writing well and often helped her to preserve that bright American façade she unfailingly presented to the world. In common with her other friends of that period, I chose to believe in this cheerfulness against all the evidence of the poems. Or rather, I believed in it, and I didn't believe. But what could one do? I felt sorry for her but she clearly didn't want that. Her jauntiness forestalled all sympathy, and, if only by her blank refusal to discuss them otherwise, she insisted that her poems were purely poems, autonomous. If attempted suicide is, as some psychiatrists believe, a cry for help, then Sylvia at this time was not suicidal. What she wanted was not help but confirmation: she needed someone to acknowledge that she was coping exceptionally well with her difficult routine life of children, nappies, shopping, and writing. She needed, even more, to know that the poems worked and were good, for although she had gone through a gate Lowell had opened, she was now far along a peculiarly solitary road on which not many would risk following her. So it was important for her to know that her messages were coming back clear and strong. Yet not even her determinedly bright self-reliance could disguise the loneliness that came from her almost palpably, like a heat haze. She asked for neither sympathy nor help but, like a bereaved widow at a wake, she simply wanted company in her mourning. I suppose it provided confirmation that, despite the odds and the internal evidence, she still existed.

One gloomy November afternoon she arrived at my studio greatly excited. As usual, she had been trudging the chill streets, house-hunting despondently and more or less aimlessly. A block away from the square near Primrose Hill where she and Ted had lived when they first came to London she saw a "To Let" notice up in front of a newly refurbished house. That in itself was something of a miracle in those impossible, overcrowded days. But more important, the house bore a blue plaque announcing that Yeats had once lived there. It was a sign, the confirmation she had been looking for. That summer she had visited Yeats' Tower at Ballylea and wrote to a friend that she thought it "the most beautiful and peaceful place in the world"; now there was a possibility of finding another Yeats tower in her favorite part of London which she could in some way share with the great poet. She hurried to the agent's and found, improbably, that she was the first to apply. Another sign. On the spot she took a five-year lease of the flat, although the rent was more than she could afford. Then she walked across dark, blowy Primrose Hill to tell me the news.

She was elated not just because she had at last found a flat but because the place and its associations seemed to her somehow preordained. In varying degrees, both she and her husband seemed to believe in the occult. As artists, I suppose, they had to, since both were intent on finding voices for their unquiet, buried selves. But there was, I think, something more to their belief than that. Ted has written that "her psychic gifts, at almost any time, were strong enough to make her frequently wish to be rid of them." That could simply have been her poet's knack of sensing the unspoken content of every situation and, later, her easy, instinctive access to her own unconscious. Yet although both of them talked often enough about astrology, dreams, and magic—enough, anyway, to imply that this was not just a casually interesting subject—I had the impression that at heart their attitudes were utterly different. Ted constantly and carefully mocked himself and deflated his pretensions, yet there was always a sense of his being in touch with some primitive area, some dark side of the self which had nothing to do with the young literary man. This, after all, was what his poems were about: an immediate, physical apprehension of the violence both of animal life and of the self—of the animality of the self. It was also part of his physical presence, a quality of threat beneath his shrewd, laconic manner. It was almost as though, despite all the reading and polish and craftsmanship, he had never properly been civilized or had, at least, never properly believed in his civilization. It was simply a shell he sardonically put up with for the sake of convenience. So all that astrology, primitive religion, and black magic he talked about, however, ironically, was a kind of metaphor for the shaking but obscure creative powers he knew himself to possess. For this reason those dubious topics took on for him an immediacy which may not have implied any belief but which certainly transformed them into something beyond mere fad. Perhaps all I am describing is, quite simply, a touch of genius. But it is a genius that has little to do with the traditional Romantic concept of the word: with Shelley's canny other-worldliness or Byron's equally canny sense of his own drama. Ted, too, is canny and practical, like most Yorkshiremen, unwillingly fooled and with a fine, racing mechanic's ear for the rumblings of the literary machine. But he is also, in a curiously complete way, an original: his reactions are unpredictable, his frame of reference different. I imagine the most extreme example of this style of genius was Blake. But there are also many people of genius—perhaps the majority—who have almost nothing of that dislocating and dislocated quality: T. S. Eliot, for example, the Polish poet Zbigniew Herbert, John Donne and Keats—all men whose unusual creative intelligence and awareness seem not essentially at odds with the reality of their everyday worlds. Instead, their particular gift is to clarify and intensify the received world.

Sylvia, I think, belonged with these latter. Her intensity was of the nerves, something urban and near screaming-point. It was also, in its way, more intellectual than Ted's. It was part of the fierceness with which she had worked as a student, passing exam after exam brilliantly, easily, hungrily. With the same intensity she immersed herself in her children, her riding, her beekeeping, even her cooking; everything had to be done well and to the fullest. Since her husband was interested in the occult—for whatever clouded personal reasons—she threw herself into that, too, almost out of the desire to excel. And because her natural talents were very great, she discovered she had "psychic gifts." No doubt the results were genuine and even uncanny, but I suspect they were a triumph of mind over ectoplasm. It is the same in the poems: Ted's gain their effect by expressing his sense of menace and violence immediately, unanswerably; in Sylvia's the expression, though often more powerful, is a by-product of a compulsive need to understand.

On Christmas Eve, 1962, Sylvia telephoned me: she and the children had finally settled into their new apartment; could I come round that evening to see the place, have a meal, and hear some new poems? As it happened, I couldn't, since I had already been invited to dinner by some friends who lived a few streets away from her. I said I'd drop in for a drink on my way.

She seemed different. Her hair, which she usually wore in a tight, schoolmistressy bun, was loose. It hung straight to her waist like a tent, giving her pale face and gaunt figure a curiously desolate, rapt air, like a priestess emptied out by the rites of her cult. When she walked in front of me down the hall passage and up the stairs to her apartment—she had the top two floors of the house—her hair gave off a strong smell, sharp as an animal's. The children were already in bed upstairs and the flat was silent. It was newly painted, white and chill. There were, as I re-member, no curtains up yet, and the night pressed in coldly on the win-dows. She had deliberately kept the place bare: rush matting on the floor, a few books, bits of Victoriana, and cloudy blue glass on the shelves, a couple of small Leonard Baskin woodcuts. It was rather beau-tiful, in its chaste, stripped-down way, but cold, very cold, and the oddments of flimsy Christmas decoration made it seem doubly forlorn, each seeming to repeat that she and the children would be alone over Christmas. For the unhappy, Christmas is always a bad time: the terrible false jollity that comes at you from every side, braying about goodwill and peace and family fun, makes loneliness and depression particularly hard to bear. I had never seen her so strained.

We drank wine and, as usual, she read me some poems. One of them was "Death & Co." This time there was no escaping the meaning. When she had written about death before, it was as something survived, even surpassed: "Lady Lazarus" ends with a resurrection and a threat, and even in "Daddy" she manages finally to turn her back on the grinning, beckoning figure—"Daddy, daddy, you bastard, I'm through." Hence, perhaps, the energy of these poems, their weird jollity in the teeth of everything, their recklessness. But now, as though poetry really were a form of black magic, the figure she had invoked so often, only to dismiss triumphantly, had risen before her, dank, final, and not to be denied. He appeared to her in both his usual shapes: like her father, elderly, unforgiving, and very dead, and also younger, more seductive, a creature of her own generation and choice.* This time there was no way out for her; she could only sit still and pretend they hadn't noticed her:

> I do not stir.
> The frost makes a flower,
> The dew makes a star,
> The dead bell,
> The dead bell.
>
> Somebody's done for.

Perhaps the bell was tolling for "somebody" other than herself; but she didn't seem to believe so.

I didn't know what to say. The earlier poems had all insisted, in their different ways, that she wanted nobody's help—although I suddenly realized that maybe they had insisted in such a manner as to make you understand that help might be acceptable, if you were willing to make the effort. But now she was beyond the reach of anyone. In the beginning she had called up these horrors partly in the hope of exorcising them, partly to demonstrate her omnipotence and invulnerability. Now she was shut in with them and knew she was defenseless.

I remember arguing inanely about the phrase "The nude/Verdigris of the condor." I said it was exaggerated, morbid. On the contrary, she replied, that was exactly how a condor's legs looked. She was right, of course. I was only trying, in a futile way, to reduce the tension and take her mind momentarily off her private horrors—as though that could be done by argument and literary criticism! She must have felt I was stupid and insensitive. Which I was. But to have been otherwise would have meant accepting responsibilities I didn't want and couldn't, in my own depression, have coped with. When I left about eight o'clock to go on to my dinner party, I knew I had let her down in some final and unforgivable way. And I knew she knew. I never again saw her alive.

* In her own note on the poem, which she wrote for the BBC, Sylvia said: "This poem—'Death & Co.'—is about the double or schizophrenic nature of death—the marmoreal coldness of Blake's death mask, say, hand in glove with the fearful softness of worms, water, and other katabolists. I imagine these two aspects of death as two men, two business friends, who have come to call."

It was an unspeakable winter, the worst, they said, in a hundred and fifty years. The snow began just after Christmas and would not let up. By New Year the whole country had ground to a halt. The trains froze on the tracks, the abandoned trucks froze on the roads. The power stations, overloaded by million upon pathetic million of hopeless electric fires, broke down continually; not that the fires mattered, since the electricians were mostly out on strike. Water pipes froze solid; for a bath you had to scheme and cajole those rare friends with centrally heated houses, who became rarer and less friendly as the weeks dragged on. Doing the dishes became a major operation. The gastric rumble of water in outdated plumbing was sweeter than the sound of mandolins. Weight for weight, plumbers were as expensive as smoked salmon, and harder to find. The gas failed and Sunday joints went raw. The lights failed and candles, of course, were unobtainable. Nerves failed and marriages crumbled. Finally, the heart failed. It seemed the cold would never end. Nag, nag, nag.

In December *The Observer* had published a still uncollected poem by Sylvia called "Event"; in mid-January they published another, "Winter Trees." Sylvia wrote me a note about it, adding that maybe we should take our children to the zoo and she would show me "the nude verdigris of the condor." But she no longer dropped into my studio with poems. Later that month I met the literary editor of one of the big weeklies. He asked me if I had seen Sylvia recently.

"No. Why?"

"I was just wondering. She sent us some poems. Very strange."

"Did you like them?"

"No," he replied. "Too extreme for my taste. I sent them all back. But she sounds in a bad state. I think she needs help."

Her doctor, a sensitive, overworked man, thought the same. He prescribed sedatives and arranged for her to see a psychotherapist. Having been bitten once by American psychiatry, she hesitated for some time before writing for an appointment. But her depression did not lift, and finally the letter was sent. It did no good. Either her letter or that of the therapist arranging a consultation went astray; apparently the postman delivered it to the wrong address. The therapist's reply arrived a day or two after she died. This was one of several links in the chain of accidents, coincidences, and mistakes that ended in her death.

I am convinced by what I know of the facts that this time she did not intend to die. Her suicide attempt ten years before had been, in every sense, deadly serious. She had carefully disguised the theft of the sleeping pills, left a misleading note to cover her tracks, and hidden herself in the darkest, most unused corner of a cellar, rearranging behind her the old firelogs she had disturbed, burying herself away like a skeleton in the nethermost family closet. Then she had swallowed a bottle of fifty sleeping pills. She was found late and by accident, and survived only by a miracle. The flow of life in her was too strong even for the violence she had done it. This, anyway, is her description of the act in *The Bell Jar*; there is no reason to believe it false. So she had learned the hard way the odds against successful suicide; she had learned that despair must be counterpoised by an almost obsessional attention to detail and disguise.

By these lights she seemed, in her last attempt, to be taking care not to succeed. But this time everything conspired to destroy her. An employment agency had found her an *au pair* girl to help with the children and housework while Sylvia got on with her writing. The girl, an Australian, was due to arrive at nine o'clock on the morning of Monday, February 11th. Meanwhile, a recurrent trouble, Sylvia's sinuses were bad; the pipes in her newly converted flat froze solid; there was still no telephone, and no word from the psychotherapist; the weather continued monstrous. Illness, loneliness, depression, and cold, combined with the demands of two small children, were too much for her. So when the weekend came she went off with the babies to stay with friends in another part of London. The plan was, I think, that she would leave early enough on Monday morning to be back in time to welcome the Australian girl. Instead, she decided to go back on the Sunday. The friends were against it but she was insistent, made a great show of her old competence and seemed more cheerful than she had been for some time. So they let her go. About eleven o'clock that night she knocked on the door of the elderly painter who lived below her, asking to borrow some stamps. But she lingered in the doorway, drawing out the conversation until he told her that he got up well before nine in the morning. Then she said goodnight and went back upstairs.

God knows what kind of a sleepless night she spent or if she wrote any poetry. Certainly, within the last few days of her life she wrote one of her most beautiful poems, "Edge," which is specifically about the act she was about to perform:

> The woman is perfected.
> Her dead
>
> Body wears the smile of accomplishment,
> The illusion of a Greek necessity
>
> Flows in the scrolls of her toga,
> Her bare

Feet seem to be saying:
We have come so far, it is over.

Each dead child coiled, a white serpent,
One at each little

Pitcher of milk, now empty.
She has folded

Them back into her body as petals
Of a rose close when the garden

Stiffens and odors bleed
From the sweet, deep throats of the night flowers.

The moon has nothing to be sad about,
Staring from her hood of bone.

She is used to this sort of thing.
Her blacks crackle and drag.

It is a poem of great peace and resignation, utterly without self-pity. Even with a subject so appallingly close she remains an artist, absorbed in the practical task of letting each image develop a full, still life of its own. That she is writing about her own death is almost irrelevant. There is another poem, "Words," also very late, which is about the way language remains and echoes long after the turmoil of life has passed; like "Edge" it has the same translucent calm. If these were the last things she wrote, I think she must in the end have accepted the logic of the life she had been leading, and come to terms with its terrible necessities.

Around six A.M. she went up to the children's room and left a plate of bread and butter and two mugs of milk, in case they should wake hungry before the *au pair* girl arrived. Then she went back down to the kitchen, sealed the door and window as best she could with towels, opened the oven, laid her head in it, and turned on the gas.

The Australian girl arrived punctually at nine A.M. She rang and knocked a long time but could get no answer. So she went off to search for a telephone kiosk in order to phone the agency and make sure she had the right address. Sylvia's name, incidentally, was not on either of the doorbells. Had everything been normal, the neighbor below would have been up by then; even if he had overslept, the girl's knocking should have aroused him. But as it happened, the neighbor was very deaf and slept without his hearing aid. More important, his bedroom was immediately below Sylvia's kitchen. The gas seeped down and knocked him out cold. So he slept on through all the noise. The girl returned and tried again, still without success. Again she went off to telephone the agency and ask what to do; they told her to go back. It was now about eleven o'clock. This time she was lucky: some builders had arrived to work in the frozen-up house, and they let her in. When she knocked on Sylvia's door there was no answer and the smell of gas was overpowering. The builders forced the lock and found Sylvia sprawled in the kitchen. She was still warm. She had left a note saying, "Please call Dr.—" and giving his telephone number. But it was too late.

Had everything worked out as it should—had the gas not drugged the man downstairs, preventing him from opening the front door to the *au pair* girl—there is no doubt she would have been saved. I think she wanted to be; why else leave her doctor's telephone number? This time, unlike the occasion ten years before, there was too much holding her to life. Above all, there were the children: she was too passionate a mother to want to lose them or them to lose her. There were also the extraordinary creative powers she now unequivocally knew she possessed: the poems came daily, unbidden and unstoppable, and she was again working on a novel about which, at last, she had no reservations.

Why, then, did she kill herself? In part, I suppose, it was "a cry for help" which fatally misfired. But it was also a last, desperate attempt to exorcise the death she had summoned up in her poems. I have already suggested that perhaps she had begun to write obsessively about death for two reasons. First, when she and her husband separated, however mutual the arrangement, she went through again the same piercing grief and bereavement she had felt as a child when her father, by his death, seemed to abandon her. Second, I believe she thought her car crash the previous summer had set her free; she had paid her dues, qualified as a survivor, and could now write about it. But, as I have written elsewhere, for the artist himself art is not necessarily therapeutic; he is not automatically relieved of his fantasies by expressing them. Instead, by some perverse logic of creation, the act of formal expression may simply make the dredged-up material more readily available to him. The result of handling it in his work may well be that he finds himself living it out. For the artist, in short, nature often imitates art. Or, to restate the cliché, when an artist holds a mirror up to nature he finds out who and what he is; but the knowledge may change him irredeemably so that he becomes that image.

I think Sylvia, in one way or another, sensed this. In an introductory note she wrote to "Daddy" for the BBC, she said of the poem's narrator, "she has to act out the awful little allegory once over before she is free of it." The allegory in question was, as she saw it, the struggle in her between a fantasy Nazi father and a Jewish mother. But perhaps it was also a fantasy of containing in herself her own dead father, like a woman possessed by a demon (in the poem she actually calls him a vampire). In order for her to be free of him, he has to be released like a genie from a bottle. And this is precisely what the poems did: they bodied forth the death within her. But they also did so in an intensely living and creative way. The more she wrote about death, the stronger and more fertile her imaginative world became. And this gave her everything to live for.

I suspect that in the end she wanted to have done with the theme once and for all. But the only way she could find was "to act out the awful little allegory once over." She had always been a bit of a gambler, used to taking risks. The authority of her poetry was in part due to her brave persistence in following the thread of her inspiration right down to the Minotaur's lair. And this psychic courage had its parallel in her physical arrogance and carelessness. Risks didn't frighten her; on the contrary, she found them stimulating. Freud has written, "Life loses in interest, when the highest stake in the game of living, life itself, may not be risked." Finally, Sylvia took that risk. She gambled for the last time, having worked out that the odds were in her favor, but perhaps, in her depression, not much caring whether she won or lost. Her calculations went wrong and she lost.

It was a mistake, then, and out of it a whole myth has grown. I don't think she would have found it much to her taste, since it is a myth of the poet as a sacrificial victim, offering herself up for the sake of her art, having been dragged by the Muses to that final altar through every kind of distress. In these terms, her suicide becomes the whole point of the story, the act which validates her poems, gives them their interest, and proves her seriousness. So people are drawn to her work in much the same spirit as *Time* featured her at length: not for the poetry but for the gossipy, extraliterary "human interest." Yet just as the suicide adds nothing at all to the poetry, so the myth of Sylvia as a passive victim is a total perversion of the woman she was. It misses altogether her liveliness, her intellectual appetite and harsh wit, her great imaginative resourcefulness and vehemence of feeling, her control. Above all, it misses the courage with which she was able to turn disaster into art. The pity is not that there is a myth of Sylvia Plath but that the myth is not simply that of an enormously gifted poet whose death came recklessly, by mistake, and too soon.

I used to think of her brightness as a façade, as though she were able, in a rather schizoid way, to turn her back on her suffering for the sake of appearances, and pretend it didn't exist. But maybe she was also able to keep her unhappiness in check because she could write about it, because she knew she was salvaging from all those horrors something rather marvelous. The end came when she felt she could stand the subject no longer. She had written it out and was ready for something new.

> The blood-jet is poetry,
> There is no stopping it.

The only method of stopping it she could see, her vision by then blinkered by depression and illness, was the last gamble. So having, as she thought, arranged to be saved, she lay down in front of the gas oven almost hopefully, almost with relief, as though she were saying, "Perhaps this will set me free."

On Friday, February 15th, there was an inquest in the drab, damp coroner's court behind Camden Town: muttered evidence, long silences, the Australian girl in tears. Earlier that morning I had gone with Ted to the undertakers in Mornington Crescent. The coffin was at the far end of a bare, draped room. She lay stiffly, a ludicrous ruff at her neck. Only her face showed. It was gray and slightly transparent, like wax. I had never before seen a dead person and I hardly recognized her; her features seemed too thin and sharp. The room smelled of apples, faint, sweet but somehow unclean, as though the apples were beginning to rot. I was glad to get out into the cold and noise of the dingy streets. It seemed impossible that she was dead.

Even now I find it hard to believe. There was too much life in her long flat, strongly boned body, and her longish face with its fine brown eyes, shrewd and full of feeling. She was practical and candid, passionate and compassionate. I believe she was a genius. I sometimes catch myself childishly thinking I'll run into her walking on Primrose Hill or the Heath, and we'll pick up the conversation where we left off. But perhaps that is because her poems still speak so distinctly in her accents: quick, sardonic, unpredictable, effortlessly inventive, a bit angry, and always utterly her own.

KATHERINE ANNE PORTER

Katherine Anne Porter (1894–) won the National Book Award in 1966 for her *Collected Stories,* following *Flowering Judas* (1935) and *Pale Horse, Pale Rider* (1939). Like many other writers of her generation, she lived for some time in Paris.

PARIS: A LITTLE INCIDENT IN THE RUE DE L'ODÉON

This anecdote comes surprisingly upon Hemingway, as it amusingly illuminates his pride and insecurity, but it tells more about Sylvia Beach
and her famous Paris bookshop, founded in the twenties. It also tells of
the transitoriness of life, as Katherine Anne Porter recalls to mind, and
puts before us, two vivid pictures of people, both of whom have vanished into the night. Notice Porter's remarkable pictorial and metaphorical gift as she takes us on a spatial tour, room by room.

Last summer in Paris I went back to the place where Sylvia Beach
had lived, to the empty bookshop, Shakespeare and Company, and the
flat above, where she brought together for sociable evenings the most
miscellaneous lot of people I ever saw: persons you were surprised to
find on the same planet together, much less under the same roof.

The bookshop at 12 Rue de l'Odéon has been closed ever since the
German occupation, but her rooms have been kept piously intact by a
faithful friend, more or less as she left them, except for a filmlike cob-
web on the objects, a grayness in the air, for Sylvia is gone, and has
taken her ghost with her. All sorts of things were there, her walls of
books in every room, the bushels of papers, hundreds of photographs,
portraits, odd bits of funny toys, even her flimsy scraps of underwear
and stockings left to dry near the kitchen window; a coffee cup and a
small coffeepot as she left them on the table; in her bedroom, her looking glass, her modest entirely incidental vanities, face powder, beauty
cream, lipstick. . . .

Oh, no. She was not there. And someone had taken away the tiger
skin from her bed—narrow as an army cot. If it was not a tiger, then
some large savage cat with good markings; real fur, I remember, spotted
or streaked, a wild woodland touch shining out in the midst of the pure,
spontaneous, persevering austerity of Sylvia's life: maybe a humorous
hint of some hidden streak in Sylvia, this preacher's daughter of a
Baltimore family, brought up in unexampled high-mindedness, gentle
company and polite learning; this nervous, witty girl whose only expressed ambition in life was to have a bookshop of her own. Anywhere
would do, but Paris for choice. God knows modesty could hardly take
denser cover, and this she did at incredible expense of hard work and
spare living and yet with the help of quiet dozens of devoted souls one
after the other; the financial and personal help of her two delightful
sisters and the lifetime savings of her mother, a phoenix of a mother
who consumed herself to ashes time and again in aid of her wild
daughter.

For she *was* wild—a wild, free spirit if ever I saw one, fearless, untamed to the last, which is not the same as being reckless or prodigal, or wicked, or suicidal. She was not really afraid of anything human, a most awe-inspiring form of courage. She trusted her own tastes and instincts and went her own way; and almost everyone who came near her trusted her too. She laid her hands gently, irresistibly on hundreds of lives, and changed them for the better: she had second sight about what each person really needed.

James Joyce, his wife, his children, his fortunes, his diet, his eyesight, and his book *Ulysses* turned out to be the major project of her life; he was her unique darling, all his concerns were hers. One could want a rest cure after merely reading an account of her labors to get that book written in the first place, then printed and paid for and distributed even partially. Yet it was only one, if the most laborious and exhausting, of all her pastimes, concerned as she was solely with bringing artists together—writers preferred, any person with a degree of talent practicing or connected with the art of Literature, and in getting their work published and set before the eyes of the world. Painters and composers were a marginal interest. There was nothing diffused or shapeless in Sylvia's purpose: that bizarre assortment of creatures shared a common center—they were artists or were trying to be. Otherwise many of them had only Sylvia in common. She had introduced many of them to each other.

We know now from many published memoirs what Ford Madox Ford thought of Hemingway, what Hemingway thought of Ford and F. Scott Fitzgerald, how William Carlos Williams felt about Paris literary life, how Bryher felt herself a stranger to every one but Sylvia, and going back to an early book of Robert McAlmon's, *Being Geniuses Together*, what he thought of the whole lot. These recorded memories glitter with malice and hatred and jealousy, and one sees ten versions of the same incident in as many books: there are admirations and friendships and kindnesses, too, in most of them; I have not seen one that spoke meanly of Sylvia. They seemed to be agreed about her, she was a touchstone.

She was a thin, twiggy sort of woman, quick-tongued, quick-minded and light on her feet. Her nerves were as tight as a tuned-up fiddle string and she had now and then attacks of migraine that stopped her in her tracks before she spun herself to death, just in the usual run of her days.

When I first saw her, in the early spring of 1932, her hair was still the color of roasted chestnut shells, her light golden brown eyes with greenish glints in them were marvelously benign, acutely attentive, and they sparkled upon one rather than beamed, as gentle eyes are supposed to do. She was not pretty, never had been, never had tried to be: she was attractive, a center of interest, a delightful presence not accountable to any of the familiar attributes of charm. Her power was in the unconscious, natural radiation of her intense energy and concentration upon those beings and arts she loved.

Sylvia loved her hundreds of friends, and they all loved her—many of whom loved almost no one else except perhaps himself—apparently without jealousy, each one sure of his special cell in the vast honeycomb of her heart; sure of his welcome in her shop with its exhilarating air of something pretty wonderful going on at top speed. Her genius was for friendship; her besetting virtue, generosity, an all-covering charity in its true sense; and courage that reassured even Hemingway, the distrustful, the wary, the unloving, who sized people up on sight, who couldn't be easy until he had somehow got the upper hand. Half an hour after he was first in her shop, Hemingway was sitting there with a sock and shoe laid aside, showing Sylvia the still-painful scars of his war wounds got in Italy. He told her the doctors thought he would die and he was baptized there in the hospital. Sylvia wrote in her memoirs, "Baptized or not—and I am going to say this whether Hemingway shoots me or not—I have always felt he was a deeply religious man."

Hemingway tried to educate her in boxing, wrestling, any kind of manly sport, but it seemed to remain to Sylvia mere reeling and writhing and fainting in coils: but Hemingway and Hadley his wife, and Bumby the Baby, and Sylvia and Adrienne Monnier, her good friend, all together at a boxing match must have been one of the sights of Paris. Sylvia tells it with her special sense of comedy; very acute, and with tenderness. Hemingway rather turns out to be the hero of her book, helping to bootleg copies of *Ulysses* into the United States, shooting German snipers off her roof on the day the American army entered Paris: being shown in fact as the man he wished and tried to be. . . .

As I say, Sylvia's friends did not always love each other even for her sake, nor could anyone but Sylvia expect them to: yet it is plain that she did. At parties specially, or in her shop, she had a way, figuratively, of taking two of her friends, strangers to each other, by the napes of their necks and cracking their heads together, saying in effect always, and at times in so many words, "My dears, you *must* love one another!" and she could cite the best of reasons for this hope, compounding her error by describing them in turn as being of the highest rank and quality each in his own field.

Usually the strangers would give each other a straight, skeptical stare, exchange a few mumbling words under her expectant, fostering eyes; and the instant she went on to other greetings and exchanges, they faced about from each other and drifted away. There may have been some later friendships growing from this method, but I don't know of any: it never made one for me, nor, I may say, the other way about.

It was in Sylvia's shop that I saw Ernest Hemingway for the first and last time. If this sounds portentous now, it is only because of all that has happened since to make of him a tragic figure. Then he was still the *beau garçon* who loved blood sports, the black-haired, sunburned muscle boy of American literature; the war hero with scars to show for it: the unalloyed male who had licked Style to a standstill. He had exactly the right attitude toward words like "glory" and so on. It was not particularly impressive: I preferred Joyce and Yeats and Henry James, and I had seen all the bullfights and done all the hunting I wanted in Mexico before I ever came to Paris. He seemed to me then to be the walking exemplar of the stylish literary attitudes of his time: he may have been, but I see now how very good he was; he paid heavily, as such men do, for their right to live on beyond the fashion they helped to make, to play out to the end not the role wished on them by their public but the destiny they cannot escape because there was a moment in their lives when they chose that destiny.

It was such a little incident, and so random and rather comic at the time, and Sylvia and I laughed over it again later, the last time I saw her in New York.

I had dropped into Sylvia's shop looking for something to read, just at early dark on a cold, rainy winter evening, maybe in 1934, I am not sure. We were standing under the light at the big round table piled up with books, talking; and I was just saying good-bye when the door burst open, and Hemingway unmistakably Ernest stood before us, looking just like the snapshots of him then being everywhere published—tall, bulky, broadfaced (his season of boyish slenderness was short), cropped black moustache, watchful eyes, all reassuringly there.

He wore a streaming old raincoat and a drenched floppy rain hat pulled over his eyebrows. Sylvia ran to him calling like a bird, both arms out; they embraced in a manly sort of way (quite a feat, sizes and sexes considered), then Sylvia turned to me with that ominous apostolic sweetness in her eyes. Stil holding one of Hemingway's hands, she reached at arm's length for mine. "Katherine Anne Porter," she said, pronouncing the names in full, "this is Ernest Hemingway. . . . Ernest, this is Katherine Anne, and I want the two best modern American writers to know each other!" Our hands were never joined.

"Modern" was a talismanic word then, but this time the magic failed. At that instant the telephone rang in the back room, Sylvia flew to answer, calling back to us merrily, merrily, "Now you two just get acquainted and I'll be right back." Hemingway and I stood and gazed unwinkingly at each other with poker faces for all of ten seconds, in silence. Hemingway then turned in one wide swing and hurled himself into the rainy darkness as he had hurled himself out of it, and that was all. I am sorry if you are disappointed. All personal lack of sympathy and attraction aside, and they were real in us both, it must have been galling to this most famous young man to have his name pronounced in the same breath as writer with someone he had never heard of, and a woman at that. I nearly felt sorry for him.

Sylvia seemed mystified that her hero had vanished. "Where did he go?" "I don't know." "What did he say?" she asked, still wondering. I had to tell her: "Nothing, not a word. Not even good-bye." She continued to think this very strange. I didn't, and don't.

SUGGESTIONS FOR WRITING

1. Find an experience that once taught you some general truth about man and the universe, or one in which you now can see some such significance, though it seemed unimportant at the time. Very few students have shot an elephant, but perhaps you were in an automobile accident or stole your best friend's storybook or doll or broke a promise. The incident may be small; the lesson may be obvious. The point is that in this incident you learned the lesson for the first time, first realized that the abstract truths actually operate in daily scrapes and quibbles. Your aim in doing the exercise is to make your readers, through vivid and figurative detail after detail, see and feel exactly how it was. To keep yourself within the expository traces, write out a clear thesis—"One day something happened that taught me the real nature of robbery: that you really steal more from yourself than from others"—and then set it at the end of a good beginning paragraph, or at least after a reasonable introduction that sets the scene and lets the reader know where he is going.

2. Write an essay about your own neighborhood, following Baldwin in mixing childhood memories with present observations and pertinent sociological facts, and similarly keeping your language vivid with sharp figurative detail.

3. Trace out what you know and do not know about your ancestry, supporting or attacking a thesis that it matters.

4. Describe a contest that brought you something of the satisfaction that White Bull feels.

5. Describe a person you have seen from time to time over the years—
   your mother, your grandfather, an aunt, a friend—trying to aim for
   some illuminating point. Try to emulate Alvarez as he blends physical description with conversation and analysis in presenting Sylvia
   Plath.

6. Give us a "little incident" similar to the one described by Katherine
   Anne Porter.

Eight
The Ironic Essay

Nothing teaches the connotations of words more surely than trying to write irony—because in irony some words say the opposite of what they mean and some say exactly what they mean and others speak subtleties in between. The three quite different essays in this section show how this ironic blending of straight and veiled statement works. You will see how the ironist takes a fictitious pose, a pretense he shares in secret with his reader. You will see how the blend of straight and veiled statement varies with the pose taken, and how irony may enter into a perfectly straight essay for a time, tongue in cheek.

Swift's pose is the most thoroughly assumed, and his irony is the most complete: most of his words say the opposite of his true message. To bring home the abominations of eighteenth-century Ireland, Swift pretends to be a man of logical but weirdly limited mind, as he makes his most immodest proposal. Carlyle ironically poses as an admirer of Coleridge, a cloudy Zeus and *guru* snuffling among his worshipers, but the claims of biographical accuracy and fair play continually break through the ironic clouds. De Voto allows a straightforward summary of a book to damn it ironically.

As you read, be alert to these ironic slants and inversions. Why are they more effective than sober statement?

JONATHAN SWIFT

Jonathan Swift (1667–1745), an Anglican clergyman, author of *Gulliver's Travels* (1726), was born in Ireland of English parents. He was prominent in London's highest political and literary circles until he became Dean of St. Patrick's Cathedral, Dublin, in 1714. He published *A Modest Proposal* in 1729.

A MODEST PROPOSAL FOR PREVENTING THE CHILDREN OF IRELAND FROM BEING A BURDEN TO THEIR PARENTS OR COUNTRY

This is the world's greatest ironic essay, prompted by real anger at English landlords for the Irish poverty they caused but never saw. See if you can sort out the actual details from the ironic exaggerations, as well as Swift's intended proposals from his immodest ironic one. Notice that the speaker is not Swift himself, but a comically dramatized character of limited and absurdly rational mind. He, with Swift, views Dublin as a melancholy object; he does not see the enormity of his logic. Do you see any parallels with the Baldwin essay?

It is a melancholy object to those who walk through this great town [Dublin], or travel in the country, when they see the streets, the roads, and cabin-doors, crowded with beggars of the female sex, followed by three, four, or six children, all in rags, and importuning every passenger for an alms. These mothers, instead of being able to work for their honest livelihood, are forced to employ all their time in strolling to beg sustenance for their helpless infants; who, as they grow up, either turn thieves for want of work, or leave their dear native country to fight for the Pretender in Spain, or sell themselves to the Barbadoes.

I think it is agreed by all parties, that this prodigious number of children in the arms, or on the backs, or at the heels of their mothers, and frequently of their fathers, is, in the present deplorable state of the kingdom, a very great additional grievance; and, therefore, whoever could find out a fair, cheap, and easy method of making these children sound, useful members of the commonwealth, would deserve so well of the public, as to have his statue set up for a preserver of the nation.

But my intention is very far from being confined to provide only for the children of professed beggars; it is of a much greater extent, and shall take in the whole number of infants at a certain age, who are born of parents in effect as little able to support them, as those who demand our charity in the streets.

As to my own part, having turned my thoughts for many years upon this important subject, and maturely weighed the several schemes of our projectors, I have always found them grossly mistaken in their computation. It is true, a child, just dropped from its dam, may be supported by her milk for a solar year, with little other nourishment; at most, not above the value of two shillings, which the mother may certainly get, or the value in scraps, by her lawful occupation of begging; and it is exactly, at one year old that I propose to provide for them in such a manner, as, instead of being a charge upon their parents, or the parish, or wanting food and raiment for the rest of their lives, they shall, on the contrary, contribute to the feeding and partly to the clothing, of many thousands.

There is likewise another great advantage in my scheme, that it will prevent those voluntary abortions, and that horrid practice of women murdering their bastard children, alas, too frequent among us! sacrificing the poor innocent babes, I doubt more to avoid the expense than the shame, which would move tears and pity in the most savage and inhuman breast.

The number of souls in this kingdom being usually reckoned one million and a half, of these I calculate there may be about two hundred thousand couple whose wives are breeders; from which number I subtract thirty thousand couple, who are able to maintain their own children (although I apprehend there cannot be so many, under the present distresses of the kingdom); but this being granted, there will remain a hundred and seventy thousand breeders. I again subtract fifty thousand, for those women who miscarry, or whose children die by accident or disease within the year. There only remain a hundred and twenty thousand children of poor parents annually born. The question therefore is, How this number shall be reared and provided for? which, as I have already said, under the present situation of affairs, is utterly impossible by all the methods hitherto proposed. For we can neither employ them in handicraft or agriculture; we neither build houses (I mean in the country), nor cultivate land: they can very seldom pick up a livelihood by stealing, till they arrive at six years old, except where they are of towardly parts; although I confess they learn the rudiments much earlier; during which time they can, however, be properly looked upon only as probationers; as I have been informed by a principal gentleman in the county of Cavan, who protested to me, that he never knew above one or two instances under the age of six, even in a part of the kingdom so renowned for the quickest proficiency in that art.

I am assured by our merchants, that a boy or a girl before twelve years old is no saleable commodity; and even when they come to this age they will not yield above three pounds, or three pounds and half-a-crown at most, on the exchange; which cannot turn to account either to the parents or kingdom, the charge of nutriment and rags having been at least four times that value.

I shall now, therefore, humbly propose my own thoughts, which I hope will not be liable to the least objection.

I have been assured by a very knowing American of my acquaintance in London, that a young healthy child, well nursed, is, at a year old, a most delicious, nourishing, and wholesome food, whether stewed, roasted, baked, or boiled; and I make no doubt that it will equally serve in a fricassee or a ragout.

I do therefore humbly offer it to public consideration, that of the hundred and twenty thousand children already computed, twenty thousand may be reserved for breed, whereof only one-fourth part to be males; which is more than we allow to sheep, black-cattle, or swine; and my reason is, that these children are seldom the fruits of marriage, a circumstance not much regarded by our savages, therefore one male will be sufficient to serve four females. That the remaining hundred thousand may, at a year old, be offered in sale to the persons of quality and fortune through the kingdom; always advising the mother to let them suck plentifully in the last month, so as to render them plump and fat for a good table. A child will make two dishes at an entertainment for friends; and when the family dines alone, the fore or hind quarter will make a reasonable dish, and, seasoned with a little pepper or salt, will be very good boiled on the fourth day, especially in winter.

I have reckoned, upon a medium, that a child just born will weigh twelve pounds, and in a solar year, if tolerably nursed, will increase to twenty-eight pounds.

I grant this food will be somewhat dear, and therefore very proper for landlords, who, as they have already devoured most of the parents, seem to have the best title to the children.

Infant's flesh will be in season throughout the year, but more plentifully in March, and a little before and after: for we are told by a grave author, an eminent French physician, that fish being a prolific diet, there are more children born in Roman Catholic countries about nine months after Lent, than at any other season; therefore, reckoning a year after Lent, the markets will be more glutted than usual, because the number of Popish infants is at least three to one in this kingdom; and therefore it will have one other collateral advantage, by lessening the Papists among us.

I have already computed the charge of nursing a beggar's child (in which list I reckon all cottagers, labourers, and four-fifths of the farmers) to be about two shillings per annum, rags included; and I believe no

gentleman would repine to give ten shillings for the carcass of a good
fat child, which, as I have said, will make four dishes of excellent nutri-
tive meat, when he has only some particular friend, or his own family,
to dine with him. Thus the squire will learn to be a good landlord, and
grow popular among his tenants; the mother will have eight shillings net
profit, and be fit for work till she produces another child.

Those who are more thrifty (as I must confess the times require) may
flay the carcass; the skin of which, artificially dressed, will make admirable gloves for ladies, and summer-boots for fine gentlemen.

As to our city of Dublin, shambles [slaughter houses] may be ap-
pointed for this purpose in the most convenient parts of it, and butchers,
we may be assured, will not be wanting; although I rather recommend
buying the children alive, then dressing them hot from the knife, as we
do roasting pigs.

A very worthy person, a true lover of his country, and whose virtues
I highly esteem, was lately pleased, in discoursing on this matter, to offer
a refinement upon my scheme. He said, that many gentlemen of this
kingdom, having of late destroyed their deer, he conceived that the want
of venison might be well supplied by the bodies of young lads and
maidens, not exceeding fourteen years of age, nor under twelve; so great
a number of both sexes in every country being now ready to starve for
want of work and service; and these to be disposed of by their parents,
if alive, or otherwise by their nearest relations. But, with due deference
to so excellent a friend, and so deserving a patriot, I cannot be altogether
in his sentiments; for as to the males, my American acquaintance assured
me, from frequent experience, that their flesh was generally tough and
lean, like that of our schoolboys, by continual exercise, and their taste
disagreeable; and to fatten them would not answer the charge. Then as
to the females, it would, I think, with humble submission, be a loss to
the public, because they soon would become breeders themselves: and
besides, it is not improbable that some scrupulous people might be apt
to censure such a practice (although indeed very unjustly), as a little
bordering upon cruelty; which, I confess, has always been with me the
strongest objection against any project, how well soever intended.

But in order to justify my friend, he confessed that this expedient
was put into his head by the famous Psalmanazar, a native of the island
Formosa, who came from thence to London above twenty years ago; and
in conversation told my friend, that in his country, when any young person happened to be put to death, the executioner sold the carcass to
persons of quality as a prime dainty; and that in his time the body of a
plump girl of fifteen, who was crucified for an attempt to poison the
emperor, was sold to his imperial majesty's prime minister of state, and

other great mandarins of the court, in joints from the gibbet, at four hundred crowns. Neither indeed can I deny, that, if the same use were made of several plump young girls in this town, who, without one single groat to their fortunes, cannot stir abroad without a chair, and appear at playhouse and assemblies in foreign fineries which they never will pay for, the kingdom would not be the worse.

Some persons of a desponding spirit are in great concern about that vast number of poor people, who are aged, diseased, or maimed; and I have been desired to employ my thoughts, what course may be taken to ease the nation of so grievous an encumbrance. But I am not in the least pain upon that matter, because it is very well known, that they are every day dying, and rotting, by cold and famine, and filth and vermin, as fast as can be reasonably expected. And as to the young labourers, they are now in almost as hopeful a condition: they cannot get work, and consequently pine away for want of nourishment, to a degree, that if at any time they are accidentally hired to common labour, they have not strength to perform it; and thus the country and themselves are happily delivered from the evils to come.

I have too long digressed, and therefore shall return to my subject. I think the advantages by the proposal which I have made are obvious and many, as well as of the highest importance.

For first, as I have already observed, it would greatly lessen the number of Papists, with whom we are yearly over-run, being the principal breeders of the nation, as well as our most dangerous enemies; and who stay at home on purpose to deliver the kingdom to the Pretender, hoping to take their advantage by the absence of so many good Protestants, who have chosen rather to leave their country than stay at home and pay tithes against their conscience to an Episcopal curate.

Secondly, The poorer tenants will have something valuable of their own, which by law may be made liable to distress, and help to pay their landlord's rent; their corn and cattle being already seized, and money a thing unknown.

Thirdly, Whereas the maintenance of a hundred thousand children, from two years old and upwards, cannot be computed at less than ten shillings a piece per annum, the nation's stock will be thereby increased fifty thousand pounds per annum, beside the profit of a new dish introduced to the tables of all gentlemen of fortune in the kingdom, who have any refinement in taste. And the money will circulate among ourselves, the goods being entirely of our own growth and manufacture.

Fourthly, The constant breeders, beside the gain of eight shillings sterling per annum by the sale of their children, will be rid of the charge of maintaining them after the first year.

Fifthly, This food would likewise bring great custom to taverns; where the vintners will certainly be so prudent as to procure the best receipts for dressing it to perfection, and, consequently, have their houses frequented by all the fine gentlemen, who justly value themselves upon their knowledge in good eating: and a skilful cook, who understands how to oblige his guests, will contrive to make it as expensive as they please.

Sixthly, This would be a great inducement to marriage, which all wise nations have either encouraged by rewards, or enforced by laws and penalties. It would increase the care and tenderness of mothers toward their children, when they were sure of a settlement for life to the poor babes, provided in some sort by the public, to their annual profit or expense. We should see an honest emulation among the married women, which of them could bring the fattest child to the market. Men would become as fond of their wives during the time of their pregnancy as they are now of their mares in foal, their cows in calf, their sows when they are ready to farrow; nor offer to beat or kick them (as is too frequent a practice) for fear of a miscarriage.

Many other advantages might be enumerated. For instance, the addition of some thousand carcasses in our exportation of barrelled beef; the propagation of swine's flesh, and improvement in the art of making good bacon, so much wanted among us by the great destruction of pigs, too frequent at our table; which are no way comparable in taste or magnificence to a well-grown, fat, yearling child, which, roasted whole, will make a considerable figure at a lord mayor's feast, or any other public entertainment. But this, and many others, I omit, being studious of brevity.

Supposing that one thousand families in this city would be constant customers for infants' flesh, beside others who might have it at merry-meetings, particularly at weddings and christenings, I compute that Dublin would take off annually about twenty thousand carcasses; and the rest of the kingdom (where probably they will be sold somewhat cheaper) the remaining eighty thousand.

I can think of no one objection, that will prossibly be raised against this proposal, unless it should be urged, that the number of people will be thereby much lessened in the kingdom. This I freely own, and it was indeed one principal design in offering it to the world. I desire the reader will observe, that I calculate my remedy for this one individual kingdom of Ireland, and for no other that ever was, is, or I think ever can be, upon earth. Therefore let no man talk to me of other expedients: of taxing our absentees at five shillings a pound: of using neither clothes, nor household furniture, except what is our own growth and manufacture:

of utterly rejecting the materials and instruments that promote foreign luxury: of curing the expensiveness of pride, vanity, idleness, and gaming in our women: of introducing a vein of parsimony, prudence, and temperance: of learning to love our country, in the want of which we differ even from LAPLANDERS, and the inhabitants of TOPINAMBOO: of quitting our animosities and factions, nor acting any longer like the Jews, who were murdering one another at the very moment their city was taken: of being a little cautious not to sell our country and conscience for nothing: of teaching landlords to have at least one degree of mercy toward their tenants: lastly, of putting a spirit of honesty, industry, and skill into our shopkeepers; who, if a resolution could now be taken to buy only our native goods, would immediately unite to cheat and exact upon us in the price, the measure, and the goodness, nor could ever yet be brought to make one fair proposal of just dealing, though often and earnestly invited to it.

Therefore I repeat, let no man talk to me of these and the like expedients, till he has at least some glimpse of hope, that there will be ever some hearty and sincere attempt to put them in practice.

But, as to myself, having been wearied out for many years with offering vain, idle, visionary thoughts, and at length utterly despairing of success, I fortunately fell upon this proposal; which, as it is wholly new, so it has something solid and real, of no expense and little trouble, full in our own power, and whereby we can incur no danger in disobliging ENGLAND. For this kind of commodity will not bear exportation, the flesh being of too tender a consistence to admit a long continuance in salt, although perhaps I could name a country, which would be glad to eat up our whole nation without it.

After all, I am not so violently bent upon my own opinion as to reject any offer proposed by wise men, which shall be found equally innocent, cheap, easy, and effectual. But before something of that kind shall be advanced in contradiction to my scheme, and offering a better, I desire the author, or authors, will be pleased maturely to consider two points. First, as things now stand, how they will be able to find food and raiment for a hundred thousand useless mouths and backs. And, secondly, there being a round million of creatures in human figure throughout this kingdom, whose whole subsistence put into a common stock would leave them in debt two million of pounds sterling, adding those who are beggars by profession, to the bulk of farmers, cottagers, and labourers, with the wives and children who are beggars in effect; I desire those politicians who dislike my overture, and may perhaps be so bold as to attempt an answer, that they will first ask the parents of these mortals, whether they would not at this day think it a great happiness to have been sold for food at a year old, in the manner I prescribe, and thereby have avoided such a perpetual scene of misfortunes, as they have since gone through, by the oppression of landlords, the impossibility of paying rent without money or trade, the want of common sustenance, with neither house nor clothes to cover them from the inclemencies of the weather, and the most inevitable prospect of entailing the like, or greater miseries, upon their breed for ever.

I profess, in the sincerity of my heart, that I have not the least personal interest in endeavouring to promote this necessary work, having no other motive than the public good of my country, by advancing our trade, providing for infants, relieving the poor, and giving some pleasure to the rich. I have no children by which I can propose to get a single penny; the youngest being nine years old, and my wife past child-bearing.

THOMAS CARLYLE

Thomas Carlyle (1795–1881), a Scotsman from the ranks of the peasantry, entered Edinburgh University at the age of fifteen. After making his mark as a German scholar and literary critic, especially with *Sartor Resartus* (1833–1834), an ironically Swiftian book of philosophy, he moved to London, where he met Coleridge, whom he describes in this selection from his *The Life of John Sterling* (London, 1851).*

COLERIDGE

This portrait of Coleridge, well past his prime but still at the height of his literary fame, is not without its irresistible cruelty. Carlyle's ironic imaginative metaphors are hard to surpass, as he develops Coleridge's "flood of utterance" from an overflowing bucket to a drowned world— and then sets Coleridge out on it with all kinds of water wings and life preservers of argumentative qualification. Notice how Carlyle's honesty pulls him back to concede a point to Coleridge, but then how his contempt for what seems empty-headed theory and egocentric rambling launches him into irony again. Note that Carlyle's irony depends mostly on exaggeration, compared to Swift's "modest" understatement.

Coleridge sat on the brow of Highgate Hill, in those years, looking down on London and its smoke-tumult, like a sage escaped from the inanity of life's battle; attracting towards him the thoughts of innumerable brave souls still engaged there. His express contributions to poetry,

* John Sterling (1806–1844) was a British author most renowned for his critical works. He is remembered today primarily as the subject of Carlyle's biography.—Ed.

philosophy, or any specific province of human literature or enlightenment had been small and sadly intermittent; but he had, especially
among young inquiring men, a higher than literary, a kind of prophetic
or magician character. He was thought to hold, he alone in England, the
key of German and other Transcendentalisms; knew the sublime secret
of believing by "the reason" what "the understanding" had been obliged
to fling out as incredible; and could still, after Hume and Voltaire had
done their best and worst with him, profess himself an orthodox Christian, and say and point to the Church of England, with its singular old
rubrics and surplices at Allhallowtide, *Esto perpetua*.* A sublime man;
who, alone in those dark days, had saved his crown of spiritual man-
hood; escaping from the black materialisms, and revolutionary deluges,
with "God, Freedom, Immortality" still his: a king of men. The practical
intellects of the world did not much heed him, or carelessly reckoned
him a metaphysical dreamer: but to the rising spirits of the young generation he had this dusky sublime character; and sat there as a kind of
Magus, girt in mystery and enigma; his Dodona oak-grove† (Mr. Gilman's house at Highgate) whispering strange things, uncertain whether
oracles or jargon.

The Gilmans did not encourage much company, or excitation of any
sort, round their sage; nevertheless access to him, if a youth did rever-
ently wish it, was not difficult. He would stroll about the pleasant garden with you, sit in the pleasant rooms of the place—perhaps take you
to his own peculiar room, high up, with a rearward view, which was the
chief of all. A really charming outlook, in fine weather. Close at hand,
wide sweep of flowery leafy gardens, their few houses mostly hidden,
the very chimney-pots veiled under blossomy umbrage, flowed gloriously
down hill, gloriously issuing in wide-tufted undulating plain-country,
rich in all charms of field and town. Waving blooming country of the
brightest green; dotted all over with handsome villas, handsome groves;
crossed by roads and human traffic, here inaudible or heard only as a
musical hum: and behind all swam, under olive-tinted haze, the illimit-
able limitary ocean of London, with its domes and steeples definite in
the sun, big Paul's and the many memories attached to it hanging high
over all. Nowhere, of its kind, could you see a grander prospect on a
bright summer day, with the set of the air going southward,—south-

---

* "Be everlasting."—Ed.
† The oak grove at the town of Dodona, in northern Greece, contained the temple
of a famous oracle of Zeus. A Magus was a Persian (and Median) "Wise Man," a
Zoroastrian priest or astrologer.—Ed.

ward, and so draping with the city-smoke not *you* but the city. Here for hours would Coleridge talk, concerning all conceivable or inconceivable things; and liked nothing better than to have an intelligent, or failing that, even a silent and patient human listener. He distinguished himself to all that ever heard him as at least the most surprising talker extant in this world,—and to some small minority, by no means to all, as the most excellent.

The good man, he was now getting old, towards sixty perhaps; and gave you the idea of a life that had been full of sufferings; a life heavy-laden, half-vanquished, still swimming painfully in seas of manifold physical and other bewilderment. Brow and head were round, and of massive weight, but the face was flabby and irresolute. The deep eyes, of a light hazel, were as full of sorrow as of inspiration; confused pain looked mildly from them, as in a kind of mild astonishment. The whole figure and air, good and amiable otherwise, might be called flabby and irresolute; expressive of weakness under possibility of strength. He hung loosely on his limbs, with knees bent, and stooping attitude; in walking, he rather shuffled than decisively stept; and a lady once remarked, he never could fix which side of the garden walk would suit him best, but continually shifted, in corkscrew fashion, and kept trying both. A heavy-laden, high-aspiring and surely much-suffering man. His voice, naturally soft and good, had contracted itself into a plaintive snuffle and sing-song; he spoke as if preaching,—you would have said, preaching earnestly and also hopelessly the weightiest things. I still recollect his "object" and "subject," terms of continual recurrence in the Kantean province; and how he sang and snuffled them into "om-m-mject" and "sum-m-mject," with a kind of solemn shake or quaver, as he rolled along. No talk, in his century or in any other, could be more surprising.

Sterling, who assiduously attended him, with profound reverence, and was often with him by himself, for a good many months, gives a record of their first colloquy.* Their colloquies were numerous, and he had taken note of many; but they are all gone to the fire, except this first, which Mr. Hare has printed,—unluckily without date. It contains a number of ingenious, true and half-true observations, and is of course a faithful epitome of the things said; but it gives small idea of Coleridge's way of talking;—this one feature is perhaps the most recognisable, "Our interview lasted for three hours, during which he talked two hours and three quarters." Nothing could be more copious than his talk;

---

* In J. C. Hare, ed., *John Sterling, Essays and Tales*, 2 vols. (1848), I: 16–26.

and furthermore it was always, virtually or literally, of the nature of a monologue; suffering no interruption, however reverent; hastily putting aside all foreign additions, annotations, or more ingenuous desires for elucidation, as well-meant superfluities which would never do. Besides, it was talk not flowing anywhither like a river, but spreading every-whither in inextricable currents and regurgitations like a lake or sea; terribly deficient in definite goal or aim, nay often in logical intelligibility; *what* you were to believe or do, on any earthly or heavenly thing, obstinately refusing to appear from it. So that, most times, you felt logically lost; swamped near to drowning in this tide of ingenious vocables, spreading out boundless as if to submerge the world.

To sit as a passive bucket and be pumped into, whether you consent or not, can in the long-run be exhilarating to no creature; how eloquent soever the flood of utterance that is descending. But if it be withal a confused unintelligible flood of utterance, threatening to submerge all known landmarks of thought, and drown the world and you!—I have heard Coleridge talk, with eager musical energy, two stricken hours, his face radiant and moist, and communicate no meaning whatsoever to any individual of his hearers,—certain of whom, I for one, still kept eagerly listening in hope; the most had long before given up, and formed (if the room were large enough) secondary humming groups of their own. He began anywhere: you put some question to him, made some suggestive observation: instead of answering this, or decidedly setting out towards answer of it, he would accumulate formidable apparatus, logical swim-bladders, transcendental life-preservers and other precautionary and vehiculatory gear, for setting out; perhaps did at last get under way,—but was swiftly solicited, turned aside by the glance of some radiant new game on this hand or that, into new courses; and ever into new; and before long into all the Universe, where it was uncertain what game you would catch, or whether any.

His talk, alas, was distinguished, like himself, by irresolution: it disliked to be troubled with conditions, abstinences, definite fulfillments;—loved to wander at its own sweet will, and make its auditor and its claims and humble wishes a mere passive bucket for itself! He had knowledge about many things and topics, much curious reading; but generally all topics led him, after a pass or two, into the high seas of theosophic philosophy, the hazy infinitude of Kantean transcendentalism, with its "sum-m-mjects" and "om-m-mjects." Sad enough; for with such indolent impatience of the claims and ignorances of others, he had not the least talent for explaining this or anything unknown to them; and you swam and fluttered in the mistiest wide unintelligible deluge of things, for the most part in a rather profitless uncomfortable manner.

Glorious islets, too, I have seen rise out of the haze; but they were few, and soon swallowed in the general element again. Balmy sunny islets, islets of the blest and the intelligible:—on which occasions those secondary humming groups would all cease humming, and hang breathless upon the eloquent words; till once your islet got wrapt in the mist again, and they could recommence humming. Eloquent artistically expressive words you always had; piercing radiances of a most subtle insight came at intervals; tones of noble pious sympathy, recognisable as pious though strangely coloured, were never wanting long: but in general you could not call this aimless, cloud-capt, cloud-based, lawlessly meandering human discourse of reason by the name of "excellent talk," but only of "surprising"; and were reminded bitterly of Hazlitt's account of it: "Excellent talker, very,—if you let him start from no premises and come to no conclusion." Coleridge was not without what talkers call wit, and there were touches of prickly sarcasm in him, contemptuous enough of the world and its idols and popular dignitaries; he had traits even of poetic humour: but in general he seemed deficient in laughter; or indeed in sympathy for concrete human things either on the sunny or on the stormy side. One right peal of concrete laughter at some convicted flesh-and-blood absurdity, one burst of noble indignation at some injustice or depravity, rubbing elbows with us on this solid Earth, how strange would it have been in the Kantean haze-world, and how infinitely cheering amid its vacant air-castles and dim-melting ghosts and shadows! None such ever came. His life had been an abstract thinking and dreaming, idealistic, passed amid the ghosts of defunct bodies and of unborn ones. The moaning singsong of that theosophico-metaphysical monotony left on you, at last, a very dreary feeling.

In close colloquy, flowing within narrower banks, I suppose he was more definite and apprehensible; Sterling in aftertimes did not complain of his unintelligibility, or imputed it only to the abstruse high nature of the topics handled. Let us hope so, let us try to believe so! There is no doubt but Coleridge could speak plain words on things plain: his observations and responses on the trivial matters that occurred were as simple as the commonest man's, or were even distinguished by superior simplicity as well as pertinency. "Ah, your tea is too cold, Mr. Coleridge!" mourned the good Mrs. Gilman once, in her kind, reverential and yet protective manner, handing him a very tolerable though belated cup.— "It's better than I deserve!" snuffled he, in a low hoarse murmur, partly courteous, chiefly pious, the tone of which still abides with me: "It's better than I deserve!"

But indeed, to the young ardent mind, instinct with pious nobleness, yet driven to the grim deserts of Radicalism for a faith, his speculations had a charm much more than literary, a charm almost religious and prophetic. The constant gist of his discourse was lamentation over the sunk condition of the world; which he recognised to be given-up to Atheism and Materialism, full of mere sordid misbeliefs, mispursuits and misresults. All Science had become mechanical; the science not of men, but of a kind of human beavers. Churches themselves had died away into a godless mechanical condition; and stood there as mere Cases of Articles, mere Forms of Churches; like the dried carcasses of once-swift camels, which you find left withering in the thirst of the universal desert,—ghastly portents for the present, beneficent ships of the desert no more. Men's souls were blinded, hebetated; and sunk under the influence of Atheism and Materialism, and Hume and Voltaire: the world for the present was as an extinct world, deserted of God, and incapable of welldoing till it changed its heart and spirit. This, expressed I think with less of indignation and with more of long-drawn querulousness, was always recognisable as the ground-tone:—in which truly a pious young heart, driven into Radicalism and the opposition party, could not but recognise a too sorrowful truth; and ask of the Oracle, with all earnestness, What remedy, then?

The remedy, though Coleridge himself professed to see it as in sunbeams, could not, except by processes unspeakably difficult, be described to you at all. On the whole, those dead Churches, this dead English Church especially, must be brought to life again. Why not? It was not dead; the soul of it, in this parched-up body, was tragically asleep only. Atheistic Philosophy was true on its side, and Hume and Voltaire could on their own ground speak irrefragably for themselves against any Church: but lift the Church and them into a higher sphere of argument, *they* died into inanition, the Church revivified itself into pristine florid vigour,—became once more a living ship of the desert, and invincibly bore you over stock and stone. But how, but how! By attending to the "reason" of man, said Coleridge, and duly chaining-up the "understanding" of man: the *Vernunft* (Reason) and *Verstand* (Understanding) of the Germans, it all turned upon these, if you could well understand them,—which you couldn't. For the rest, Mr. Coleridge had on the anvil various Books, especially was about to write one grand Book *On the Logos*, which would help to bridge the chasm for us. So much appeared, however: Churches, though proved false (as you had imagined), were still true (as you were to imagine): here was an Artist who could burn you up an old Church, root and branch; and then as the Alchymists professed to do with organic substances in general, distil you an "Astral Spirit" from the ashes, which was the very image of the old burnt article, its airdrawn counterpart,—this you still had, or might get, and draw use from if you could. Wait till the Book on the Logos were done;—alas, till your terrene eyes, blind with conceit and the dust of logic, were purged, subtilised and spiritualised into the sharpness of vision requisite for discerning such an "om-m-mject."—The ingenuous young English head, of those days, stood strangely puzzled by such revelations; uncertain whether it were getting inspired, or getting infatuated into flat imbecility; and strange effulgence, of new day or else of deeper meteoric night, coloured the horizon of the future for it.

Let me not be unjust to this memorable man. Surely there was here, in his pious, ever-labouring, subtle mind, a precious truth, or prefigurement of truth; and yet a fatal delusion withal. Prefigurement that, in spite of beaver sciences and temporary spiritual hebetude and cecity, man and his Universe were eternally divine; and that no past nobleness, or revelation of the divine, could or would ever be lost to him. Most true, surely, and worthy of all acceptance. Good also to do what you can with old Churches and practical Symbols of the Noble: nay, quit not the burnt ruins of them while you find there is still gold to be dug there. But, on the whole, do not think you can, by logical alchymy, distil astral spirits from them; or if you could, that said astral spirits, or defunct logical phantasms, could serve you in anything. What the light of your mind, which is the direct inspiration of the Almighty, pronounces incredible,—that, in God's name, leave uncredited; at your peril do not try believing that. No subtlest hocus-pocus of "reason" *versus* "understanding" will avail for that feat;—and it is terribly perilous to try it in these provinces!

The truth is, I now see, Coleridge's talk and speculation was the emblem of himself: in it, as in him, a ray of heavenly inspiration struggled, in a tragically ineffectual degree, with the weakness of flesh and blood. He says once, he "had skirted the howling deserts of Infidelity"; this was evident enough: but he had not had the courage, in defiance of pain and terror, to press resolutely across said deserts to the new firm lands of Faith beyond; he preferred to create logical fatamorganas for himself on this hither side, and laboriously solace himself with these.

To the man himself Nature had given, in high measure, the seeds of a noble endowment; and to unfold it had been forbidden him. A subtle lynx-eyed intellect, tremulous pious sensibility to all good and all beautiful; truly a ray of empyrean light;—but imbedded in such weak laxity of character, in such indolences and esuriences as had made strange work with it. Once more, the tragic story of a high endowment with an insufficient will. An eye to discern the divineness of the Heaven's splendours and lightnings, the insatiable wish to revel in their godlike radiances and brilliances; but no heart to front the scathing terrors of them, which is the first condition of your conquering an abiding place there. The courage necessary for him, above all things, had been denied this man. His life, with such ray of the empyrean in it, was great and terrible to him; and he had not valiantly grappled with it, he had fled from it; sought refuge in vague day-dreams, hollow compromises, in opium, in theosophic metaphysics. Harsh pain, danger, necessity, slavish harnessed toil, were of all things abhorrent to him. And so the empyrean element, lying smothered under the terrene, and yet inextinguishable there, made sad writhings. For pain, danger, difficulty, steady slaving toil, and other highly disagreeable behests of destiny, shall in no wise be shirked by any brightest mortal that will approve himself loyal to his mission in this world; nay, precisely the higher he is, the deeper will be the disagreeableness, and the detestability to flesh and blood, of the tasks laid on him; and the heavier too, and more tragic, his penalties, if he neglect them.

For the old Eternal Powers do live forever; nor do their laws know any change, however we in our poor wigs and church-tippets may attempt to read their laws. To *steal* into Heaven,—by the modern method, of sticking ostrich-like your head into fallacies on Earth, equally as by the ancient and by all conceivable methods,—is forever forbidden. High-treason is the name of that attempt; and it continues to be punished as such. Strange enough: here once more was a kind of Heaven-scaling Ixion*; and to him, as to the old one, the just gods were very stern! The ever-revolving, never-advancing Wheel (of a kind) was his, through life; and from his Cloud Juno did not he too procreate strange Centaurs, spectral Puseyisms,† monstrous illusory Hybrids, and ecclesiastical Chimeras,—which now roam the earth in a very lamentable manner.

---

* A Greek king admitted into Olympus as a guest by Zeus. He attempted to seduce Hera (Juno), Zeus's wife, but she substituted a cloud for herself, by which he became the father of the Centaurs. For his offence, Zeus bound him to a fiery wheel forever turning in the river Tartarus in Hades.—Ed.

† Edward Pusey, English clergyman, started a movement at Oxford, running from 1833 to 1841 (also called the Tractarian movement), which aimed to bring the English church back toward simple, primitive Christianity.—Ed.

BERNARD DE VOTO

Bernard De Voto (1897–1955) was born in Ogden, Utah. He transferred from the University of Utah to Harvard, where he earned his Bachelor of Arts degree in 1920. He taught at Northwestern University (1922–1927) and Harvard (1929–1936), resigning to become editor of *The Saturday Review of Literature* for two years, before becoming an independent man of letters. Journalist, critic, novelist, historian, with three books on Mark Twain, he was widely known for "The Easy Chair," his column for many years in *Harper's Magazine*. He won the Pulitzer Prize for his book on the Rocky Mountain fur trade, *Across the Wide Missouri* (1948), the first of a trilogy on American continentalism followed by *The Year of Decision: 1846* (1961) and *The Course of Empire* (1952).

GREEN LIGHT

This amusing and devastating review of a pious best-seller makes its point by merely describing the book's contents. But in this description, irony points the way. It, too, like Carlyle's, is exaggerative, though quieter, simply letting the exaggeration in sentimental clichés do its ironic work, as in *shattered lives, mighty preacher, sways multitudes.* To help you appreciate them, underline these touches as you read. What is the effect of *not* calling this book *bilge?*

A summary of the Reverend Dr. [Lloyd C.] Douglas's [*Green Light*] will indicate its classification. In a city never quite identified as Chicago a crippled clergyman named Dean Harcourt mends shattered lives by discovering to their possessors their own Personal Adequacy and bringing them into knowledge of the Irresistible Onward Drive of God's purpose. (Hence the symbolic title: the road is clear before you—Go Forward.) The dean is a mighty preacher and so sways multitudes, but also he is a mystical psychoanalyst, a priest in the consulting room, and thus exercises his inspiration on individuals. Persons who come in contact with him are never again quite the same. Once a patient of his has heard the message, he has thereafter a harmonious personality, makes a success in his career, and achieves a happy marriage—except Sonia Duquesne, who has committed adultery and has to be content with becoming the dean's secretary. Several minor couples are conducted to God-consciousness and the marriage bed, but both the dean and his message are focused on Newell Paige and Phyllis Dexter. Paige is the most brilliant young surgeon anywhere. He is about to succeed to the place of the most brilliant older surgeon, whom he loves and idolizes,

Dr. Bruce Endicott. (Note the influence of Mrs. Southworth in the characters' names.) A patient whom Dr. Paige is treating has received Dean Harcourt's message and seems to the doctor the most inspiring woman he has ever known. But alas, on the day when Dr. Endicott is to operate on her, the bottom falls out of the stock market and so he botches the job. The patient dies, Dr. Paige accepts the responsibility for his chief's mistake, Dr. Endicott permits him to, and he begins to wander over the earth, disenchanted, very bitter, his life a ruin. Being a great soul, he can't help doing good here and there, but he is still Hamlet when he drops in on Dean Harcourt. In the dean's office he meets the daughter of the dead woman, and though they love greatly they misunderstand. Paige therefore wanders some more and the dean finally has to discover him in a laboratory where deckle-edge scientists are risking their lives with Rocky Mountain spotted fever before he can make his message clear. Even so a setter bitch is killed and she has carried some of the most touching scenes in the book. Dr. Endicott repents and everyone, including the adulteress, is saved.

It would be absurd to call this sort of thing bilge. It belongs to one of the oldest traditions of literature, the mystically therapeutic. Its equivalent is always with us and always serves an important end. Dr. Douglas is, briefly, a Harold Bell Wright—a streamlined Wright with knee-action wheels and chased silver dials on the cowl, to be sure, but with the identical engine under the hood. His milieu has changed from the desert to the metropolis, he deals with the maladjusted rather than the impure of heart, fear and frustration rather than lust and dishonesty are his monsters, but he tells us exactly what Mr. Wright used to tell us and he employs exactly the same technique. He tells us: one increasing purpose runs. He tell us: let not your hearts be troubled. He tells us no more—but do not be disdainful. He tells us what Mary Baker Eddy and Ralph Waldo Trine told us—or, if you like, what Emerson and Whitman told us. Or Woodrow Wilson. Or Karl Marx.

Millions want to be told just that. This audience combines wish-fulfillment with its spiritual sustenance, and it is Dr. Douglas's audience. He gives them what they need and desperately desire: assurance. In a time of economic chaos, it is comforting to be told that the Long Parade is moving onward in God's plan. In a time of disaster, it is comforting to be told that one is being Dragged Up. It is always comforting to frightened, weary, and discouraged men, to be told that they are the masters of their fate, that they have a spiritual power which will bring them through, that they have the Kingdom of Heaven within them, that the God-spirit of which they are a part has given them unused and even unguessed capacities for heroism and eventual success. It is comforting and, when told in terms of metrical and crepuscular vagueness, it is convincing. Thoughts so noble, so impalpable, so incapable of precise statement, must be true.

Comfort is what his readers ask of Dr. Douglas and comfort is what they get. His books would not sell by the carload—as at least *The Magnificent Obsession* did, which had the same message—unless his public found what they were looking for. It is a legitimate literary quest. He works with the humbler symbols of art, but they are eternal symbols. Their success on the lower levels of literature, in the sub-basements where yearning and exhortation and incantation dictate their form, requires no explanation. Does *Molly-Make-Believe* need to be explained? Or *St. Elmo*? Or *Tempest and Sunshine*? Or *If Winter Comes*?

SUGGESTIONS FOR WRITING

1. Write an ironic essay, with Swift as your model. It need not be profound. Take some notorious collegiate fact or trait, and write, for instance, "A Modest Proposal to Encourage Recreation on Weekends." Imagine yourself a myopic do-gooder, and write an earnest, and modest, appeal to pry the students away from their books. Or, if you can keep the surface ironically cool, you may wish to try one of the burning issues of the day—student politics, classified research, inflation, pollution.

    Build your essay, as Swift does, on a regular argumentative structure with beginning, middle, and end. Your thesis will be ironic, of course; but develop it as you would any argumentative thesis, using one of the pro-con structures on pages 68–69. Since irony depends on a shared understanding between writer and reader, you must pick some topic of common knowledge—or your irony will not be understood, and you will be talking in riddles. Since, to write ironically, you must be personally concerned, the world-shaking issues may be a little too impersonal for effective irony. If so, pick something perfectly familiar, something even playful and trivial, such as blind dates, roommates, dormitory food, eight o'clock classes, co-ops and communes, long hair and blue eyelids, style of dress, cluttering the walks with parked bicycles, or cluttering the lanes with parked cars.

2. Write an ironic sketch of someone overly admired by himself and others, borrowing some malicious hints from Carlyle and trying to use his ironic exaggeration and metaphor.

3. Try to devastate a book, movie, or television program in the mode of De Voto.

Nine
The Critical Review

A critical review is both a discovery and an evaluation. It may evaluate any artistic work, but it usually deals with books or, more recently, films. And in evaluating, of course, it describes. The critics in this section try to locate a central meaning, since the novel and the film act things out, in a kind of vocal charade, rather than proclaiming their ultimate significance. The review, like the essay, has its thesis—a combination of what the artist has implied, what that implication is worth, and how well he has implied it. The critic may make his thesis explicit at the outset, as with Faulkner's bold "His best," or he may let it accumulate inductively to Gill's final "catastrophe." He may also write an independent, stimulating essay about several books or films of a kind, as Warshow has done with the Western. As you read, notice how the description of what is in each work not only conveys a sense of the work but also reinforces the critic's judgment of it.

WILLIAM FAULKNER

William Faulkner (1897–1962), born in Oxford, Mississippi, where he lived for most of his life, gained full stature as a writer with *The Sound and the*

Fury (1929), a stream-of-consciousness novel, southern style, influenced by James Joyce's *Ulysses* (1922). It was the first of a rich accumulation of novels and stories concerning Yoknapatawpha County, its people and social history—a fictional land much like Faulkner's own Mississippi county, Lafayette.

HEMINGWAY'S THE OLD MAN AND THE SEA

Faulkner shied away from commenting on his literary rival, and the two kept their distance throughout life. But here he speaks out with unqualified praise. Can you tell from this review what Faulkner's opinion of Hemingway's work, in general, would be?

His best. Time may show it to be the best single piece of any of us, I mean his and my contemporaries. This time, he discovered God, a Creator. Until now, his men and women had made themselves, shaped themselves out of their own clay; their victories and defeats were at the hands of each other, just to prove to themselves or one another how tough they could be. But this time, he wrote about pity: about something somewhere that made them all: the old man who had to catch the fish and then lose it, the fish that had to be caught and then lost, the sharks which had to rob the old man of his fish; made them all and loved them all and pitied them all. It's all right. Praise God that whatever made and loves and pities Hemingway and me kept him from touching it any further.

THE NEW YORKER

Founded in 1925 by Harold Ross (1892–1951), a boy from Aspen, Colorado (on rebound from service in France in World War I as editor of *Stars and Stripes*, the army's newspaper), *The New Yorker* soon established itself (with the finances of Raoul Fleischmann, a millionaire poker-acquaintance of Ross's) as a unique American institution, one of the world's great magazines. Today, under the editorship of William Shawn, it continues its reputation for timeliness, humor, literature, astute social commentary, and excellent writing in all departments.

NOTES ON THREE FILMS

In addition to the crisp annihilation of these films, which were reviewed in 1973, notice the comments on acting and directing.

Man of La Mancha (1972)—The lyrics still sound as if they had been translated from Esperanto, and it's a slow haul to a sentimental haven, but toward the middle, Peter O'Toole, looking like an elongated Alec Guinness, is so wafer-thin and stylized, and his woefulness is so deeply silly that the contrast between his Don Quixote and the full-bodied, realistic Aldonza of Sophia Loren becomes affecting. Loren, with her great, sorrowing green-brown eyes, is magnificently sensual and spiritual; she brings the soul of Italian opera to this Broadway bastardization, which combines Cervantes' life with his novel. Arthur Hiller directed.

The Man Who Played God (1932)—George Arliss is the great concert violinist who is deafened by a bomb thrown by anarchists; Bette Davis is the young girl infatuated with his celebrity status. His despair is cured after he begins to use binoculars and read lips and, eavesdropping on the people in the park opposite his house, involves himself in their lives. This maudlin monstrosity about the therapeutic benefits of voyeurism was actually refurbished in 1955 (by Irving Wallace—who else?) for the film début of Liberace, shamelessly titled "Sincerely Yours." The Arliss version (which is bad enough) has in its cast Ray Milland, Hedda Hopper, Violet Heming, Donald Cook, and Louise Closser Hale. John Adolfi directed; it is generally considered the film in which Bette Davis first showed her talent.

Marie Antoinette (1938)—A resplendent bore. M-G-M built a grand ballroom that was several feet longer than the original at Versailles, and Adrian designed twelve hundred and fifty gowns, as well as costumes for two poodles. The efforts to create a sympathetic interpretation of Marie that would be suitable for Norma Shearer—M-G-M's "first lady" and, as Irving Thalberg's widow, a large stockholder—resulted in a lugubriously noble central character. Since King Louis XVI (Robert Morley) wasn't much of a love interest, Shearer was given Tyrone Power (as a Swedish count) for a bit of romance; meant for leavening, this doomed affair only adds to the soggy weight. W. S. Van Dyke directed; with John Barrymore, Gladys George, Anita Louise, and Joseph Schildkraut.

BRENDAN GILL

Brendan Gill (1914–), born in Connecticut and educated at Yale, became drama critic of *The New Yorker* and has served on that magazine since 1936, with reams of reviews, "Talk of the Town" columns, short stories, and finely etched profiles.

A RAGE TO LIVE

John O'Hara wrote *A Rage to Live* to culminate his fame. Gill, his friend and fellow *New Yorker* writer, thought to give it an honest review. But the failure that Gill saw in the book, and perhaps in human nature, combined with the acidulous *New Yorker* stance and wit, blew the book (deservedly) and the friendship apart. But we can still admire, with a wry smile for all things human, the review's honesty, wit, and style.

"The present volume is a progress report from a case history study on human sex behavior." So, bumpily but with a certain grandeur, begins the first chapter of the Kinsey-Pomeroy-Martin whodunit, "Sexual Behavior in the Human Male." Translated into less gravelly English, this quotation from last year's romantic best-seller would make a pretty accurate description of what will probably be one of the year's best-sellers, the enormous new novel by John O'Hara, entitled "A Rage to Live" (Random House). The parallels between the Kinsey Report and the O'Hara Report are unmistakable. The authors not only share a major theme but have a similar interest in determining the extent to which the various classes in our society can be distinguished from one another in terms of what they do about sex and then in terms of what they *think* about what they do about sex. Dr. Kinsey is perhaps the leading professional student of this subject and as such has had the advantage of having numerous assistants, as well as the financial backing of the Rockefeller Foundation. Dr. O'Hara, our leading amateur, has had to go it alone, at his own expense. On the other hand, O'Hara has long been one of the most prominent figures in the profession of letters, while Kinsey, an old gall-wasp man, is a taxonomist first and a literary craftsman second.

Granted that Kinsey has the edge in statistics and O'Hara in style, the layman's immediate response to "A Rage to Live," as to the earlier, pioneer work, is likely to be one of uncritical admiration for the amount of scholarly research involved. This feeling is soon displaced, however, by one of depression, and eventually of suffocation, for the reader who begins by being ashamed of having paid so little heed to the true nature of the human condition ends by being convinced, half against his will, that the investigation of sexual practices had better be left, as it always used to be, not to the expert but to the young. It was predicted last year that the Kinsey Report would open our eyes and jolt us into a lively awareness of the complexity of our sexual problems; now it appears that the Report put more people to sleep than it awakened, and numbed our minds instead of jolting them. The recurrent passages of maudlin sexuality in "A Rage to Live," complete even to so worn a stencil as the prostitute with a loving heart and a high I.Q., may have the same effect. If so, it will be all the sadder, because the author has plainly intended to do more than out-Kinsey Kinsey; he has intended, indeed, to write nothing less than a great American novel.

There was reason enough for this ambition. "A Rage to Live" is O'Hara's first novel in eleven years and comes exactly fifteen years after "Appointment in Samarra," which was, and is, an almost perfect book —taut, vivid, tough-minded, and compassionate. In the period between "Appointment in Samarra" and "A Rage to Live," O'Hara published two other novels—the successful "Butterfield 8" and the inconclusive "Hope of Heaven"—and five volumes of short stories, many of which are as good as anything in the language. Within the tight framework of these stories, apparently so small in compass but nearly always so explosive in force, O'Hara was able to take the measure of an astonishing variety of subjects, describing for us, with or without sex but with every appearance of authenticity, the customs of such dissimilar outposts of civilization as Hollywood, Stockbridge, Washington, D.C., and Hobe Sound, as well as half a dozen New Yorks—Wall Street, Jackson Heights, the Village, Fifty-second Street, Beekman Place, Riverside Drive. But it is an unbreakable convention of our time that a man who has written novels goes on writing novels, and perhaps partly for this reason, but surely for other deeper and more compelling reasons, O'Hara sat down and doggedly accumulated "A Rage to Live," which must be about as long as his three previous novels put together and which bears little or no resemblance to any of them.

A sprawling book, discursive and prolix, ranging in time from 1877 to 1947, and full of a multitude of semi-detached characters and subplots, what "A Rage to Live" *does* resemble is one of those "panoramic," three-or-four-generation novels that writers of the third and fourth magnitude turn out in such disheartening abundance. Dr. O'Hara's handy guide to healthy sex practices has been tucked inside the disarming wrapper of the formula family novel, and one result of this odd combination is the loss of the old sure-fire, ice-cold O'Hara dialogue. Here, for example, is Sidney Tate, addressing his wife, Grace Caldwell Tate, the heroine of the novel, on the subject of her affair with a cheap, lower-middle-class Irish contractor:

". . . you see, in this world you learn a set of rules, or you don't learn them. But assuming you learn them, you stick by them. They may be no damn good, but you're who you are and what you are because they're your rules and you stick by them. And of course when it's easy to stick by them, that's no test. It's when it's hard to obey the rules, that's when they mean something. That's what I believe, and I always thought you did too. I'm the first, God knows, to grant that you, with your beauty, you had opportunities or invitations. But you obeyed the rules, the same rules I obeyed. But then you said the hell with them. What it amounts to is you said the hell with my rules, and the hell with me. So Grace—the hell with you. I love you, but if I have any luck, that'll pass, in my new life."

Now, if this sounds like something out of an old *Redbook*, one is prepared at first to account for it on the ground that Tate is a Yale man, but no, he is the closest thing to a hero in the novel, and his ethics appear to be those of the author. That passage is, in fact, the intellectual high point of the book, and from there it grinds slowly downhill, through Sidney's death and a few more love affairs for Grace, to a sinister postlude, in which we learn that all the surviving characters have turned more or less physically into swine. In "Appointment in Samarra," there was nothing about Julian English that we did not know and want to know, but Grace Caldwell Tate is a fatally uninteresting woman, and her rage to live rarely amounts to more than pique. It is hard to understand how one of our best writers could have written this book, and it is because of O'Hara's distinction that his failure here seems in the same nature of a catastrophe.

EUDORA WELTY

Eudora Welty (1909–), born in Jackson, Mississippi, and educated at the University of Wisconsin and Columbia, started writing stories as a child but did not publish until 1936. Then a steady stream of stories followed, exploring the tensions of modern life in a southern setting. She published her first novel, *Delta Wedding*, in 1946. Her novel *The Optimist's Daughter* (1972) won the Pulitzer Prize.

THE UNDERGROUND MAN

A mere detective novel depicts, as Welty sees it, the whole trip of modern society, in its escapes into fantasy and hallucination. Note how she
blends description—her description of the novel's descriptions—into her
analysis of what it all implies.

Curled up, with an insulted look on his upturned face, and wearing a
peppermint-striped shirt, the fresh corpse of a man is disclosed in a hole
in the ground. From the scene of the crime, the victim's little boy is carried off, nobody knows why, by a pair of troubled teen-agers. And at
the same time, a deadly forest fire gets its start in these hills above Santa
Teresa; whoever murdered Stanley Broadhurst must have caused him to
drop his cigarillo into the dry grass. So opens the new novel by Ross
Macdonald, *The Underground Man*. It comes to stunning achievement.

A Forest Service man looks into the killing to find out who was responsible for the fire; but Lew Archer goes faster and farther into his
own investigation, for a personal reason. That morning, he had met that
little boy; they fed blue jays together. He promises the young widow,
the child's mother, to find her son and bring him back.

The double mystery of Santa Teresa cries urgency but is never going
to explain itself in an ordinary way. For instance, it looks as if the victim himself might have dug the hole in which he lies. ("Why would a
man dig his own grave?"—"He may not have known it was going to be
his.") With the fire coming, Archer has to work fast. The corpse must
be quickly buried again, or be consumed with his murder unsolved.
This, the underground man of the title, waits the book out, the buried
connection between present threat and something out of the past.

"I don't believe in coincidences," Archer says, as the investigation
leads him into a backward direction, and he sees the case take on a
premonitory symmetry. And it is not coincidence indeed, or anything so
simple, but a sort of spiral of time that he goes hurtling into, with an
answer lying fifteen years deep.

He is to meet many strange and lonely souls drawing their inspiration
from private sources. On the periphery are those all but anonymous
characters, part of the floating population of the city, evocative of all
the sadness that fills a lonely world, like some California versions of
those Saltimbanques of Picasso's ("even a little more fleeting than ourselves") drifting across the smoke-obscured outskirts. They are the sentinels of a case in which everybody has something to lose, and most of
the characters in this time-haunted, fire-threatened novel lose it in the
course of what happens—a son, or a husband, or a mountain retreat; a

sailing boat, a memory; the secret of fifteen years or the dream of a lifetime; or a life.

Brooding over the case is the dark fact that for some certain souls the past does not let go. They nourish the conviction that its ties may be outlived but, for hidden reasons, can be impossible to outgrow or leave behind.

Stanley Broadhurst died searching for his long-lost father. The Oedipus story, which figured in Mr. Macdonald's *The Galton Case* and *The Chill*, has echoes here too. But another sort of legend takes a central place in *The Underground Man*. This is the medieval tale of romance and the faerie.

It is exactly what Archer plunges into when he enters this case. Finding his way, through their lies and fears, into other people's obsessions and dreams, he might as well be in a fairy tale with them. The mystery has handed him what amounts to a set of impossible tasks: Find the door that opens the past. Unravel the ever-tangling threads of time. Rescue the stolen child from fleeing creatures who appear to be under a spell and who forbid him to speak to them. Meet danger from the aroused elements of fire and water. And before the tower.

But Archer's own role in their fairy tale is clear to him: from the time he fed the blue jays with the little boy, he never had a choice. There is the maze of the past to be entered and come out of alive, bringing the innocent to safety. And in the maze, there lives a monster; his name is Murder.

All along the way, the people he questions shift their stands, lie as fast as they can, slip only too swiftly out of human reach. Their ages are deceiving, they put on trappings of disguise or even what might be called transformations. As Archer, by stages, all the while moving at speed, connects one character with the next, he discovers what makes the sinister affinity between them.

"Robert Driscoll Falconer, Jr., was a god come down to earth in human guise," the older Mrs. Broadhurst, mother of the murder victim, has written in a memoir of her father, and here her Spencerian handwriting went to pieces: "It straggled across the lined yellow page like a defeated army." Mrs. Crandall, the mother of the runaway girl, is "one of those waiting mothers who would sit forever beside the phone but didn't know what to say when it finally rang." Another character being questioned plays "a game that guilty people play, questioning the questioner, trying to convert the truth into a shuttlecock that could be batted back and forth and eventually lost." And the violence and malice of another character "appeared to her as emanations from the external world."

These people live in prisons of the spirit, and suffer there. The winding, prisonlike stairs that appear and reappear under Archer's hurrying feet in the course of the chase are like the repeated questionings that lead most often into some private hell.

And of course unreality—the big underlying trouble of all these people—was back of the crime itself: the victim was obsessed with the lifelong search for his father; oblivious of everything and everybody else, he invited his own oblivion. In a different way, unreality was back of the child-stealing. "As you can see, we gave her everything," says the mother standing in her runaway daughter's lovely white room. "But it wasn't what she wanted." The home environment of the girl and others like her, Archer is brought to observe, was "an unreality so bland and smothering that the children tore loose and impaled themselves on the spikes of any reality that offered. Or made their own unreality with drugs."

The plot is intricate, involuted, and complicated to the hilt; and this, as I see it, is the novel's point. The danger derives from the fairy tales into which people make their lives. In lonely, fearful, or confused minds, real-life facts can become rarefied into private fantasies. And when intensity is accepted—welcomed—as the measure of truth, how can the real and the fabricated be told apart?

We come to a scene where the parallel with the fairy tale is explicit —and something more. It is the best in the book—I can give but a part.

"I made my way up the washed-out gravel drive. The twin conical towers standing up against the night sky made the house look like something out of a medieval romance. The illusion faded as I got nearer. There was a multi-colored fanlight over the front door, with segments of glass fallen out, like missing teeth in an old smile. . . . The door creaked open when I knocked."

Here lives a lady "far gone in solitude," whose secret lies hidden at the heart of the mystery. She stands there in "a long full skirt on which there were paint stains in all three primary colors." She is a painter— of spiritual conditions, she says; to Archer her pictures resemble "serious contusions and open wounds" or "imperfectly remembered hallucinations."

" 'I was born in this house,' she said, as if she'd been waiting fifteen years for a listener." (And these are the fifteen years that have done their worst to everybody in the novel.) "It's interesting to come back to your childhood home, . . . like becoming 'very young and very old both at the same time.' That was how she looked, I thought, in her archaic long skirt—very young and very old, the granddaughter and the grandmother in one person, slightly schizo."

"There were romantic tears in her eyes" when her story is out. "My own eyes remained quite dry."

Fairy tale and living reality alternate on one current to pulse together in this remarkable scene. The woman is a pivotal character, and Archer has caught up with her; they are face to face, and there comes a moment's embrace. Of the many brilliant ways Mr. Macdonld has put his motif to use, I believe this is the touch that delighted me most. For of course Archer, this middle-aging Californian who has seen everything in a career of going into impossible trouble with his eyes open, who has always been the protector of the weak and the rescuer of the helpless, is a born romantic. Here he meets his introverted and ailing counterpart—this lady is the chatelaine of the romantic-gone-wrong. He is not by nature immune, especially to what is lovely or was lovely once. At a given moment, they may brush close—as Archer, the only one with insight into himself, is aware.

Time pressing, time lapsing, time repeating itself in dark acts, splitting into two in some agonized or imperfect mind—time is the wicked fairy to troubled people, granting them inevitably the thing they dread. While Archer's investigation is drawing him into the past, we are never allowed to forget that present time has been steadily increasing its menace. Mr. Macdonald has brought the fire toward us at closer and closer stages. By the time it gets as close as the top of the hill (this was the murder area), it appears "like a brilliant omniform growth which continued to grow until it bloomed very large against the sky. A sentinel quail on the hillside below it was ticking an alarm." Then, reaching the Broadhurst house, "the fire bent around it like the fingers of a hand, squeezing smoke out of the windows and then flame."

Indeed the fire is a multiple and accumulating identity, with a career of its own, a super-character that has earned itself a character's name—Rattlesnake. Significantly, Archer says, "There was only one good thing about the fire. It made people talk about the things that really concerned them."

What really concerns Archer, and the real kernel of the book, its heart and soul, is the little boy of six, good and brave and smart. He constitutes the book's emergency; he is also entirely believable, a full-rounded and endearing character. Ronny is the tender embodiment of everything Archer is by nature bound to protect, infinitely worthy of rescue.

When Archer plunges into a case, his reasons are always personal reasons (this is one of the things that make us so much for Archer). The little boy, for as long as he's missing, will be Archer's own loss. And without relinquishing for a moment his clear and lively identity, the child takes on another importance as well: "The world was changing," says Archer, "as if with one piece missing the whole thing had come loose and was running wild."

If it is the character of the little boy that makes the case matter to Archer, so it is the character of Archer, whose first-person narrative forms all Mr. Macdonald's novels, that makes it matter to us. Archer, from the start, has been a distinguished creation; he was always an attractive figure and in the course of the last several books has matured and deepened in substance to our still greater pleasure. Possessed even when young of an endless backlog of stored information, most of it sad, on human nature, he tended once, unless I'm mistaken, to be a bit cynical. Now he is something much more, he is vulnerable. As a detective and as a man, he takes the human situation with full seriousness. He cares. And good and evil both are real to him.

Archer knows himself to be a romantic, would call it a weakness—as he calls himself a "not unwilling catalyst" for trouble; he carries the knowledge around with him—that's how he got here. But he is in no way archaic. He is at heart a champion, but a self-questioning, often a self-deriding champion. He is of today, one of ours. *The Underground Man* is written so close to the nerve of today as to expose most of the apprehensions we live with.

In our day, it is for such a novel as *The Underground Man* that the detective form exists. I think it also matters that it is the detective form, with all its difficult demands and its corresponding charms, that makes such a novel possible. What gives me special satisfaction about this novel is that no one but a good writer—*this* good writer—could have possibly brought it off. *The Underground Man* is Mr. Macdonald's best book yet, I think. It is not only exhilaratingly well done; it is also very moving.

Ross Macdonald's style, to which in large part this is due, is one of delicacy and tension, very tightly made, with a spring in it. It doesn't allow a static sentence or one without pertinence. And the spare, controlled narrative, built for action and speed, conveys as well the world through which the action moves and gives it meaning, brings scene and character, however swiftly, before the eyes without a blur. It is an almost unbroken series of sparkling pictures.

The style that works so well to produce fluidity and grace also suggests a mind much given to contemplation and reflection on our world. Mr. Macdonald's writing is something like a stand of clean, cool, well-branched, well tended trees in which bright birds can flash and perch. And not for show, but to sing.

A great deal of what this writer has to tell us comes by way of beautiful and audacious similes. "His hairy head seemed enormous and grotesque on his boy's body, like a papier-mâché saint's head on a stick": the troubled teen-ager's self-absorption, his sense of destiny—theatrical but maybe in a good cause—along with the precise way he looks and carries himself, are given us all in one. At the scene of evacuation from the forest fire, at the bottom of a rich householder's swimming pool "lay a blue mink coat, like the headless pelt of a woman." A sloop lying on her side, dismantled offshore, "flopped in a surge like a bird made helpless by oil." The Snows, little old lady and grown son: "The door of Fritz's room was ajar. One of his moist eyes appeared at the crack like the eye of a fish in an underwater crevice. His mother, at the other door, was watching him like a shark."

Descriptions so interpretive are of course here as part and parcel of the character of Archer who says them to us. Mr. Macdonald's accuracy of observation becomes Archer's detection—running evidence. Mr. Macdonald brings characters into sudden sharp focus, too, by arresting them in an occasional archetypical pose. The obsessed Stanley is here in the words of his wife: "Sometimes he'd be just sitting there shuffling through his pictures and his letters. He looked like a man counting his money." And Fritz in the lath house, where Archer is leaving him, complaining among his plants: "The striped shadow fell from the roof, jailbirding him."

ROBERT WARSHOW

Robert Warshow (1917–1955), born in New York City, was educated at the University of Michigan and served as translator and researcher for the U.S. Army's Security Agency in Washington, D.C., during World War II, after which he joined the staff of *Commentary* magazine in New York. He began writing about the movies in 1947, and was planning to do a book on them (while applying for a Guggenheim Fellowship) when he died suddenly of a heart attack at age thirty-seven. His essays were collected in *The Immediate Experience* (1970), with an introduction by his friend Lionel Trilling.

THE WESTERNER

Warshow analyzes the mythical drive behind our filmed fantasies of violence, whether of gangland, frontier, or interstellar space. Our popular films, he argues, reflect a new popular myth on the primordial framework of individual wit against the structures of power. What myths do you see acted out in the films and programs of today?

They that have power to hurt and will do none,
That do not do the thing they most do show,
Who, moving others, are themselves as stone,
Unmoved, cold, and to temptation slow;
They rightly do inherit heaven's graces,
And husband nature's riches from expense;
They are the lords and owners of their faces,
*Others but stewards of their excellence.**

The two most successful creations of American movies are the gangster and the Westerner: men with guns. Guns as physical objects, and the postures associated with their use, form the visual and emotional center of both types of films. I suppose this reflects the importance of guns in the fantasy life of Americans; but that is a less illuminating point than it appears to be.

The gangster movie, which no longer exists in its "classical" form, is a story of enterprise and success ending in precipitate failure. Success is conceived as an increasing power to work injury, it belongs to the city, and it is of course a form of evil (though the gangster's death, presented usually as "punishment," is perceived simply as defeat). The peculiarity of the gangster is his unceasing, nervous activity. The exact nature of his enterprises may remain vague, but his commitment to enterprise is always clear, and all the more clear because he operates outside the field of utility. He is without culture, without manners, without leisure, or at any rate his leisure is likely to be spent in debauchery so compulsively aggressive as to seem only another aspect of his "work." But he is graceful, moving like a dancer among the crowded dangers of the city.

Like other tycoons, the gangster is crude in conceiving his ends but by no means inarticulate; on the contrary, he is usually expansive and noisy (the introspective gangster is a fairly recent development), and can state definitely what he wants: to take over the North Side, to own a hundred suits, to be Number One. But new "frontiers" will present themselves infinitely, and by a rigid convention it is understood that as soon as he wishes to rest on his gains, he is on the way to destruction.

The gangster is lonely and melancholy, and can give the impression of a profound worldly wisdom. He appeals most to adolescents with their impatience and their feeling of being outsiders, but more generally he appeals to that side of all of us which refuses to believe in the "normal" possibilities of happiness and achievement; the gangster is the "no" to the great American "yes" which is stamped so big over our official culture and yet has so little to do with the way we really feel

* Shakespeare, Sonnet 94.—Ed.

about our lives. But the gangster's loneliness and melancholy are not "authentic"; like everything else that belongs to him, they are not honestly come by: he is lonely and melancholy not because life ultimately demands such feelings but because he has put himself in a position where everybody wants to kill him and eventually somebody will. He is wide open and defenseless, incomplete because unable to accept any limits or come to terms with his own nature, fearful, loveless. And the story of his career is a nightmare inversion of the values of ambition and opportunity. From the window of Scarface's bullet-proof apartment can be seen an electric sign proclaiming: "The World Is Yours," and, if I remember, this sign is the last thing we see after Scarface lies dead in the street. In the end it is the gangster's weakness as much as his power and freedom that appeals to us; the world is not ours, but it is not his either, and in his death he "pays" for our fantasies, releasing us momentarily both from the concept of success, which he denies by caricaturing it, and from the need to succeed, which he shows to be dangerous.*

The Western hero, by contrast, is a figure of repose. He resembles the gangster in being lonely and to some degree melancholy. But his melancholy comes from the "simple" recognition that life is unavoidably serious, not from the disproportions of his own temperament. And his loneliness is organic, not imposed on him by his situation but belonging to him intimately and testifying to his completeness. The gangster must reject others violently or draw them violently to him. The Westerner is not thus compelled to seek love; he is prepared to accept it, perhaps, but he never asks of it more than it can give, and we see him constantly in situations where love is at best an irrelevance. If there is a woman he loves, she is usually unable to understand his motives; she is against killing and being killed, and he finds it impossible to explain to her that there is no point in being "against" these things: they belong to his world.

Very often this woman is from the East and her failure to understand represents a clash of cultures. In the American mind, refinement, virtue, civilization, Christianity itself, are seen as feminine, and therefore women are often portrayed as possessing some kind of deeper wisdom, while the men, for all their apparent self-assurance, are fundamentally childish. But the West, lacking the graces of civilization, is the place "where men are men"; in Western movies, men have the deeper wisdom and the women are children. Those women in the Western

* I discussed gangster movies at greater length in an article called "The Gangster as Tragic Hero" (*PR*, February 1948).

movies who share the hero's understanding of life are prostitutes (or, as they are usually presented, bar-room entertainers)—women, that is, who have come to understand in the most practical way how love can be an irrelevance, and therefore "fallen" women. The gangster, too, associates with prostitutes, but for him the important things about a prostitute are her passive availability and her costliness: she is part of his winnings. In Western movies, the important thing about a prostitute is her quasi-masculine independence: nobody owns her, nothing has to be explained to her, and she is not, like a virtuous woman, a "value" that demands to be protected. When the Westerner leaves the prostitute for a virtuous woman—for love—he is in fact forsaking a way of life, though the point of the choice is often obscured by having the prostitute killed by getting into the line of fire.

The Westerner is *par excellence* a man of leisure. Even when he wears the badge of a marshal or, more rarely, owns a ranch, he appears to be unemployed. We see him standing at a bar, or playing poker—a game which expresses perfectly his talent for remaining relaxed in the midst of tension—or perhaps camping out on the plains on some extraordinary errand. If he does own a ranch, it is in the background; we are not actually aware that he owns anything except his horse, his guns, and the one worn suit of clothing which is likely to remain unchanged all through the movie. It comes as a surprise to see him take money from his pocket or an extra shirt from his saddle-bags. As a rule we do not even know where he sleeps at night and don't think of asking. Yet it never occurs to us that he is a poor man; there is no poverty in Western movies, and really no wealth either: those great cattle domains and shipments of gold which figure so largely in the plots are moral and not material quantities, not the objects of contention but only its occasion. Possessions too are irrelevant.

Employment of some kind—usually unproductive—is always open to the Westerner, but when he accepts it, it is not because he needs to make a living, much less from any idea of "getting ahead." Where could he want to "get ahead" to? By the time we see him, he is already "there": he can ride a horse faultlessly, keep his countenance in the face of death, and draw his gun a little faster and shoot it a little straighter than anyone he is likely to meet. These are sharply defined acquirements, giving to the figure of the Westerner an apparent moral clarity of his physical image against his bare landscape; initially, at any rate, the Western movie presents itself as being without mystery, its whole universe comprehended in what we see on the screen.

Much of this apparent simplicity arises directly from those "cinematic" elements which have long been understood to give the Western theme its special appropriateness for the movies: the wide expanses of land, the free movement of men on horses. As guns constitute the visible moral center of the Western movie, suggesting continually the possibility of violence, so land and horses represent the movie's material basis, its sphere of action. But the land and the horses have also a moral significance: the physical freedom they represent belongs to the moral "openness" of the West—corresponding to the fact that guns are carried where they can be seen. (And, as we shall see, the character of land and horses changes as the Western film becomes more complex.)

The gangster's world is less open, and his arts not so easily identifiable as the Westerner's. Perhaps he too can keep his countenance, but the mask he wears is really no mask: its purpose is precisely to make evident the fact that he desperately wants to "get ahead" and will stop at nothing. Where the Westerner imposes himself by the appearance of unshakable control, the gangster's pre-eminence lies in the suggestion that he may at any moment lose control; his strength is not in being able to shoot faster or straighter than others, but in being more willing to shoot. "Do it first," says Scarface expounding his mode of operation, "and keep on doing it!" With the Westerner, it is a crucial point of honor *not* to "do it first"; his gun remains in its holster until the moment of combat.

There is no suggestion, however, that he draws the gun reluctantly. The Westerner could not fulfill himself if the moment did not finally come when he can shoot his enemy down. But because that moment is so thoroughly the expression of his being, it must be kept pure. He will not violate the accepted forms of combat though by doing so he could save a city. And he can wait. "When you call me that—smile!"—the villain smiles weakly, soon he is laughing with horrible joviality, and the crisis is past. But it is allowed to pass because it must come again: sooner or later Trampas will "make his play," and the Virginian will be ready for him.

What does the Westerner fight for? We know he is on the side of justice and order, and of course it can be said he fights for these things. But such broad aims never correspond exactly to his real motives; they only offer him his opportunity. The Westerner himself, when an explanation is asked of him (usually by a woman), is likely to say that he does what he "has to do." If justice and order did not continually demand his protection, he would be without a calling. Indeed, we come upon him often in just that situation, as the reign of law settles over the West and he is forced to see that his day is over; those are the pictures which end with his death or with his departure for some more remote frontier. What he defends, at bottom, is the purity of his own image—in fact his honor. This is what makes him invulnerable. When the gangster is killed, his whole life is shown to have been a mistake, but the image the Westerner seeks to maintain can be presented as clearly in defeat as in victory: he fights not for advantage and not for the right, but to state what he is, and he must live in a world which permits that statement. The Westerner is the last gentleman, and the movies which over and over again tell his story are probably the last art form in which the concept of honor retains its strength.

Of course I do not mean to say that ideas of virtue and justice and courage have gone out of culture. Honor is more than these things: it is a style, concerned with harmonious appearances as much as with desirable consequences, and tending therefore toward the denial of life in favor of art. "Who hath it? he that died o' Wednesday." On the whole, a world that leans to Falstaff's view is a more civilized and even, finally, a more graceful world. It is just the march of civilization that forces the Westerner to move on; and if we actually had to confront the question it might turn out that the woman who refuses to understand him is right as often as she is wrong. But we do not confront the question. Where the Westerner lives it is always about 1870—not the real 1870, either, or the real West—and he is killed or goes away when his position becomes problematical. The fact that he continues to hold our attention is evidence enough that, in his proper frame, he presents an image of personal nobility that is still real for us.

Clearly, this image easily becomes ridiculous: we need only look at William S. Hart or Tom Mix, who in the wooden absoluteness of their virtue represented little that an adult could take seriously; and doubtless such figures as Gene Autry or Roy Rogers are no better, though I confess I have seen none of their movies. Some film enthusiasts claim to find in the early, unsophisticated Westerns a "cinematic purity" that has since been lost; this idea is as valid, and finally as misleading, as T. S. Eliot's statement that *Everyman* is the only play in English that stays within the limitations of art. The truth is that the Westerner comes into the field of serious art only when his moral code, without ceasing to be compelling, is seen also to be imperfect. The Westerner at his best exhibits a moral ambiguity which darkens his image and saves him from absurdity; this ambiguity arises from the fact that, whatever his justifications, he is a killer of men.

In *The Virginian*, which is an archetypal Western movie as *Scarface* or *Little Caesar* are archetypal gangster movies, there is a lynching in which the hero (Gary Cooper), as leader of a posse, must supervise the hanging of his best friend for stealing cattle. With the growth of American "social consciousness," it is no longer possible to present a lynching in the movies unless the point is the illegality and injustice of the lynching itself; *The Ox-Bow Incident,* made in 1943, explicitly puts forward the newer point of view and can be regarded as a kind of "anti-Western." But in 1929, when *The Virginian* was made, the present inhibition about lynching was not yet in force; the justice, and therefore the necessity, of the hanging is never questioned—except by the schoolteacher from the East, whose refusal to understand serves as usual to set forth more sharply the deeper seriousness of the West. The Virginian is thus in a tragic dilemma where one moral absolute conflicts with another and the choice of either must leave a moral stain. If he had chosen to save his friend, he would have violated the image of himself that he had made essential to his existence, and the movie would have had to end with his death, for only by his death could the image have been restored. Having chosen instead to sacrifice his friend to the higher demands of the "code"—the only choice worthy of him, as even the friend understands—he is none the less stained by the killing, but what is needed now to set accounts straight is not his death but the death of the villain Trampas, the leader of the cattle thieves, who had escaped the posse and abandoned the Virginian's friend to his fate. Again the woman intervenes: Why must there be *more* killing? If the hero really loved her, he would leave town, refusing Trampas's challenge. What good will it be if Trampas should kill him? But the Virginian does once more what he "has to do," and in avenging his friend's death wipes out the stain on his own honor. Yet his victory cannot be complete: no death can be paid for and no stain truly wiped out; the movie is still a tragedy, for though the hero escapes with his life, he has been forced to confront the ultimate limits of his moral ideas.

This mature sense of limitation and unavoidable guilt is what gives the Westerner a "right" to his melancholy. It is true that the gangster's story is also a tragedy—in certain formal ways more clearly a tragedy than the Westerner's—but it is a romantic tragedy, based on a hero whose defeat springs with almost mechanical inevitability from the outrageous presumption of his demands: the gangster is *bound* to go on until he is killed. The Westerner is a more classical figure, self-contained and limited to begin with, seeking not to extend his dominion but only to assert his personal value, and his tragedy lies in the fact that even this circumscribed demand cannot be fully realized. Since the Westerner is not a murderer but (most of the time) a man of virtue, and since he is always prepared for defeat, he retains his inner invulnerability and his story need not end with his death (and usually does not); but what we finally respond to is not his victory but his defeat.

Up to a point, it is plain that the deeper seriousness of the good West-ern films comes from the introduction of a realism, both physical and psychological, that was missing with Tom Mix and William S. Hart. As lines of age have come into Gary Cooper's face since *The Virginian*, so the outlines of the Western movie in general have become less smooth, its background more drab. The sun still beats upon the town, but the camera is likely now to take advantage of this illumination to seek out more closely the shabbiness of buildings and furniture, the loose, worn hang of clothing, the wrinkles and dirt of the faces. Once it has been discovered that the true theme of the Western movie is not the freedom and expansiveness of frontier life, but its limitations, its material bare-ness, the pressures of obligation, then even the landscape itself ceases to be quite the arena of free movement it once was, but becomes instead a great empty waste, cutting down more often than it exaggerates the stature of the horseman who rides across it. We are more likely now to see the Westerner struggling against the obstacles of the physical world (as in the wonderful scenes on the desert and among the rocks in *The Last Posse*) than carelessly surmounting them. Even the horses, no longer the "friends" of man or the inspired chargers of knight-errantry, have lost much of the moral significance that once seemed to belong to them in their careering across the screen. It seems to me the horses grow tired and stumble more often than they did, and that we see them less fre-quently at the gallop.

In *The Gunfighter*, a remarkable film of a couple of years ago, the landscape has virtually disappeared. Most of the action takes place in-doors, in a cheerless saloon where a tired "bad man" (Gregory Peck) contemplates the waste of his life, to be senselessly killed at the end by a vicious youngster setting off on the same futile path. The movie is done in cold, quiet tones of gray, and every object in it—faces, clothing, a table, the hero's heavy mustache—is given an air of uncompromising authenticity, suggesting those dim photographs of the nineteenth-century West in which Wyatt Earp, say, turns out to be a blank untidy figure posing awkwardly before some uninteresting building. This "authen-ticity," to be sure, is only aesthetic; the chief fact about nineteenth-century photographs, to my eyes at any rate, is how stonily they refuse to yield up the truth. But that limitation is just what is needed: by pre-serving some hint of the rigidity of archaic photography (only in tone and décor, never in composition), *The Gunfighter* can permit us to feel that we are looking at a more "real" West than the one the movies have accustomed us to—harder, duller, less "romantic"—and yet without forc-ing us outside the boundaries which give the Western movie its validity.

We come upon the hero of *The Gunfighter* at the end of a career in which he has never upheld justice and order, and has been at times, apparently, an actual criminal; in this case, it is clear that the hero has been wrong and the woman who has rejected his way of life has been right. He is thus without any of the larger justifications, and knows himself a ruined man. There can be no question of his "redeeming" himself in any socially constructive way. He is too much the victim of his own reputation to turn marshal as one of his old friends has done, and he is not offered the sentimental solution of a chance to give up his life for some good end; the whole point is that he exists outside the field of social value. Indeed, if we were once allowed to see him in the days of his "success," he might become a figure like the gangster, for his career has been aggressively "anti-social" and the practical problem he faces is the gangster's problem: there will always be somebody trying to kill him. Yet it is obviously absurd to speak of him as "anti-social," not only because we do not see him acting as a criminal, but more fundamentally because we do not see his milieu as a society. Of course it has its "social problems" and a kind of static history: civilization is always just at the point of driving out the old freedom; there are women and children to represent the possibility of a settled life; and there is the marshal, a bad man turned good, determined to keep at least his area of jurisdiction at peace. But these elements are not, in fact, a part of the film's "realism," even though they come out of the real history of the West; they belong to the conventions of the form, to that accepted framework which makes the film possible in the first place, and they exist not to provide a standard by which the gunfighter can be judged, but only to set him off. The true "civilization" of the Western movie is always embodied in an individual, good or bad is more a matter of personal bearing than of social consequences, and the conflict of good and bad is a duel between two men. Deeply troubled and obviously doomed, the gunfighter is the Western hero still, perhaps all the more because his value must express itself entirely in his own being—in his presence, the way he holds our eyes—and in contradiction to the facts. No matter what he has done, he *looks* right, and he remains invulnerable because, without acknowledging anyone else's right to judge him, he has judged his own failure and has already assimilated it, understanding—as no one else understands except the marshal and the bar-room girl—that he can do nothing but play out the drama of the gun fight again and again until the time comes when it will be he who gets killed. What "redeems" him is that he no longer believes in this drama and nevertheless will continue to play his role perfectly: the pattern is all.

The proper function of realism in the Western movie can only be to deepen the lines of that pattern. It is an art form for connoisseurs, where the spectator derives his pleasure from the appreciation of minor variations within the working out of a pre-established order. One does not want too much novelty; it comes as a shock, for instance, when the hero is made to operate without a gun, as has been done in several pictures (e.g., *Destry Rides Again*), and our uneasiness is allayed only when he is finally compelled to put his "pacifism" aside. If the hero can be shown to be troubled, complex, fallible, even eccentric, or the villain given some psychological taint or, better, some evocative physical mannerism, to shade the colors of his villainy, that is all to the good. Indeed, that kind of variation is absolutely necessary to keep the type from becoming sterile: we do not want to see the same movie over and over again, only the same form. But when the impulse toward realism is extended into a "reinterpretation" of the West as a developed society, drawing our eyes away from the hero if only to the extent of showing him as the one dominant figure in a complex social order, then the pattern is broken and the West itself begins to be uninteresting. If the "social problems" of the frontier are to be the movie's chief concern, there is no longer any point in re-examining these problems twenty times a year; they have been solved, and the people for whom they once were real are dead. Moreover, the hero himself, still the film's central figure, now tends to become its one unassimilable element, since he is the most "unreal."

The Ox-Bow Incident, by denying the convention of the lynching, presents us with a modern "social drama" and evokes a corresponding response, but in doing so it almost makes the Western setting irrelevant, a mere backdrop of beautiful scenery. (It is significant that *The Ox-Bow Incident* has no hero; a hero would have to stop the lynching or be killed in trying to stop it, and then the "problem" of lynching would no longer be central.) Even in *The Gunfighter* the women and children are a little too much in evidence, threatening constantly to become a real focus of concern instead of simply part of the given framework; and the young tough who kills the hero has too much the air of juvenile criminality: the hero himself could never have been like that, and the idea of a cycle being repeated therefore loses its sharpness. But the most striking example of the confusion created by a too conscientious "social" realism is in the celebrated *High Noon*.

In *High Noon* we find Gary Cooper still the upholder of order that he was in *The Virginian*, but twenty-four years older, stooped, slower moving, awkward, his face lined, the flesh sagging, a less beautiful and weaker figure, but with the suggestion of greater depth that belongs almost automatically to age. Like the hero of *The Gunfighter*, he no longer has to assert his character and is no longer interested in the drama of combat; it is hard to imagine that he might once have been so youthful as to say, "When you call me that—smile!" In fact, when we come upon him he is hanging up his guns and his marshal's badge in order to begin a new, peaceful life with his bride, who is a Quaker. But then the news comes that a man he had sent to prison has been pardoned and will get to town on the noon train; three friends of this man have come to wait for him at the station, and when the freed convict arrives the four of them will come to kill the marshal! He is thus trapped; the bride will object, the hero himself will waver much more than he would have done twenty-four years ago, but in the end he will play out the drama because it is what he "has to do." All this belongs to the established form (there is even the "fallen woman" who understands the marshal's position as his wife does not). Leaving aside the crudity of building up suspense by means of the clock, the actual Western drama of *High Noon* is well handled and forms a good companion piece to *The Virginian*, showing in both conception and technique the ways in which the Western movie has naturally developed.

But there is a second drama along with the first. As the marshal sets out to find deputies to help him deal with the four gunmen, we are taken through the various social strata of the town, each group in turn refusing its assistance out of cowardice, malice, irresponsibility, or venality. With this we are in the field of "social drama"—of a very low order, incidentally, altogether unconvincing and displaying a vulgar anti-populism that has marred some other movies of Stanley Kramer's. But the falsity of the "social drama" is less important than the fact that it does not belong in the movie to begin with. The technical problem was to make it necessary for the marshal to face his enemies alone; to explain *why* the other townspeople are not at his side is to raise a question which does not exist in the proper frame of the Western movie, where the hero is "naturally" alone and it is only necessary to contrive the physical absence of those who might be his allies, if any contrivance is needed at all. In addition, though the hero of *High Noon* proves himself a better man than all around him, the actual effect of this contrast is to lessen his stature: he becomes only a rejected man of virtue. In our final glimpse of him, as he rides away through the town where he has spent most of his life without really imposing himself on it, he is a pathetic rather than a tragic figure. And his departure has another meaning as well; the "social drama" has no place for him.

But there is also a different way of violating the Western form. This is to yield entirely to its static quality as legend and to the "cinematic" temptations of its landscape, the horses, the quiet men. John Ford's famous *Stagecoach* (1938) had much of this unhappy preoccupation with style, and the same director's *My Darling Clementine* (1946), a soft and beautiful movie about Wyatt Earp, goes further along the same path, offering indeed a superficial accuracy of historical reconstruction, but so loving in execution as to destroy the outlines of the Western legend, assimilating it to the more sentimental legend of rural America and making the hero a more dangerous Mr. Deeds. (*Powder River*, a recent "routine" Western shamelessly copied from *My Darling Clementine*, is in most ways a better film; lacking the benefit of a serious director, it is necessarily more concerned with drama than with style.)

The highest expression of this aestheticizing tendency is in George Stevens' *Shane*, where the legend of the West is virtually reduced to its essentials and then fixed in the dreamy clarity of a fairy tale. There never was so broad and bare and lovely a landscape as Stevens puts before us, or so unimaginably comfortless a "town" as the little group of buildings on the prairie to which the settlers must come for their supplies and to buy a drink. The mere physical progress of the film, following the style of *A Place in the Sun*, is so deliberately graceful that everything seems to be happening at the bottom of a clear lake. The hero (Alan Ladd) is hardly a man at all, but something like the Spirit of the West, beautiful in fringed buckskins. He emerges mysteriously from the plains, breathing sweetness and a melancholy which is no longer simply the Westerner's natural response to experience but has taken on spirituality; and when he has accomplished his mission, meeting and destroying in the black figure of Jack Palance a Spirit of Evil just as metaphysical as his own embodiment of virtue, he fades away again into the more distant West, a man whose "day is over," leaving behind the wondering little boy who might have imagined the whole story. The choice of Alan Ladd to play the leading role is alone an indication of this film's tendency. Actors like Gary Cooper or Gregory Peck are in themselves, as material objects, "realistic," seeming to bear in their bodies and their faces mortality, limitation, the knowledge of good and evil. Ladd is a more "aesthetic" object, with some of the "universality" of a piece of sculpture; his special quality is in his physical smoothness and serenity, unworldly and yet not innocent, but suggesting that no experience can really touch him. Stevens has tried to freeze the Western myth once and for all in the immobility of Alan Ladd's countenance. If *Shane* were "right," and fully successful, it might be possible to say there was no point in making any more Western movies; once the hero is apotheosized, variation and development are closed off.

Shane is not "right," but it is still true that the possibilities of fruitful variation in the Western movie are limited. The form can keep its freshness through endless repetitions only because of the special character of the film medium, where the physical difference between one object and another—above all, between one actor and another—is of such enormous importance, serving the function that is served by the variety of language in the perpetuation of literary types. In this sense, the "vocabulary" of films is much larger than that of literature and falls more readily into pleasing and significant arrangements. (That may explain why the middle levels of excellence are more easily reached in the movies than in literary forms, and perhaps also why the status of the movies as art is constantly being called into question.) But the advantage of this almost automatic particularity belongs to all films alike. Why does the Western movie especially have such a hold on our imagination?

Chiefly, I think, because it offers a serious orientation to the problem of violence such as can be found almost nowhere else in our culture. One of the well-known peculiarities of modern civilized opinion is its refusal to acknowledge the value of violence. This refusal is a virtue, but like many virtues it involves a certain willful blindness and it encourages hypocrisy. We train ourselves to be shocked or bored by cultural images of violence, and our very concept of heroism tends to be a passive one: we are less drawn to the brave young men who kill large numbers of our enemies than to the heroic prisoners who endure torture without capitulating. In art, though we may still be able to understand and participate in the values of the Iliad, a modern writer like Ernest Hemingway we find somewhat embarrassing: there is no doubt that he stirs us, but we cannot help recognizing also that he is a little childish. And in the criticism of popular culture, where the educated observer is usually under the illusion that he has nothing at stake, the presence of images of violence is often assumed to be in itself a sufficient ground for condemnation.

These attitudes, however, have not reduced the element of violence in our culture but, if anything, have helped to free it from moral control by letting it take on the aura of "emancipation." The celebration of acts of violence is left more and more to the irresponsible: on the higher cultural levels to writers like Céline, and lower down to Mickey Spillane or Horace McCoy, or to the comic books, television, and the movies. The gangster movie, with its numerous variations, belongs to this cultural "underground" which sets forth the attractions of violence in the face of all our higher social attitudes. It is a more "modern" genre than the Western, perhaps even more profound, because it confronts industrial society on its own ground—the city—and because, like much of our advanced art, it gains its effects by a gross insistence on its own narrow logic. But it is anti-social, resting on fantasies of irresponsible freedom. If we are brought finally to acquiesce in the denial of these fantasies, it is only because they have been shown to be dangerous, not because they have given way to a better vision of behavior.*

In war movies, to be sure, it is possible to present the uses of violence within a framework of responsibility. But there is the disadvantage that modern war is a co-operative enterprise; its violence is largely impersonal, and heroism belongs to the group more than to the individual. The hero of a war movie is most often simply a leader, and his superiority is likely to be expressed in a denial of the heroic: you are not supposed to be brave, you are supposed to get the job done and stay alive (this too, of course, is a kind of heroic posture, but a new—and "practical"—one). At its best, the war movie may represent a more civilized point of view than the Western, and if it were not continually marred by ideological sentimentality we might hope to find it developing into a higher form of drama. But it cannot supply the values we seek in the Western.

Those values are in the image of a single man who wears a gun on his thigh. The gun tells us that he lives in a world of violence, and even that he "believes in violence." But the drama is one of self-restraint: the moment of violence must come in its own time and according to its special laws, or else it is valueless. There is little cruelty in Western movies, and little sentimentality; our eyes are not focused on the sufferings of the defeated but on the deportment of the hero. Really, it is not violence at all which is the "point" of the Western movie, but a certain image of man, a style, which expresses itself most clearly in violence. Watch a child with his toy guns and you will see: what most interests him is not (as we so much fear) the fantasy of hurting others, but to work out how a man might look when he shoots or is shot. A hero is one who looks like a hero.

Whatever the limitations of such an idea in experience, it has always been valid in art, and has a special validity in an art where appearances are everything. The Western hero is necessarily an archaic figure; we do not really believe in him and would not have him step out of his rigidly conventionalized background. But his archaicism does not take away from his power; on the contrary, it adds to it by keeping him just a

---

* I am not concerned here with the actual social consequences of gangster movies, though I suspect they could not have been so pernicious as they were thought to be. Some of the compromises introduced to avoid the supposed bad effects of the old gangster movies may be, if anything, more dangerous, for the sadistic violence that once belonged only to the gangster is now commonly enlisted on the side of the law and thus goes undefeated, allowing us (if we wish) to find in the movies a sort of "confirmation" of our fantasies.

little beyond the reach both of common sense and of absolutized emotion, the two usual impulses of our art. And he has, after all, his own kind of relevance. He is there to remind us of the possibility of style in an age which has put on itself the burden of pretending that style has no meaning, and, in the midst of our anxieties over the problem of violence, to suggest that even in killing or being killed we are not freed from the necessity of establishing satisfactory modes of behavior. Above all, the movies in which the Westerner plays out his role preserve for us the pleasures of a complete and self-contained drama—and one which still effortlessly crosses the boundaries which divide our culture—in a time when other, more consciously serious art forms are increasingly complex, uncertain, and ill-defined.

SUGGESTIONS FOR WRITING

1. Write a review of a book or movie in one pungent paragraph, taking *The New Yorker's* squibs and Faulkner's paragraph on Hemingway as models.

2. With the reviews in this chapter in mind, write a review of some book or movie you strongly liked or disliked, preferably one by a writer or director whose work you have seen before. Try to locate in your recollected reaction just what displeased or delighted you, and why, transforming your reactions into reasons that would convince others.

3. If you have been following some television serial from infancy onward, or if you have been raised on some series of books like *The Bobbsey Twins,* or have been addicted to some comic strip, write a generalizing or mythologizing essay about it based on the pattern of Warshow's analysis of Westerns.

Ten

Evidence and the Author's Voice

This section celebrates human variety. Here are four people seriously engaged in convincing us to see important matters as they see them, speaking to issues that concern us all. Yet each voice speaks for itself, as a person, and this personality persuades us of our common cause. If such people are concerned, we feel, the issues cannot be vain. Each brings evidence of various shapes and sizes, whether in a word, a sentence, an example of several paragraphs, or an extended description, to illustrate his points, to help us *see* them. But we see the evidence through his eyes and hear him describe it in his personal voice, as if on a guided tour. Such is the persuasive force of the human personality, the human voice, as it speaks through written prose. To write well, find this center from which your own personality and its natural idiom can carry your convictions to all, with the power of the concerned human being.

JEREMY R. AZRAEL

Jeremy R. Azrael (1935–), born in Baltimore and educated at Harvard, is currently a professor of political science at the University of Chicago. His expertise in Soviet politics is evidenced in his book *Managerial Power and Soviet Politics* (1966).

MURDER TRIAL IN MOSCOW

Here, in swift narrative prose, in straight sentences, with little more than
keen vignette and quotation—virtually all evidence and no comment—
is a case against injustice and the myths the majority forms to smother
the scapegoat. Notice how Azrael's thesis emerges only at the end, and
then obliquely, after his vivid detail has implied the point.

We first learned of the case of Aleksandr Ivanovich Bazhenov from an
announcement on the bulletin board of Moscow University's law faculty
which signaled forthcoming trials of special interest to aspiring Soviet
jurists. However, despite this publicity, we were the only representatives
of the university present in the small courtroom of the Moscow Oblast
Court when, at 10 A.M. on November 10, the Bazhenov case was called.
The rest of the audience consisted of sundry courtroom hangers-on, a
sizable group of Bazhenov's neighbors, Bazhenov's wife, and the mother
and several relatives of Bazhenov's victim. For Bazhenov was charged
under Article 136a of the Criminal Code of the Russian republic, the
article dealing with premeditated murder from base motives.

People's Judge Ivan Sergeyevich Shepilov summarized the bare details
of the charge from the record of the pre-trial investigation which lay on
his desk. First, however, he confirmed the identity and vital statistics of
the accused, made sure that the latter did not object to the defense
attorney who had been assigned him, and, after reading the law covering
perjury, registered the witnesses who were slated to be heard.

Bazhenov, it was established, had been born in 1926, was a resident
of a small village in Penza province, was of peasant origin and Russian
nationality, was married but childless, had had six years of education,
had served in the army from 1943 to 1950, was not a member of the
Communist Party, had never before been accused or convicted of any
crime, and, prior to his arrest, had been employed as a carpenter in a
small factory. He was accused of having shot one Vladimir Silkin, aged
fourteen, when the latter, along with three youthful companions, invaded
his private apple orchard at midnight on August 9, 1958.

This was the sum and substance of the formal charge, although, informed as it was by such technical details as the number (78) and location (the chest) of the gunshot wounds found on Silkin's body, it took
Judge Shepilov a full fifteen minutes to read it through. When he had
finished, he asked Bazhenov whether he acknowledged the charge and
asked the defense and prosecuting attorneys and the two people's
assessors, lay jurymen assigned to decide the case along with him,
whether they had any questions about it. Receiving an affirmative

answer from Bazhenov and a negative answer from the attorneys and assessors, Shepilov requested the accused to rise and give his own version of the case.

Bazhenov, it quickly became clear, was precisely what his appearance suggested: a simple, inarticulate peasant. He was obviously bewildered and terrified by his current predicament and could scarcely speak. Moreover, he was given no opportunity to compose himself, for, at almost every word he uttered, Judge Shepilov interjected an acid comment or supercilious question, thus frightening and bewildering the accused yet further. As a result, Bazhenov's testimony added little to our knowledge of the events of the case. All it really did was give us our first insight into the character of Judge Shepilov, or, at least, into his attitude toward the case at hand:

BAZHENOV: I shot into the air.

SHEPILOV: But a man fell. Do you think we're fools? You shot at people.

BAZHENOV: I didn't want to kill anyone.

SHEPILOV: Really? Did you think that if you shot a man he would become healthier?

BAZHENOV: I didn't want to kill.

SHEPILOV: I didn't ask what you wanted.

BAZHENOV: I didn't want to.

SHEPILOV: Why did you do it, if you didn't want to?

(Silence)

SHEPILOV: Did you think nothing was more important than apples? Why did you kill?

BAZHENOV: On account of apples. . . .

BAZHENOV: I wanted to shoot up.

SHEPILOV: Where did you shoot?

BAZHENOV: In the air.

SHEPILOV: Impossible! That, you yourself fully understand. You are speaking nonsense. Where did you in fact shoot?

BAZHENOV: In the chest.

SHEPILOV: If you had wanted to shoot up, at most the head would have been hit. What was the direction of the shot?

BAZHENOV: Upwards.

SHEPILOV: You spent seven years in the army and didn't learn how to shoot? Really! Where did you shoot?

And so on. Bazhenov continued to insist that he had not wanted to kill and had fired into the air. Shepilov continued to insist that both propositions were nonsensical, and the merry-go-round went on for about twenty minutes.

The prosecutor, a sallow, self-satisfied-looking young man, also questioned Bazhenov. "You killed on account of apples? But what could your loss have been? Five or ten apples? Does that justify your shot?"

The examination of Bazhenov then passed into the hands of the defense attorney. Naum Viktorovich Bykovsky, with his carefully trimmed goatee, wavy gray hair, and comfortably well-groomed look, was the sort of elderly Russian who almost automatically inspires the confidence and trust of Westerners and frequently arouses the suspicion and hostility of Soviet activists. His questioning of Bazhenov was quiet and solicitous, and gave us our first substantial information about the circumstances of the Bazhenov case.

Bykovsky drew from Bazhenov the following history. The accused was dependent for half his income on the two cubic meters of apples which his small thirteen-tree orchard annually yielded him. However, ever since the orchard had begun to yield fruit, it had been beset by thieves. Often up to half the crop was stolen. During the past summer, Bazhenov testified, losses had been particularly heavy, reaching such proportions in the weeks immediately preceding the crime that he had finally taken to sleeping in the orchard in order to fend off the thieves.

Finally, only two weeks before Silkin's death, he had managed to catch two thieves in the orchard. However, when he attempted to detain them, he was set upon and badly beaten. He had reported this to the militia, but, so far as he knew, no investigation had been conducted. In any event, his assailants had not been apprehended. With this experience behind him, he had decided to buy a shotgun, and it was with this weapon that he had shot Silkin when, upon being awakened at midnight, he had seen four figures in the orchard. He had not, in the darkness, been able to perceive that the intruders were adolescents, but he had given a warning whistle before firing, and he had fired—or, at least, had intended to fire—into the air.

With his client's version of the case fully recorded, Bykovsky closed his examination. Judge Shepilov thereupon started to call the first witness, but the prosecutor interrupted with a request to ask the accused just one more question. His purpose was not clarification but reiteration of what was clearly the foundation stone of the prosecution's case: "You intended merely to save apples, and that's all?" Again Bazhenov responded affirmatively, and the parade of witnesses was permitted to begin.

The first three witnesses were Silkin's companions on the fateful midnight raid. All three were sixteen-year-old factory apprentices; all three told substantially the same story. They were returning home from a public dance and, on passing Bazhenov's orchard, suddenly decided to filch a few apples. All testified that Silkin had been reluctant to take part in the foray but had finally followed them over the orchard's fence. All vigorously denied having stolen apples from Bazhenov or anyone else earlier. The only point on which they disagreed was whether or not the fatal shot had been preceded by a warning whistle.

The first of the boys to testify, the only one of the three who told his story clearly and coherently, claimed to remember such a whistle. The second, who insisted that the tragedy had occurred in July, not August, denied that there had been a whistle, and he was supported by the third. The point was clearly important to the attorneys as an index of Bazhenov's intent, and both pursued the issue vigorously. Apart from this question, however, the prosecutor examined the boys only cursorily, and Bykovsky sought to establish that the boys, each of whom earned three hundred rubles a month, could have afforded to buy apples.

The last witness was Bazhenov's wife, whose testimony confirmed that of her husband as to the care they had lavished on their orchard, its economic importance to them, the high losses they had sustained at the hands of thieves, the disruption of their normal lives brought about by the need for Bazhenov to sleep in the orchard, and the severity of Bazhenov's injuries from the incident two weeks prior to Silkin's death. She reported that when Bazhenov ran into the house on the fateful night and announced that he had just killed a man, her first words were, "You had better go to the militia," and this rang true to her general character as it was revealed in the tone of her testimony. She spoke without the least trace of emotion, throughout referred to Bazhenov as "he," and cast nary a glance toward the prisoner's dock. And yet one somehow felt that there was more of peasant fatalism than of conjugal distance or betrayal in all this.

When the witnesses finished their testimony, Judge Shepilov asked the attorneys whether they had any further evidence to introduce before beginning their summaries and pleas. The defense attorney introduced the accused's war record and work record. Bazhenov had won two citations for wounds received in battle and a First of May citation for good work. The mention of war wounds had obviously won the respect of the audience, but the mention of the work citation called forth a low roll of laughter that clearly said, "Who hasn't received such a certificate? You're really scraping the bottom of the barrel." It was, therefore, on a slightly less than overwhelming note that Bykovsky resumed his seat, and a ten-minute recess was declared before the court would reconvene for final arguments.

Like the majority of the courtroom spectators, we took advantage of the recess to stretch our legs in the corridor. However, despite the obvious desire of several of the spectators to talk to us, we moved off a bit and simply listened and watched.

The mother of the victim, Silkin, sat sobbing quietly on a bench just outside the courtroom door. She had already caused some commotion in the courtroom, first by fainting as Judge Shepilov read the indictment with its gruesome description of the state of the corpse, and then by going into hysterics during the testimony of her son's companions. On both occasions there had been a murmur of sympathy from the audience, which subsided only after Judge Shepilov rapped sharply for silence and warned that "This is a trial, not a spectacle."

Now, however, the sobbing mother seemed to arouse the ire of the waiting crowd. Several elderly men from among the courtroom hangers-on in the audience turned on her and began to upbraid her for having raised a thief. "What but a bad end," they demanded, "could be anticipated for such a son?"

The mother broke into yet louder and more bitter sobs. Over and over she shrieked, "No, no, he was a good boy." But her protests seemed simply to increase the vehemence of her tormentors, who let loose a flood of cruel, mocking laughter interspersed with asides about the fate of thieves, the just deserts of delinquents, the way children reflect their parents' character.

No one intervened, no one said, "Leave the poor, bereaved woman alone!" Even the woman herself did not plead to be left in peace.

Immediately upon reconvening the court, Judge Shepilov called upon the prosecutor to sum up his case. The latter spoke rapidly and without passion—indeed, almost without expression. His summation, which was chaotically organized, reinforced our impression that he was so certain of the outcome of the case that he attached little importance to its presentation. The main themes of his summation could, of course, have been predicted from his prior arguments, but what was surprising was the cavalier fashion in which he handled the two legal problems on which the outcome of the case would presumably hinge: was the murder premeditated and was it, as the relevant article of the code insisted it had to be, committed from base motives?

As for premeditation, the prosecutor's argument was simple: Bazhenov's intent to murder was proved by the fact that he had loaded his shotgun with live ammunition and had incontrovertibly, his professions to the contrary notwithstanding, fired not into the air but directly at a person. The fact that Bazhenov had perhaps not intended the specific murder which occurred was, he asserted, irrelevant.

The issue of motivation seemed to him equally clear-cut. Soviet law, he said, was always especially severe where the protection of life was concerned, but it had to be doubly so when life was taken in defense of a few apples. Bazhenov himself had admitted repeatedly that he had murdered for the sake of apples. "What," the prosecutor asked, "could be more miserly or base than to take the life of a fourteen-year-old boy for the sake of ten apples?" Bazhenov had a full range of defensive measures available for the protection of his orchard, but willfully chose to kill, and that without even a warning. The motive, the prosecutor reiterated, was to save a few apples; the victim was a young boy who had not even begun to live. "In the light of these facts," he concluded, "I ask for a finding of guilty under the Article 136a of the Criminal Code and request that the court return the normal maximum sentence of ten years' deprivation of liberty."

The entire tone and style of the prosecutor's speech, which it had taken him only twelve minutes to deliver, contrasted sharply with that of defense attorney Bykovsky, who now rose to deliver his summation. The argument was both tightly organized and forceful, and skillfully blended four distinct elements. First, there was a careful reference to rulings and instructions from higher courts which bore on the case at hand. Second, there was a moving appeal, in the best tradition of Russian courtroom pleading, that the court put the case in the proper human perspective and judge only the individual who faced it. Third, there was a reinterpretation of the evidence in terms of the preceding elements—in terms of the rulings of higher courts and the individual circumstances of the accused. And finally, there was a striking reference to the possibilities of true justice, which had been introduced into Soviet judicial practice after Stalin's death and were being put to the test in the present case.

Bykovsky stressed the fact that Bazhenov had been subjected to extreme provocation and that every Soviet citizen had the right to defend his property against thieves. However, he went much further. He opened his remarks by expressing his sympathy to Silkin's relatives. He spoke with great emotion of how blessed was the gift of life, of how easy it was to snuff out and how impossible to restore. And then, wheeling toward the bench, he reminded the court that, though Silkin's life was gone, Bazhenov was still alive, and that his fate, the fate of a living human being, rested now with the court.

Bazhenov, Bykovsky expostulated, was a poor and simple soul. He had given seven years of his life to the service of his country and upon returning to civilian life had sought, above all, peace and quiet. He had worked diligently and had devoted every spare moment to his small orchard. The orchard, Bykovsky argued, was much more than a source of profit to Bazhenov; it was a source of stability and personal satisfaction. However, as soon as the orchard had begun to flourish, it had been beset by thieves. Bazhenov had been forced to abandon his hearth and sleep amidst his precious trees in order to protect them and all they stood for. His whole life had been disrupted. And when he at last managed to catch some thieves, he had been badly beaten. Yet, even then the militia had done nothing except file a report on the assault.

It was only at this point, Bykovsky went on, only after he had been harassed, insulted, and injured, only after he had looked in vain to the public authorities for support, that Bazhenov, in desperation, had purchased a gun. There could be no doubt, Bykovsky asserted, that a Soviet citizen possessed the right to defend his property against hooligans and thieves. How, he demanded, could one attribute the exercise of this right to base motives, and hence bring it under Article 136a? Must one simply yield to a thief who demands one's clothing or watch? Could resistance to the thief in such a case be attributed to base motives?

Previously, Bykovsky remonstrated in a low voice, it had been an accepted part of Soviet court practice to attribute the worst imaginable motives to the accused and to avoid inquiry into the specific circumstances which surrounded an alleged crime. Then, Bykovsky continued, it had been customary to consider the trial nothing more than a ceremonial ritual, after which the accused was automatically given the severest possible sentence. But now, Bykovsky emphatically reminded the court, all that had changed. Apropos of the present case, one could see the change in the Judicial Instruction handed down in 1956 by the U.S.S.R. Supreme Court, directing all lower courts to recognize that all citizens had the right of active defense of their property as well as their bodies and lives against hooligans.

How, Bykovsky thundered, could any prosecutor in 1958 claim that Bazhenov's act was one of premeditated murder from base motives? Try as he might, Bykovsky asserted, he could find nothing in any authoritative judicial text or contemporary directive which suggested that Bazhenov's act was anything more than active defense of property.

It was true, Bykovsky conceded, that active defense was justified only in response to a "socially dangerous attack," but that was precisely the nature of the robbery attempted by the unfortunate Silkin and his comrades. The boys could have bought apples, yet they stole; and Silkin was shot in the act of theft itself. "Socially dangerous? Of course! If one asks, 'Where can one go from apples?', the answer is, 'A long way. One can go to a watch, a jacket, a suit, and so forth.' The populace demands that the fruits of its labors be protected."

The only relevant question, Bykovsky maintained, was that of the degree of proportionality between attack and defense. The prosecutor, he insisted, was wrong to suggest that any question of proportionality between apples and lives was involved. No jurist would frame the question in this way. As for the really relevant question, Bykovsky went on, the defense itself was persuaded that Bazhenov had adopted a disproportionate defensive response. Bykovsky asserted that for this reason he himself did not consider it possible to recommend the simple acquittal of his client. However, the maximum sentence which could be tolerated was three years, and even that would be grossly excessive.

> Bazhenov's crime clearly falls under Article 139 of the Criminal Code—the article which deals specifically with overly extreme measures of defense. Under this article, Bazhenov is guilty. He should have shot into the air or perhaps toward the boy's feet. But some sort of *active* defense was appropriate and necessary. Even if Silkin and his comrades had simply been innocently strolling through the orchard, the court would have to make a distinction between the objective situation and the motives of the accused. In even this hypothetical case, the relevant article would still be 139. In the actual case at hand, where not innocent strolling but criminal theft characterized the objective situation, there is clearly no way to go beyond Article 139. Neither sympathy for the relatives of the deceased nor outdated judicial habit should or can lead us to apply the wrong article.

The prosecutor, who was visibly stunned by the vigor of the defense, demanded rebuttal time. There was real wonder in his voice as he admitted, "My, my . . . so to speak . . . opponent is right about the instruction of the U.S.S.R. Supreme Court." However, the prosecutor went on to say that his "opponent" had failed to mention that the Criminal Code of the Russian republic, while not denying citizens the right to active defense of their private property, specifically directed that great caution be exercised where only gardens or orchards were involved. This, he argued, constituted a warning to the courts that such things as the theft of apples by children did not justify active measures of defense.

To this Bykovsky, in his very brief rebuttal of the prosecutor's rebuttal, pointed out that at midnight on a dark night one could neither distinguish adolescents from adults nor be expected to ascertain the age of one's assailants before acting in self-defense. He did not contest the prosecutor's characterization of the Russian code, but simply reiterated the instruction of the U.S.S.R. Supreme Court and suggested that it was precisely because an orchard was involved that he had conceded Bazhenov's action was excessive. Certainly, Bykovsky concluded, there was nothing in the code to support the prosecutor's suggestion that action in defense of one's orchard was automatically tantamount to action inspired by base motives.

With the summations and rebuttals completed, Judge Shepilov declared a one-hour luncheon recess, to be followed by the final statement of the accused. As his four guards with their bayoneted rifles led Bazhenov from the room, we approached Bykovsky and congratulated him on his conduct of the case. We explained that we were American students of Soviet affairs and told him that it would be a pleasure to report that the quality of defense in Soviet trials was so high. We told him that, to our minds, he had made the prosecutor's case appear exceedingly flimsy.

Bykovsky thanked us with real warmth, but quickly changed the subject and began to inquire further about our special interests, our status in the Soviet Union, the nature of American legal training. Every time we tried to turn the discussion back to the Bazhenov case, he became distinctly ill at ease.

It was impossible, under the circumstances, to press him hard, but finally, after he had begun to glance at his watch, we asked what sort of decision he expected the court to return. We ourselves were quite optimistic, for we had by now adopted Bykovsky's case as well as been persuaded by it, and therefore were rather surprised when Bykovsky, after hesitating just a second, said in a voice that seemed to us strangely sober and resigned, "You will see." And with that he disappeared into his chamber.

After lunch, Bazhenov made his last statement in a whispered mutter. His head was cast down and his brow furrowed, and the words came out jerkily and expressionless: "I did not want to kill. I received two wounds in the war. I was beaten only ten days before the accident, and the militia did nothing. I loved my orchard and only wanted to protect it. I paid over six hundred rubles for my trees." And with this last exalted sentiment, Bazhenov resumed his seat. His mercenary conclusion surely had not been advised by Bykovsky and showed perhaps more clearly than anything else Bazhenov's own true character and total lack of sensitivity to the process in which he was caught up. It would, we feared, hardly turn the court's final deliberations in his favor. However, Judge Shepilov evidently did not contemplate that lengthy deliberations would be necessary in any case. Immediately after Bazhenov's statement, he announced that the court would reconvene for sentencing in fifty minutes.

When the court reconvened, Judge Shepilov immediately began to read an almost interminable but carefully organized decision which rehearsed all the facts of the case and all of the interpretations adduced.

Two pages were devoted to a new description of the condition of Silkin's body after the shotgun blast. Shepilov's view of the case was clear-cut: the murder was ghastly, it was committed for the sake of a few apples, base motives were unmistakably at its root, it clearly fell under Article 136a, defining premeditated murder. The argument of the prosecution had carried the day, and the prosecutor leaned back in his chair with a sigh of satisfaction. Bykovsky did not raise his head from his papers. The audience waited for the sentence to be pronounced in a silence that was electric with anticipation.

"The crime," Judge Shepilov said slowly, "is not merely horrible; it is full of implications which justify our considering it a socially dangerous crime. In light of this fact, the crime falls outside the limits visualized in the scale of normal penalties attached to Article 136a. Because his crime was particularly socially dangerous, the court sentences the accused to the extreme measure of social defense, death by shooting." And then, fairly screaming at the defendant, "Clear enough?"

There was a gasp through the courtroom, and then, for the minute it took the shock to set in, there was silence. The first sound to be heard was a long, low sob from Bazhenov's wife, followed immediately, as if in response, by shouts of "Correct, correct, thank God, thank God" from Silkin's mother and several of her friends. These worn *babas* struggled to their feet and began frantically to cross themselves as they shouted. As the members of the bench filed out, these women pushed toward the aisle and reached out to touch Judge Shepilov as he passed, stern-faced, eyes straight ahead. "Thank God." "Correct, correct." "Thank you, thank you, thank you," they cried.

They turned with curses and imprecations on Bazhenov, who sat slumped in his seat. His wife, who had broken into uncontrollable sobs, they simultaneously belabored with derisive howls of glee and consoled with comments on her still young years and new-won freedom. Finally, they noticed us staring at them, and evidently they sensed a challenge in our look. "The verdict was right; the verdict was right, wasn't it?" several voices demanded.

We shrugged, but the demand was put again and again, more and more imperatively, and, at the same time, more and more imploringly, as if all their conclusions and the rectitude of all their actions hinged on our assent. At last, braving we knew not what, we said that we could not agree with either the verdict or the sentence. They must know as well as we, we said, that the fatal words "socially dangerous" were ordinarily applied only to crimes of high political import or to serious crimes committed by recidivists. The Soviet Union boasted to the entire world that to all intents and purposes it had no death penalty, and the entire world believed that this was so to all intents and purposes, even when it knew about the existence of the extraordinary provision dealing with "socially dangerous crimes."

There was a sudden silence, and then one wrinkled old woman leaned forward and, as the others drew around, whispered, "You don't know Bazhenov. He's a monster, a fiend. Why, just before he killed Silkin, he gnawed the hand from a five-year-old baby whom he caught in his orchard. He's a cannibal. He's had six children of his own, but he's boiled them all in oil. You don't know Bazhenov." The eyes of our aged confidante grew narrower as she spoke; her tone grew ever more mysterious. At first the crowd around us listened with as much wonder as we, but soon they began to nod vigorously. "He ate off a boy's hand," one repeated. "Boiled his own children," rasped another. A village legend, the legend of the monster Bazhenov, was being created. It was as if, having seen Bazhenov's fate, his neighbors had concluded that the accused had to be a satanic fiend. As if this were the only way they could make the outcome of the trial comprehensible. We were the catalysts that called their response forth, but once the moral was established, our belief or disbelief became irrelevant, and no one tried to detain us as we edged out of the circle.

It was only after we had found a café in which to collect our breaths and our thoughts that we realized that perhaps there was a sense in which the response of Bazhenov's fellow villagers was more than merely psychologically noteworthy. Perhaps the trial we had just witnessed had been intended not merely to uphold the law but to point a broader moral.

There was the fact that the Bazhenov case had been singled out for its special interest to law students. There was the whole tenor of Judge Shepilov's initial examination of the accused. There was the prosecutor's concentration on the nonjuridical aspects of the case and his obvious complacency about the outcome. There was the surprise shown at the vigor of Bykovsky's defense of the accused. There was Bykovsky's stress on the illegitimacy of ceremonial trials, coupled, however, with his unwillingness to ask that his client be acquitted. Finally, there was Bykovsky's message to us. Retrospectively, his "You will see" seemed to suggest: "No matter that you are persuaded and impressed by my defense; the key to this case lies outside my influence."

However, though they had, in a sense, been less naïve than we, Bazhenov's neighbors had surely drawn the wrong lesson from the trial. Their legend completely blunted the political and ideological moral the regime intended, which was not that Bazhenov was evil incarnate but raher that he had *become* evil incarnate under the corrupting influence of acquisitiveness and selfishness rooted in the possession of private property. It was not Bazhenov's having succumbed to evil instincts that was to be stressed, but his having succumbed to evil and "backward" instincts—the retrograde instincts of capitalism. The trial, we concluded, was very probably intended to serve as an especially significant object lesson in the regime's perpetual, and recently intensified, campaign against manifestations of the psychology of private ownership.

Yet there remained a puzzle. The regime's campaign against manifestations of the "bourgeois property instinct," while it had been energetic, had not been outrightly terroristic in recent years, especially where the rural population, with its deep-rooted attachment to its garden plots, was concerned. Judge Shepilov's sentence, however, had smacked of outright terrorism. It was, therefore, with some interest that we learned that on appeal by the *prosecutor* the Supreme Court of the Russian republic had reduced Bazhenov's sentence to ten years. Unfortunately, the Supreme Court did not explain the rationale behind its decision. What seemed likely, if our interpretative hypothesis was correct, was that at the original trial Judge Shepilov, aware that the case before him had special political and ideological significance, had overreacted. The purpose of the appeal, then, apart from salving the prosecutor's pride, was to rebuke the judge for his excessive zeal and the distortion of the "true" moral of the trial which was its consequence.

Another possibility was that the Supreme Court was striking against the continued presence of much wider tendencies on the part of some Soviet judges to invoke the "socially dangerous" escape clause in the law code as readily as they had prior to Stalin's death. The reduction of sentence might, that is, have been a partial vindication of legality in the Western sense—an attack on judicial terror in general and not merely on its clumsy use in a politically sensitive situation. But if this had been the intended implication, it would have been conveyed much more effectively had the Supreme Court reviewed the case on an appeal not from the prosecutor but from defense lawyer Bykovsky, or, at the very least, had the Supreme Court followed Bykovsky's recommendations as to the proper article to apply to the case and the appropriate sentence to impose. In short, we still felt that the Bazhenov case was a miscarriage of justice and that the probable explanation lay outside the legal system proper. Certainly Bykovsky was not formally vindicated by the Supreme Court. And yet we were aware that in a long-term perspective, the most significant thing about the Bazhenov trial might well be that Bykovsky's voice was heard.

NORMAN MAILER

Norman Mailer (1923–), born in Long Branch, New Jersey, served in the infantry in the Pacific from 1944 to 1946 and emerged with his first book, *The Naked and the Dead* (1948), to become one of the leading postwar novelists. He and journalist James Breslin ran for mayor and deputy mayor, respectively, in the 1969 New York City Democratic primary election, but Mailer lost to Mario Procaccino, who lost to John Lindsay in the fall.

WHAT IS WRONG WITH THE CITY?

This is the text of the major speech of Mailer's campaign, the more pertinent in the mid-seventies as New York City's financial troubles deepen, and pollution and traffic thicken. The *Detroit Free Press* added the "real politician's" version when it printed Mailer's remarks simultaneously with the *New York Times'* text on May 18, 1969. Compare the two voices thus produced. What differences do you see in language and evidence? Do Orwell's comments on politics and language apply? How would *you* render the "politician's" paraphrase?

How is one to speak of the illness of a city? A clear day can come, a morning in early May like the pride of June. The streets are cool, the buildings have come out of shadow, and silences are broken by the voices of children. It is as if the neighborhood has slept in the winding street of the past. Forty years go by—one can recollect the milkman and the clop of a horse. It is a great city. Everyone speaks of the delight of the day on the way to work. It is hard on such mornings to believe that New York is the victim "etherized on a table."

Yet by afternoon the city is incarcerated once more. Haze covers the sky, a grim, formless glare blazes back from the horizon. The city has become unbalanced again. By the time work is done, New Yorkers push through the acrid lung-rotting air and work their way home, avoiding

AS A REAL POLITICIAN PHRASES IT

My fellow Americans, I speak to you at a time of crisis, a time not only of crisis for our city but for all America. It is a time when great vision is called for. Our cities have many problems.

They are crowded.

Pollution is an ever-growing problem.

Our transportation networks are clogged and inadequate.

Honest citizens fear crime in the streets as never before.

Out of this, a great cry has been heard: "Something must be done." I have heard your cry.

each other's eyes in the subways. Later, near midnight, thinking of a walk to buy the *Times*, they hesitate—in the darkness a familiar sense of dread returns, the streets are not quite safe, the sense of waiting for some apocalyptic fire, some night of long knives hangs over the city. We recognize one more time that the city is ill, that our own New York, the empire city, is not too far from death.

Recollect: When we were children we were told air was invisible, and it was. Now we see it shift and thicken, move in gray depression over a stricken sky. Now we grow used to living with colds all year, and viruses suggestive of plague. Tempers shorten in our hideous air. The sick get sicker, the violent more violent. The frayed tissue of New York manners seems ready to splatter on every city street. It is the first problem of the city, our atrocious air. People do not die dramatically like the one-day victims of Donora,* rather they dwindle imperceptibly, die five years before their time, ten years before, cough or sneeze helplessly into the middle of someone else's good mood, stroll about with the hot iron of future asthma manacled to their lungs.

Contaminants of our air have by now far exceeded acceptable levels.

That is our pervasive ill. It is fed by a host of tributary ills which flow into the air, fed first by our traffic, renowned through the world for its incapacity to move. Midtown Manhattan is next to impenetrable by vehicle from midday to evening—the average rate of advance is, in fact, six miles an hour, about the speed of a horse at a walk. Once free of the center, there is the threat of hourlong tie-ups at

Frankly, the great traffic networks which we viewed with such pride only a few short years ago are now totally inadequate.

---

* On October 30–31, 1948, a poisonous smog covering Donora, Pennsylvania, killed 20 people and made 5,000 ill.—Ed.

every bridge, tunnel, and expressway if even a single car breaks down in a lane. In the course of a year, people lose weeks of working time through the sum of minutes and quarter-hours of waiting to crawl forward in traffic. Tempers blow with lost schedules, work suffers everywhere. All the while stalled cars gun their motors while waiting in place, pumping carbon monoxide into air already laden with caustic sulphur-oxide from fuel oil we burn to make electricity.

Given this daily burden, this air pollution, noise pollution, stagnant transport, all but crippled subways, routes of new transportation twenty years unbuilt— every New Yorker sallies forth into an environment which strips him before noon of his good cheer, his charity, his calm nerve, and his ability to discipline his anger.

Yet, beneath that mood of pestilential clangor, something worse is ticking away— our deeper sense of a concealed and continuing human horror. If there are eight million people in New York, one million live on welfare, no, the figure is higher now, it will be one million two hundred thousand by the end of the year. Not a tenth of these welfare cases will ever be available for work; they are women and children first, then too old, too sick, too addicted, too illiterate, too unskilled, too ignorant of English. Fatherless families and motherless families live at the end of an umbilical financial cord which perpetuates them in an embryonic economic state. Welfare is the single largest item in the city budget—two years ago it surpassed the figure we reserve for education, yet it comes down to payments of no more than $3,800 a year for a family of four. Each member of that family is able to

Let me make myself perfectly clear. The entire system of welfare has broken down. It needs to be restructured along more realistic lines. More than that, we need to make welfare meaningful. We must learn not to give more, but how to give more efficiently.

spend a dollar a day for food, at most $1.25 a day.

Our finances are intolerable. If New York state delivers $17 billion in income tax and $5 billion in corporate taxes to the federal government, it is conservative to assume that $14 billion of the total of $22 billion has come from the people of New York City. But our city budget is about $7½ billion: of that sum only $3 billion derives from the state and from Washington. New York must find another $4½ billion in real estate and other local taxes.

Consider then: we pay $14 billion in income tax to the federal government and to Albany. Back comes $3 billion. We put out five dollars for every dollar which returns. So we live in vistas of ironbound civic poverty. Four of those lost five dollars are going to places like Vietnam and Malmstrom in North Dakota where the ABM will find a site, or dollars are going to interstate highways which pass through regions we probably will never visit. In relation to the federal government, the city is like a sharecropper who lives forever in debt at the company store.

Yes, everything is wrong. The vocations of the past disintegrate. Jewish teachers who went into the education system twenty years ago to have security for themselves and to disseminate enlightenment among the children of the poor, now feel no security in their work, and are rejected in their liberal sociological style of teaching. The collective ego of their life-style is shattered. They are forced to comprehend that there are black people who would rather be taught by other black people than by experts.

The need for authenticity has become the real desire in education. "Who am I? What is the meaning of my skin, my pas-

This city is now operating under an antiquated tax base.

We don't get our money's worth from Uncle Sam . . .

America is still the great melting pot. Our differences are our strengths as well as our weaknesses. We must be able to give to people, whatever their ethnic persuasions, a sense of identity.

sion, my dread, my fury, my dream of glories undreamed, my very need for bread?"—these questions are now becoming so powerful they bring the pumps of blood up to pressure and leave murder in the womb of a dying city and a fury to discover for oneself whether one is victim or potential hero, stupid or too bright for old pedagogical ways. Rage at the frustration of the effort to find a style became the rage at the root of the uproar in the schools last year, and the rage will be there until the schools are free to discover a new way to learn. Let us not be arrogant toward the ignorant—their sensitivity is often too deep to dare the knowledge of numbers or the curlicue within a letter. Picasso, age of eleven, could still not do arithmetic because the figure 7 looked like a nose upside down to him.

Our parks deteriorate, and after duty our police go home to suburbs beyond the city—they come back to govern us from without. And municipal employes drift in the endless administrative bogs of Wagnerian systems of apathy and attrition. Work gets done at the rate of work accomplished by a draft army in peacetime at a sullen out-of-the-way post. The poverty program staggers from the brilliance of its embezzlements. But, of course, if you were a bright young black man, might you not want to steal a million from the feds?

Part of the tragedy, part of the unbelievable oncoming demise of New York is that none of us can simply believe it.

It's hard to believe it's happening to us.

Now all our problems have the magnitude of junkie problems—they are so coexistent with our life that New Yorkers do not try to solve them but escape them. Our fix is to put the blame on the blacks

A lot of us want to blame others, and run from the problem. But, my friends, I think together we can—and will—make things better.

and Puerto Ricans. But everybody knows that nobody can really know where the blame resides. It is the only way he can have the optimism to run. So the prospective candidate writing these words has the heart to consider entering the Democratic primary on June 17 because he thinks he sees a way out of the swamp; better, he believes he glimpses a royal road.

The face of the solution may reside in the notion that the left has been absolutely right on some critical problems of our times, and the conservatives have been altogether correct about one enormous matter—which is that the federal government has no business whatever in local affairs. The style of New York life has shifted since the second world war (along with the rest of the American cities) from a scene of local neighborhoods and personalities to a large dull impersonal style of life which deadens us with its architecture, its highways, its abstract welfare, and its bureaucratic reflex to look for government solutions which come into the city from without (and do not work). So the old confidence that the problems of our life were roughly equal to our abilities has been lost. Our authority has been handed over to the federal power.

How can we begin? By the most brutal view, New York City is today a legislative pail of dismembered organs strewn from Washington to Albany. We are without a comprehensive function or a skin. We cannot begin until we find a function which will become our skin.

It is simple: our city must become a state.

We must look to become a state of the United States separate from New York state: the fifty-first, in fact, of the United

It is simple: Our city must become a state.

States. New York city state, or the state of New York city. It is strange on the tongue, but not so strange.

Think on the problem of this separation. People across the state are oriented toward Buffalo or Albany or Rochester or Montreal or Toronto or Boston or Cleveland. They do not think in great numbers of coming to New York City to make their life. In fact the good farmers and small-town workers of New York State rather detest us. They hear of the evils of our city with quiet thin-lipped glee; in the state legislature they rush to compound those evils. Every time the city needs a program which the state must approve, the city returns with a part of its package —the rest has been lost in deals, compromises, and imposts. The connection of New York City to New York state is a marriage of misery, incompatibility, and abominable old quarrels.

What do the farmers care about urban problems? They don't like us any more than we like them.

Look, we have received no money so far for improving our city transit lines, yet the highway program for America in 1968 was $5 billion. Of this, New York state received at least $350,000,000 for its roads. New York City received not a dollar from Washington or Albany for reconstruction of its 6,000 miles of streets and avenues.

One suggestion is that we could spend our own money, rather than have it spent by all those farmers upstate.

As a city-state we could speak to the federal government in the unmistakable tones of a state. We could claim that a comparable amount is required for our transportation problems which can better be solved by the construction of new rapid transit.

We give to Washington and Albany almost five tax dollars for every dollar which returns; Mississippi, while declaiming the virtues and inviolability of states' rights, still gets four federal dollars for every income-tax dollar she pays up.

Power to the neighborhoods! In the new city-state, every opportunity would be offered to neighborhoods to vote to become townships, villages, hamlets, subboroughs, tracts, or small cities, at which legal point they would be funded directly by the fifty-first state. Many of these neighborhoods would manage their own municipal services, their police, sanitation, fire protection, education, parks, or, like very small towns, they could, if they wished, combine services with other neighborhoods. Each neighborhood would thus begin to outline the style of its local government by the choice of its services.

The grass roots must again be permitted to speak out. Where there is no grass, we must plant it. [laughter] I know what you young people are thinking.

Poorer neighborhoods would obviously look to establish themselves upon their immediate problems. So Harlem, Bedford-Stuyvesant, and the Barrio in East Harlem might be the first to vote for power to their own neighborhoods so that they might be in position to administer their own poverty program, own welfare, their own education systems, and their own—if they so voted—police and sanitation and fire protection for which they would proceed to pay out their funds. They would then be able to hire their own people for their own neighborhood jobs and services.

And so, I say we must return to self-determination. To control by the people of their own destiny.

Power to the neighborhoods would mean that any neighborhood could constitute itself on any principle, whether spiritual, emotional, economical, ideological, or idealistic.

To the degree that we have lost faith in the power of the government to conduct our lives, so would the principle of power to the neighborhoods begin to thrive, so too would the first spiritual problem of the twentieth century—alienation from the self—be given a tool by which to rediscover oneself.

In New York, which is to say, in the twentieth-century, one can never know whether the world is vastly more or less violent than it seems. Nor can we discover which actions in our lives are authentic or which belong to the art of the put-on. Conceive that society has come to the point where tolerance of others' idea has no meaning unless there is benumbed acceptance of the fact that we must accept their lives. If there are young people who believe that human liberty is blockaded until they have the right to take off their clothes in the street—and more! and more!—make love on the hood of an automobile—there are others who think it is a sin against the eyes of the Lord even to contemplate the act in one's mind.

Both could now begin to build communities on their separate faith—a spectrum which might run from compulsory free love to mandatory attendance in church on Sunday! Grant us to recognize that wherever there is a common desire among people vital enough to keep a community alive, then there must be also the presence of a clue that some kind of real life resides in the desire. Others may eventually discern how.

Which is where we go now—into the campaign: To talk in the days ahead of what power to the neighborhoods will mean. We will go down the steps of the position papers and talk of jobs and housing and welfare, of education, municipal unions, and law and order, finance, the names of laws, the statistics of the budget, the problems of traffic and transportation. There will be a paucity of metaphor and a taste of stale saliva to the debates, for voters are hard-working people who trust

Whatever you believe, well, ladies and gentlemen, you could do your thing.

the plain more than the poetic. How then can Mailer and Breslin, two writers with reputations notorious enough for four, ever hope to convince the voting hand of the electorate? What would they do if, miracle of political explosions, they were to win?

Well, they might cry like Mario Procaccino, for they would never have a good time again; but they would serve, they would learn on the job, they would conduct their education in public. They would be obliged to. And indeed the supposition could remain that they might even do well, better than the men before them. How else could they have the confidence to run?

As for the fact that they were literary men—that might be the first asset of all. They would know how to talk to the people—they would be forced to govern by the fine art of the voice. And best of all, what a tentative confidence would reign in the eye of New York that her literary men, used to dealing with the proportions of worlds hitherto created only in the mind, might now have a sensitive nose for the balances and the battles, the tugs, the pushing, the heaves of that city whose declaration of new birth was implicit in the extraordinary fact that him, Mailer! and him, Breslin! had been voted in.

Sweet Sunday, dear friends, and take a chance. We are out of the lottery of the years.

You say we can't govern because of our background. Well, I say give us a try.

So let us try. Get out and vote for us!

JAMES HARVEY ROBINSON

James Harvey Robinson (1863–1936), a historian at Columbia with degrees from Harvard and Freiburg, resigned in 1919 to protest a violation of academic freedom and wrote his most famous book, *The Mind in the Making* (1921), from which this selection comes.

ON VARIOUS KINDS OF THINKING

This essay gets behind our rationalizations to our real reasons as compared to those defenses we call our "good" reasons. Robinson makes an
important point, but the making would be as dry as straw were it not for
his informed and intelligent ease. His voice is pleasant. Somebody is
home. Notice his metaphorical alertness: "not compromise us too *nakedly*," "the *spigot* of speech." In addition to these metaphors, which
give his thoughts visualization, observe the other illustrations and examples that help us to *see* his points.

The truest and most profound observations on Intelligence have in
the past been made by the poets and, in recent times, by story-writers.
They have been keen observers and recorders and reckoned freely with
the emotions and sentiments. Most philosophers, on the other hand,
have exhibited a grotesque ignorance of man's life and have built up
systems that are elaborate and imposing, but quite unrelated to actual
human affairs. They have almost consistently neglected the actual process of thought and have set the mind off as something apart to be
studied by itself. *But no such mind, exempt from bodily processes,
animal impulses, savage traditions, infantile impressions, conventional
reactions, and traditional knowledge, ever existed,* even in the case of
the most abstract of metaphysicians. Kant entitled his great work *A
Critique of Pure Reason.* But to the modern student of mind pure reason seems as mythical as the pure gold, transparent as glass, with which
the celestial city is paved.

Formerly philosophers thought of mind as having to do exclusively
with conscious thought. It was that within man which perceived, remembered, judged, reasoned, understood, believed, willed. But of late
it has been shown that we are unaware of a great part of what we
perceive, remember, will, and infer; and that a great part of the thinking
of which we are aware is determined by that of which we are not conscious. It has indeed been demonstrated that our unconscious psychic
life far outruns our conscious. . . .

We do not think enough about thinking, and much of our confusion
is the result of current illusions in regard to it. Let us forget for the
moment any impressions we may have derived from the philosophers,
and see what seems to happen in ourselves. The first thing that we
notice is that our thought moves with such incredible rapidity that it is
almost impossible to arrest any specimen of it long enough to have a
look at it. When we are offered a penny for our thoughts we always
find that we have recently had so many things in mind that we can

easily make a selection which will not compromise us too nakedly. On inspection we shall find that even if we are not downright ashamed of a great part of our spontaneous thinking it is far too intimate, personal, ignoble, or trivial to permit us to reveal more than a small part of it. I believe this must be true of everyone. We do not, of course, know what goes on in other people's heads. They tell us very little and we tell them very little. The spigot of speech, rarely fully opened, could never emit more than driblets of the ever renewed hogshead of thought—*noch grösser wie's Heidelberger Fass.** We find it hard to believe that other people's thoughts are as silly as our own, but they probably are.

Reverie

We all appear to ourselves to be thinking all the time during our waking hours, and most of us are aware that we go on thinking while we are asleep, even more foolishly than when awake. When uninterrupted by some practical issue we are engaged in what is now known as a *reverie.* This is our spontaneous and favorite kind of thinking. We allow our ideas to take their own course and this course is determined by our hopes and fears, our spontaneous desires, their fulfillment or frustration; by our likes and dislikes, our loves and hates and resentments. There is nothing else anything like so interesting to ourselves as ourselves. All thought that is not more or less laboriously controlled and directed will inevitably circle about the beloved Ego. It is amusing and pathetic to observe this tendency in ourselves and in others. We learn politely and generously to overlook this truth, but if we dare to think of it, it blazes forth like the noontide sun. . . .

Deciding

The reverie, as any of us can see for himself, is frequently broken and interrupted by the necessity of a second kind of thinking. We have to make practical decisions. Shall we write a letter or no? Shall we take the subway or a bus? Shall we have dinner at seven or half past? Shall we buy U.S. Rubber or a Liberty Bond? Decisions are easily distinguishable from the free flow of the reverie. Sometimes they demand a good deal of careful pondering and the recollection of pertinent facts; often, however, they are made impulsively. They are a more difficult and

---

* "Bigger still than Heidelberg's vat": a 49,000-gallon wine-vat, built in 1751, in the cellar of Heidelberg Castle.—Ed.

laborious thing than the reverie, and we resent having to "make up our mind" when we are tired, or absorbed in a congenial reverie. Weighing a decision, it should be noted, does not necessarily add anything to our knowledge, although we may, of course, seek further information before making it.

Rationalizing

A third kind of thinking is stimulated when anyone questions our belief and opinions. We sometimes find ourselves changing our minds without any resistance or heavy emotion, but if we are told that we are wrong we resent the imputation and harden our hearts. We are incredibly heedless in the formation of our beliefs, but find ourselves filled with an illicit passion for them when anyone proposes to rob us of their companionship. It is obviously not the ideas themselves that are dear to us, but our self-esteem, which is threatened. We are by nature stubbornly pledged to defend our own from attack, whether it be our person, our family, our property, or our opinion. A United States Senator once remarked to a friend of mine that God Almighty could not make him change his mind on our Latin-America policy. We may surrender, but rarely confess ourselves vanquished. In the intellectual world at least peace is without victory.

Few of us take the pains to study the origin of our cherished convictions; indeed, we have a natural repugnance to so doing. We like to continue to believe what we have been accustomed to accept as true, and the resentment aroused when doubt is cast upon any of our assumptions leads us to seek every manner of excuse for clinging to them. *The result is that most of our so-called reasoning consists in finding arguments for going on believing as we already do.*

I remember years ago attending a public dinner to which the Governor of the state was bidden. The chairman explained that His Excellency could not be present for certain "good" reasons; what the "real" reasons were the presiding officer said he would leave us to conjecture. This distinction between "good" and "real" reasons is one of the most clarifying and essential in the whole realm of thought. We can readily give what seem to us "good" reasons for being a Catholic or a Mason, a Republican or a Democrat, an adherent or opponent of the League of Nations. But the "real" reasons are usually on quite a different plane. Of course the importance of this distinction is popularly, if somewhat obscurely, recognized. The Baptist missionary is ready enough to see that the Buddhist is not such because his doctrines would bear careful inspection, but because he happened to be born in a Buddhist family in Tokio. But it would be treason to his faith to acknowledge that his own partiality for certain doctrines is due to the fact that his mother was a member of the First Baptist church of Oak Ridge. A savage can give all sorts of reasons for his belief that it is dangerous to step on a man's shadow, and a newspaper editor can advance plenty of arguments against the Bolsheviki. But neither of them may realize why he happens to be defending his particular opinion.

The "real" reasons for our beliefs are concealed from ourselves as well as from others. As we grow up we simply adopt the ideas presented to us in regard to such matters as religion, family relations, property, business, our country, and the state. We unconsciously absorb them from our environment. They are persistently whispered in our ear by the group in which we happen to live. Opinions, on the other hand, which are the result of experience or of honest reasoning do not have this quality of "primary certitude." I remember when as a youth I heard a group of business men discussing the question of the immortality of the soul, I was outraged by the sentiment of doubt expressed by one of the party. As I look back now I see that I had at the time no interest in the matter, and certainly no least argument to urge in favor of the belief in which I had been reared. But neither my personal indifference to the issue, nor the fact that I had previously given it no attention, served to prevent an angry resentment when I heard *my* ideas questioned.

This spontaneous and loyal support of our preconceptions—this process of finding "good" reasons to justify our routine beliefs—is known to modern psychologists as "rationalizing"—clearly only a new name for a very ancient thing. Our "good" reasons ordinarily have no value in promoting honest enlightenment because, no matter how solemnly they may be marshaled, they are at bottom the result of personal preference or prejudice, and not of an honest desire to seek or accept new knowledge.

In our reveries we are frequently engaged in self-justification, for we cannot bear to think ourselves wrong, and yet have constant illustrations of our weaknesses and mistakes. So we spend much time finding fault with circumstances and the conduct of others, and shifting on to them with great ingenuity the onus of our own failures and disappointments. *Rationalizing is the self-exculpation which occurs when we feel ourselves, or our group, accused of misapprehension or error.*

The little word *my* is the most important one in all human affairs, and properly to reckon with it is the beginning of wisdom. It has the same force whether it is *my* dinner, *my* dog, and *my* house, or *my* faith, *my* country, and *my* God. We not only resent the imputation that our watch is wrong, or our car shabby, but that our conception of the canals of Mars, of the pronunciation of "Epictetus," of the medicinal value of salicine, or the date of Sargon I, is subject to revision.

Philosophers, scholars, and men of science exhibit a common sensitiveness in all decisions in which their *amour propre** is involved. Thousands of argumentative works have been written to vent a grudge. However stately their reasoning, it may be nothing but rationalizing, stimulated by the most commonplace of all motives. A history of philosophy and theology could be written in terms of grouches, wounded pride, and aversions, and it would be far more instructive than the usual treatments of these themes. Sometimes, under Providence, the lowly impulse of resentment leads to great achievements. Milton wrote his treatise on divorce as a result of his troubles with his seventeen-year-old wife, and when he was accused of being the leading spirit in a new sect, the Divorcers, he wrote his noble *Areopagitica* to prove his right to say what he thought fit, and incidentally to establish the advantage of a free press in the promotion of Truth.

All mankind, high and low, thinks in all the ways which have been described. The reverie goes on all the time not only in the mind of the mill hand and the Broadway flapper, but equally in weighty judges and godly bishops. It has gone on in all the philosophers, scientists, poets, and theologians that have ever lived. Aristotle's most abstruse speculations were doubtless tempered by highly irrelevant reflections. He is reported to have had very thin legs and small eyes, for which he doubtless had to find excuses, and he was wont to indulge in very conspicuous dress and rings and was accustomed to arrange his hair carefully.† Diogenes the Cynic exhibited the impudence of a touchy soul. His tub was his distinction. Tennyson in beginning his "Maud" could not forget his chagrin over losing his patrimony years before as the result of an unhappy investment in the Patent Decorative Carving Company. These facts are not recalled here as a gratuitous disparagement of the truly great, but to insure a full realization of the tremendous competition which all really exacting thought has to face, even in the minds of the most highly endowed mortals.

And now the astonishing and perturbing suspicion emerges that perhaps almost all that had passed for social science, political economy, politics, and ethics in the past may be brushed aside by future generations as mainly rationalizing. John Dewey has already reached this

* "Self-love."—Ed.
† Diogenes Laertius, book v.

conclusion in regard to philosophy.* Veblen† and other writers have revealed the various unperceived presuppositions of the traditional political economy, and now comes an Italian sociologist, Vilfredo Pareto, who, in his huge treatise on general sociology, devotes hundreds of pages to substantiating a similar thesis affecting all the social sciences.‡ This conclusion may be ranked by students of a hundred years hence as one of the several great discoveries of our age. It is by no means fully worked out, and it is so opposed to nature that it will be very slowly accepted by the great mass of those who consider themselves thoughtful. As a historical student I am personally fully reconciled to this newer view. Indeed, it seems to me inevitable that just as the various sciences of nature were, before the opening of the seventeenth century, largely masses of rationalizations to suit the religious sentiments of the period, so the social sciences have continued even to our own day to be rationalizations of uncritically accepted beliefs and customs.

It will become apparent as we proceed that the fact that an idea is ancient and that it has been widely received is no argument in its favor, but should immediately suggest the necessity of carefully testing it as a probable instance of rationalization.

How Creative Thought Transforms the World

This brings us to another kind of thought which can fairly easily be distinguished from the three kinds described above. It has not the usual qualities of the reverie, for it does not hover about our personal complacencies and humiliations. It is not made up of the homely decisions forced upon us by everyday needs, when we review our little stock of existing information, consult our conventional preferences and obligations, and make a choice of action. It is not the defense of our own cherished beliefs and prejudices just because they are our own—mere plausible excuses for remaining of the same mind. On the contrary, it is that peculiar species of thought which leads us to *change* our mind.

---

* *Reconstruction in Philosophy.*

† *The Place of Science in Modern Civilization.*

‡ *Traité de Sociologie Générale, passim.* The author's term *"derivations"* seems to be his precise way of expressing what we have called the "good" reasons, and his *"residus"* correspond to the "real" reasons. He well says, *"L'homme éprouve le besoin de raisonner, et en outre d'étendre un voile sur ses instincts et sur ses sentiments"* ["Man feels the need to reason, and moreover to spread a veil over his instincts and his feelings."]—hence, rationalization. His aim is to reduce sociology to the "real" reasons.

It is this kind of thought that has raised man from his pristine, sub-savage ignorance and squalor to the degree of knowledge and comfort which he now possesses. On his capacity to continue and greatly extend this kind of thinking depends his chance of groping his way out of the plight in which the most highly civilized peoples of the world now find themselves. In the past this type of thinking has been called Reason. But so many misapprehensions have grown up around the word that some of us have become very suspicious of it. I suggest, therefore, that we substitute a recent name and speak of "creative thought" rather than of Reason. *For this kind of meditation begets knowledge, and knowledge is really creative inasmuch as it makes things look different from what they seemed before and may indeed work for their reconstruction.*

In certain moods some of us realize that we are observing things or making reflections with a seeming disregard of our personal preoccupations. We are not preening or defending ourselves; we are not faced by the necessity of any practical decision, nor are we apologizing for believing this or that. We are just wondering and looking and mayhap seeing what we never perceived before.

Curiosity is as clear and definite as any of our urges. We wonder what is in a sealed telegram or in a letter in which some one else is absorbed, or what is being said in the telephone booth or in low conversation. This inquisitiveness is vastly stimulated by jealousy, suspicion, or any hint that we ourselves are directly or indirectly involved. But there appears to be a fair amount of personal interest in other people's affairs even when they do not concern us except as a mystery to be unraveled or a tale to be told. The reports of a divorce suit will have "news value" for many weeks. They constitute a story, like a novel or play or moving picture. This is not an example of pure curiosity, however, since we readily identify ourselves with others, and their joys and despair then become our own.

We also take note of, or "observe," as Sherlock Holmes says, things which have nothing to do with our personal interests and make no personal appeal either direct or by way of sympathy. This is what Veblen so well calls "idle curiosity." And it is usually idle enough. Some of us when we face the line of people opposite us in a subway train impulsively consider them in detail and engage in rapid inferences and form theories in regard to them. On entering a room there are those who will perceive at a glance the degree of preciousness of the rugs, the character of the pictures, and the personality revealed by the books. But there are many, it would seem, who are so absorbed in their personal reverie or in some definite purpose that they have no bright-eyed energy for idle curiosity. The tendency to miscellaneous observation we come by honestly enough, for we note it in many of our animal relatives.

Veblen, however, uses the term "idle curiosity" somewhat ironically, as is his wont. It is idle only to those who fail to realize that it may be a very rare and indispensable thing from which almost all distinguished human achievement proceeds. Since it may lead to systematic examination and seeking for things hitherto undiscovered. For research is but diligent search which enjoys the high flavor of primitive hunting. Occasionally and fitfully idle curiosity thus leads to creative thought, which alters and broadens our own views and aspirations and may in turn, under highly favorable circumstances, affect the views and lives of others, even for generations to follow. An example or two will make this unique human process clear.

Galileo was a thoughtful youth and doubtless carried on a rich and varied reverie. He had artistic ability and might have turned out to be a musician or painter. When he had dwelt among the monks at Valambrosa he had been tempted to lead the life of a religious. As a boy he busied himself with toy machines and he inherited a fondness for mathematics. All these facts are of record. We may safely assume also that, along with many other subjects of contemplation, the Pisan maidens found a vivid place in his thoughts.

One day when seventeen years old he wandered into the cathedral of his native town. In the midst of his reverie he looked up at the lamps hanging by long chains from the high ceiling of the church. Then something very difficult to explain occurred. He found himself no longer thinking of the building, worshipers, or the services; of his artistic or religious interests; of his reluctance to become a physician as his father wished. He forgot the question of a career and even the *graziosissime donne*.* As he watched the swinging lamps he was suddenly wondering if mayhap their oscillations, whether long or short, did not occupy the same time. Then he tested this hypothesis by counting his pulse, for that was the only timepiece he had with him.

This observation, however remarkable in itself, was not enough to produce a really creative thought. Others may have noticed the same thing and yet nothing came of it. Most of our observations have no assignable results. Galileo may have seen that the warts on a peasant's face formed a perfect isosceles triangle, or he may have noticed with boyish glee that just as the officiating priest was uttering the solemn

* "So lovely girls."—Ed.

words *ecce agnus Dei,* a fly lit on the end of his nose. To be really creative, ideas have to be worked up and then "put over," so that they become a part of man's social heritage. The highly accurate pendulum clock was one of the later results of Galileo's discovery. He himself was led to reconsider and successfully to refute the old notions of falling bodies. It remained for Newton to prove that the moon was falling, and presumably all the heavenly bodies. This quite upset all the consecrated views of the heavens as managed by angelic engineers. The universality of the laws of gravitation stimulated the attempt to seek other and equally important natural laws and cast grave doubts on the miracles in which mankind had hitherto believed. In short, those who dared to include in their thought the discoveries of Galileo and his successors found themselves in a new earth surrounded by new heavens.

On the 28th of October, 1831, three hundred and fifty years after Galileo had noticed the isochronous vibrations of the lamps, creative thought and its currency had so far increased that Faraday was wondering what would happen if he mounted a disk of copper between the poles of a horseshoe magnet. As the disk revolved an electric current was produced. This would doubtless have seemed the idlest kind of an experiment to the stanch business men of the time, who, it happened, were just then denouncing the child-labor bills in their anxiety to avail themselves to the full of the results of earlier idle curiosity. But should the dynamos and motors which have come into being as the outcome of Faraday's experiment be stopped this evening, the business man of to-day, agitated over labor troubles, might, as he trudged home past lines of "dead" cars, through dark streets to an unlighted house, engage in a little creative thought of his own and perceive that he and his laborers would have no modern factories and mines to quarrel about had it not been for the strange practical effects of the idle curiosity of scientists, inventors, and engineers.

The examples of creative intelligence given above belong to the realm of modern scientific achievement, which furnishes the most striking instances of the effects of scrupulous, objective thinking. But there are, of course, other great realms in which the recording and embodiment of acute observation and insight have wrought themselves into the higher life of man. The great poets and dramatists and our modern story-tellers have found themselves engaged in productive reveries, noting and artistically presenting their discoveries for the delight and instruction of those who have the ability to appreciate them.

The process by which a fresh and original poem or drama comes into being is doubtless analogous to that which originates and elaborates so-called scientific discoveries; but there is clearly a temperamental difference. The genesis and advance of painting, sculpture, and music offer still other problems. We really as yet know shockingly little about these matters, and indeed very few people have the least curiosity about them. Nevertheless, creative intelligence in its various forms and activities is what makes man. Were it not for its slow, painful, and constantly discouraged operations through the ages man would be no more than a species of primate living on seeds, fruit, roots, and uncooked flesh, and wandering naked through the woods and over the plains like a chimpanzee. . . .

The "real" reasons, which explain how it is we happen to hold a particular belief, are chiefly historical. Our most important opinions—those, for example, having to do with traditional, religious, and moral convictions, property rights, patriotism, national honor, the state, and indeed all the assumed foundations of society—are, as I have already suggested, rarely the result of reasoned consideration, but of unthinking absorption from the social environment in which we live. Consequently, they have about them a quality of "elemental certitude," and we especially resent doubt or criticism cast upon them. So long, however, as we revere the whisperings of the herd, we are obviously unable to examine them dispassionately and to consider to what extent they are suited to the novel conditions and social exigencies in which we find ourselves to-day.

The "real" reasons for our beliefs, by making clear their origins and history, can do much to dissipate this emotional blockade and rid us of our prejudices and preconceptions. Once this is done and we come critically to examine our traditional beliefs, we may well find some of them sustained by experience and honest reasoning, while others must be revised to meet new conditions and our more extended knowledge. But only after we have undertaken such a critical examination in the light of experience and modern knowledge, freed from any feeling of "primary certitude," can we claim that the "good" are also the "real" reasons for our opinions.

I do not flatter myself that this general show-up of man's thought through the ages will cure myself or others of carelessness in adopting ideas, or of unseemly heat in defending them just because we have adopted them. But if the considerations which I propose to recall are really incorporated into our thinking and are permitted to establish our general outlook on human affairs, they will do much to relieve the imaginary obligation we feel in regard to traditional sentiments and ideals. Few of us are capable of engaging in creative thought, but some of us can at least come to distinguish it from other and inferior kinds of thought and accord to it the esteem that it merits as the greatest treasure of the past and the only hope of the future.

ALAN PATON

Alan Paton (1903–), of English descent, was educated at the University of Natal in Pietermaritzburg, South Africa, the city of his birth. He taught in a school for Zulus in the village of Ixopo, Natal, headed a reformatory for black juvenile delinquents in Johannesburg (taking down barbed wire and planting geraniums), and eventually, on a tour of prisons in Sweden, wrote the first chapter of his great novel, *Cry, the Beloved Country* (1948). For his championship of racial freedom, he has been forbidden to leave South Africa.

THE CHALLENGE OF FEAR

This essay examines the hopeful assumptions of progress and virtue rewarded that seem to have prevailed before World War I, as well as the fear that lies behind our rationalizations, our prejudices, our inhumanities. How does Paton reinforce what Orwell says? what Robinson and Popper say? Notice the kind of evidence he adduces, and how he puts himself in evidence.

One of the big lessons that life has taught me is that my earlier understanding of man and his society was wretchedly inadequate. An extraordinary thing, is it not, that one should begin to acquire an understanding of them both when one is drawing near to the end of his acquaintance with them? The richer one grows in wisdom, the shorter becomes the time in which to use it.

Just how it happened that my understanding was so inadequate, I don't quite know. My parents certainly never taught me that man was growing better and better and that the future was therefore in some way assured. They certainly taught me to seek after righteousness, but they never taught me that righteousness would in a temporal and political sense be successful. Nor did I ever learn this at school. Yet that is what I grew up believing. Why should this be so?

I can only think that it was taught to me after all, not by father or mother or teacher or priest, but because it was a basic assumption of the pre-1914 society into which I was born. I am surprised to find that this view of man and life was shared by many all over the world who were born at that time. I am surprised because my own particular world was a very particular one indeed. It was the town of Pietermaritzburg, Natal, founded by the Afrikaner trekkers, but intensely British at the time of my birth in 1903, most of the trekkers having gone to the Transvaal after the British annexation of Natal. My world was intensely pro-

Empire, devoted to the Royal Family, moved to excitement and pride when the red-coated soldiers of the British garrison marched down the street past our home, with arms swinging and drums beating and fifes blowing, to the old Polo Ground to parade for the King's birthday.

There were 30,000 people in Pietermaritzburg in my boyhood, more than half of them Africans and Indians, of whose existence we knew and of whose lives we did not. They were not persons. The Africans were servants, or they dug up the roads. The Indians sold fruit and vegetables, in baskets fastened one to the front and the other to the back end of a flexible strip of bamboo carried on the shoulder, the baskets swaying up and down with a springy motion.

This faulty understanding of man and life has been called by some the romantic illusion, and can be entertained in different places and at different times in history, but in our illusion the might of the British Empire, the indomitable British Navy, and the *Pax Britannica* were particular elements. The world was good, and it was going to stay good, perhaps even become better.

I had no conception at that age of the way in which man could create tremendous, noble-sounding slogans, and could shout them aloud while doing ignoble actions; and what is more, the louder the shout, the greater the ignobleness could be. I had no conception of the need of so much of mankind, while it was actually employed in self-seeking and self-securing, to cling simultaneously to unself-centered religion and altruistic ethics. Nor did I realize that man could so easily deceive himself that his highest religious and ethical values were identical with his own self-interest. And there must have been a great many people like me; otherwise why did George Orwell's *1984* create such a sensation among us?

The extraordinary thing about all this is that I ought to have known it. My parents gave me a religious upbringing, and the reading of the gospel story should have prepared me better for the world with its scribes and pharisees and the crucifixion of Jesus through the instruments of church and state. I take that story seriously, for I believe that in some societies one cannot be true to one's highest beliefs without paying for it in suffering. This is more true in the totalitarian and the semitotalitarian societies (of which Nazi Germany is an example of the first and South Africa an example of the second) than in countries such as America and Britain. In South Africa, one may say with safety that apartheid is misguided, but it is dangerous to say that it is cruel or to oppose it too vigorously.

Not only the Gospel, but history also should have taught me to know better. There is, for one thing, the tale of man's innumerable wars, and of his inhumanity to other men. The early Christians were persecuted by the state, but when Christianity became a state religion, it was not long before the church began persecuting and burning heretics. For centuries, the Jews suffered unspeakably at the hands of Christians, who had no difficulty in believing that they were doing a good thing, and doing it in the name of Christ, who taught that one must love one's neighbor as oneself and had made it very clear who one's neighbor was.

Not even the World War of 1914 shattered my pre-1914 world, though today to read of the terrible and useless slaughter of the bright youth of Britain, France, and Germany leaves one appalled. It was Adolf Hitler who finally destroyed for me—and for many others—the romantic illusion. Dachau, Belsen, Auschwitz—these places gave me an education which was not available in Pietermaritzburg. So one suddenly learns in age the truth of a saying heard in youth; namely, that life is the greatest teacher of them all.

What Hitler taught me about man and nature was sobering enough, but life taught me two further lessons. The first was that, whatever Hitler had taught me about man, I must on no account forget that all over the world men and women, both young and old, would offer their lives in the fight against totalitarian rule and the doctrine of race superiority because they believed them to be evil. The second lesson was quite different, and that was that some of these same men and women twenty years later would begin to support the very things that they had fought against, and to approve of the punishment without trial of those who opposed the doctrine of apartheid, but had committed no known offense.

And why do they behave like this? Have they suddenly, or even gradually, become corrupted? And if so, why? Surely the answer is that the nature of their security—and that means the nature of their self-interest—has changed. In 1939, their security was the British Empire and the Navy. In 1967, amid the turbulence and uncertainties of modern Africa, their security appears to them to lie in white supremacy and apartheid. With the change of one's self-interest, there comes also a change in one's ideology, one's values, one's principles.

This discovery of the complexity of human nature was accompanied by another—the discovery of the complexity and irrationality of human motive, the discovery that one could love and hate simultaneously, be honest and cheat, be arrogant and humble, be any pair of opposites that one had supposed to be mutually exclusive. This, I believe, is not common knowledge and would be incomprehensible to many. It has always been known, of course, by the dramatists and the novelists. It is, in fact, a knowledge far more disturbing to other people than to writers, for to writers it is the grist to their mills.

Nor was I aware when I was young (both as boy and as man) how powerful a motive is fear, even though I myself had many fears. As I write this, I am searching for an explanation of the fact that under some circumstances men readily admit fear, and under other circumstances do not. I assume that readiness to admit fear is part of a general readiness to look at the world as it is, and therefore at oneself as one is, while unwillingness to admit fear may be a strong element in self-esteem. One does not readily admit to a fear of which one is ashamed.

Now, while fear has its important uses, such as causing an outflow of adrenalin which helps one run away faster, it is a wretched determinant of conduct. There is nothing more pitiable than a human being whose conduct is largely determined by fear. Furthermore, it is a destroyer of reason and the rational life. What can be done to control it, check it, or even eliminate it?

Here I must use language which will be out of fashion for some, and I must use reasoning which will seem quite unreal to others. Life has taught me that John uttered the plain and simple truth when he wrote that there is no fear in love, but that perfect love casts out fear. In one sense, the opposite of fear is courage, but in the dynamic sense the opposite of fear is love, whether this be love of man or love of justice.

It is clearly not enough to tell a fearful man that if he would only love more, he would fear less. In an age when leprosy was feared much more than it is today, that rich and spoiled young man, Francis of Assisi, impelled by some sudden and irresistible emotion, got down from his gaily caparisoned horse and embraced a leper in the road. From that day, he feared nothing, and taught thousands of others to fear nothing. Yet few of us are visited by such irresistible emotion.

How does one help ordinary men and women, if not to eliminate fear, at least to keep it within bounds, so that reason may play a stronger role in the affairs of men and nations and so that men may cease to pursue policies which must lead to the very disasters they fear? To me, this is the most important question that confronts the human race.

I note that it is more and more widely held that poverty and inequality of opportunity are among the greatest causes of tension between man and man, between race and race, and between nation and nation. I believe that race tension in my own country would be amazingly abated if the disparity between average white income and average black income were not so overwhelming. I believe that tension between America and Russia has declined since Russia became one of the productive nations. Yet when men are ruled by fear, they strive to prevent the very changes that will abate it.

Fear of change is, no doubt, in all of us, but it most afflicts the man who fears that any change must lead to loss of his wealth and status. When this fear becomes inordinate, he will, if he has political power, abrogate such things as civil rights and the rule of law, using the argument that he abrogates them only to preserve them. In my own country, the government, in order to preserve Christian civilization, uses methods incompatible with Christianity and abrogates values which are essential to any civilization which calls itself Christian. If only a man would say, "I do this because I'm afraid," one could bear it; but when he says, "I do this because I'm good," that is a bit too much.

I see no hope for the peace of society or the peace of the world so long as this fear of change is so powerful. And this fear will remain powerful so long as the one side has so much to gain and the other so much to lose.

I should like to make one point clear, and that is that I do not believe that a more equitable distribution of wealth will automatically bring the Great Society. The point I am trying to make is that if it is not done, there will never be any Great Society. Nor will there be any peace for the world.

Can a school prepare our children for the complexity and waywardness of man? Is it not more likely that these lessons can be taught only by living? There would be the danger that some children might learn to believe a contrary illusion, namely, that man is cruel, cunning, and deceitful. If I remember my childhood and boyhood correctly, and perhaps even my experience as a young teacher, one actually protected children against knowing too much of the worse sides of man's nature. My readers know, no doubt, the story of the businessman who put his young son on the roof of the house, and, standing below, said, "Jump, son, and Daddy will catch you." So the boy jumped, and Daddy didn't catch him, but instead said to him, "Son, that will teach you to trust nobody." One could hardly do that. But one could, while holding up the goals of honesty, kindness, loyalty, tolerance, integrity, tell children a bit of what the world is like. I would also assume that the children of 1967 know far more about man and his nature and society than did the children of the pre-1914 days; it must be almost impossible for children of today to cherish the old romantic illusion.

One must not suppose, however, that because children have lost the romantic illusion and look upon life and the world and their parents with a more calculating eye that they are now free of illusions. In South Africa, many white children cherish the illusion that they are, in many important ways, superior to other children, and I regret to add that many non-white children entertain the illusion that they are, in many important ways, inferior to white children. Another powerful illusion handed down to many white children is that their country is perfect and their government wholly just and benign, so that they lose all faculty for self-criticism.

I have known people who, when their romantic illusion is finally destroyed, cease to believe anything except that man is bad and life intolerable; who feel that they have come, to use Thomas Wolfe's magnificent words, from the prison of their mothers' flesh "into the unspeakable and incommunicable prison of this earth." I presume they would say that this is what life has taught them. It is my fortune to be able to say that though life destroyed my romantic illusion, she did not teach me the contrary illusion. It would appear either that she does not teach the same lessons to everybody, or that other factors operate besides experience, such as temperament, character, religious faith, and sheer luck and good fortune.

I certainly had good fortune in marriage and children and friends —especially those friends who, with me, have challenged the beliefs and practices of a color-bar society—and it is these personal relationships that have saved me from the melancholy that besets the wholly disillusioned. I call this my luck because it is very difficult, and perhaps impossible, to achieve such a state by act of will. You may say to a friend, "Don't worry; worry changes nothing," but that in itself will not stop him from worrying. Life has taught me—and this is my luck— that active loving saves one from a morbid preoccupation with the shortcomings of society and the waywardness of men.

I should again make it clear at this point that I am not saying that human society is unimprovable. What I am saying is that the problems of creating the Great Society are immensely greater than many of us were taught to believe and that we would have been better equipped to deal with them if we had understood their nature and difficulty better. To give up the task of reforming society is to give up one's responsibility as a free man. The task itself is endless, and large parts of it, sometimes the whole of it, must be performed anew by each succeeding generation.

Now, while life was teaching me these lessons, she was leading me in what would appear to be a quite contrary or at least contradictory direction. Here I must refer directly to my own local and particular situation as a white South African. While, on the one hand, I was discarding the romantic illusion about men and society, on the other I was beginning to rebel against the man-made barriers of race and color that divided man from man and to cherish a new ideal of society, which would be judged by some to be an illusion no less romantic than the one it was replacing.

When I first set out in this direction, the road was certainly unusual, whereas later it was to become dangerous, owing to the coming to power of a government which took to itself supra-legal powers enabling it to banish, silence, confine to small areas, debar from certain occupations and from attending any social or political gathering, any person who in the opinion of the Minister was "furthering the aims of Communism." Many non-Communists were dealt with in this way, without charge, trial, or sentence; some of these were my own fellow liberals, whose only offenses had been that they had ignored conventional race barriers or had been active in providing legal defense for political prisoners and aid for their dependents.

Whereas South Africa teaches many of its people to fear and to hate racial mixing (and I use the word "mixing" in its widest, not its narrowest sense), here it was teaching me the opposite, and teaching me to see our future as being that of one nonracial society and not a collection of strictly separated and individual race groups. The whole philosophy of apartheid is based on the fundamental assumption that there can be no such thing as a nonracial society, and that each individual realizes himself only through his membership in his own racial group, and that, therefore, it is the duty of the government to preserve these racial differences, in language, education, sex, marriage, sport, entertainment, and so on and so on. The apostle of apartheid would further declare that it is only another romantic illusion to imagine that an Afrikaner Calvinist, an English-speaking Anglican (Episcopalian), a colored (that is, of mixed blood) Roman Catholic, an African Methodist, an African ancestor-worshipper, an Indian Hindu, and an Indian Muslim—not to mention those who profess no particular faith—could operate a common nonracial society. The apostle of apartheid says he is a realist and that a person like myself is a sentimental idealist. But when this apostle is angry with me he would call me dangerous, and could, if he wished, restrict my freedom in the ways I have mentioned above.

He will, almost certainly in 1968, make it an offense to operate a nonracial (and multiracial) political party. One learns the lesson at first hand that the practice of the art of political persuasion can be made impossible by the state. One learns how the whole character of a people can be changed by a powerful state. Having Germany in mind, I do not say fundamentally changed; but even if the change is not fundamental, it is terrible enough.

Yet, in spite of all this one goes on believing in a nonracial unity that can transcend racial difference. This is something that one has come to believe through experience of personal relationships, and it may be that what is possible in personal relationships is not possible in society. There have been many examples in history where two individuals from mutually hostile groups have greatly loved one another.

Now, is it possible or is it not possible to realize in society what one has realized in personal relationships? I believe one cannot answer the question. All that one can say is that there is within one an impulse to try to realize it, that this impulse is an integral part of one's self, and that it must be obeyed, for to disobey it is to do damage to the integrity of one's self. And what is more, one has fortunately already learned the lesson that a failure, or a measure of failure, to realize some social or political aim can be compensated for to a tremendous degree by the depth and warmth of one's personal relationships.

What has life then taught me after all? She has taught me not to expect too much, though not in the sense of the cynical beatitude, "Blessed is he who expecteth nothing, for he shall not be disappointed." Life has not taught me to expect nothing, but she has taught me not to expect success to be the inevitable result of my endeavors. She has taught me to seek sustenance from the endeavor itself, but to leave the result to God. And the strange thing is that my parents taught me all this more than half a century ago. It is a lesson that—for me—had to be learned at least twice. When I learned it in my youth, it meant Sir Galahad and the Holy Grail. When I learned it in my age, it meant Christ and the road to Golgotha. And looking back upon it all, I would not wish it otherwise. Indeed, I cannot see how it could have been otherwise.

To try to be free of self-deception, to try to see with clear eyes oneself and others and the world, does not necessarily bring an undiluted kind of happiness. Yet it is something I would not exchange for any happiness built on any other foundation. There is only one way in which one can endure man's inhumanity to man and that is to try, in one's own life, to exemplify man's humanity to man. "Teach me, oh Lord, to seek not so much to be consoled as to console."

SUGGESTIONS FOR WRITING

1. With evidence from these five selections, write an essay on the thesis "In the modern world, the individual is far from free."

2. With evidence from your own experience, write an essay on the pressures of conformity, such as "The Individual Versus the Demon-

stration," "The Bowling Club Versus Solitude," or "The Code of the Group."

3. Write an essay following Azrael's lead in which you describe some instance of a group picking a scapegoat.

4. Write a critique of Mailer's essay in which you analyze the source and means of its power, considering both thought and expression, for which the "political" phrasing alongside should provide clues.

5. Using Robinson and Paton and evidence from observation of yourself and others, write an essay on the prevalence of rationalization.

6. Write an essay on becoming disillusioned, "on learning the truth," using something from Paton and quoting Popper's suggestion that we

6. Write an essay on Paton's idea of "one's responsibility as a free man."

7. Write a research paper based on some issued raised by any of the essays in this book. Your problem will be essentially the same as that in an essay built of your own ideas: you will find a thesis and then flesh it out in an essay with beginning, middle, and end. But you will go beyond your own speculations as you document and challenge your thesis with what others have said. Pick some controversial topic, with much said on both sides, and make up your mind about where you stand. Contrary to common misconception, it is better to go into your research with your thesis (or hypothesis) clearly in mind, your own side chosen. Write out a thesis before you begin. Doing so will clarify your thoughts. But your mind need not be closed. As you read the pros and cons of the matter, you may modify your thesis—or even switch to the other side. With no thesis beforehand, though, your mind may be too wide open for anything to formulate.

Your thesis drafted, your reading done, and your notes taken, write an introductory paragraph, with thesis funneled at the end of it, and then proceed to set up your cons and to knock them down with your pros. You will be writing your own argument, simply quoting and citing the arguments of others as you present your case.

Here are some suggested topics for research, stated as theses to attack or support:

(a) Federal aid to our colleges means creeping dictatorship.

(b) The cure for juvenile crime begins at home.

(c) The American press is unfair to Russian justice (for example, the recent trials of dissenting writers).

(d) Schweitzer's Lambaréné did little permanent good.

(e) Euthanasia conflicts with Schweitzer's "reverence for life."
(f) Racial desegregation by force denies democratic rights.
(g) The Puritans were right in suppressing Christmas.
(h) Black Power means freedom for all.

Refutations. The Growth of Scientific Knowledge. Basic Books, New York, 1962, 1965; Harper Torch Books, 1968, and Routledge and Kegan Paul, London, 1963, fifth edition, 1974.

————, "Utopia and Violence" in *Conjectures and Refutations. The Growth of Scientific Knowledge.* Basic Books, New York, 1962, 1965; Harper Torch Books, 1968, and Routledge and Kegan Paul, London, 1963, fifth edition, 1974.

Katherine Anne Porter, "Paris: A Little Incident in the Rue de l'Odeon," *Ladies Home Journal* (August 1964). Copyright © 1964 by Katherine Anne Porter. Reprinted by permission of Joan Daves, Literary Agent.

James Harvey Robinson, "On Various Kinds of Thinking." Abridgment of Chapters 3–5 in *The Mind in the Making* by James Harvey Robinson. Copyright 1921 by Harper & Row, Publishers, Inc. By permission of the publishers.

George Santayana, "Cervantes," in *Essays in Literary Criticism,* ed. Irving Singer. Copyright 1956 by Charles Scribner's Sons. Reprinted by permission of Charles Scribner's Sons.

Edward Sapir, "Language and Literature," in *Language* by Edward Sapir. Copyright 1921 by Harcourt Brace Jovanovich, Inc.; copyright 1949 by Jean V. Sapir. Reprinted by permission of the publisher.

Albert Schweitzer, "The Evolution of Ethics," *The Atlantic Monthly* (November 1958). The National Arts Foundation arranged for the publication of "The Evolution of Ethics" in the United States. Translation from the German by Mrs. Carleton Smith.

Walter T. Stace, "Man Against Darkness," *The Atlantic Monthly* (September 1948). Copyright © 1948 by The Atlantic Monthly Company, Boston, Mass. Reprinted with permission.

Stanley Vestal, "The Man Who Killed Custer," in *Sitting Bull: Champion of the Sioux.* New edition copyright © 1957 by the University of Oklahoma Press. Reprinted by permission.

Robert Warshow, "The Westerner," *Partisan Review* 21, no. 2 (March–April 1954). From *The Immediate Experience* by Robert Warshow (Doubleday, 1970). Reprinted by permission of *Partisan Review* and Paul Warshow.

Eudora Welty, "Review of *The Underground Man,*" *The New York Times Book Review* (February 14, 1971). Copyright © 1971 by The New York Times Company. Reprinted by permission.

E. B. White, "A Slight Sound at Evening," (Allen Cove, Summer 1954) in *The Points of My Compass* by E. B. White. Copyright 1954 by E. B. White. Originally appeared in *The Yale Review* under the title "Walden—1954." Reprinted by permission of Harper & Row, Publishers, Inc.

Virginia Woolf, "How Should One Read a Book?" in *The Second Common Reader* by Virginia Woolf. Copyright 1932 by Harcourt Brace Jovanovich, Inc.; copyright © 1960 by Leonard Woolf. Reprinted by permission of the publishers.

77 78 79 80 81 7 6 5 4 3 2